Military Health Care

This edited volume surveys critical aspects of modern military health care in the US and various other Western countries with troops in Iraq and Afghanistan.

In the United States, the military medical system, including care for veterans, is large and diverse and involves two institutions, the US Department of Defense (DoD) and the US Department of Veterans Affairs (VA). Studying the system gives practitioners and policy-makers an understanding of the larger picture of the military medical structure, facilitating thought about some of the difficulties and opportunities for coordinating treatments and preparing for the future.

This book covers health care issues prior to deployment, such as screening for mental health, evaluating long-term consequences of exposure to military service, and provision of insurance; care during a conflict, primarily battlefield clinics, battlefield trauma care, and evacuation procedures; and post-combat care, including serious war injuries, psychiatric, and long-term care. Bringing together research from a wide range of contributors, the volume provides readers with an extensive, up-to-date source of information on military medicine.

This book will be of great interest to students of public health, military sociology, the Iraq war, US public policy, and war and conflict studies in general.

Jomana Amara is Associate Professor of Economics at the Defense Resources Management Institute and Naval Postgraduate School in Monterey, California and a Fulbright Scholar.

Ann M. Hendricks directed Health Care Financing & Economics, a research center at the VA Boston Healthcare System. She is also an Associate Professor of Health Policy and Management at Boston University's School of Public Health.

Cass Military Studies

Military Health Care

From pre-deployment to post-separation

**Edited by Jomana Amara and
Ann M. Hendricks**

LONDON AND NEW YORK

First published 2013
by Routledge
2 Park Square, Milton Park, Abingdon, Oxon, OX14 4RN

Simultaneously published in the USA and Canada
by Routledge
711 Third Avenue, New York, NY 10017

Routledge is an imprint of the Taylor & Francis Group, an informa business

© 2013 US Government

British Library Cataloguing in Publication Data
A catalogue record for this book is available from the British Library

Library of Congress Cataloging in Publication Data
Military health care : from pre-deployment to post-separation /
edited by Jomana Amara and Ann M. Hendricks.
    p. cm.
    Includes bibliographical references and index.
    1. United States – Armed Forces – Medical care. 2. Veterans –
    Medical care – United States. 3. Medicine, Military – United
    States. I. Amara, Jomana, 1961– II. Hendricks, Ann M., 1947–
    UH223.M633 2013
    355.3´450973–dc23   2012039549

ISBN: 978-0-415-52402-5 (hbk)
ISBN: 978-0-203-56849-1 (ebk)

Typeset in Baskerville
by HWA Text and Data Management, London

Printed and bound in Great Britain by MPG Printgroup

Contents

Figures

Tables

Contributors

About the Editors

Jomana Amara PhD, PE is Associate Professor of Economics at the Defense Resources Management Institute at the Naval Postgraduate School in Monterey, California and a Fulbright Scholar. Dr. Amara worked with Shell Oil as a project leader before joining the Naval Postgraduate School. She currently researches and publishes on international economics, defense economics, health economics, and the economics of the public sector. She has addressed various national and international academic organizations, institutions and conferences. She has published in numerous peer-reviewed journals. Dr. Amara is a member of the American Economic Association (AEA) and the International Institute of Strategic Studies (IISS).

Ann M. Hendricks PhD directed Health Care Financing & Economics, a research center at the VA Boston Healthcare System. She is also an associate professor of health policy and management at Boston University's School of Public Health. Her current research focuses on the demand for health care, long-term care utilization, utilization across health care systems by patients with conditions such as schizophrenia, PTSD related to sexual trauma, diabetes and Parkinson's disease, and the costs of care. She has numerous publications to her credit and has been guest editor for special VA-focused issues of *Medical Care* and *Medical Care Research and Review*.

List of contributors

Elizabeth Bass is Associate Analyst in the National Security Division of the Congressional Budget Office. She is a health economist interested in health insurance, veterans' health care, and military personnel issues. Dr. Bass worked previously as a researcher at the James A. Haley VAMC in Tampa for six years, and as Assistant Professor at the University of South Florida. She holds a doctorate in Economics from the University of Illinois at Chicago. Before pursing her doctorate she worked as a financial broker in Germany.

David G. Brown PsyD is the Chief, Behavioral Health, Pacific Regional Medical Command. He previously served at the Office of the Secretary of Defense as the Director and Clinical Subject Matter Expert of the Defense Suicide Prevention Oversight Council, responsible for the creation of the Suicide Prevention Office and responding to all Congressional and Senate Armed Services Committee testimonies on suicide. He supported the Secretary of Defense and Secretary of the Veterans Administration to develop and implement processes, procedures, and standards for the transition of service members from care and treatment through DoD and the VA.

Theodore R. Brown DO, MPH currently serves as the Division Surgeon, 25th Infantry Division, Schofield Barracks, Hawaii. He previously served as the Preventive Medicine Physician, Office of the Command Surgeon, Headquarters, United States Central Command (USCENTCOM). In that capacity, he was responsible for updating and revising predeployment medical policy and standards for personnel deploying to the USCENTCOM area of responsibility. He is board certified in Family, Preventive, and Occupational and Environmental Medicine.

Tim A. Bullman MA is a biostatistician with the Department of Veterans Affairs, Office of Environmental Epidemiology Service in Washington DC. For the past 23 years he has served as an investigator for various veteran cohort studies. Many of these studies were retrospective cohort mortality studies, focusing on risk of suicide among formerly deployed veterans. He currently serves as a co-investigator on several mortality studies of veterans from Operations Enduring Freedom and Iraqi Freedom. Many of his studies have been published in peer reviewed journals.

Jonviea Chamberlain MS obtained her MS in Epidemiology from University of Massachusetts Amherst. While completing her master's degree, she performed research on military health consequences of environmental exposures. Her research interests include epidemiology of infectious disease and environmental exposures.

David X. Cifu MD is Chairman and the Herman J. Flax, MD Professor of the Department of PM&R at the Virginia Commonwealth University (VCU) School of Medicine in Richmond, Virginia, the Chief of PM&R Services of the VCU Health System, the Executive Director of the VCU-Center for Rehabilitation Sciences and Engineering, National Director of PM&R Program Office and a member of the Senior Executive Staff for the Department of Veterans Affairs. Dr. Cifu's research interests include efficacy studies on diagnostic and management strategies for combat and non-combat injuries to the neurologic system of veterans and service members.

Tammy Crowder MD, PhD has been Chief of Staff for the Defense and Veterans Brain Injury Center since 2009. She is responsible for day-to-day management and execution of all DVBIC programs within the DVBIC network to include many US Army, Navy, Marine, and Air Force installations throughout the US and at Landstuhl Regional Medical Center in Germany as well as two civilian TBI treatment facilities. Dr. Crowder served as the Contracting Officer Representative for the Psychological Health and Traumatic Brain Injury and Deployment Related Medical Research Programs at the Medical Research and Material Command, Congressionally Directed Medical Research Program.

Nancy F. Crum-Cianflone MD, MPH is Principal Investigator of the Millennium Cohort Study and the Head of the Department of Deployment Health Research Center at the Naval Health Research Center, San Diego, California. She is a former US Naval Officer and a board certified Internal Medicine physician. Dr. Crum-Cianflone has a distinguished research career in the field of military medicine with over 125 peer-reviewed publications. She is also currently a staff physician at the Naval Medical Center San Diego, an adjunct Professor at San Diego State University, and a Voluntary Associate Professor of Medicine at the University of California San Diego.

Ryan Edwards is Associate Professor of economics at Queens College, City University of New York. He holds a 2002 doctorate in economics from the University of California at Berkeley, where he received predoctoral funding from the National Institute on Aging. He is a faculty researcher of the National Bureau of Economic Research, a member of the doctoral faculty at the CUNY Graduate Center; his research focuses on the economics of population health and aging.

Bryan Fisk is a Lieutenant Colonel in the US Army and a member of the American Board of Internal Medicine. He is currently Assistant Chief of Critical Care Medicine Service, Department of Surgery, Walter Reed Army Medical Center and Director of Tactical, Operational, and Disaster Medicine resident rotation. He is also a SWAT team physician with the US Park Police, Washington, DC. Dr. Fisk was deployed to Operation Iraqi Freedom in 2003, 2004 and Operation Enduring Freedom 2010. He has published extensively in journals, most recently in *Anticancer Research*, *Critical Care Medicine*, *Journal of Special Operations Medicine*, and *Journal of Immunology*.

Stacy Garrett-Ray MD, MPH, MBA is the Deputy Director of Comprehensive Women's Health for Women Veterans Health Strategic Health Care Group within VHA Office of Patient Care Services. In this capacity, she serves to expand initiatives for women veterans' health and enhance comprehensive primary care services for women veterans nationally. She is currently the New Models of Care Women's Health Sub-initiative Lead for the VA T21 Transformational Initiatives. Dr. Garrett-Ray, a Board-certified Family Practitioner, came to VA from the University of Maryland, where she served as Medical Director of the Baltimore City Cancer Program of the University of Maryland Greenebaum Cancer Center.

Heidi Golding is Principal Analyst for the National Security Division of the Congressional Budget Office. Her specific areas of interest include military personnel, compensation and financing reform, and veterans' issues. With nearly 15 years of work as a defense analyst, her extensive research has involved not only historical data analysis but also survey design and inquiry. Her most recent work included estimating VA's health care costs to treat OIF/OEF veterans, the retention impact of the new veterans' educational benefits, and the recruiting and retention considerations of extensive war-time deployments.

Jay P. Granier MD, PhD is a Polytrauma Fellow at the McGuire VA Medical Center in Richmond, VA. Dr. Granier received his Doctor of Philosophy in Speech and Hearing Science from the University of Iowa in 2002 and his medical degree from Louisiana State University Health Sciences Center in New Orleans, LA, in 2007. He completed internship and residency training in PM&R at East Carolina University. His clinical and research interests involve the rehabilitation of individuals with TBI and CVA.

Deborah L. Grassman is a Nurse Practitioner at Bay Pines VAMC in St. Petersburg, Florida. She has been with the VA for 26 years and has been the Director of the Bay Pines Hospice program for the last 15 years. She has published numerous articles on providing hospice care to veterans. She pioneered identifying the effects of past trauma on the quality of a person's dying process, as well as ways to effectively respond to issues that surface at the end of life. She is the author of the book, *Peace at Last: Stories of Hope and Healing for Veterans and Their Families.*

Jamie Grimes MD has been the National Director of the Defense and Veterans Brain Injury Center since 2010. Prior to that, she had been the DVBIC Site Director at Wilford Hall Medical Center (WHMC) and Brooke Army Medical Center (BAMC), now combined as the San Antonio Military Medical Center (SAMMC), since 2007. She is board certified in Vascular Neurology, Neurology, and Psychiatry and has extensive clinical experience with the combat wounded warriors from Operations Enduring and Iraqi Freedom, having served tours of duty in OIF (2004) and OEF (2011).

Jason Guthrie is a Strategy & Operations Associate with Deloitte Consulting LLP and the historian for the Defense Centers of Excellence for Psychological Health and Traumatic Brain Injury. From within the DCoE Chief of Staff's office, Jason works closely with the directorates to develop the organization's history program, manage the development of historical projects, support program and policy initiatives, and educate internal and external stakeholders about the history of psychological health and traumatic brain injury diagnoses and treatment in the US military. He has completed research projects in the United States and abroad, and contributed articles to academic journals and other publications.

Sally Haskell MD is Acting Director of Comprehensive Women's Health for the Women Veterans' Health Strategic Healthcare Group in VA Central Office. She is a general internist, clinician educator, and women's health researcher at VA Connecticut and Associate Professor of Medicine at Yale University School of Medicine. Since 2007 Dr. Haskell has been a co-principal investigator on the HSR&D funded Women Veterans' Cohort Study. Her research interests include gender differences in post-deployment health, chronic pain in women veterans, gender disparities in cardiovascular risk prevention, and menopause and hormone therapy.

Katherine Helmick currently serves as the Deputy Director for Traumatic Brain Injury (TBI) at the Defense Centers of Excellence for Psychological Health and Traumatic Brain Injury (DCoE). She brings considerable clinical and research experience in the field of neuroscience to her position as well as over 100 regional, national and international presentations to include many peer-reviewed publications. Ms. Helmick has served in a variety of leadership, advisory, and operational roles, including positions such as deputy director for the Clinical and Educational Affairs Office for Defense and Veterans Brain Injury Center (DVBIC); and manager with the Office of Clinical Standards at DVBIC.

Marjan Ghahramanlou Holloway is Associate Professor of Medical and Clinical Psychology and Psychiatry at Uniformed Services University of the Health Sciences (USUHS) in Bethesda, Maryland. She is a licensed Maryland Psychologist and a certified therapist of the Academy of Cognitive Therapy with a private clinical practice in Chevy Chase, Maryland. Dr. Holloway is the author of several peer reviewed manuscripts, book chapters, and encyclopedia entries. She has presented at numerous symposia, workshops, clinical roundtables, national and international conferences. Dr. Holloway's laboratory at USUHS focuses on programmatic research in the area of suicide prevention for the United States military.

Robert Ireland USAF, Medical Corps, Chief Flight Surgeon (Retired), served in the Office of the Assistant Secretary of Defense (Health Affairs), Clinical and Program Policy, as Program Director for Mental Health Policy from 2005 to 2009. He led standardization of DoD suicide data as Chair of the DoD Suicide Prevention and Risk Reduction Committee, and facilitated joint prevention efforts of the military, VA, and other federal suicide specialists. Previously, he was the Chief of the Neuropsychiatry function at the USAF School of Aerospace Medicine Consultation Service and USAF Psychiatry Consultant to the Surgeon General.

Han K. Kang MD, PhD is an epidemiologist with the Department of Veterans Affairs and is also an adjunct associate professor in the Department of Epidemiology and Biostatistics of the George Washington University and adjunct associate professor of Preventive Medicine/Biometrics at the Uniformed Services

University of the Health Sciences. For the last three decades, his research interest has been focused primarily on the health of US military and veteran populations who were potentially exposed to environmental/occupational hazards during their military service. He has published over 100 scientific articles in peer-reviewed journals.

Rachel Kimerling PhD is a Clinical Psychologist at the Dissemination and Training Division of the National Center for PTSD at the VA Palo Alto Health Care System. She is also an Investigator at the Center for Health Care Evaluation. She is the Director of Monitoring for the VA Office of Mental Health Services Military Sexual Trauma Support Team. Dr. Kimerling is a health services researcher with a focus on issues of women and gender in the detection and treatment of traumatic stress. She is currently a member of the VA Under Secretary for Health's Special Committee on Post-traumatic Stress Disorder.

Maxine Krengel PhD earned her doctorate at SUNY Albany. Dr. Krengel has worked in the clinical neuropsychology service as a staff clinician and supervisor for 19 years. She is part of a group private practice at Boston University in the Department of Neurology. She continues to teach neuropsychology practicum students, interns and postdoctoral fellows at the Boston University School of Medicine and she teaches classes in assessment and brain behavior relationships at Lesley University, Boston University and Boston College. Research interests include effects of toxicant exposures on cognition, Gulf War related illnesses, and the cognitive effects of blast injury.

Henry L. Lew is Professor of Physical Medicine & Rehabilitation at the University of Hawaii. He is an international expert on TBI and National Consultant for the Defense and Veterans Brain Injury Center (DVBIC). Prior to that he was Chief of Physical Medicine & Rehabilitation and Polytrauma Network Site Director at VA Boston, and an Executive Committee member of the VA Polytrauma and Blast-related Injuries QUERI. Dr. Lew's research interests include coordination of care for TBI patients.

Patricia Janulewicz Lloyd obtained her MPH and DSc in Environmental Health from Boston University. She completed pre- and post-doctoral training in neuropsychology at the Boston University School of Public Health and neurotoxicology and teratology the University of Massachusetts Boston. Dr. Janulewicz Lloyd is currently a part-time Research Assistant Professor in the Psychology Department at the University of Massachusetts Boston and part-time Post-Doctoral Associate at Boston University School of Public Health in the Environmental Health Department. Dr. Janulewicz Lloyd's research interests include studying the neurobehavioral effects in children exposed to teratogens and the behavioral effects of neurotoxicant exposures in military veterans.

Alair MacLean is Associate Professor of Sociology at Washington State University Vancouver in Vancouver, WA. She received her PhD from the University of Wisconsin at Madison in 2004, where she studied with Robert Hauser. Prior to joining WSU, MacLean spent two years as an NIA postdoctoral fellow in aging at the RAND Corporation in Santa Monica, CA. She has published extensively on veterans' experiences and has written a review of military life-course studies with Glen Elder, Jr. that appeared in the *Annual Review of Sociology*.

Shira Maguen is a Staff Psychologist on the Posttraumatic Stress Disorder Clinical Team at the San Francisco VA Medical Center and Assistant Professor in the Dept. of Psychiatry, UCSF School of Medicine. Dr. Maguen is the recipient of a VA Health Services Research and Development Grant that examines the impact of killing in veterans and Department of Defense grants that examine PTSD and co-morbid conditions in OEF/OIF/OND women veterans and mild TBI and PTSD in OEF/OIF/OND veterans. Her research interests fall under the umbrella of PTSD and include risk and resilience factors, and gender differences in mental health diagnoses among veterans.

Kristin Mattocks PhD is the Associate Chief of Staff/Research at VA Central Western Massachusetts and an assistant professor of medicine at University of Massachusetts Medical School. Dr. Mattocks is a health services researcher who focuses on understanding reproductive health issues among women veterans, and her most recent research examines women using dual sources of care to address their reproductive health needs. Dr. Mattocks also serves as the chair of a women's reproductive health working group in the VA.

Susan McCutcheon EdD, RN is the National Director, Family Services, Women's Mental Health and Military Sexual Trauma for the VA Office of Mental Health Services. She has recently completed a three-year term as a board member of the National Alliance on Mental Illness of Ohio. In 2001, Dr. McCutcheon was selected as a Robert Wood Johnson Executive Nurse Fellow. In 2005, she was selected to participate in Leadership VA. Dr. McCutcheon has received the Cleveland Federal Executive Employee Recognition Award from the Cleveland Federal Executive Board and the Mental Health Professional of the Year award from the National Alliance of the Mentally Ill Metro Cleveland.

Ajit B. Pai MD is the Medical Director of the Polytrauma Rehabilitation Center at the McGuire VA Medical Center in Richmond, VA, the Assistant Residency Director for the Virginia Commonwealth University PM&R Residency and the McGuire VA Medical Center Polytrauma Fellowship Programs. After completing his internship and residency training in PM&R at Virginia Commonwealth University, he spent an additional year of specialty training as a Spinal Cord Injury Medicine fellow at the Richmond VA Medical Center. His clinical and research interests involve rehabilitation of individuals with TBI, SCI and complex war injuries.

Allison Percy is Principal Analyst in the National Security Division of the Congressional Budget Office. Her areas of expertise include military health care, veterans' medical care, veterans' disability compensation, health information technology, and health care quality. Before joining CBO in June 2001, Allison Percy was a postdoctoral fellow with the Department of Veterans Affairs in Philadelphia. She received her PhD in health economics from the Wharton School at the University of Pennsylvania in 2000. Earlier she worked as a health financing analyst for John Snow, Inc., an international public health consulting firm.

Anke Richter, Associate Professor at the Defense Resources Management Institute, Naval Postgraduate School, received a PhD in Operations Research from Stanford University. Her research interests include resource allocation for epidemic control, disease modeling and economic impact assessment, and bio-terrorism. She has published in numerous journals. Dr. Richter is a member of the Institute for Operations Research and the Management Sciences (INFORMS) and the International Society for Pharmacoeconomics and Outcomes Research (ISPOR). She has published in several peer-reviewed journals, including the *Journal of the American Medical Association*, *Journal of Clinical Epidemiology*, *PharmacoEconomics*, *Medical Decision Making*, *Clinical Therapeutics*, and *Managed Care Interfaces*.

Christopher Robinson, Deputy Director at the Psychological Health Defense Centers of Excellence for Psychological Health and Traumatic Brain Injury, is a clinical health psychologist who brings expertise in public behavioral health and health policy to his role as the deputy director. Robinson previously served as the director of the Strategies, Plans and Programs Directorate and recently returned from a deployment to Afghanistan where he served as the Combat Stress Detachment Commander for RC-East. Robinson served as the 78th Medical Operations Squadron commander at Robins Air Force Base in Georgia, where he led all health care operations.

Roberto J. Rona is Emeritus Professor of Public Health Medicine at King's College London. His research experience includes nutritional surveillance, growth in children, obesity, respiratory illness, food allergy, evaluation of new technology in medicine and epidemiological work in Latin America. He entered the field of military health in 1999–2000 to assess the current health information systems available in the Armed Forces. His research has been on public health issues of mental health in the UK military, especially screening and risk factors for mental ill-health. He has published more than 200 papers in medicine and psychiatry.

Scott T. Shreve, DO, has been the National Director of the Hospice and Palliative Care Program for the Veterans Healthcare Administration since June 2004. Dr. Shreve spends half his time as the Medical Director of the Hospice Unit at the Lebanon VA Medical Center in Lebanon, Pennsylvania where he has been since 1993. Dr. Shreve is an Associate Professor of Clinical Medicine at the Pennsylvania State University and is board certified in internal medicine, geriatrics and hospice and palliative care. He has co-authored articles on measuring quality of care, geriatric medicine and hospice care.

Kimberly Sullivan is a Research Assistant Professor at the Boston University School of Public Health department of Environmental Health and the Scientific Coordinator for the congressionally directed Research Advisory Committee (RAC) on Gulf War Veterans Illnesses. Dr. Sullivan has worked in the field of behavioral neurotoxicology since 1995. She has coordinated field studies in neurotoxicology (i.e., pesticides, methylmercury), neurobehavioral outcomes and the effects of stressors and genetic predisposition to disease on cognitive functioning. Most recently, she was the Principal Investigator on a study of cognition and structural MRI in pesticide-exposed Gulf War veterans.

Laure Veet MD is the Director of Women's Health Education in the Women Veterans Health Strategic Healthcare Group in VA Central Office. In this role, she is responsible for leading development and implementation of initiatives related to heath education for provision of care to Women Veterans for the Department of Veterans Affairs. Prior to that she served as the Associate Chief of Staff for Education at the Philadelphia VA Medical Center, overseeing programs for more than 1,000 residents and students from the University of Pennsylvania School of Medicine and nearly 50 other educational institution affiliations that rotated to PVAMC each year

Natalie Webb, Associate Professor at the Defense Resources Management Institute, Naval Postgraduate School, received a PhD in economics from Duke University. She currently conducts research on nonprofit and voluntary organizations, including their interaction with defense and other government agencies and non-governmental organizations, and performance management. She has published in several peer-reviewed journals including *Nonprofit and Voluntary Sector Quarterly*, *Defense & Security Analysis*, *Public Finance and Management* and *Applied Economics*. Dr. Webb is a member of the American Economic Association and the Association for Research on Nonprofit Organizations and Voluntary Action.

Simon Wessely is Director of the King's Centre for Military Health Research, Chair of Psychological Medicine and Vice Dean of the Institute of Psychiatry, King's College London. After medical training he specialized in psychiatry, as well as gaining a Master's and Doctorate in epidemiology. He has authored or co-authored over 600 papers covering many aspects of medicine and psychiatry, and has a long-standing interest in the health of the Armed Forces.

Acknowledgements

The editors wish to thank all the contributors to the book for their hard work and dedication. The editors also wish to thank Vandamere Press for permission to use the art on page 61 of *Peace at Last: Stories of Hope and Healing for Veterans and Their Families*.

Part I
Overview

1 Survey of military medical care from pre-deployment to post-separation

Jomana Amara and Ann M. Hendricks

Introduction

In the United States, the military medical system, including care for veterans, is large and diverse and involves two institutions, the US Department of Defense (DoD) and the US Department of Veterans Affairs (VA). The military medical care system has changed in significant ways in the last few decades in response to major policy and operational changes. One of the major changes is a result of the health care system dealing with a large influx of veterans from previous wars (Korea and Vietnam Wars) and the acceptance of new diagnoses such as PTSD after the conclusion of the Vietnam War. Some other issues influencing medical care include the policy decision to move to an all-volunteer force in the mid-1970s; expanding the role of female service members; extending deployment of members of the National Guard and Reserves. At a minimum, studying current and past systems of military medical care, permits practitioners to appreciate the changes that might improve care in the future (DeBakey, 1996) and allows practitioners and policy makers an understanding of the larger picture of the military medical system to facilitate thinking about some of the difficulties and opportunities for coordinating treatments and preparing for the future.

Operation Enduring Freedom and Operation Iraqi Freedom (OEF/OIF) are the first major large-scale military engagements that the US and many of its allies have been involved in since the end of the Vietnam War, necessitating the deployment of large numbers of troops for extended periods of time. These engagements have severely strained and tested military medical resources and the resources of the VA. In addition, these conflicts mark a shift to a new form of warfare. Consequently, this new form of warfare has resulted in injuries and medical concerns that existed for veterans of past conflicts, but have been labeled "signature" injuries of OEF/OIF. In particular, traumatic brain injury (TBI) and post-traumatic stress disorder (PTSD) have led to more attention to service members' physical and mental health pre-deployment as well as after. In addition, the US deployed its reserve and National Guard forces at an unprecedented rate, changing the age distribution of deployed and subsequent veteran cohorts. Furthermore, the extent of female service members' involvement in OEF/OIF in terms of both the number of women deployed and the scope of their involvement is unparalleled. Finally, the period between the Vietnam War and OEF/OIF witnessed tremendous advances in general medical care that translated to progress in care for war wounded.

Today, there are roughly 23 million veterans in the US (United States Census Bureau, 2011). For the majority of these veterans, the period of military service is relatively brief, averaging about 6.5 years among respondents in the 2001 National Survey of Veterans (Department of Veteran's Affairs, 2002). In the same survey, 39 percent of respondents reported having served in a combat or war zone and 36 percent reported exposure to dead, dying, or wounded people (Department of Veteran's Affairs, 2002). Some military service members receive medical care in the combat theater for injuries or other medical conditions sustained while deployed. Other service members have combat-related medical conditions that are identified and treated after they return from war either in the DoD's health care system for active-duty personnel or in the VA for veterans, including deactivated reservists. VA provides health care services through the Veterans Health Administration (VHA), which treats eligible veterans for these service-connected conditions and other ailments.

There are many overt influences of military service on later-life health such as combat-related physical injuries. Less apparent are the psychological wounds that have been a persistent injury of warfare throughout human history, but only recently have we begun to develop more consistent methods of diagnosis and treatment. While exposure to the physical and psychological harms of combat is the clearest channel through which military service may harm physical and mental health, there are many other ways in which military service can affect health. More indirect channels include the development of unhealthy behaviors that may arise either in response to the stresses of combat or the command structure, or more or less independently while the individual is engaged in military service. Military medicine includes treatment for the results of these as well.

History

Since the Revolutionary War and with every military operation since, the structure of the medical care provided to the armed forces has evolved and become more effective in treating the wounded. As technology advanced, wounded soldiers who previously were beyond the capabilities of the care available, survived and the military was able to develop and sustain medical care in remote and inhospitable locations under extremely hectic and dangerous conditions. For example, the concept of military triage was developed in the early years of the twentieth century because, for the first time, improved evacuation systems resulted in more severely wounded soldiers reaching medical care than ever before and the military medical systems of that time had to contend with an overwhelming volume of casualties.

The innovative use of combat medics to provide care at the forward location of wounding became a constant presence on the battlefields during the American Civil War. Since then, the combat medic has been expected to render immediate first aid, including stopping bleeding, splinting fractures, dressing wounds, and administering pain medication (DeBakey, 1996). The use of intravenous fluids, plasma, and antibiotic powder by combat medics were introduced during World War II. However, since World War I, in addition to training combat medics, the military provided medical training for soldiers. The training emphasized control of hemorrhage, wound dressing, and fracture splinting. The focus on training combat medics seems to have had an impact on the percentage of soldiers killed in action in the current war, with the current rate dropping significantly (Hetz, 2006). Current practice dictates that casualties receive care immediately after wounding. The injured are rapidly returned to duty or carry on along the continuum of care until they reach the level appropriate to their medical need. There are five levels of treatment within the military health care system. Each level has the same capabilities as the level before it, but adds a new treatment capability that distinguishes it from the previous level. Care is usually initiated by the wounded soldier's companions or the combat medic assigned to that particular combat unit. The first three levels of care are in the combat theater field with some Level 4 care available in the battle theater. The first level of full surgical and hospital capability occurs at Level 3. The US Army moved from Mobile Surgical Hospitals to a single, modular hospital (Medical Re-engineering Initiative) during OIF. Level 4 capability can also be found outside of the immediate vicinity of the combat theater such as Landstuhl Army Regional Medical Center in Germany. Level 5 care includes stateside Army Medical Centers like Walter Reed and Brooke where definitive care and rehabilitation of war wounded have become a significant focus (Hetz, 2006).

US experience

The US is unique in that the federal government has established two institutions to administer medical care to members of the armed forces and veterans. The DoD maintains care of service members until separation, at which point the VA commences care of those eligible. Even though these two institutions are separate, they cooperate and try to attempt a seamless transition between active duty and retirees (Government Accountability Office, 2005). This is a unique arrangement in that most nations do not have a separate entity to deal with the medical needs of veterans and veterans usually resort to accessing the existing general health care systems.

Following World War II, VHA was primarily a hospital system for patients with war injuries or psychiatric disorders. By law, outpatient services were available only to veterans with prior VHA inpatient admissions. Nursing home units were often long-term homes for veterans with a variety of disabilities. As World War II veterans aged, the system did not provide adequate or equal access for veterans around the country, many or even most of whom were ambulatory patients with multiple chronic conditions. For decades, the system's focus on inpatient and specialty care lagged behind health care delivery in the private sector, where many medical procedures had moved to an outpatient setting and preventive or coordinated care was emphasized. In fact, rules that prohibited outpatient care in many cases raised concerns that VHA could not provide coordinated primary care (USGAO, 1995, 1996).

VHA addressed Congress's demands to increase access to care for veterans when VHA's then-Undersecretary for Health Dr. Kenneth Kizer led an effort to reengineer the Department's health care system in the 1990s. The changes were intended for better management of performance and systemic improvements in quality and innovation (Kizer, *Prescription for Change*, March 1995; Iglehart, 1996). A substantial revision of eligibility rules and expanded services made care more accessible to veterans and in the most medically appropriate setting.

In addition to the changes in benefits brought by the VHA reengineering, in 1995, VHA medical centers, outpatient clinics, and other facilities were reorganized into regional networks, currently numbering 21 and typically including 7 to 10 medical centers and a large number of outpatient clinics and other facilities. A focus of VHA's reorganization has been the movement of care from inpatient to outpatient settings. For example, as the patient population grew, use of VHA nursing homes for post-acute rehabilitation treatment increased and the number of long stays decreased.

Another area of change was in the provision of substance abuse treatment for veterans with substance use disorders (SUDs) where the inpatient programs were "virtually eliminated" between 1994 and 2004 (Tracy et al., 2004). Between 2004 and 2009, a number of initiatives redefined SUD treatment within VHA with emphasis on evidence-based practices and outpatient programs (Tracy et al., 2011). The measures of success have focused on continuity of follow-up care and patient engagement in treatment.

These are just two of the transformations that have taken place throughout the VHA in the past two decades. The changes have promoted patient-centered, evidence-based care that delivers high quality treatment to all eligible veterans (Perlin, 2004).

Focus of the book

The purpose of this book is to provide the reader with an overview of the recent changes and advances in medical care policy for active duty and separated members of the armed forces. This book is also intended to assist personnel studying, providing care, and understanding policy for the medical care options available to active duty and retired service members. Since the United States has the majority of the forces currently deployed and is the nation with the institutions in place to address medical needs at all phases of the deployment cycle and post-separation, the book primarily has a US focus.

In thinking about the book, the editors chose authors recognized for their expertise. The authors were encouraged to focus on and highlight the recent changes that they have observed in their field of expertise. While there are many ways to organize the material in the book, an approach tied to the military career cycle was followed. This approach allows the reader to follow the service member's exposure to health services from enlistment to end-of-life care. The book is divided into four parts with each part covering a time period in the cycle of health care provided to veterans. The parts are: overview, pre-deployment, deployment, and post-deployment. The book begins with the overview part that defines the background against which the discussions in the book take place.

Overview

This part sets the background and surveys the needs of the various cohorts of veterans accessing US health care services. The part also describes the access that active duty, reserve and former military service members typically have to health care programs and health insurance during service and after their discharge from the forces. For US readers, this institutional information may be directly relevant. Non-US readers may find this background helps them draw appropriate parallels to their own national systems.

Chapter 2 reviews the demographics of the US OEF/OIF cohort and compares it with previous cohorts from other military engagements. It places the demands for immediate post-deployment health services by the OEF/OIF veterans in relation to the demands of the aging Korean and Vietnam War veterans in terms of the number of patients and the average costs of their care. It examines the impact of injured OEF/OIF veterans especially in the area of TBI, PTSD, and physical disability services.

The third Overview chapter describes the access that active duty, reserve and former military service members typically have to US health care programs and health insurance during service and after their discharge from the forces. The chapter lists the options available for the TRICARE system, the military's health care plan that includes both military medical treatment facilities and civilian providers and describes the medical programs available to veterans through the VHA, the medical program of the VA. The chapter also details the eligibility of service personnel (active duty, National Guard, Reserves), veterans, retirees, and dependents to health care and the challenges to providing health care through DoD and VHA.

Pre-deployment

The military services recognize that appropriate health care begins with an understanding of the pre-deployment physical and mental conditions of their members. Especially important are the factors that may affect resilience after events and injuries in the combat zone. Military service confers unique occupational exposures and intense stressors that may have profound impact on long-term health. An understanding and base-lining of service members' health is crucial in an environment of high military operating tempo where personnel can expect to deploy multiple times in the course of their careers. Part II of the book will discuss policy and data pertinent to this concern.

Pre-deployment medical policy establishes, among other requirements, the criteria used to determine an individual's medical suitability for deployment. Such policy is necessary for a number of reasons, the first of which is to ensure the deployment of a fit and ready force that is able to withstand the unique occupational and environmental exposures and stressors associated with deployment. Secondly, it reduces the potential for unnecessary medical evacuation for medical conditions that are not suitable for a particular deployment. Chapter 4 expounds on the myriad considerations made when establishing pre-deployment medical policy. The chapter focuses on the perspective from US Central Command (CENTCOM), the command in the US military that is responsible for a 20-country region including Iraq and Afghanistan – the two major post-Vietnam theaters of war. While other Geographic Combatant Commands (CCMDs) have similar policies, for the most part they mirror CENTCOM's policy and make minor adjustments. Additionally, no other CCMD requires as robust a policy as CENTCOM. The chapter also addresses potential adverse outcomes and costs associated with the lack of an effective application of pre-deployment medical policy.

While most studies of military related exposures are limited by retrospective and cross-sectional design, convenience sampling, and/or short follow-up, the Millennium Cohort Study is the largest population-based prospective health study in military history, designed to evaluate the long-term health impact of military service and to allow policymakers to relate pre-deployment health conditions to later events and outcomes. The Millennium Cohort Study was launched by 2001. Chapter 5 details how the Millennium Cohort Study is answering long-term health concerns of military service members by complementing and integrating with existing military health system data. The cohort consists of four separate panels enrolled in 2001, 2004, 2007, and 2010 which total over 200,000 participants from all service branches and includes both active-duty and reserve and National Guard personnel. Participants are surveyed at three-year intervals for 21 years while in service and post service. The Millennium Cohort Study is setting a new standard for prospective evaluation of the long-term health consequences of military occupational exposures, both among active military personnel as well as among the growing number of cohort members who have separated or retired from military service and entered the civilian population. The rigorous design and strength of this study will allow the project to address complex issues of military and national public health importance for years to come.

Screening for mental health is a frequent topic of discussion in the military, many supporting its introduction, but some recommending caution. Chapter 6 describes the reasons why screening for mental health is an important health service topic and the criteria which should be fulfilled before implementing a screening program. The chapter describes the opportunities for screening and reviews the evidence in favor of and against screening. The chapter also discusses the possible reasons why the US has been supportive of screening for mental illness while the UK response has been less enthusiastic so far.

The final chapter in this part focuses on the military's public health approach to suicide prevention. Given the public health significance of military suicide and the impact of a service member's suicide on his or her family, unit, and the military community, the DoD has adopted a comprehensive approach to suicide prevention within the armed forces. A key theme throughout the chapter is the critical role of collaboration among key DoD organizations with experts from other federal agencies and academic institutions to continuously improve upon existing surveillance, programmatic, and research components of various suicide prevention efforts within the large military system. The chapter also provides information about recent organized efforts within the armed forces to minimize the devastating toll of suicide on service members and their families as well as on the military system. A sustained scientific dialogue about military suicide prevention efforts, as presented in this chapter, will equip healthcare and helping services providers, military leaders, researchers, and policy makers with a greater appreciation of the complexity of suicide and its prevention among a young and predominantly male force under the current stressors of high military operational tempo and multiple conflicts.

Deployment

The primary mission of the military medical corps is to preserve the fighting force. During war, the components of this mission include treatment and rehabilitation of war injuries and non-battle-related injuries, and prevention of disease and injury. To best accomplish this mission, medical officers need to anticipate and recognize the most common medical disorders to ensure a fit and ready force able to fulfill its mandate.

The military health system provides a continuum of care encompassing the forward stabilization on the battlefield to definitive care and rehabilitation at military medical centers in the continental United States. The focus of Chapter 8 is care that is rendered at the battle aid station by the initial responder and includes aid provided by combat life-savers and/or the combat line medics. The provision of far forward medical care in the combat theater is essential to both mission success and the well-being of individual service members. Medical teams at the front lines have gone to extraordinary measures for the past decade to provide the best possible medical care in austere locations. Providing front-line medical care in a combat theater can be one of the most challenging and at the same time rewarding experiences available to a medical provider at any level of training. The challenge includes balancing the sometimes competing interests of mission goals versus individual patient needs, limited supplies, professional isolation, and presence of increased threats.

The chapter reviews the medical capabilities available to provide medical treatment to the forward-deployed service member as well as the means by which mild traumatic brain injury and post-traumatic stress disorder are addressed by the forward provider. The dedication of the initial responder medical team, in combination with advances in the medical equipment, protective equipment, and military systems have resulted in lower killed-in-action rates and the highest survivability rate after injury than during any past conflict. However, the nature of the current conflict, along with increased awareness, is giving rise to an increasing number of service members suffering from mild traumatic brain injury and posttraumatic stress disorder. Research and training are underway to prevent, identify, and initiate early treatment for these casualties at the front lines of conflict.

Chapter 9 focuses on the use of hospital ships to provide medical care to forces in combat. Traditional hospital ship missions provided combat support and training; however, hospital ships now routinely perform humanitarian assistance and disaster relief missions. The authors focus on goals for and desired outcomes of navy hospital ships to include addressing health and welfare conditions of local populations, security and stability in a region, and attitudes towards Americans and the West. As humanitarian assistance and disaster relief missions grow in importance for combatant commanders, deployed forces, senior government leaders and the international community, leaders must better understand lessons learned from other missions and integrate policy and direction for the missions. They must consider the disparate forces influencing these missions and be willing to devote resources to better understand stakeholders and outcomes they affect. Building on earlier surveys of literature and government documents on hospital ship missions, the authors recommend greater focus on planning for, staffing, resourcing, and managing hospital ships in accordance with more current missions. The chapter concludes by recommending greater coordination with the allies in providing medical care internationally.

Post-deployment and separation

The final part of the book addresses the medical issues that service members struggle with when returning from deployment, when they leave service, and finally as they and their families contend with end-of-life issues.

The first three chapters in the part, Chapters 10, 11, and 12, tackle mental health issues from three very different perspectives. Chapter 10 steps back and broadly traces the history and evolution of traumatic brain injury; Chapter 11 details the DoD response to psychological health and traumatic brain injury issues; Chapter 12 gauges the VA response to suicide.

The authors of Chapter 10 draw on vast experience working in the two major US institutions responsible for the health care of service members and veterans, DoD and VA. The authors examine how casualties resulting from major wars in the past, starting from the US Civil War to the present day conflicts in Iraq and Afghanistan, led to the establishment of the current model of evaluation and treatment of TBI. They review how the field has expanded in response to the growing cohort of young, brain-injured veterans. The chapter provides an overview of the polytrauma system of care, established as collaboration between the DoD, the VA, and civilian partners, with the goal to integrate specialized TBI care, research, and education across the military, veteran, and civilian medical care. The chapter concludes by detailing the innovative research conducted and the future of TBI treatment.

Chapter 11 examines the Defense Department response to psychological health (PH) and TBI from an historical and a programmatic perspective: it provides background and context for current program and policy decisions, highlights the most important elements of the current DoD approach, and demonstrates the importance of continued integration and collaboration across agencies. The authors suggest that the PH/TBI program development within the DoD has yielded significant advances in medical understanding and dramatically raised the quality of care available to service members. The chapter concludes by summarizing the Defense Department's coordinated response to the challenges of PH/TBI: a focus on promoting early detection, thus early treatment; ensuring force readiness and addressing cultural barriers to care; improving collaborations with VHA, other federal agencies and academic and civilian organizations; improving deployment related assessments; deploying effective treatments based on the most up-to-date clinical standards; and conducting military relevant research and enhancing information technology systems to promote data sharing and tracking.

In response to congressional mandates and public interest, VHA has increased its efforts to monitor and prevent veteran suicides. Chapter 12 examines the many suicide prevention efforts designed to inform veterans and their caretakers about possible warning signs that might precede suicide behavior and about the various suicide prevention resources available. The efforts include media campaigns and adding personnel to more closely monitor, track, and provide counseling to veterans at risk for suicide. The authors point out that the legislated mission of providing suicide rates for all veterans has still not been realized. The difficulty with enumerating all veteran suicides is primarily related to the difficulty of identifying all veterans.

However, VHA has had greater success regarding suicide prevention, either meeting or progressing towards meeting its obligations relative to providing resources to prevent veteran suicides.

Chapter 13 provides a brief overview of the toxicant exposures experienced by veterans during three eras of military conflict. The authors contend that environmental exposures during deployment have been encountered since the earliest conflicts and will continue to be an important issue in future deployments. However, the crucial yet difficult issue is to determine the appropriate levels of interventional chemicals to reduce the risk of disease from pests and possible chemical warfare agent exposures while decreasing the likelihood of negative effects from the chemical toxicant exposures themselves. Exposures to chemical agents will be an ongoing concern in future deployments. The ideal practice would protect troops from disease and exposure but not cause adverse health outcomes in troops at the same time. This approach could help avoid future episodes of Agent Orange chronic sequelae or Gulf War multisymptom illness or cancer incidence as a result of hexavalent chromium exposures. In addition it may also help answer the questions that remain including, "what is the impact of genetic factors interacting with exposures on resultant health symptom concerns?", "what are the effects on an aging population with prior exposures?" and "are there potential treatments to diminish the multiple medical, neuropsychological and psychological effects of these exposures?"

Over the past decade, the number of women veterans using the VA care has nearly doubled, and numbers will continue to rise. In Chapter 14, Kimerling et al. point out that women veterans of Operation Enduring Freedom, Operation Iraqi Freedom, and Operation New Dawn (OEF/OIF/OND) are substantially more likely to seek VHA health care than women from previous eras. This influx of new women veterans represents a changing face of women in VHA. With more than two-thirds of the OEF/OIF/OND cohort in reproductive age groups, there is a projected need for enhanced services across many domains, including reproductive health care, such as the issues of contraception and childbirth. These age groups also represent the peak years for utilization of mental health services among women. The authors conclude by recommending increased attention to access for mental health services, including treatment of war-zone exposures, and attention to couples and family issues that are especially relevant to women's readjustment after deployment.

The book concludes with two chapters addressing the aging and end-of-life issues that veterans contend with. Chapter 15 summarizes and discusses the literature examining the health of aging veterans, the literature on the effects of military service on veterans' mortality and health, and the relationships between military service and later-life health and well-being. MacLean and Edwards outline the challenges to assessing whether and how military service affects health. In addition, they analyze the trends in the experiences of surviving veterans focusing on shifts in war and peace. They offer a broader view of the effects of military service on health and other outcomes that may not be limited to disabilities or health conditions formally diagnosed by the VHA by recognizing that military service has far-reaching influences on the minds and perspectives of all veterans whether they saw combat or not, and whether or not they were wounded. They posit that a far more difficult question to answer is whether and how military service may have exerted a treatment effect on the health of the average veteran independent of measurable service-related trauma.

Grassman and Shreve, in the last chapter of the book, movingly describe the challenges of the final battle that 1,800 veterans face daily: dying peacefully. Military service influences soldiers in ways that can sometimes complicate peaceful dying, even though their death may not occur until many years after they leave military service. The authors point out that survival-mode mentality interferes with letting go and a veteran's "attack and defend" instincts make death the enemy and dying a battle. The very characteristics that are prized in service members, such as stoicism and wisdom, and some members' traumatic experience and paralyzing guilt resulting from combat experience become a complication and may impact how veterans and their families cope with the dying process. In addition, veterans may struggle with a sense of "unfinished business" resulting from behaviors used either to avoid confronting locked-up feelings or to numb traumatic memories. Veterans and their families have unique bereavement needs to be considered by those charged with caring for terminally ill veterans and their families. The literature is only beginning to evolve in providing guidance for addressing these needs. Pharmacologic interventions for select conditions can be helpful but when a provider is faced with a veteran refusing to admit he or she is in pain when the grimace says otherwise, care often extends well beyond the medicine cabinet.

References

DeBakey, M.E., 1996. History, the Torch that Illuminates: Lessons from Military Medicine. *Military Medicine*, 161(12), pp. 711–16.

Department of Veteran's Affairs, 2002. *United States Department of Veteran's Affairs*. [Online] Available at: http://www.virec.research.va.gov/DataSourcesName/NationalSurveyVet erans/2001NationalSurveyofVeterans.htm [Accessed 15 April 2012].

Government Accountability Office, 2005. *United States Government Accountability Office*. [Online] Available at: http://www.gao.gov/new.items/d05722t.pdf [Accessed 16 April 2012].

Hetz, S.P., 2006. Introduction to Military Medicine: A Brief Overview. *Surgical Clinics of North America*, 86, pp. 675–688.

Iglehart, J.K., 1996. Reform of the Veterans Affairs Health Care System. *New England Journal of Medicine*, 335, pp. 1407–12.

Kizer, K.W., 1995. *Prescription for Change: The Guiding Principles and Strategic Objectives Underlying the Transformation of the Veterans Healthcare System*. [Online] Available at: http://www.va.gov/HEALTHPOLICYPLANNING/rxweb.pdf [Accessed 22 April 2012].

Perlin J.B., Kolodner R.M & Roswell R.H., 2004. The veterans health administration: quality, value, accountability, and information as transforming strategies for patient-centered care. *American Journal of Managment Care*, 10, pp. 828–36.

Tracy, S., Trafton J. & Humphries K., 2004. *The Department of Veterans Affairs Substance Abuse Treatment System: Results of the 2003 Drug and Alcohol Program Survey*. Palo Alto: US Department of Veterans Affairs.

Tracy S.W., Tavakoli S., Stolpner S. & Trafton J.A., 2011. Treating Substance Use Disorders within the Veterans Affairs Health Care System. In T. Miller, ed. *Veterans Health Reference*. New York: Praeger.

United States Census Bureau, 2011. *United States Census Bureau*. [Online] Available at: http://www.census.gov/compendia/statab/ [Accessed 15 April 2012].

(USGAO) United States Government Accountability Office, Tuesday May 9 1990. *GAO Testimony Before the Subcommittee on Human Resources and Intergovernmental Relations*. Federal Health Care Delivery Issues, Health, Education, and Human Services Division.

(USGAO) US Government Accountability Office, VA Health Care: Issues Affecting Eligibility Reform (GAO/T-HEHS-95-213, July 19, 1995).

(USGAO) United States Government Accountability Office, Thursday June 27 1996. Efforts to Improve Veterans' Access to Primary Care Services (GAO/T-HEHS-96-134, Apr. 24, 1996).

2 OEF/OIF demographics compared with previous cohorts

Implications for medical care

Ann M. Hendricks and Jomana Amara

Introduction

Since 2001, the United States (US) has deployed more than 2 million troops to Afghanistan and Iraq for Operation Enduring Freedom and Operation Iraqi Freedom (OEF/OIF), often for more than one tour of duty (Tan, 2009). These major international conflicts were the first since the Vietnam War that required a great number of troops on the ground. About 50 nations have contributed troops to both conflict areas, but the majority of those deployed at any one time have been from the US. For example, in 2009, 90,000 of the 130,000 troops deployed in Afghanistan were from the US with the next largest contingents from the United Kingdom (9,500) and Germany (4,818) (ISAF, 2012).

The nature of the OEF/OIF conflicts has translated into health care needs that have concerned not only US service members and their families, but also the US Congress, the Department of Defense (DoD) and the Department of Veterans Affairs (VA) (e.g., see S. HRG 112–95 or S. HRG. 112–267). The signature conditions of the wars for US veterans are traumatic brain injury (TBI) and post-traumatic stress disorder (PTSD), but the majority of health complaints for both active duty military and veterans are relatively mundane, such as gastro-intestinal or musculo-skeletal complaints. For example, Deyton (2008) reported that the largest proportion (46.6 percent) of OEF/OIF veterans accessing VA health care had diagnoses for musculo-skeletal conditions. Haskell et al. (2012) found that the odds for musculo-skeletal and joint problems were even greater for female OEF/OIF veterans compared with males.

The concern about the nation's ability to provide medical care for service members returning from active war duty must be assessed in the context of the other demands on the system, however. For example the Vietnam War cohort outnumbers the OEF/OIF cohort more than threefold and is entering old age, the period of life with the greatest health burden from chronic disease. In fact, demand for immediate post-deployment services by the OEF/OIF veterans is overshadowed nationally by the demands of the Korean and Vietnam War cohorts in terms of the number of patients and the average cost of care.

This chapter describes the US veteran population today and places the OEF/OIF cohort in the context of all living US veterans. It relies on publicly available data and information. It does not explore the ramifications for veterans' education, insurance, loans, burial, compensation, or pensions. Although the pressing needs of newly discharged veterans require immediate attention, long-term care needs for aging veterans is a concern not only for the future of the OEF/OIF cohort, but more immediately for the veterans of past conflicts.

We first present information about overall trends in the total numbers of US veterans and compare demographic characteristics of OEF/OIF veterans and the overall veteran population. The discussion then moves to some of the health care needs of veterans who separated from the military in the past ten years.

The US veteran population

Over the past seventy years, the number of veterans grew following the nation's involvement in World War II, the Korean conflict, and the Vietnam War, all of which used drafts to enlist military personnel (Figure 2.1). The total number of veterans peaked around 1980. Since then it has generally declined as many older veterans died and the military downsized at the end of the Cold War. However, the large cohorts from World War II, the Korean conflict and the Vietnam War still make up the majority of today's veterans. In 2012, most (55.5 percent) of the 21.8 million US veterans are age 60 or older; only 5.5 percent are age 30 or younger (US DVA 2007).

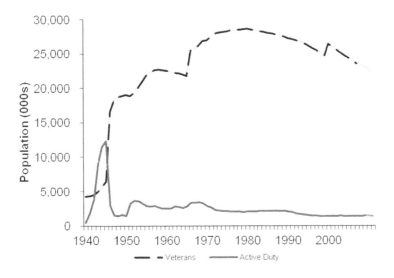

Figure 2.1 Active duty and veteran populations, 1940–2012

US Department of Defense, Personnel, Publications, Selected Manpower Statistics, Annual, http://siadapp.dior.whs.mil/personnel/Pubs.htm.

Note: The increase in the veteran population is an artifact of the decennial census in 2000, which identified more veterans than had been projected from the 1990 census. Some experts believe that increased life expectancy was the reason for this difference.

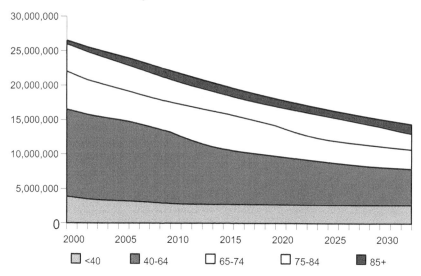

Figure 2.2 Forecast of veteran population by age group, 2000 through 2033

Source: http://www1.va.gov/vetdata/docs/1l.xls, accessed April 23, 2012

Military conscription ended in 1973 and today's members of the armed forces join voluntarily. Across all services, there are over 1.4 million active military personnel today (http://siadapp.dmdc.osd.mil/personnel/MILITARY/ms0.pdf). The relatively stable or perhaps declining (Feickert & Henning, 2012) numbers of active military projected for the next few decades imply that the total number of veterans will continue to decline through 2030 to about 14 million (Figure 2.2). By that time, the number of veterans over age 75 will be greater than the number under the age of 40.

Women make up 8.7 percent of all living veterans, almost 1.9 million individuals (US DVA, 2007). They are younger than male veterans; about half of women veterans are currently younger than 50 while only about a quarter of the men are that young. This difference in age reflects increased military opportunities for women after the Vietnam War, which in turn increased the number of female recruits. Women have been a much larger proportion of active military from the 1980s onward.

Projections through 2030 show the total number of women veterans increasing to over 2.1 million or one out of every seven veterans (USDVA, 2007). In the 1990s, DoD changed the way women are assigned and the positions they are assigned to. The combat exclusion was removed and the number of positions to which women could be assigned increased. Given these changes in the active military, OEF/OIF are the first military engagements to result in substantial numbers of female service members in the theater of war.

The racial make-up of the US veteran population is also changing. In the early 1990s, non-Hispanic white Americans were 85 percent of all veterans; in 2012, the proportion has fallen to 78 percent. Another 11.8 percent are non-

Hispanic African Americans. Hispanic Americans make up 6.1 percent and the remaining 3 to 4 percent are Native Americans, Asian Americans, those of Pacific Island descent, or people who identify as having mixed racial heritage. Based on current active military enrollments, the racial composition of veterans in 2033 is projected to become more diverse, but non-Hispanic white Americans will still be the majority (over 70 percent) with the other groups proportionately larger than they are today (US DVA, 2007).

The largest cohort of current veterans, almost 7 million, is from the Vietnam War (http://www.va.gov/VETDATA/Demographics/Demographics.asp, Table 5L). Another 5.5 million or so are counted as "peacetime" veterans with service between major conflicts. There are more than 3.4 million living veterans from World War II and the Korean War combined, but in another twenty years, there will be virtually no veterans still alive from either of these wars. About 2.5 million Vietnam veterans will still be alive, but the rest of the veteran population will have served from 1980 onward.

The impact of OEF/OIF on veterans

What is the impact of the last decade's actions in Iraq and Afghanistan on the number of US veterans? The number of veterans who separated from the military since 2002 and served in OEF/OIF is about 2 million, over half of whom were reservists or members of the National Guard and may have already had veteran status from service in the regular Army, Navy, Marines or Air Force. During those same years, the total number of veterans discharged is estimated at about 2.7 million, approximately 12.4 percent of all living veterans. Thus, OEF/OIF did not increase the numbers or change the characteristics of US veterans compared with expected separations in the absence of these conflicts. However, these conflicts did affect the health conditions of veterans.

Physical casualties in recent wars are far more numerous than deaths. Table 2.1 details the US military deaths and casualties from the Civil War to OEF/OIF. The table indicates the ratio of casualties to deaths increased over time starting at about one casualty per death during the Civil War and ending at about 7.5 casualties per death for OEF/OIF. This change can be attributed to the improvement in medical services, particularly those located close to hostilities, over the years. Battlefield medicine, evacuation procedures, and battlefield medical support services have evolved tremendously, leading to greater survival rates for troops. In addition, the very high ratio of casualties to deaths for OEF/OIF may be due in part to the use of body armor and helmets, among other changes. This protective gear shields the user from bullets and shrapnel, improving overall survival rates.

Despite the high ratios of casualties to deaths, the absolute number of physical casualties in OEF/OIF is small compared with the number of disabled veterans from earlier actions. For example, veterans from the Vietnam War era still comprise over 40 percent of today's disabled veterans, in large part because the largest number of veterans who are still alive served during those years. In addition, several important conditions were recognized as service-connected only after the

Table 2.1 US military deaths and casualties from principal wars [a]

Conflict	Number Serving Worldwide	Death	Casualty	Ratio Casualty:Death
Civil War (1861–1865)	2,213,363	364,511	281,881	1:1
Spanish-American War	306,760	2,446	1,662	1:2
World War I	4,734,991	116,516	204,002	2:1
World War II	16,112,566	405,399	671,846	2:1
Korea (1950–1953)	5,720,000	36,574	103,284	3:1
Vietnam (1964–1973)	8,744,000	58,209	153,303	3:1
Persian Gulf War (1990–1991)	2,225,000	382	467	3:1
OEF/OIF [b] (2001 to present)	2,200,000	6,386	47,784	7.5:1

a   Data as of April 2, 2012, Department of Defense, http://siadapp.dmdc.osd.mil/personnel/
CASUALTY/gwot_reason.pdf accessed May 1, 2012.
b   Number of deployed service members from Analysis of VA Health Care Utilization Among US
Southwest Asian War Veterans, VHA Office of Public Health and Environmental Hazards.

Vietnam War, adding to the ranks of the disabled. The primary one is PTSD, which the American Psychiatric Association added as an official diagnosis only in 1980. Because this condition may not be recognized as disabling until years after a service member has become a veteran, the number of Vietnam veterans with disabling mental or emotional conditions far exceeds the 153,000 recognized by the military at the end of the war.

Signature conditions

The OEF/OIF wars are the most sustained combat operations since Vietnam. Two major veteran health conditions stemming from these conflicts have received particular attention from Congress and Veterans Health Affairs (VHA): TBI and PTSD. Neither of these is unique to OEF/OIF, but the needs of these two groups of patients have garnered attention. In addition, amputations have been prominent in the news, even though the absolute numbers are relatively small: fewer than 1,500 as of September 1, 2010 (Fischer, 2010). Congress, recognizing the special needs of OEF/OIF veterans, included funds for prosthetic research and increased funding for the Defense and Veteran's Brain Injury Center (DVBIC), the facility that coordinates treatment and research for TBIs. Additional funding for programs for mental health care in general and PTSD specifically has also been made available.

TBI

According to DVBIC (2012), from 2000 through the fourth quarter of 2011, 233,425 soldiers had had a TBI, either combat- or non-combat-related. Non-combat-related brain injuries can result from vehicle accidents, falls, and blows that

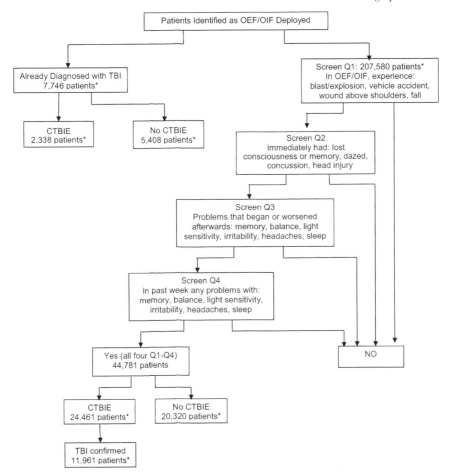

Figure 2.3 VHA TBI screening process (October 2007–March 2009)

could occur during training, recreational activities or other pursuits. Symptoms of TBI may not be evident on first examination since some cases of closed brain injury are not diagnosed properly at the time and may manifest later (Okie 2005). DVBIC (2012) reports that 2.7 percent (over 6,000 cases) were penetrating or severe injuries and 76.7 percent (almost 180,000) were "mild".

The VHA has instituted a post-deployment TBI screening and evaluation process for veterans accessing its services. The screening involves four sets of questions about events, immediate and current symptoms. A positive screen (answering "yes" to at least one question in each of the four sets of questions) leads to a referral for a comprehensive evaluation by a clinician (Figure 2.3). In fiscal 2008 and 2009, the rate of positive screens was 21.6 percent.

Not all patients who have had a TBI will screen positive, because they do not have current symptoms. On the other hand, not all patients who screen positive have a history of TBI. Positive screens may be due to the presence of other conditions, such as PTSD or inner ear injury (Iverson et al., 2009). Based on experience from past conflicts, VHA screening aims to be inclusive, evaluating veterans with lower probability of having TBI to ensure that all those potentially needing care receive appropriate assessment and treatment, especially those with mild injury (US GAO, 2008; Hoge et al., 2006).

On average, veterans with a diagnosis of combat-related TBI report a larger variety of symptoms than those with TBI that is not combat-related. Vision impairment, sensitivity to light or noise, sleep disturbance, and PTSD are among the symptoms experienced more by those veterans with combat-related injury. Receiving timely treatment and rehabilitation may, at a minimum, help veterans adapt to the physical outcomes caused by mild or moderate TBI. For example, understanding the cause of physical symptoms like loss of hearing or feeling in the extremities and learning coping strategies may forestall a variety of negative feelings. In this way, getting treatment earlier is more cost effective than getting it at a later time. For a history of the development of treatment, see Chapters 10 and 11 in this volume.

PTSD

The VHA has undertaken many efforts to improve PTSD care delivered to veterans. It has developed a guide for clinicians and implemented a clinical reminder to prompt clinicians to assess OEF/OIF veterans for PTSD, depression, and substance abuse. The VHA has implemented a national system of 144 PTSD programs in all states and required all VHA outpatient clinics to have either a psychiatrist or a psychologist on staff full time. VHA has also established Mental Illness Research, Education, and Clinical Centers (MIRECCs) to focus on issues of post-deployment health of OEF/OIF veterans such as PTSD and suicide prevention.

In the case of OEF/OIF, 15.6 to 17.1 percent of veterans deployed to Iraq reportedly displayed symptoms of PTSD and 11.2 percent of veterans deployed to Afghanistan reportedly did so (Hoge et al. 2004). Of the OEF/OIF veterans who have used VHA services, however, almost 37 percent had a diagnosis for any mental health condition (Deyton, 2008). Within this broad category, PTSD was the most common diagnosis listed, with substance use disorders, major depression, and neurotic disorders also reported for at least a quarter of the patients (VHA Office of Public Health and Environmental Hazards 2007). Among women OEF/OIF veterans, PTSD is potentially identified for at least as large a proportion of women as men (see Chapter 14).

Studies indicate that more frequent and more intense involvement in combat operations increases the risk of developing mental health problems (Office of the Surgeon Multinational Force, 2006). Due to the intensity of combat in OEF/OIF, returning veterans are at a high risk for mental health problems—specifically those resulting from TBI or PTSD. These two injuries often coincide. Because of its chronic nature, it is difficult to predict the pattern of utilization and therefore the costs for treatment of PTSD (Hendricks et al., 2012). Outpatient treatment for mental health issues is the norm in VHA; some specialized residential treatment programs do exist, but these programs are not located in every state.

VHA and health care for OEF/OIF veterans

Both DoD and the VHA are responsible for the wellbeing and welfare of veterans, especially those who were injured or disabled while on active military duty. Bass et al. (Chapter 3, this volume) show that veterans with disabilities connected to their military service (whether from combat or non-hostile activities) are given the highest priority for care within the VHA. This emphasis on service-related injuries and disabilities was also the case under precursors to the VHA, which were first established in 1930 when Congress authorized the President to consolidate the activities of all government activities affecting war veterans. World War II resulted in a massive increase in the number of veterans. Congress enacted a large number of new benefits for veterans, most significantly the World War II GI bill of 1944. Further acts were passed for the benefit of veterans of the Korean conflict, the Vietnam War, and the all-volunteer force. In 1989, the Department of Veterans Affairs was established as a cabinet-level position. It is second in size only to the DoD.

The VHA health care benefit is funded by discretionary allocations that Congress reviews every year. Thus, the level of VHA funding for veterans' health care is not guaranteed and changes year to year. Since 2001, it has expanded from $21 billion to about $53 billion requested for FY 2013, a 151 percent increase (Testimony, Secretary Shinseki, Feb 29, 2012). VHA's national health care delivery system is divided into 21 Veterans Integrated Service Networks (VISNs). Each network includes between five and eleven hospitals as well as community-based outpatient clinics (CBOCs), nursing homes, and readjustment counseling centers (Vet Centers). In 2012, VHA operated 157 hospitals, 134 nursing homes, 43 residential rehabilitation treatment centers, and 711 CBOCs. In addition, the VHA provides grants for construction of state-owned nursing homes and domiciliary facilities.

VHA estimates that in 2013 it will treat over 600,000 OEF/OIF veterans, about 9 percent of all veterans expected to receive VHA health care that year. OEF/OIF veterans receive care in all of the VHA networks around the country, but are disproportionately affecting VHA medical centers in California, Texas, Florida, and the southeastern states. These include states with some of the largest veteran populations, but the OEF/OIF patient loads represent larger percentages of this veteran cohort than is true for other veterans. This pattern may be due to the existence in these states of more military bases where military families reside and to which the veterans return. The pattern has important implications for the future costs of care for OEF/OIF veterans because it may indicate the need to expand VHA capacity more in these states than in other areas of the country.

Costs for care

It is currently difficult to quantify the costs and the amount of care that the OEF/OIF cohort requires because of all the unknowns:

* Politically mandated changes in eligibility
* The nature, severity, and number of PTSD, TBI, and physical disabilities
* To which VHA centers the veterans will turn for care
* Medical discoveries and new treatments
* How much the veterans rely on VHA for care from one year to the next.

Because the range of estimates for OEF/OIF veterans with severe physical or mental conditions is so large (e.g., 15 to 40 percent of OEF/OIF veterans possibly have PTSD, depending on the sample and the measure of PTSD), translating those lower and upper bounds into amounts of utilization or funding for more than a few years into the future is not policy relevant today.

Conventional wisdom holds that caring for returning veterans is placing a large burden on the VHA system (Bilmes 2007). However, demand for immediate post-deployment VHA services by the OEF/OIF veterans will be overshadowed nationally by the demands of the aging Korean and Vietnam Wars cohorts in terms of the number of patients and the average cost of their care (Hendricks and Amara 2008). The importance of the aging veteran cohort is apparent from Figures 2.1 and 2.2. In 2012, not only were more than half of all veterans over age 60, almost two-thirds were 55 and older. The healthcare needs of these older veterans are those of most elderly Americans with complex chronic conditions such as diabetes or heart failure. Elderly veterans, however, often have additional complications from disabilities sustained during military service, including mental health disorders. These veterans will continue to comprise most of the demand on VHA funding and services until the majority of the World War II, Korean War, and Vietnam War cohort pass through the system. By 2030, veterans from OEF/OIF will be middle-aged or older and will have additional disabilities that are not service-connected, but that will require health services nevertheless.

References

Amara, J. & Hendricks. A. (2009). The deferred cost of war: Short and long term impact of OEF/OIF on veterans' health care. *Defense & Security Analysis*, 25(3), 285–298.

Bilmes, L. (2007). *Soldiers Returning from Iraq and Afghanistan: The Long-Term Costs of Providing Veterans Medical Care and Disability Benefits (RWP07-001)*. Working paper. John F. Kennedy School of Government-Harvard University, Cambridge, MA.

Buddin, R., & Kapur, K. (2005). *An Analysis of Military Disability Compensation*. Santa Monica, CA: RAND National Defense Research Institute.

Congressional Research Support Report for Congress. (2006a). *Veterans' Medical Care: FY2007 Appropriations* (Order Code RL33409). Washington, DC: Library of Congress.

Congressional Research Support Report for Congress. (2006b). *Veterans' Health Care Issues in the 109th Congress* (Order Code RL 32961). Washington, DC: Library of Congress.

Congressional Research Support Report for Congress. (2007). *Veterans' Benefits: Issues in the 110th Congress* (Order Code RL33985). Washington, DC: Library of Congress.

Department of Veterans Affairs Office of Research and Development, National Institute of Mental Health, United States Army Medical Research and Materiel Command. (2006). *Mapping the Landscape of Deployment Related Adjustment and Mental Disorders. A Meeting Summary of a Working Group to Inform Research.* Rockville, MD: US Department of Veterans Affairs.

Deyton, L., (2008) Analysis of VA Health Care Utilization Among US Global War on Terrorism (GWOT) Veterans, Presentation at AcademyHealth, June 2008, *Accessed April 29, 2012, h*ttp://www.academyhealth.org/files/2008/monday/tmarshalls/6_9_2008_11_30/deytonl.pdf.

DVBIC (2012) DoD Worldwide Numbers for TBI (Non-combat and Combat Injuries). *Defense Medical Surveillance System (Dmss) And Theater Medical Data Store (TMDS) Prepared by Armed Forces Health Surveillance Center (AFHSC)* http://www.dvbic.org/TBI-Numbers.aspx accessed April 4, 2012.

Feickert, A., & Henning, C.A., (2012) Army Drawdown and Restructuring: Background and Issues for Congress, April 20, 2012, Congressional Research Service, 7-5700, www.crs.gov, R42493.

Fischer, H., (2010) U.S. Military Casualty Statistics: Operation New Dawn, Operation Iraqi Freedom, and Operation Enduring Freedom, September 28, 2010, Congressional Research Service Report for Congress, 7-5700, www.crs.gov , RS22452.

Haskell, S.G., Ning, Y., Krebs, E., Goulet, J., Mattocks, K., Kerns, R., & Brandt, C., (2012) Prevalence of painful musculoskeletal conditions in female and male veterans in 7 years after return from deployment in Operation Enduring Freedom/Operation Iraqi Freedom, *Clinical Journal of Pain*, 28(2):163–167. doi: 10.1097/AJP.0b013e318223d951, accessed May 4, 2012 at http://journals.lww.com/clinicalpain/Abstract/2012/02000/Prevalence_of_Painful_Musculoskeletal_Conditions.11.aspx.

Hendricks, A., & Amara, J. (2008). Demographics of the current veterans population and its implication for the future disability and health care needs of veterans. In N. Ainspan, & W. Penk (Eds.), *War's Returning Wounded, Injured and Ill: A Handbook.* (pp. 13–29). Westport, CN: Praeger Publishers.

Hendricks, A., Krengel, M., Iverson, K.M., Kimerling, R., Tun, C., Amara, J., Lew, & H.L. (2012). Estimating the costs of care for co-morbid mild TBI and PTSD, in Vasterling J.J., Bryant R.A., & Keane T.M. (eds.) *PTSD and Mild Traumatic Brain Injury*, New York: Guildford Press.

Hoge, C., Castro, C., Messer, S., McGurk, M., Cotting, D., & Koffman, R. (2004). Combat duty in Iraq and Afghanistan, mental health problems, and barriers to care. *The New England Journal of Medicine*, 351 (1), 13–22.

Hoge, C.W., Auchterlonie, J.L., & Milliken, C.S. (2006) Mental health problems, use of mental health services, and attrition from military service after returning from deployment to Iraq or Afghanistan. *JAMA*. 295:1023–1032.

ISAF (International Security Assistance Force), (2012) Troop Numbers and Contributions. Accessed April 2, 2012 at http://www.isaf.nato.int/troop-numbers-and-contributions/index.php.

Iverson, G.L., Langlois, J.A., McCrea, M.A., & Kelly, J.P., (2009), Challenges associated with post-deployment screening for mild traumatic brain injury in military personnel, *The Clinical Neuropsychologist*, 23:1299–1314.

Lew, H.L., Poole, J., Guillory, S., Salerno, R.M., Leskin, G., & Sigford, B. (2006). Persistent problems after traumatic brain injury: the need for long-term follow up and coordinated care. *Journal of Rehabilitation Research Development*, 43 (2), 7–10.

National Center for Veterans, Analysis and Statistics, Assistant Secretary for Policy and Planning. (1995). *National Survey of Veterans (Depot stock no. P92493)*. Washington, DC: US Department of Veterans Affairs.

National Center for Veterans, Analysis and Statistics, Assistant Secretary for Policy and Planning. (2003). *National Survey of Veterans*. Washington, DC: US Department of Veterans Affairs.

Office of the Surgeon Multinational Force – Iraq and Office of the Surgeon General, United States Army Medical Command. (2006). *Mental Health Advisory Team (MHAT) IV Operation Iraqi Freedom 05–07*.

Okie, S. (2005). Traumatic brain injury in the war zone. *New England Journal of Medicine*, 352 (20), 2043–2047.

S. HRG. 112–95, The Fiscal Year 2012 Budget for Veterans' Programs Hearing Before the Committee on Veterans' Affairs United States Senate, One Hundred Twelfth Congress First Session, March 2, 2011 at http://www.gpo.gov/fdsys/pkg/CHRG-112shrg65905/pdf/CHRG-112shrg65905.pdf, accessed April 29, 2012.

S. HRG. 112–267, VA Mental Health Care: Addressing Wait Times and Access to Care, November 30, 2011 at http://www.gpo.gov/fdsys/pkg/CHRG-112shrg72248/pdf/CHRG-112shrg72248.pdf, accessed April 29, 2012.

Tan, M. (2009) 2 Million Troops have Deployed since 9/11, *Marine Corps Times* Dec. 18, 2009.

US Department of Veterans Affairs (2007), Demographics, VetPop2007 National Tables, Table 1L http://www.va.gov/VETDATA/Demographics/Demographics.asp Accessed April 4, 2012.

US Government Accountability Office. (2006a). *Disability Benefits. Benefit Amounts for Military Personnel and Civilian Public Safety Officers Vary by Program Provisions and Individual Circumstances (GAO-06-04)*. Washington, DC: US GAO.

US Government Accountability Office. (2006b). *Veterans Disability Benefits. VA Should Improve Its Management of Individual Unemployability Benefits by Strengthening Criteria, Guidance, and Procedures. (GAO-06-309)*. Washington, DC: US GAO.

US Government Accountability Office. (2008), VA Health Care: Mild Traumatic Brain Injury Screening and Evaluation Implemented of OEF/OIF Veterans, but Challenges Remain, Report to Congressional Requesters, February 2008, GAO 08-276.

Veterans Health Administration Office of Public Health and Environmental Hazards. (2007). *Analysis of VA Health Care Utilization among US Southwest Asian War Veterans: Operation Iraqi Freedom, Operation Enduring Freedom*. Washington, DC: US Department of Veterans Affairs.

3 Health care and insurance for US military service members

Active duty, national guard, reserve, veterans, and retired

Elizabeth Bass, Heidi Golding, and Allison Percy[1]

Active duty, national guard and reserve, and former military service members typically have access to several health care programs during service and after separation. Active duty service members are covered by TRICARE, the Department of Defense's (DoD's) health care program.[2] Active duty dependents, guard and reservists, retirees, survivors, and their dependents may also be covered. TRICARE provides medical care to military beneficiaries using both military and civilian providers. The program includes direct care at Military Treatment Facilities (MTFs), which are medical centers, hospitals, and clinics owned and operated by DoD, and also civilian care through regional networks of contracted providers and by a large number of non-contracted providers. More than 9 million people were eligible for TRICARE in 2010, and nearly 8 million of them used TRICARE that year. While supporting the health and readiness of the active duty force is the primary mission of military health care, the bulk of TRICARE utilization and spending reflects services provided to retirees, dependents, and survivors, who together are over 80 percent of the eligible population (Congressional Budget Office 2009: 8).

When most service members transition out of uniform and become veterans, they lose access to TRICARE benefits unless they qualify for military retirement. Veterans may be eligible for care through the Veterans Health Administration (VHA), the medical program of the Department of Veterans Affairs (VA). With the number of veterans in the US population totaling 23 million in 2010, VHA delivered services to more than 5 million patients. VHA provides care directly in its own hospitals, clinics, and other facilities, though in certain circumstances a veteran may access outside providers at VHA's expense. Many veterans also have private employer-sponsored insurance or are eligible for other public programs such as Medicare or Medicaid. These multiple sources of health care often overlap, and this can make coordination of care and cost constraint challenging. Compared with health care plans offered in the private sector, the out-of-pocket costs associated with using most benefits provided by DoD and VHA are low.

This chapter presents an overview of the health care and health insurance options available to these service members as they age, from active duty or reserve status, to separation, to Medicare eligibility.

Active duty and dependents

Active duty personnel are automatically enrolled in TRICARE, effective the first day of reporting to active duty. Similar to most health plans, TRICARE has options that cover dependents, such as spouses and children.[3] Health care is free for active duty members and provided at minimal cost for their dependents under the most popular TRICARE plan.

The Army, Navy, and Air Force operate hospitals and clinics in the United States and overseas. Active duty members typically receive all of their health care directly from those MTFs. The MTFs may also provide care to other groups of beneficiaries, and with minor exceptions services in MTFs are free to all users. Statutes regulate the order in which different groups of beneficiaries may receive care. Priority is always given to active duty personnel; thereafter precedence usually goes to active duty dependents, then retirees, their dependents, and survivors. A small number of other eligible beneficiaries may use MTFs when space and resources are available. As a practical matter, access to the direct care system also depends on whether beneficiaries live close enough to an MTF to depend on it as their primary source of care. Since MTFs may be inconvenient, not preferred, or not available, most TRICARE users who are not active duty or do not live near MTFs receive care through TRICARE's civilian providers.

TRICARE offers several health plan options, as well as pharmacy and dental benefits, using a combination of MTFs and civilian networks. The governance structure for this system is the TRICARE Management Activity (TMA). TMA organizes health plan provision geographically, with three regions in the United States, and one for the rest of the world. Each area is bid out competitively to regional private contractors (who, in turn, may use sub-contractors) to administer the plans for DoD: developing networks of civilian providers, processing claims, monitoring network quality and customer satisfaction, and other administrative functions. National contractors are used for claims processing for users who are also Medicare eligible, as well as for dental and pharmacy claims processing. TMA has access-to-care standards that address appointment and office wait times, accessibility in emergencies, and the composition of network specialists.

The three largest TRICARE plans—Prime, Standard, and Extra—offer coverage to most DoD beneficiaries. Prime (a health maintenance organization-type plan) is the sole option for uniformed service members on active duty, including activated members of the guard and reserves; dependents, however, may choose from Prime, Standard (a fee-for-service plan), or Extra (a preferred provider plan).[4] The majority of family members of active duty personnel choose Prime. TRICARE Prime has fewer out-of-pocket costs than TRICARE Standard and Extra, but less freedom of choice in providers. Both Standard and Extra have an annual outpatient deductible for active duty dependents, but no premiums or enrollment fees. Several additional smaller programs serve limited populations; for example, beneficiaries who live where regular networks of TRICARE providers are not available. TRICARE has a number of variants to ensure coverage for all active duty members and their dependents regardless of worldwide location or special considerations.

TRICARE Prime is operated much like a civilian health maintenance organization (HMO). Primary care clinicians for active duty members are located within the MTFs. Active duty dependents, however, may use a primary care clinician at the MTF or turn to the TRICARE civilian network. The primary care clinicians provide most care and any referrals to specialists; such referrals are generally required under TRICARE Prime. Benefits are comprehensive, including vision, preventive services, and travel reimbursement for some specialty care. Service members and their dependents are charged nothing whether they use military or civilian providers as long as they remain in the network: no enrollment fees, premiums, deductibles, or other cost-sharing. Care received without a referral is subject to some cost sharing in the form of point-of-service fees, which means that beneficiaries may use providers outside the recognized network yet retain some Prime insurance benefits.[5]

TRICARE Standard is a traditional fee-for-service plan. Standard allows participants the most freedom in selection of providers, but requires higher out-of-pocket costs than Prime or Extra. Out-of-network providers may accept the TRICARE reimbursement rate as payment in full, or they may charge up to 15 percent above the TRICARE allowable charge; if the provider does so, the beneficiary is responsible for the extra cost, in addition to the normal coinsurance amount.[6]

TRICARE Extra is similar to the Standard plan, but uses a preferred provider network. Under this version, network providers accept a negotiated payment rate from TRICARE and agree to file all claims for participants. Beneficiaries using Extra generally incur lower out-of-pocket costs than those who use Standard.[7]

The basic structure of both TRICARE Standard and Extra is akin to many plans commonly offered by civilian employers. TRICARE may act as dependents' primary insurance or supplement other health insurance coverage. Because enrollment in the Standard and Extra plans is not required, the distinction between the two lies in whether beneficiaries choose a TRICARE-authorized provider in the network (in which case DoD processes the medical encounter under the Extra plan) or non-network provider (DoD processes the medical encounter under the Standard plan). Thus, a single beneficiary may participate in both Standard and Extra plans over the course of a year. Beneficiaries who reach an annual catastrophic cap face no more cost sharing for the remainder of the year for allowable charges of covered services.[8]

TRICARE Young Adult is a health care plan initiated in 2011 offering coverage to certain adult children of TRICARE beneficiaries: unmarried adult children between the ages of 21 and 26, not eligible for an employer-sponsored health plan through their own employment, or otherwise eligible for TRICARE coverage. Initially, only the Standard option was available, but Prime coverage began in 2012. Both options have monthly premiums; Standard also has an annual outpatient deductible, and other cost sharing.[9] These fees are intended to cover all the costs of the Young Adult program.

Beneficiaries have several options with *TRICARE's Pharmacy Program*. Prescriptions are filled for free in MTFs when written by any qualified provider, whether military or civilian, in or out of network. Beneficiaries may also fill MTF prescriptions at retail pharmacies in the TRICARE network or use TRICARE's mail order pharmacy. Copayments vary by the type of drug: beneficiaries pay the least for generic drugs, more for brand-name drugs from TRICARE's approved list of pharmaceuticals (the formulary), and the most for brand-name drugs that are not part of the formulary.

All non-active duty beneficiaries who live in the United States face the same cost sharing for prescriptions obtained in network retail pharmacies.[10]

TRICARE Dental Programs provide dental care without cost to active duty personnel either at military dental treatment facilities or within the network of civilian dentists. Other military beneficiaries do not automatically receive dental benefits under TRICARE, but have the option to enroll in various premium-based programs. Cost sharing depends on the sponsor's rank and type of care provided.[11]

National Guard, Reserve, and dependents

In the past decade, DoD has relied more and more on reservists to support contingency operations, such as the conflicts in Iraq and Afghanistan. Congress, in turn, has increased the health care benefits available to reservists and their dependents. Since 2005, the selected reserve, a component of the ready reserve which includes the Army National Guard, Army Reserve, Navy Reserve, Marine Corps Reserve, Air National Guard, and Air Force Reserve, has had access to TRICARE through a new program, TRICARE Reserve Select. Previously, reservists were eligible for TRICARE only while on active duty for more than 30 days.[12]

Selected reserve members have a cycle of coverage during which they are eligible for different TRICARE options based on duty status: pre-activation, active duty, deactivation, and inactive. Pre-activation eligibility for TRICARE is triggered when members of the selected reserve are notified that they will serve on active duty to supplement regular armed forces either in support of contingency operations or other federal service. At this point, members become eligible for TRICARE Prime, and their families are eligible for TRICARE Prime, Standard, and Extra on the date the order was issued or 180 days before reporting to active duty, whichever is later. This is commonly referred to as "early eligibility" and may continue uninterrupted once members begin active duty. Like all active duty personnel, guard and reserve members enroll in TRICARE Prime upon reaching their final duty station. They and their families receive the same coverage as active duty service members and their dependents. After deactivation, reserve members return to inactive status, and may be eligible for certain transitional or temporary plans or for the TRICARE plan designed for drilling reservists. (Active duty members separating from the military before retirement may also have access to one or more of these plans.)

Transitional Assistance Management Program (TAMP) offers 180 days of continued TRICARE coverage as an interim benefit for service members transitioning out of active duty service. The TAMP period begins on the day after separation from active duty. Members and dependents who enroll use TRICARE Prime, Standard, or Extra under the same cost sharing rules that apply to active duty families.

TRICARE Reserve Select (TRS) is for reservists who have completed the TAMP period and wish to stay with a TRICARE plan. TRS is similar to TRICARE Standard and Extra with the same coverage, cost sharing, and annual outpatient deductible applicable to active duty family members. The main difference is that inactive reservists and their families must pay monthly premiums.[13] These premiums cover 28 percent of estimated program cost, updated annually based on costs during the preceding calendar year. Only selected reservists in a drill pay status (not on active duty orders) who are not eligible for the Federal Employees Health Benefits Program (either through their own current or former employment or that of a family member) may qualify for TRS, and qualification lasts the duration of time the sponsor remains in the reserve (while not activated). Upon activation, the member and dependents become eligible for TRICARE, including for the pre-activation period, and TRS coverage ends.

Guard and reserve members—and former active duty members (not retired)—whose TAMP eligibility has expired and who have not yet acquired other health insurance post-separation, or who are not eligible for TAMP or TRS, may qualify to purchase another plan, the *Continued Health Care Benefit Program (CHCBP)*. This premium-based plan offers temporary health coverage for 18–36 months after TRICARE eligibility ends, serving as a transition between military health benefits and any new (civilian) health plan.[14] CHCBP acts much like extended health insurance benefits provided under the Consolidated Omnibus Budget Reconciliation Act of 1985 (commonly called COBRA) for a worker leaving a civilian employer. Those who qualify must purchase CHCBP within 60 days of losing TRICARE coverage. The program is comparable to TRICARE Standard with the same coverage, cost sharing, and annual outpatient deductible. Premiums are based on average rates for a comparable plan in the Federal Employees Health Benefits Program, including both the employee and employer share of the premium plus an administrative fee.

Post separation: veterans and retired

Veterans, who are former military members who have served on active duty (including certain members of the guard and reserve components who have completed their periods of activation), may be eligible for multiple sources of health care or health insurance depending on past service and other factors. Immediately after separation from active duty, a veteran may use TAMP or CHCBP. Veterans may have access to health care provided by the VHA, other public sources such as Medicare or Medicaid, or private health insurance. Retirees from the military (generally those who have at least 20 years of active duty service or have retired before that because of illness or injury, or guard and reserve with 20 qualifying years of service) and their dependents have additional coverage options. Because many former military members are eligible for several programs, use of multiple provider systems within a single year is common.

Health care for veterans in the Veterans Health Administration

VHA provides comprehensive health care to veterans including routine health assessments, inpatient and outpatient surgery, and specialty care for most conditions. Limited long-term custodial care in nursing homes is also available. VHA operates a health care system consisting of about 150 medical centers, 970 ambulatory care and community-based outpatient clinics, 300 Vet Centers (which provide readjustment counseling and outreach services), 135 nursing homes and more than 150 rehabilitation and home care programs. Most care is given directly in those facilities by providers employed by VHA, although in certain circumstances a veteran may receive care from outside providers paid for by VHA.

Eligibility for VHA's health care services is based primarily on a veteran's military service. Generally, veterans must have served 24 continuous months on active duty and been discharged under other than dishonorable conditions. Guard and reserve members who were called to active duty under a federal order also qualify for VHA health care if they completed the term for which they were called and were granted an other than dishonorable discharge.[15]

Those broad criteria, however, do not always translate into access to services. Care paid for by VHA is not an entitlement, but rather is funded by annual federal appropriation acts. In 1996, Congress mandated that VHA set up and maintain a system of enrollment to help allocate resources. VHA assigns each veteran seeking care to one of eight categories that indicate priority for enrollment (priority group 1 has highest priority, priority group 8 the lowest) (see Table 3.1). The groups reflect such factors as the presence and extent of a disability, income, or recent combat service. Disabled and low-income veterans are given a higher priority, while veterans with more financial resources who do not have a compensable service-connected disability (that is, a medical condition incurred or exacerbated during military service that is disabling to the extent that VA provides compensation) receive a lower priority. Some veterans who would be in the lowest priority group have been restricted from enrolling for VHA health care at various points in time. The Veterans Programs Enhancement Act of 1998 (Public Law 105-368) guarantees access to VHA's health care system, after separation from active military service, to members of the armed forces including guard and reservists who have served on active duty in combat operations since the law was enacted. The law gave combat veterans two years to enroll in VHA's health care system after leaving active duty without requiring those veterans to document either income below established thresholds or a service-connected disability. In 2008, lawmakers modified the eligibility period so that recent combat veterans may enroll for VHA services within five years after leaving active duty regardless of their income or disability status (see Title XVII of the National Defense Authorization Act for Fiscal Year 2008, P.L. 110-181, 122 Stat. 493).

In 2010, about 8 million of the 23 million veterans in the US had enrolled in the VHA. More than 5 million of them used VHA's services in that year. Of those veterans who enroll, most do not use VHA for all of their health care needs; indeed enrollees received less than one-third of their total health care from VHA

Table 3.1 Enrollment priority groups at the Veterans Health Administration

Priority 1	Veterans with service-connected disabilities (SCDs) rated 50% or more disabling (or two or more SCDs that together are 50% or more disabling)
Priority 2	Veterans with SCDs rated 30–40% disabling
Priority 3	Veterans who are former prisoners of war; were awarded the Purple Heart; were discharged because of SCDs; have SCDs rated 10–20% disabling; or were disabled by treatment or vocational rehabilitation
Priority 4	Veterans who are receiving aid and attendance or housebound benefits; or who VHA has determined to be catastrophically disabled as a result of a non-service-connected illness or injury
Priority 5	Veterans who do not have SCDs or who have non-compensable SCDs rated 0% disabling and whose annual income and net worth are below VA's national means-test thresholds; veterans who receive a VA pension; veterans eligible for Medicaid benefits
Priority 6	All other eligible veterans not required to make copayments: veterans of World War I or the Mexican Border War; veterans seeking care for disorders associated with exposure to chemical, nuclear, or biological agents in the line of duty; veterans who have compensable SCDs rated 0% disabling; and recently discharged combat veterans who are within a five-year period of eligibility (most veterans of the ongoing overseas contingency operations are initially assigned to P6)
Priority 7	Veterans with no compensable SCDs whose annual income and net worth are each above the VA means-test thresholds, but whose income is below the VA national geographic income thresholds, and who agree to make copayments
Priority 8	Veterans who have no SCDs (or who have non-compensable SCDs rated 0% disabling) whose annual income and net worth are each above the VA means-test thresholds and the VA national geographic income thresholds, and who agree to make copayments

in 2008. The amount of care veterans receive depends on many factors including the convenience of VHA facilities, perceptions of quality of care, out-of-pocket costs, and the availability of other health care options. In 2010, about 79 percent of enrolled veterans had other sources of health care available to them, such as employer-based insurance or public sources of insurance (Department of Veterans Affairs, Office of the Assistant Deputy Under Secretary for Health for Policy and Planning 2011: 25).

Out-of-pocket expenses for veterans using VHA are relatively modest or zero. Veterans enrolled in VHA pay no annual enrollment fees or deductible. In addition, VHA provides medical care for service-connected disabilities free of charge. It also treats those veterans with severe service-connected disabilities (those rated by VA as 50 percent or greater) for non-service connected conditions for free. However, other veterans may be charged to treat conditions not related to their military service unless they are able to demonstrate financial need.[16] Depending on a veteran's priority group and whether the condition being treated is service-connected, veterans may be charged copayments for outpatient visits, to fill a prescription, and for inpatient care.[17] VHA updates some of the copayment charges annually, but has not changed the outpatient fees since fiscal year 2002 or earlier.

Other health insurance for veterans and dependents

As noted earlier, many veterans do not turn to VHA for health care, instead relying on private health insurance or other public sources. In 2009, 93 percent of all veterans in the United States had some type of insurance coverage: most (69 percent) had private health insurance (Department of Veterans Affairs, National Center for Veterans Analysis and Statistics 2011: Table 1). With about 40 percent of veterans over the age of 65, more than half of those enrolled in VHA receive additional public insurance coverage, mainly Medicare (Department of Veterans Affairs, Office of the Assistant Deputy Under Secretary for Health for Policy and Planning 2011: 25).

TRICARE for military retirees and dependents

Military retirees are different from other veterans in that they receive a retirement annuity from DoD. Because most people who join the military do so by age 25, many retire from it between the ages of 38 and 45. Military retirees may thus be subdivided into two groups: those not eligible for Medicare (under the age of 65), and those who are Medicare-eligible (age 65 and older, or have end-stage renal disease, or are permanently disabled). In 2009, fewer than half of all military retirees were over the age of 65, although that portion is growing. The benefits that the two groups of retirees receive under TRICARE, if they choose to continue with this military benefit, differ based on their Medicare eligibility.

The 3.4 million retirees and their dependents who are not yet eligible for Medicare have several options under TRICARE. They may use Prime or they may choose benefits under the Standard or Extra plans. Retirees in Prime pay an annual enrollment fee and small copayments based on type of care received. Retirees in Standard or Extra face annual outpatient deductibles, pay a percentage of each provider's fee, and have a higher catastrophic cap than active duty beneficiaries.[18]

Dental care is also available through the *TRICARE Retiree Dental Program (TRDP)*. This coverage requires monthly premiums that are deducted automatically from retired pay, and enrollees also pay some deductibles and coinsurance, and have annual maximum benefit limits.[19] While DoD negotiates the contract for this coverage with a dental insurance provider, premiums are not subsidized by the federal government like they are for the TRICARE Dental Program.

Service members who retire from the guard or reserves must normally wait until age 60 to begin receiving retirement pay. Until recently, retired reservists who had left the military but were not yet receiving retirement pay were not eligible for TRICARE coverage.[20] In 2010, DoD began offering *TRICARE Retired Reserve (TRR)* as a premium-based program for such "gray area" reservists: those who have accumulated enough service to qualify for military retirement, but are not old enough to receive their military pension. TRR is like TRS for retired reservists who are not yet drawing retirement pay, and for their dependents.[21] TRR permits care by any TRICARE-authorized provider and operates much like Standard or Extra. Monthly premiums, annual outpatient deductibles, and cost sharing varies based on whether a patient seeks care from a TRICARE network provider. Current law requires members to pay the full cost of coverage under TRR with no government subsidy.[22]

According to a 2006 survey conducted by the research organization RAND for DoD, 87 percent of military retirees aged 60 years or younger were employed, as were 53 percent of those between 61 and 64 years (Mariano et al. 2007: 17). Over half of retirees had working spouses. Among those surveyed, 78 percent had access to civilian health plans. But less than half used private insurance, citing high premiums and cost sharing compared with TRICARE. Military retirees and their dependents who have other health insurance may supplement private plans with benefits from TRICARE Standard or Extra as much or as often as they choose without enrolling beforehand.[23]

Military retirees and dependents who are eligible for Medicare (at age 65) may enroll in *TRICARE For Life (TFL)*.[24] This wrap-around benefit for those with Medicare has dramatically reduced out-of-pocket costs for Medicare-eligible military retirees and dependents seeking care from civilian providers. Beneficiaries must enroll in Medicare Part B in order to be eligible for TFL, but there is no separate enrollment fee or premium for TFL.[25] For medical services that are covered by both Medicare and TRICARE, Medicare pays first and TFL pays any remaining coinsurance or copayment amounts, so that the bill is paid in full by the combination of Medicare and TFL. If a medical service is covered by one program but not the other, such as chiropractic care, beneficiaries may face a deductible and coinsurance payments. While both Medicare and TRICARE offer some coverage for care at a skilled nursing facility after an inpatient stay, long-term custodial care in a nursing home or other institutional setting is not covered by either program.

Prescription medications are available through the same TRICARE Pharmacy Program offered other beneficiaries, with prescriptions provided free at MTFs, for a modest copayment via mail-order (except for generics, which are free), or from retail network pharmacies. As with the under-65 retirees, dental care is available through the TRICARE Retiree Dental Program.

Challenges to providing health care through DoD and VHA

DoD and VHA face many challenges to their health care programs, especially in coordinating care for beneficiaries and addressing the rapid growth in health spending. Particular attention has been given to managing health care information and benefits between DoD and VHA. In addition, there are ongoing concerns by policy makers and others that DoD and VHA continue providing affordable levels of care that they believe service members and veterans deserve. Within a time of tightening federal budget constraints, however, rising spending levels may draw attention to the tradeoffs between spending on this health care and other spending.

Military personnel, veterans, and their dependents may have several different health care options at any given time, creating an extensive and complex system that can make coordination of care challenging (see Table 3.2). In particular, many have voiced concerns that navigating the change from DoD to VHA care for wounded service members and others can be difficult. In general, severely ill or disabled service members are assigned a care coordinator or nurse manager—sometimes several—to oversee the transition; others newly discharged often apply directly for VHA enrollment without assistance. Coordination between the two departments at separation from service varies. The Wounded Warrior Act, part of the National Defense Authorization Act for Fiscal Year 2008 (Public Law 110-181), requires that both departments coordinate health care management, disability evaluation, and transition of service members from the conflicts in Iraq and Afghanistan from DoD to VHA. Although not all requirements of the Wounded Warrior Act have been implemented, DoD and VA have taken considerable steps forward. As of 2011, VHA and DoD did not have the ability to fully share health information between their different computer systems. Technical and organizational challenges have made it difficult to construct a unified electronic medical record, but DoD and VHA do have data sharing agreements and information exchange projects. One example is the Virtual Lifetime Electronic Record (VLER), a program to share select parts of a veteran's medical and administrative information electronically, safely, and privately with health care providers—military and civilian—who are part of the Nationwide Health Information Network Exchange.

Both departments are also confronting the costs associated with providing comprehensive medical care to the large number of beneficiaries eligible either for DoD or VHA care, or both. Medical spending has risen rapidly in recent years. In fiscal year 2000, DoD spent about $22 billion (in 2010 dollars) on providing health care to military service members, retirees, and dependents. Due in part to a broadening of benefits and a lag in out-of-pocket costs compared with civilian options, by 2010 DoD's health care spending had risen to $49 billion, which was 124 percent real growth within a decade, or about 8 percent annually. Health care spending increased from 6 percent in 2000 to 9 percent in 2010 of DoD's annual base budget (that is, its budget excluding funds for overseas contingency operations). According to Congressional Budget Office estimates, that spending is expected to surpass $58 billion in inflation-adjusted 2010 dollars by 2015.[26] In March 2011, then Secretary of Defense Robert Gates argued before the House Appropriations Committee that the current TRICARE arrangement is "unsustainable," joining other military leaders in expressing concern over DoD's sharply rising health care costs.

VHA spending has increased from $25 billion in 2000 (in 2010 dollars) to $48 billion in 2010, an increase of nearly 7 percent annually. Both increases in the costs per veteran patient (including rapid medical inflation), and to a lesser extent rising numbers of veterans using VHA, contributed to spending growth in recent years. CBO estimates that, under various assumptions, the total resources

Table 3.2 Health care options for military and former military, and dependents

Beneficiary Type	Program Options
Active duty service members, including National Guard and Reserve activated for more than 30 consecutive days	Military Treatment Facilities (first priority) TRICARE Prime TRICARE Active Duty Dental Program
Active duty dependents, including those of activated National Guard and Reserve, and eligible survivors	TRICARE Prime TRICARE Standard TRICARE Extra TRICARE Dental Program Military Treatment Facilities (space available basis) Private insurance Government programs (if eligible)
National Guard and Reserve members, not activated, and dependents	TRICARE Transitional Assistance Management Program Continued Health Care Benefit Program TRICARE Reserve Select TRICARE Dental Program Private insurance Government programs (if eligible)
Separated former military, not retired	TRICARE Transitional Assistance Management Program Continued Health Care Benefit Program Veterans Health Administration (if eligible) Private insurance Medicare (if age 65 or disabled) Government programs (if eligible)
Retired National Guard and Reserve members, not yet receiving retirement pay, and dependents	TRICARE Retired Reserve Private insurance Government programs (if eligible)
Retired service members and their dependents and survivors, and retired National Guard and Reserve members receiving retired pay and their dependents and survivors not yet eligible for Medicare	TRICARE Prime TRICARE Standard TRICARE Extra TRICARE Retiree Dental Program Military Treatment Facilities (space available basis) Private insurance Government programs (if eligible)
Medicare-eligible retired service members and their dependents and survivors, and retired National Guard and Reserve members and their dependents and survivors	Medicare TRICARE For Life (TFL) TRICARE Retiree Dental Program Military Treatment Facilities (space available basis) Veterans Health Administration (if eligible) Private insurance Government programs (if eligible)

necessary to provide health care services to all veterans who seek treatment at VHA would range from about $59 billion to $66 billion in inflation-adjusted 2010 dollars by 2015.[27] Given recent discussions on reducing the size of the federal debt, additional scrutiny may be focused on the rapid growth in VHA's spending and how to best allocate available resources to VHA and other programs.

Notes

1 The views expressed in this work are those of the authors and should not be interpreted as those of the Congressional Budget Office.

2 The uniformed services within the Department of Defense are composed of the US Air Force, US Army, US Navy, and the US Marine Corps. Also covered by TRICARE but outside the Department of Defense are the following uniformed services: the US Coast Guard, the Commissioned Corps of the US Public Health Service, and the Commissioned Corps of the National Oceanic and Atmospheric Administration. Members of the latter services are eligible for the same health benefits as military personnel, but the population and spending figures in this chapter refer only to the portion of TRICARE serving DoD beneficiaries.

3 The definition of an eligible dependent may vary from one TRICARE benefit to another. For additional details, visit the TRICARE website at www.tricare.mil.

4 The US Family Health Plan is an additional TRICARE Prime option available through networks of community-based, not-for-profit health care systems in only six areas of the United States. Active duty family members pay no enrollment fees and no out-of-pocket costs as long as care is received from the US Family Health Plan provider. All other beneficiaries have annual enrollment fees and small copays that are the same as for TRICARE Prime.

5 There is no point-of-service option for active duty service members.

6 In 2012 the outpatient deductible ranged from $50 (for individual plans) to $300 (for family plans) for active duty dependents, depending on the sponsor's rank. Dependents of activated guard and reserve have no deductible. Coinsurance rates for most services are 20% of the TRICARE allowable charge.

7 Outpatient deductibles are the same as under Standard, but coinsurance rates for active duty dependents are 15% of negotiated network rates for most services.

8 As of 2012 this cap was set at $1,000 per year for families of active duty service members. By comparison, in 2012 the Blue Cross Blue Shield Standard Option (a mix of preferred and non-preferred providers) for federal employees had an out-of-pocket maximum of $7,000.

9 In 2012 the monthly premiums for TYA Standard were $176, and $201 for TYA Prime.

10 In 2012 copays for the TRICARE Mail Order Pharmacy Program pharmacies were $0 for generics, $9 for brand name, $25 for non-formulary prescriptions; network retail pharmacies were $5 for generics, $12 for brand name, and $25 for non-formulary prescriptions. TRICARE Mail Order Pharmacy Program copays cover a 90-day supply, compared with a 30-day supply in retail drug stores. Cost shares for prescriptions filled in non-network retail pharmacies for Prime enrollees were 50% after meeting the point-of-service deductible, and for Standard and Extra users $12 or 20% (whichever was greater) for generic and brand name drugs or $25 or 20% (whichever was greater) for non-formulary drugs.

11 Monthly premiums for active duty family members in 2012 were about $13 for individuals and about $32 for family plans. Annual maximum benefit limits were $1,200. Diagnostic and preventive services had no copay, and most other cost sharing was 20% to 50% of negotiated network rates, with some variation by pay grade of the active duty sponsor.

12 National guard and reserve members may also enroll in the TRICARE Dental Program when not on active duty orders, but family plans have higher monthly premiums than when the member has been activated.

13 In 2012 these premiums were about $55 per month for member-only coverage or about $200 per month for family coverage.

14 In 2012 these premiums were about $355 per month for member-only coverage or about $800 per month for family coverage, paid quarterly.

15 Dependents of veterans are generally not eligible for care from the VHA, although some spouses and children of totally disabled veterans or of service members who died on active duty may receive benefits from the Civilian Health and Medical Program of the Department of Veterans Affairs (CHAMPVA). That program provides health insurance to eligible beneficiaries who use providers that accept CHAMPVA. VHA facilities may provide care to CHAMPVA beneficiaries when they have the capacity.

16 If veterans seeking care have other private insurance, VHA may bill those insurers for any treatment of conditions not due to military service.

17 Copayment for an outpatient visit in 2011 was $15. The maximum cost for a prescription was $9. The maximum cost for the first 90 days of inpatient care was $1,132. (Other copayments may also be assessed.)

18 In 2012 the annual enrollment fees for Prime were $260 for individual retirees and $520 for family coverage of new enrollees ($230 and $460 for renewing enrollees). Examples of copayment rates for retirees and their dependents using Prime in civilian facilities were $12 for an outpatient visit and $11 per day for inpatient stays. For retirees and their dependents using Standard or Extra, annual deductibles were $150 for individuals and $300 for families. Under Standard, coinsurance rates for most services were 25% of the TRICARE allowable charge. For Extra, coinsurance rates for most services were 20% of negotiated network rates. The catastrophic cap for retirees in 2012 was $3,000.

19 Premiums for TRDP vary by location and type of plan (individual or family). The annual deductibles in 2012 were $50 per individual or $150 per family. Annual maximum benefit limits were $1,200. Diagnostic and preventive services had no copay; most other cost sharing was 40% to 50% of negotiated network rates (higher if care received from a non-participating provider).

20 Some guard and reserve members who have been activated recently may be eligible to begin drawing retired pay before age 60; the age requirement is reduced by 3 months for each cumulative period of 90 days of service on active duty or in response to a national emergency after January 28, 2008. These members must still wait until age 60 to be eligible for the same TRICARE Prime, Standard, or Extra benefits available to active component retirees.

21 Retired reservists and dependents eligible for the Federal Employees Health Benefits program may not enroll in TRR. Once retired reservists start drawing retired pay, they and their dependents become eligible for the same TRICARE Prime, Standard, or Extra benefits available to active component retirees, and TRR coverage ends.

22 In 2012 TRR member-only coverage was about $420 per month while family coverage was about $1,025 per month.

23 By law, TRICARE is the second payer after any other health insurance plan, except those plans specifically designated as TRICARE supplements.

24 Until TFL implementation in 2001, TRICARE beneficiaries who turned 65 were expected to rely on Medicare to cover any civilian medical services received. While military retirees and their dependents may be seen at MTFs as space allows, their lower priority may make it difficult to obtain regular care. MTFs with sufficient capacity offer TRICARE Plus, a primary care enrollment program (not an HMO or other health plan). The primary care manager at the MTF serves as the principal health care provider, even though patients may continue to receive care from civilian providers. There is no enrollment fee, and access priority is the same as for non-active duty beneficiaries with TRICARE Prime.

25 Premiums in 2012 for Medicare Part B ranged from $99.90 to $319.70 per month, depending on income and other factors.
26 CBO's projection of DoD health spending in 2015 was converted to 2010 dollars using the GDP price deflator.
27 See Congressional Budget Office (October 2010), *Potential Cost of Veterans' Health Care*, for an analysis of future costs for VHA.

References

Congressional Budget Office. (2009) *The Effects of Proposals to Increase Cost Sharing in TRICARE.* Available HTTP: < http://www.cbo.gov/ftpdocs/102xx/doc10261/ TRICARE.pdf> (accessed July 5, 2011).

Congressional Budget Office. (2010) *Potential Cost of Veterans' Health Care.* Available at: http://www.cbo.gov/sites/default/files/cbofiles/ftpdocs/118xx/doc11811/2010_10_7_vahealthcare.pdf (accessed November 17, 2012).

Congressional Budget Office. (2011) *Long-Term Implications of the 2012 Future Years Defense Program.* Available HTTP: <http://www.cbo.gov/ftpdocs/122xx/doc12264/06-30-11_FYDP.pdf > (accessed July 5, 2011).

Department of Veterans Affairs, National Center for Veterans Analysis and Statistics. (2011) *Health Insurance Coverage by Veteran Status and Type of Insurance: 2000 to 2009.* Available HTTP: <http://www.va.gov/vetdata/docs/SpecialReports/HealthIns tables_FINAL.pdf> (accessed July 21, 2011).

Department of Veterans Affairs, Veterans Health Administration, Office of the Assistant Deputy Under Secretary for Health for Policy and Planning. (2011) *2010 Survey of Veteran Enrollees' Health and Reliance upon VA.* Available HTTP: <http://www.va.gov/ HEALTHPOLICYPLANNING/Soe2010/SoE_2010_Final.pdf> (accessed September 1, 2011).

Mariano, L.T., Kirby, S.N., Eibner, C. and Naftel, S. (2007) *Civilian Health Insurance Options of Military Retirees: Findings from a Pilot Study.* RAND. Available HTTP: <http://www.rand.org/pubs/monographs/MG583.html> (accessed September 6, 2011).

TRICARE Management Activity. Available HTTP: < http://www.tricare.mil> (accessed June–September 2011).

US Department of Health and Human Services, Office of the National Coordinator for Health Information Technology. (2011) *Nationwide Health Information Network: Overview.* Available HTTP: < http://healthit.hhs.gov/portal/server.pt?open=512&,mode=2&cached=true&objID=1142> (accessed September 2, 2011).

US Department of Veterans Affairs. Available HTTP: http://www.va.gov/> (accessed June–September 2011).

Part II
Pre-deployment

4 Pre-deployment medical policy development

Perspectives from the experience of US Central Command

Theodore R. Brown

Introduction

A number of policies establish pre-deployment requirements for military service members and units preparing for deployment. In addition to dealing with personnel, finance and training, Department of Defense (DoD) and service specific policies establish deployment medical standards and requirements for service members, DoD civilians and contractor personnel.[1] To reconcile different standards set forth in various policies and establish a single, minimum medical standard for deployment, many of the Geographic Combatant Commands (CCMDs) also establish CCMD-specific medical deployment policies. Such is the case with United States Central Command (USCENTCOM), the CCMD responsible for the 20-nation region that includes Afghanistan and Iraq.

The USCENTCOM medical deployment policy is set forth in what is known as "the MOD", the most recent modification to the original USCENTCOM Individual Protection and Individual/Unit Deployment Policy. The Under Secretary of Defense for Personnel and Readiness (USD(P&R)), in a 2006 memorandum, established the Geographic Combatant Commander (GCC) as the waiver authority for services seeking to "deploy a Service member who [did] not meet its deployment standards."[2] As such, a primary function of USCENTCOM deployment policy is to communicate what medical conditions are considered non-deployable for the USCENTCOM area of responsibility (AOR) and under what conditions a waiver would be considered. This chapter focuses on the considerations required to develop criteria for the deployment of personnel with specific medical conditions. The USCENTCOM deployment policy also enforces or establishes requirements regarding: pre- and post-deployment health assessments; force health protection considerations such as immunizations and force health protection prescription products (e.g. malaria chemoprophylaxis); women's health; pharmaceuticals and durable medical equipment; pre-deployment testing (e.g. laboratory, tuberculosis, automated neuropsychological assessment metrics); and chemical, biological, radiological and nuclear countermeasures.[3]

Before further discussion about pre-deployment policy development, it might not be readily apparent to all readers why such a policy is necessary. Most, if not all, will understand the need for a policy that delineates the requirements listed above. To some, however, it might seem unnecessary to include discussion, either general or specific, about medical conditions and treatments – after all, aren't all service members screened for disqualifying conditions when they enter service as well as recurrently throughout their time in the military? That is true. Service members must pass a physical exam, conducted in accordance with accession medical standards, to enter service. These standards may differ between the services. However, service members incur injuries and develop diseases during military service. Their ability to remain in the military is governed by a separate, typically less restrictive, set of medical standards known as retention standards. For this reason, and for others that will become apparent throughout the rest of this chapter, there must also be standards that govern a service member's fitness for deployment. Additionally, a large cohort of civilian personnel, who never endured a process such as accession medical screening, must also be found fit or unfit for deployment by application of a standard. These overarching reasons highlight the need for a deployment standard.

Deployment policy goals

Discussion regarding a specific policy should include discussion of the goals of the policy. For medical deployment policy, it can be argued there are many goals, but two are primary, overarching goals to which others are either supporting or secondary. In terms of occupational medicine, these primary goals seek to protect the worker from the workplace and the workplace from the worker. In this analogy, the worker represents the deploying individual and the workplace represents both the deployed environment and the mission. In the final analysis, the mission must be accomplished, which requires a fit force that can operate in unique environments. Pre-deployment medical policy should both minimize potential detriments to the mission and prevent untoward health effects to the individual. Each of these policy goals will now be discussed in greater detail.

The first of these goals focuses on the individual to ensure the deployment of fit and ready personnel that not only can perform the mission, but also can do so in the operational environment to which they are deploying. They must be able to withstand the unique occupational and environmental exposures and stressors associated with deployment without being placed at undue risk for adverse short- or long-term health effects. Service members and civilians alike are called upon to perform their jobs in unique and very challenging environments. Even individuals who are deployed to perform jobs that might otherwise be considered purely administrative are faced with routine deployment stressors such as carrying equipment, extensive walking (perhaps at higher-than-normal altitudes), sleep disturbance, and entering/exiting unique military vehicles. These stressors, and many others, are present in addition to physical or mental stressors contributed by routine military operations or enemy actions.

The second policy goal focuses on the mission by reducing the potential for unnecessary medical treatment and/or evacuation resulting from pre-deployment related conditions. While related to the first goal, the second is more concerned with successful mission completion. Any medical resources that must be expended on evaluation, treatment, and evacuation for conditions that existed pre-deployment are resources that are potentially not available for support of operational forces. Such support is the primary mission of medical units and personnel in theater – as stated on the Army Medical Department Regiment's insignia, "to conserve fighting strength."[4] Not only does the treatment and evacuation for pre-deployment related conditions utilize resources that were primarily meant for operational forces, it potentially places the mission at risk for failure. It also places evacuation personnel at risk in conducting evacuation missions that they might not have otherwise had to conduct.

Many questions regarding medical pre-deployment policy development for a CCMD are easy to answer. For example, determining which immunizations should be required for a specific region is relatively straightforward; some immunizations are dictated by DoD policy, others have clear recommendations from organizations such as the Centers for Disease Control and Prevention. However, the discussion here focuses on the complex issues of medical conditions and medications and what considerations inform whether or not personnel are deemed fit for deployment. Specific examples will relate to the USCENTCOM AOR and policy, but the same thought process could be applied by any CCMD in developing its own policy.

Pre-deployment medical policy

The development of pre-deployment medical policy has been a continuous and iterative process over the last 10 years. CCMDs, and specifically USCENTCOM, have been more responsive to lessons learned in theater than DoD at large, incorporating them into pre-deployment policy more frequently. The policy is continuously reviewed and is updated approximately every 18 months, allowing lessons learned to have a more immediate impact on the medical preparation for deployment. As a result of the iterative nature of policy changes (i.e. DoD policy incorporating USCENTCOM requirements and vice versa), the DoD and USCENTCOM policies address many of the same areas of concern.

Due to the nature of medical advances, including diagnostics and therapeutics, no pre-deployment policy can list all possible medical conditions and medications, though it may address some specifically. In order to address, in broad terms, the primary policy goals as well as to provide overarching guidance to healthcare providers evaluating potential deploying personnel, the policy should include some general guidelines. These guidelines should describe the nature of medical conditions, as well as their treatment, that would or would not make an individual suitable for deployment. USCENTCOM policy provides such guidance in terms of both the individual and the mission. Noting the extreme excursions in both environmental (temperature, physiologic demand, air quality) and operational factors (circadian rhythm disturbance, diet, emotional stress), it notes that those whose health is dependent on avoiding such extremes should not deploy.

USCENTCOM policy also notes that those whose condition prevents use of personal protective measures (i.e. wearing personal protective equipment or receiving immunizations and/or chemoprophylaxis) should not deploy.[5] This goes back to protecting the worker from the workplace. In this vein, those with impaired daily function or for whom the operational environment would worsen the underlying condition should also not deploy. At the very least, such individuals should be considered for a functional assessment and examination to objectively measure whether they can adequately perform specific functions in the deployed environment – and whether they can do so without risk of harm to themselves or others.

General guidance should also address those conditions that might place the mission, or other personnel, at risk – protecting the workplace from the worker. USCENTCOM policy addresses this risk by providing a list of general conditions that should be considered when determining the deployability of an individual. These conditions include: the anticipated use of medical resources; the need for routine evacuation; the need for follow-up or ongoing evaluation; any limitation of duty; and the potential for a grave outcome if the condition worsens.[6] Individuals who have medical conditions that are stable and meet the above general guidance, as determined by an evaluating healthcare provider, are likely deployable. With that said, DoD and CCMD policies go beyond this general guidance to specify certain medical conditions as well as medications that require additional consideration and possibly more extensive evaluation to determine whether they are suitable for deployment.

From the CCMD perspective, certain non-deployable medical conditions or types of conditions are spelled out in DoD policy. While the CCMD must follow DoD policy, it can also be more proscriptive, since its focus is on a specific AOR that is unique from other AORs. The uniqueness of each AOR requires an individual assessment in order to effectively mitigate individual and operational risk. In addition to DoD policy, a number of inputs inform the formulation of CCMD pre-deployment policy. For purposes of discussion, these inputs will be grouped as follows: evidence base; operational experience and need; and clinical judgment.

Over the past few years, the medical establishment as a whole has embraced the concept of evidence-based medicine (EBM). EBM seeks to provide evidence, ideally gained through scientific methods of study, to support clinical practice and decision-making. Two primary sources provide input to the formulation of pre-deployment policy – the medical literature and subject-matter expert (SME) recommendation.

The medical literature should be referenced when determining what medical conditions should either be non-deployable or require additional evaluation to make a determination. A few of the areas include: new diagnostics, outcomes-based research, and improved understanding of underlying pathophysiology. In one case, the literature may demonstrate there are no long-term health effects resulting from condition "X"; this may cause a change in policy deeming condition "X" deployable when previously it was non-deployable. In another case, research on the underlying pathophysiology of condition "Y" may demonstrate effects on the immune system, raising susceptibility to infectious disease; this may cause a policy change deeming condition "Y" non-deployable so as not to cause untoward health effects for the individual.

Either in conjunction with the medical literature or in the absence of the same, SME opinions and recommendations are essential in formulating medical pre-deployment policy. In the past, USCENTCOM has involved SMEs both at the time of policy review and revision as well as on a case-by-case basis either in determining whether a policy change was needed or in considering an individual waiver request. The topic of medical waivers and their review and disposition will be discussed in detail later, but the involvement of SMEs in the policy revision process will be covered here.

As discussed above, USCENTCOM medical deployment policy is reviewed and updated at least every 18 months. The frequency of this review is based on factors such as: changes in guiding DoD policy, operational need, and personnel changes (either in CCMD leadership or CCMD medical staff). In anticipation of policy revision, the relevant SMEs should be sought out and requested to review the current policy and provide their recommendations regarding its adequacy or any necessary changes. A starting point for USCENTCOM in obtaining SME input has been the Army specialty consultants to The Surgeon General (TSG).

The Army TSG has a consultant for each of over 60 medical specialties, from allergy to preventive medicine to urology. Thus, TSG has both a senior specialist for each area and a single point of contact through which to reach the rest of the specialty branch. While SME input is also sought from the other services and civilian experts, the Army consultants are uniquely poised to provide such input to the CCMD for the following reasons: their input to other policies is routinely sought; most have experienced first-hand the deployed environment; and they represent the preponderance of the deployed force – the Army. Once the revised policy is drafted, SME input should again be sought to ensure adequate incorporation of recommendations and to solicit any additional input.

In addition to purely clinical SME input, that of other medical SMEs should be sought and included, especially experts in force health protection, environmental science, pharmacy, medical logistics, and medical maintenance. If the determination is made that a specific condition, medication, or piece of medical equipment is suitable for deployment, it must also be determined if the resources and mechanisms are in place to support such a deployment. These considerations, especially at the local and individual level, may prevent the deployment of an individual who is, on purely clinical grounds, deployable.

The second major input to CCMD pre-deployment medical policy, after the evidence base, is operational experience and need. Operational experience is that experience gained primarily by personnel involved in theater medical operations from the tactical to the strategic level. Such experience might be gained by a physician or physician's assistant providing Role 1 medical care at a forward operating base who finds that a specific condition is either unsuitable for deployment or unsupportable in that environment.[7] Operational experience might also be gained by medical personnel at Role 2 or 3 facilities as they see numerous referrals for evaluation or treatment for a specific condition. One of the primary sources of operational experience contributing to USCENTCOM pre-deployment policy comes from theater aeromedical evacuation personnel. Those involved in theater evacuations have a unique perspective for gauging which conditions, despite in-theater medical capabilities, were in the end unsuitable for deployment or were exacerbated by the deployment. Important information can be gleaned by monitoring evacuation data and discussing trends with theater evacuation personnel (e.g., the theater validating flight surgeon). This brings us to operational need.

Operational need can be viewed from the perspective of both the ground commander and the medical evaluator. The ground commander's need is a fit and ready force, in sufficient numbers to accomplish the mission. The ability to ensure such a force medically requires a pre-deployment policy that is not so restrictive as to prevent sufficient numbers of deployable personnel, but is also not so liberal as to present an unnecessary level of risk to the commander or the mission. Balance between these two extremes is frequently difficult, and despite what is written in any policy, the determination as to whether an individual is medically deployable or not often falls to the individual healthcare provider. This highlights the operational need of the medical evaluator.

While there are general guidelines in pre-deployment policy that describe the characteristics of a non-deployable condition, within those guidelines there is a certain degree of interpretation that could potentially lead one evaluator to deem an individual deployable and another to deem the same individual non-deployable. Granted, such cases are significantly outnumbered by cases on which two different evaluators would agree. However, if it is either noted by, or brought to the attention of, the CCMD that a specific condition or medication more often than not results in disagreement, it is an operational need for greater policy specificity that the pre-deployment policy should address. USCENTCOM addresses this need by going beyond the general guidelines and including more detailed guidance regarding specific conditions and treatments.

The final input for CCMD pre-deployment medical policy discussed here is, for lack of a better term, clinical judgment. This clinical judgment is different and distinct from SME recommendations discussed above. It is the judgment exercised primarily by the CCMD medical advisor, the CCMD surgeon, in weighing all other inputs in the context of their own unique knowledge of the AOR. As the primary advisor to the GCC on all medical issues, and as the designated medical waiver authority for that CCMD, the surgeon provides final policy recommendations to the GCC. Ideally, the medical literature, SME recommendations, and operational needs would all support the same policy recommendation, but this is infrequently the case. The GCC, as with all other medical issues affecting the CCMD, relies on the surgeon to weigh the various inputs, apply clinical judgment and unique perspective, and recommend a policy. Implied in this recommendation is judgment, and communication to the GCC, of any risk that the GCC may assume as a result of the recommended policy.

To illustrate these inputs to the formulation of CCMD pre-deployment medical policy, the example of obstructive sleep apnea (OSA) and its common treatment of continuous positive airway pressure (CPAP) will be used. The policy evolution surrounding OSA and CPAP illustrates the roles that the evidence base (both literature and SME opinion), operational experience and clinical judgment played in arriving at a final policy that differed significantly from previous policy.

Prior to March 2010, OSA treated with CPAP was a non-deployable condition for the USCENTCOM AOR and denied waiver requests for CPAP. Among the reasons for this policy was the potential for short- and long-term health effects should the individual be without CPAP due to loss of electrical power, at the time a frequent occurrence at many locations in theater. The lack of reliable electrical power also presented a safety risk due to potential daytime somnolence should those with OSA have to go untreated. The theater environment also presented a substantial probability for CPAP machine malfunction due to high levels of particulate matter in the air. Finally, the lack of medical maintenance capability to repair CPAP machines and the fact that they were not in the medical logistics supply chain posed additional risks to deploying personnel on CPAP.

In drafting its deployment policy published March 2010, USCENTCOM sought SME input on the issue of OSA and CPAP. The sleep medicine community initially provided feedback on the prior policy, in effect saying that an absolute prohibition against CPAP in theater was too restrictive and not supported by medical evidence. The evidence demonstrated that effective treatment with CPAP could prevent long-term health effects of OSA and that there were no clear long-term health effects of untreated mild OSA. In fact, the Army had changed its own policy regarding medical fitness standards, no longer requiring those diagnosed with OSA to proceed directly to a medical board, but rather allowing for a trial of CPAP to determine continued fitness to serve. The USCENTCOM Surgeon requested that the sleep medicine community draft a recommendation reflecting a deployment policy for OSA and CPAP supported by the evidence.

The sleep medicine community produced a very detailed draft, clearly outlining which personnel with OSA should be deemed deployable and under what conditions. It recommended objective measures of OSA severity and adequacy of treatment. The recommendations were based both on current medical evidence, as reported in the medical literature, and on the collective opinions of the sleep medicine community, most of whom had been deployed themselves.

While the draft recommendation was very thorough in its approach, detailing the testing to be done and specifying the cutoffs to be met in determining an individual's suitability for deployment, it was too specific – not concise enough to meet the operational need of commanders and medical personnel. Commanders require policy that is clear, concise, and provides the necessary information to accomplish the mission. In the case of medical pre-deployment policy, it should facilitate the commander's ability to determine which personnel will likely be deployable. Likewise, medical personnel who conduct pre-deployment evaluations do not have the luxury of working through an algorithm for each and every possible medical condition to make a deployability determination for each individual. To that end, the USCENTCOM Surgeon directed his staff to consolidate what was provided by the sleep medicine community and reframe it in a way that would be useful to commanders and medical personnel alike.

The resulting recommendation approved by the USCENTCOM Surgeon, and subsequently by the USCENTCOM Commander, was a concise, straightforward policy incorporating the primary components of the recommendation by the sleep medicine community. It did not retain all the detail of the initial recommendation, but those details were included in an additional reference for use by medical evaluators. The final policy did retain the overarching objective measures of OSA severity and CPAP treatment adequacy as well as specific cutoffs for determining deployability. The final policy provided the necessary guidance without being too proscriptive, thereby permitting medical providers to apply independent clinical judgment and expertise. Clinical judgment was also exercised in this case, at the population and strategic level, by the USCENTCOM Surgeon, guided by his unique perspective of the operational environment in theater. In directing formulation of a less restrictive policy than what was first recommended, thereby assuming greater risk, he supported the operational need of the commander for deployable personnel while still leaving open the possibility of a non-deployable determination by the evaluating provider.

While this example demonstrates the inputs of medical evidence, SME opinion, operational need, and clinical judgment, it should also be noted that additional factors enabled such a policy. The evolution of CPAP machine technology was one factor. Machines had become much quieter, less cumbersome and more durable. The policy also included language encouraging, if not requiring, machines with battery back-up capability to overcome any electrical power issue. Additionally, where before there was no medical maintenance or medical logistical support for CPAP, a limited repair capability had been developed as had the ability to order replacement machines through medical logistics channels. Finally, the policy directed those deploying with CPAP to do so with sufficient supplies (i.e. filters) for the duration of the deployment.

Waivers

Policy will never be responsive enough to keep up with changes in medicine and in the operational environment in which personnel are deployed. Additionally, in an area such as medicine, which must be applied to individuals with innumerable differences, it is impossible to formulate policy that is "one size fits all". For these reasons, commanders must be able to obtain a waiver of policy standards. Although an individual may be non-deployable by strict application of the policy, they may still be an asset to the unit and not represent an undue risk to themselves, others or the mission that would prevent deployment.

The USCENTCOM Surgeon is the designated waiver authority for the USCENTCOM AOR. As such, the waiver process for personnel deploying to the AOR is outlined in the pre-deployment policy. While the specific process for requesting a waiver is not particularly important, a discussion of the factors considered in the disposition of these waivers is germane. Though numerous, these factors can be classified as either individual or operational variables. Examples of individual variables include the medical condition, its stability, its treatment (previous and current, including medications), effects or limitations imposed by the condition or treatment, required follow-up or ongoing evaluation (laboratory studies, clinical evaluation), and the results of prior medical board evaluations. Operational variables include the area of operation (AO), length of deployment, deployed position or duties, the individual's criticality to the mission, and available medical resources at the deployed location. We'll first consider the individual variables in greater detail.

Of all the variables considered in waiver requests, perhaps those of greatest import are the condition itself, including its treatment and stability. While not many, there may be conditions that should be considered disqualifying for deployment in and of themselves and for which waivers should not be granted. Though they may change over time and across AORs, past examples of such absolute disqualifiers in the USCENTCOM AOR have included insulin-requiring diabetes mellitus, body mass index of 40 kg/m^2 or greater, symptomatic OSA, human immunodeficiency virus (HIV) positivity, psychotic disorders, and treatment with warfarin (Coumadin®) or varenicline (Chantix®).[8] The rationale behind each of these "no waivers granted" conditions or treatments is outside the scope of this chapter, but includes inability to ensure standard-of-care treatment in theater, insufficiency of the medical infrastructure to support the condition, risk to self or others in the deployed environment, and prohibition by DoD-level policy.

Aside from these exceptions, other conditions should demonstrate a clear pattern of stability before being considered for deployment. Conditions for which treatment has recently begun, which may require modification of treatment, or for which frequent clinical visits are required are not suitable for deployment where follow-up at the recommended interval cannot always be assured. Especially during the initial deployment to theater, it is imperative that any chronic medical conditions or acute illnesses that preceded deployment be either resolved or stabilized. As it can be weeks from the time of departure from home station until arrival at final deployment location, access to care can be difficult. If medical conditions are not stable, because of decreased access to care during movement, any deterioration in the individual's condition may result in return to home station, or lead to short-term health consequences that will reduce effectiveness on arrival at final deployment location. In either case, the individual, unit and mission suffer as a result – either through the loss of an individual for whom the unit must now request replacement or through the decreased combat effectiveness of the same individual.

Though obviously related to the condition, specific mention should be made regarding treatments. Noted in the "no waivers granted" list are a few medications or classes of medications. The rationale for their presence on this list includes risk for sudden incapacitation, specific storage/handling requirements, psychological side-effects, and significant risk to self in the event of injury. Considerations regarding pharmacotherapy are myriad, including potential side-effects. All medications should also be reviewed for potential theater-specific concerns, that is, in the context of the specific AOR – its climate, altitude, infectious disease risk, etc. Some medications may require limiting sun exposure or having a predictable, specific diet. Other medications may make one more susceptible to infectious diseases or prevent the same individual from receiving recommended vaccinations. Whatever the case, it is not simply the condition that must be considered, but also the treatment.

Once the condition and treatment have been considered, the need for ongoing follow-up or evaluation should be determined. Ideally, the only required follow-up would be on an as-needed basis, such as that for a longstanding, stable condition. At the other end of the spectrum would be a relatively new condition which has not yet demonstrated clinical stability and for which more regular follow-up is required. The USCENTCOM policy states that necessary follow-up should be no more than quarterly and should not require specialized labs or other studies not readily available in theater. Conducting follow-up should certainly not require evacuation from the deployed location.

Finally, any previous medical board referrals or findings should be reviewed. Individuals reclassified into a different occupational specialty because of their medical condition differ from someone who was retained in their primary specialty without restrictions on activity or assignment. Medical boards will occasionally comment specifically on an individual's deployability. Board results inform the final decision, but in the end the waiver authority is still the CCMD surgeon. It should be highlighted that the primary function of the medical board is to determine whether the individual can perform the routine functions of their occupational specialty, not whether they can perform this job in the deployed environment. Even if medical boards reach the point where they consistently comment on deployability, the CCMD surgeon will still make the determination as to whether the individual can perform their job in that CCMD's AOR. As the waiver authority, such a determination is the purview of the CCMD surgeon, not that of a service-specific medical board.

Turning to operational variables, first among them is the specific deployed area of operations (AO). All deployments are not equal in the level of physical, physiological, mental, and emotional stress they may cause; nor are all AOs equal in the level of risk they present to an individual with a specific medical condition or treatment. Even within a larger AO – for example, the country of Afghanistan – there are more specific regions and even more specific deployed locations that may vary greatly in terms of stressors and risk. For example, while the stressors and risks associated with deployment are ever present, the levels experienced on a fire base in southern Afghanistan are different than those experienced in the capital of Kabul. It is within the context of the specific AO that a waiver of the standards should be considered. It may be that one location poses too great a risk to the individual or mission, while deployment to a different location may be acceptable from both a medical and command perspective.

The length of deployment should be considered simultaneously with the AO, as a 6-month deployment presents a different level of risk than does a 12-month deployment to the same location. Likewise, a shorter time deployed at one location may represent an equivalent degree of risk as a year deployment at another. In addition to the location and length of deployment is the consideration of the individual's deployed position and duties while deployed. Such factors as the hours required of their position, the amount of time spent off their primary base of operations (e.g. on patrol "outside the wire"), and their potential contact with local personnel as well as enemy personnel must all be considered.

Frequently associated with an individual's deployed position or duties is the degree to which they are critical to the mission. Significant pressure to deploy at or above 100 percent of end strength typically leads units to regard all their personnel as mission-critical. While it is true that everyone has an important role to play, testified to by the fact that each waiver request is considered on an individual basis, there can be widely disparate effects on the mission depending on who is found non-deployable. For example, one of the low-density military occupational specialties (MOS) in the US Army is the Utilities Equipment Repairer 52C. One of their duties is to repair air conditioning units in vehicles. Vehicles cannot be used if the air conditioning units need repair, not only to ensure personnel comfort and health, but also to keep communication systems, which would otherwise overheat, functioning. There may be only two 52C series personnel in a brigade; determining even one to be non-deployable causes a potentially significant mission impact. On the other hand, a brigade may have more than adequate numbers of Automated Logistical Specialists, MOS 92A, and if one is not deployable, it causes less potential detriment to the mission. So not only does an individual's MOS and density matter, so does the specific deployed mission.

The final operational variable to be discussed with respect to waiver disposition is that of the medical resources at the individual's anticipated deployment location. Obviously this implies knowledge of the deployed location, previously discussed, as well as working knowledge of the medical resources and capabilities available at that location. It is for this reason that the CCMD surgeon is best suited to make the final determination as to individuals' deployment suitability. The surgeon has a unique perspective regarding the medical capabilities available in a specific location. It is within this context that they are able to consider an individual with a specific medical condition and treatment, performing specific duties and responsibilities, for a specific length of time, and the potential mission impact should that individual not deploy.

Just as operations over the last 10 years of war have evolved and adapted, so have medical policies and procedures, specifically that of the CCMD most impacted by those operations, USCENTCOM. Inherent in implementation and effectiveness of any policy is awareness at the user level. In efforts to increase that awareness, the USCENTCOM Surgeon's office established communication with, and made presentations to, key stakeholders and policy executors. The policy was also rewritten to allow its publication in unclassified form so that it could be more freely distributed and accessed than it had been before. Again, key stakeholders were instrumental in efforts to increase access and awareness by posting the policy on their respective websites. These efforts had a discernible impact, as the volume of policy inquiries and waiver requests increased significantly.

As previously discussed, the USCENTCOM Surgeon is the designated waiver authority for personnel deploying to the USCENTCOM AOR. For deploying service members, waiver authority for some conditions was delegated to the service component surgeons (the Army, Navy, Air Force, Marine, and Special Operations components under USCENTCOM). The USCENTCOM Surgeon retained authority for the disposition of other service member waivers (including behavioral health conditions) as well as all waivers for non-service-affiliated personnel (e.g. DoD civilians, contractor personnel).

Basic numbers of waivers dispositioned by the USCENTCOM Surgeon in 2010 illustrate the relative volume and approximate approval rates. They also show the effect of both the policy change and its increased socialization. Any trends demonstrated by these numbers cannot be completely attributed to the policy change, as there was a significant surge in troop levels deploying to Afghanistan in 2010; likewise, the increased troop levels likely do not completely account for the trends. It should again be noted that these figures do not represent all waivers for those deploying to the USCENTCOM AOR. They do include all non-service-affiliated personnel as well as a subpopulation of each of the military services.

In calendar year 2010, approximately 1,700 waiver requests were received by the USCENTCOM Surgeon compared with a total of 409 waivers in 2009. As a frame of reference, the updated USCENTCOM deployment policy was published in early March 2010. In the first quarter (January through March) of 2010, an average of 53 waivers was received per month. Over the next three quarters, after publication of the policy, the monthly average increased steadily from 53 to 90, to 177, to 245. The waiver approval rate remained relatively stable; while the overall 2010 rate was 78 percent, the quarterly approval rates were 74, 85, 78, and 78 percent, respectively. Two other trends highlight the impact of increased distribution of the policy and efforts to increase awareness of its requirements – waiver requests for deploying civilian personnel and for behavioral health conditions.

During 2010, the quarterly percentage of waivers submitted for civilian personnel rose from 51 percent to 80 percent of all waiver requests, with a monthly range of 15 to 231 waivers. This trend, in part due to the troop surge in Afghanistan, is also likely due to increased policy awareness. Unlike military units, which have relatively easy access to secure systems where the various policies for deployment reside, civilian personnel typically experience more difficulty obtaining all relevant policies and requirements. This difficulty is partly due to classification levels placed on policies, including those marked as "for official use only". By publishing the 2010 deployment policy as unclassified, with no caveats, USCENTCOM ensured broader access for those without readily available secure networks such as deploying civilian and contracting personnel.

The increased proportion of civilian waiver requests accompanied a decreased proportion of behavioral health waivers. In the first quarter of 2010, 49 percent of the waivers received were for behavioral health conditions, but that percentage dropped to 20 percent for the final quarter with a monthly low of 14 percent. The decrease is certainly tied to the increase in civilian waivers because all civilian waiver requests are dispositioned by USCENTCOM, regardless of the condition, whether behavioral health or non-behavioral health. As the number of civilian waiver requests increased, so did the number of waiver requests for non-behavioral health conditions. In addition, the decreasing behavioral health trend likely represents increased awareness of USCENTCOM policy amongst military personnel and units. Since DoD-level policy regarding non-deployable behavioral health conditions[9] pre-dates similar policy regarding other conditions and is much more ingrained in the pre- and post-deployment process, the primary source for guidance on non-behavioral health conditions and deployment is the CCMD policy. The decrease in percentage of behavioral health waivers demonstrates increased awareness of the USCENTCOM policy with respect to the non-behavioral health conditions it addresses.

Conclusion

This chapter presented the need for, goals of, and inputs to CCMD pre-deployment medical policy. In doing so using the USCENTCOM experience and OSA and CPAP to illustrate, it provides a model by which other CCMDs could formulate policy. At a minimum, it highlights considerations that should be made. Basic waiver data has emphasized the importance of ensuring access, awareness and understanding of the policy. Despite a clearly-written policy that fulfills the needs of commanders and evaluators alike, without access, awareness and understanding, it is no more than words on paper that do nothing to achieve the end state of a fit and ready deployed force.

Notes

1 Department of Defense Instruction (DoDI) 6490.03 'Deployment Health', 11 August 2006; DoDI 6490.07 'Deployment-Limiting Medical Conditions for Service Members and DoD Civilian Employees', 5 February 2010; DoDI 3020.41 'Contractor Personnel Authorized to Accompany the U.S. Armed Forces', 3 October 2005; Assistant Secretary of Defense for Health Affairs Memorandum 'Policy Guidance for Deployment-Limiting Psychiatric Conditions and Medications', 7 November 2006.

2 D.S.C. Chu, Under Secretary of Defense for Personnel and Readiness Memorandum 'SUBJECT: Policy Guidance for Medical Deferral Pending Deployment to Theaters of Operation', 2006, 1.

3 United States Central Command, 'MOD 10 to USCENTCOM Individual Protection and Individual/Unit Deployment Policy', 2010, 4, 6–12.

4 United States Army Medical Department. (2011) *Army Medical Department Regiment.* Online. Available HTTP: <http://ameddregiment.amedd.army.mil> (accessed 7 October 2011).

5 United States Central Command, 'PPG-TAB A: Amplification of the Minimal Standards of Fitness for Deployment to the CENTCOM AOR; to Accompany MOD 10 to USCENTCOM Individual Protection and Individual/Unit Deployment Policy', 2010, 1–2.

6 Ibid, 2.

7 The levels of health service support provided in theater are referred to by their designated Role. There are five roles of care, increasing in capability from the most

basic (Role 1) to the most advanced (Role 5). Though more thoroughly described elsewhere, brief descriptions follow. Role 1 – that care typically provided by a battalion aid station; triage, treatment, and evacuation; staffed by medics, a physician assistant, and possibly a physician; no holding capability. Role 2 – increased capability over Role 1 with limited holding capability; includes primary care, optometry, behavioral health services, dental, lab and x-ray capabilities; frequently has blood products as well as surgical capability when augmented. Role 3 – highest level of care available in the combat theater; the majority of inpatient beds are at Role 3; includes specialty care (medical and surgical), intensive care, blood bank and computed tomography (CT). Role 4 – definitive medical and surgical care outside the combat zone; provides more intensive rehabilitation or specialty needs. Role 5 – care provided in the continental US by DoD and Veterans Affairs (VA) hospitals. (Reference: Emergency War Surgery, 3rd US Revision, Department of Defense, Borden Institute, pp. 2.2–2.10.)

8 United States Central Command, 'PPG-TAB A: Amplification of the Minimal Standards of Fitness for Deployment to the CENTCOM AOR; to Accompany MOD 10 to USCENTCOM Individual Protection and Individual/Unit Deployment Policy', 2010, 3–6.

9 Assistant Secretary of Defense for Health Affairs Memorandum 'Policy Guidance for Deployment-Limiting Psychiatric Conditions and Medications', 7 November 2006.

5   The Millennium Cohort Study

Answering long-term health concerns
of US military service members by
integrating longitudinal survey data with
military health system records

Nancy F. Crum-Cianflone

Background of the Millennium Cohort Study

The impetus for the initiation of the Millennium Cohort Study was in large part a result of the events that followed the 1991 Gulf War, a conflict that deployed nearly 700,000 US service members to Kuwait after the invasion by Iraqi Forces (Committee on Measuring the Health of Gulf War Veterans, 1999). Shortly after the conflict, thousands of service members reported a variety of symptoms and illnesses. Questions arose as to whether these health issues were a result of the military deployments; however, no epidemiologic study was in place to address these concerns. Over a billion dollars were subsequently spent on post-symptom assessments, but such efforts were limited by the lack of baseline data to assess temporal associations and were subject to a variety of biases, including recall bias (Committee on Measuring the Health of Gulf War Veterans, 1999). In short, most studies of military-related exposures were limited by retrospective or cross-sectional design, convenience sampling, and/or short follow-up (Department of Veterans Affairs 1999; Gray et al. 1998; Kang et al. 1995).

In the late 1990s, the US Department of Defense (DoD) identified the need for a coordinated epidemiological research study to determine if military experiences, including deployment, affect long-term health outcomes. The Institute of Medicine (IOM) specifically advocated for a large, prospective study for evaluating exposures and their potential effects on a broad range of health outcomes, which was endorsed by Congress (Gray et al. 2002; Secretary of Defense 1998). Section 743 of the Strom Thurmond National Defense Authorization Act (1999) declared: "The Secretary of Defense is hereby authorized to establish a center devoted to a longitudinal study to evaluate data on the health conditions of members of the Armed Forces upon their return from deployment on military operations for purposes of ensuring the rapid identification of any trends in diseases, illnesses, or injuries among such members as a result of such operations" (Strom Thurmond National Defense Authorization Act for Fiscal Year 1999, 1999). For that reason, the DoD Center for Deployment Health Research was established at the Naval Health Research Center (NHRC) in San Diego, California.

In response to the recommendation for a large, longitudinal study of US military members, the Millennium Cohort Study was conceived in 1999. The study received institutional (NHRC) and DoD approval and began in July of 2001. Fortuitously, the research was initiated before the current operations (pre-9/11); hence, it established baseline pre-deployment health and behavioral data for a large cohort of US military service members.

The Millennium Cohort Study was designed in collaboration with all military services and the Department of Veterans Affairs to meet the research needs of the DoD and Veteran Service Organizations (VSOs). The Cohort consists of military members from all service branches and includes active-duty, Reserve, and National Guard personnel. Compared with the prior Gulf War registries, this study has the advantage of collecting prospective individual-level data regarding both pre- and post-deployment health data to robustly access changes over time.

The primary study objective of the ongoing Millennium Cohort is to evaluate the impact of military service, including deployments and other occupational exposures, on long-term health. Important health outcomes include both subjective measures of symptoms and functional health, as well as objective clinical diagnoses obtained from medical records. Information is collected pre-deployment and post-deployment to allow for the assessment of the impact of military deployments and other experiences. The longitudinal study design will collect data among participants over a 21-year period (allowing participants to be followed during their entire military career from shortly after entry into the military until retirement at 20 years of military service, with the addition of one year). Over the last decade (since 2001), the Millennium Cohort Study has become the largest population-based prospective health study in US military history, providing significant contributions to the understanding of the long-term health impacts of military service.

Study population

The Cohort currently consists of four panels enrolled separately in 2001, 2004, 2007, and 2011, totaling approximately 200,000 participants from all service branches. Participants are surveyed at three-year intervals (termed 'waves') for up to 21 years while in service and post-service. Participation in the study is by invitation to ensure that a random sample of the military population is enrolled; this strategy was utilized to overcome the limitation of Gulf War registry data, which may have been confounded by self-selection biases. Information on the dates and final enrollment numbers for each of the enrollment panels is shown in Table 5.1. In addition to re-surveying participants every three years, a new panel has also been enrolled every three years since 2001.

Oversampling of specific groups within the military for participation in each panel was performed in order to have adequate sample sizes to access health outcomes in specific groups of interest (Table 5.1). For example, some panels have oversampled Reserves/National Guard and women, given the higher numbers of these groups deployed in the current operations compared with previous conflicts.

Table 5.1 Composition of each panel in the Millennium Cohort Study

Panel	Dates Enrolled	Years of Service at Enrollment	Oversampled Groups	Roster Size (Date)	Number Contacted**	Total Enrolled (% Contacted)
1	July 2001–June 2003	All durations (cross-section of military population)	Females, National Guard/Reserves, and prior deployers*	256,400 (Oct 2000)	214,388	77,047 (35.9%)
2	June 2004–February 2006	1–2 years	Females and Marine Corps	150,000 (Oct 2003)	123,001	31,110 (25.3%)
3	June 2007–December 2008	1–3 years	Females and Marine Corps	200,000 (Oct 2006)	154,270	43,439 (28.2%)
4	April 2011–ongoing	2–5 years	Females and Married	250,000 (Oct 2010)	***	***

*   Deployment to southwest Asia, Bosnia, and/or Kosovo after August of 1997.
**   Invalid names/addresses and duplicates were excluded.
***   Panel currently being enrolled.

Table 5.2 Data on initial response and follow-up rates in the Millennium Cohort Study

Panel/Wave	Initial and Follow-up Response Rates*
Panel 1	
Wave 1 (2001–2003)	77,047/214,388 (35.9% response rate)
Wave 2 (2004–2006)	55,021/77,047 (71.4% follow-up rate)
Wave 3 (2007–2008)	54,790/77,047 (71.1% follow-up rate)
Panel 2	
Wave 1 (2004–2006)	31,110/123,001 (25.3% response rate)
Wave 2 (2007–2008)	17,152/31,110 (55.1% follow-up rate)
Panel 3	
Wave 1 (2007–2008)	43,439/154,270 (28.2% response rate)

*Percentage based on number of members contacted.

To illustrate how the panels for the Millennium Cohort Study were constructed, 256,400 (11 percent) of the 2.2 million uniformed personnel (October 2000) in Panel 1 were invited to join the study [data from Defense Manpower Data Center (DMDC)]). This group represented a cross-sectional sample of the entire military service population. Of those invited, 214,388 were successfully contacted to participate, and 77,047 (36 percent of the contacted group) joined the study (Table 5.1). The numbers invited and response rates are shown in Tables 5.1 and 5.2. For Panel 1, oversampling was performed to achieve an enrollment of 30 percent who had been deployed to southwest Asia, Bosnia, and/or Kosovo after August of 1997. This group, therefore, provides data on the potential impact of prior deployment on future military and health outcomes. Additionally, Panel 1 was oversampled for Reserve, National Guard, and female service personnel (Table 5.1).

Oversampling was also performed for subsequent panels, as shown in Table 5.1. For example, Panel 4 was oversampled for married service members to assist with the enrollment of the concurrent Millennium Cohort Family Study, which was initiated in 2011. Since military families may be significantly affected by a service member's deployments and health outcomes, this concurrent study will survey spouses of active duty members to better understand the needs of family members.

Characteristics of the demographic and military composition of Panels 1–3 at enrollment are shown in Table 5.3. Response rates at the first and subsequent survey cycles for the first three panels are shown in Table 5.2. The overall baseline response rate was 31 percent, and at least one follow-up survey has been completed by > 70 percent of the Cohort. As of this writing, 57 percent of the current participants (Panels 1–3) have deployed at least once in support of the wars in Iraq and Afghanistan, and 28 percent have deployed multiple times. These data exemplify that the Millennium Cohort Study has adequate numbers to compare deployed vs. non-deployed service members and their outcomes. Moreover,

Table 5.3 Characteristics of Millennium Cohort Study participants by panel

	Panel 1 n = 77,019* (%)	Panel 2 n = 31,110 (%)	Panel 3 n = 43,439 (%)
Characteristics at time of enrollment			
Sex			
Male	73.2	61.6	64.3
Female	26.8	38.4	35.7
Birth year			
Pre-1960	21.6	0.7	0.2
1960–1969	37.9	5.4	1.7
1970–1979	34.6	31.9	15.7
1980–later	5.9	62.0	82.4
Race/ethnicity**			
White, non-Hispanic	69.6	71.4	72.2
Black, non-Hispanic	13.8	11.6	11.3
Asian/Pacific Islander	7.9	4.9	5.6
Hispanic	6.4	10.1	7.8
Other	2.3	2.0	3.1
Education†			
High school or less	74.4	84.6	84.8
Some college or more	25.6	15.4	15.2
Service branch			
Army	47.3	48.2	36.4
Air Force	29.0	26.6	29.7
Navy/Coast Guard	19.0	16.9	18.2
Marine Corps	5.1	8.3	15.7
Service component			
Active duty	57.0	59.9	79.3
Reserve/National Guard	43.0	40.0	20.7
Military pay grade			
Enlisted	77.0	88.3	88.5
Officer	23.0	11.7	11.5
Characteristics at follow-up			
Deployed to current operations‡			
Yes	47.2	64.5	67.4
No	52.8	35.5	32.6
Number of deployments‡			
Two or more	23.7	31.9	31.9
One	23.5	32.6	35.5
None	52.8	35.5	32.6
% Separated from military service‡	40.4	41.5	14.4
% Deceased‡	0.9	0.4	0.2

*   Some initial participants were withdrawn from the study population.
**   Number of missing values per Panel: P1 = 61, P2 = 42.
†   Number of missing values per Panel: P1 = 5, P2 = 2, P3 = 3.
‡   Data reflected as of January 2011.

currently, 33 percent of the Cohort have left military service and continue to be followed over time, which allows for the evaluation of the potential long-term effects of service after separation or retirement (Table 5.3).

To summarize, since the end of the 2007–2008 survey cycle, the Cohort had > 150,000 participants, making it the largest prospective study in US military history. This research offers unprecedented information on the potential effects of military experience, including deployment and combat, on a variety of mental and physical health outcomes. With the 21+ year follow-up planned, this study will also assess longer-term outcomes, including those that develop after military service. With the initiation of the Millennium Cohort Family Study, data on both the service member and spouse will now be available to better inform DoD policies. Further information about the Millennium Cohort Study and Family Study can be found at http://www.MillenniumCohort.org and http://www.FamilyCohort.org.

Study methodology

Survey instrument

A questionnaire was developed using input from focus groups and tested in a pilot study ($n = 1,000$) to provide data which are not available in other DoD datasets. Specifically, the Millennium Cohort survey includes self-reported, individual-level data. It consists of 100 items, many with multiple components (total of > 450 questions), and completion takes approximately 30–45 minutes.

The questionnaire collects information on the service member's physical, behavioral, and mental health and utilizes a variety of standardized questionnaires (shown in Table 5.4). Additionally, the survey captures data on military experiences (including deployments, combat, and occupation exposures) and other metrics (e.g., sleep, diet, alcohol and tobacco use, complementary and alternate therapies, and physical activity). Specific questions assessing combat, occupational, and chemical/biological/radiological warfare exposures are shown in Table 5.5. Follow-up surveys (administered every three years) allow for capture of the changing nature of the members' experiences and health; for example, symptoms can be followed over time and characterized as new-onset, persistent, relapsed, or resolved. The survey is modifiable and has been revised during each survey cycle to expand information on new militarily relevant issues – e.g., questions on exposure to burn pits, sustaining head trauma, and resiliency factors have recently been incorporated.

Participants respond to an invitation to complete a survey via a secure website or a traditional paper survey. The Internet is of particular benefit to a highly mobile population, especially those who deploy or frequently relocate. Today, nearly 90 percent of our participants complete their surveys via the website. Advantages to the use of the Internet include more rapid use of the data, increased data reliability, and reduction in survey costs, such as postal mailings and electronic entry of the written records via Teleform, which are otherwise incurred.

Table 5.4 Standardized instruments embedded within the survey

Construct	Inventory
Physical, mental, and functional health	Short-Form 36
Psychological assessment including symptoms of depression, anxiety, panic syndrome, binge-eating, bulimia nervosa, and alcohol abuse	Patient Health Questionnaire (PHQ)
Post-traumatic stress disorder	Posttraumatic Stress Disorder (PTSD) Checklist–Civilian Version
Alcohol problems	CAGE questionnaire
Specific war-time exposures – depleted uranium, chemical or biological warfare agents	Department of Veterans Affairs Gulf War Survey
Sleep	Insomnia Severity Index

Table 5.5 Self-reported combat experiences and potential occupational exposures

Type of Questions	Specific Questions
Combat*	• Witnessing a person's death due to war, disaster, or tragic event
	• Witnessing instances of physical abuse (torture, beating, rape)
	• Dead and/or decomposing bodies
	• Maimed soldiers or civilians
	• Prisoners of war or refugees
Occupational Exposures	• Occupational hazards requiring protective equipment, such as respirators or hearing protection
	• Routine skin contact with pain and/or solvent and/or substances
	• Depleted uranium
	• Microwaves (excluding small microwave ovens)
	• Pesticides, including creams, sprays, or uniform treatments
	• Pesticides applied in the environment or around living facilities
	• Any exposure, physical or psychological, during a military deployment that had a significant impact on your health? Specify
	• Chemical or biological warfare agents
	• Medical countermeasures for chemical or biological warfare agent exposure
	• Alarms necessitating wearing of chemical or biological warfare protective gear
	• Exposure to smoke from burning trash and/or feces

*An additional battery of 13 questions about combat experiences was added to the 2011 survey. Updated items include feeling that you were in great danger of being killed, being attacked or ambushed, receiving small arms fire, clearing/searching homes or buildings, having an improvised explosive device (IED) or booby trap explode near you, being wounded or injured, seeing dead bodies or human remains, handling or uncovering human remains, knowing someone seriously injured or killed, seeing Americans who were seriously injured or killed, having a member of your unit be seriously injured or killed, being directly responsible for the death of an enemy combatant, or being directly responsible for the death of a non-combatant.

Survey methods

Standard methods for conducting the survey are utilized and have been modeled after the work of Dillman (Dillman 1978). Data on military rosters and initial contact addresses are obtained from DMDC. Information about the study is sent to participants via initial postcards, followed by emails. These messages inform service members about the study and request their voluntary participation. In order to gather a broad spectrum of military experiences, the study team encourages all military personnel who receive an invitation to complete the survey so that their unique experiences are included.

All forms of communication include the survey web link and a computer-generated study identification number. To ensure that the invited participant is the person entering the site, a 'digital signature,' comprised of both the subject identification number along with the last four digits of the member's Social Security number, is used; all transmissions of data occur over a secure and encrypted connection. Besides the web-based survey, participants receive a printed copy of the survey with a postage-paid return envelope. Repeat mailings are sent over the course of the survey cycle (typically 12–18 months to ensure those who may be deployed are able to respond during the cycle) until a completed survey is returned, the service member explicitly declines to participate, or the survey cycle concludes.

Each participant provides his or her preferred postal and email address and phone number. Updates on changes to the participants' contact information are requested on a regular basis, and returned mail (using 'Return Service Requested') is logged into a system that tracks incorrect addresses using a mail item barcode. Service members may ask to have their names deleted from the mail lists and/or to be withdrawn from the study at any time.

Retention is paramount in this 21-year longitudinal study, as it examines both short- and long-term outcomes. A variety of techniques is utilized to encourage continued participation, including a letter welcoming each participant to the Cohort, semiannual appreciatory postcards at Veterans and Memorial Day (Welch et al. 2009), and newsletters that highlight the study's findings and their impact on DoD policies. Additionally, all correspondence contains the study's recognizable logo, which has been used since the study's initiation in 2001. Finally, upon completion of each survey, participants are offered a modest incentive such as a Millennium Cohort Study coin, hat, coaster, magnet, key chain, or phone or gift card.

Challenges to the success of surveying military members encompass not only the mobility of the population, but also concerns regarding the legitimacy of the research. The Millennium Cohort Study is DoD-sponsored research supported by all service branches and Veterans Affairs. The study has been approved by the Institutional Review Board (NHRC 2000.0007) and Office of Management and Budget (OMB Approval Number 0720-0029), and has a Report Control Symbol number [RCS Number DD-HA(AR)2106] for surveying both active duty members and separated personnel. Other approaches to confirm the study's validity are utilized, including messages on members' 'Leave and Earning Statements' (LESs), press releases to military newspapers, inclusion of the study site's DSN number and .mil address on communications to participants, and endorsement letters from service members. Further, the support of both military and Veterans Service Organizations (VSOs) has been critical. Overall, the success of these techniques is exemplified by the strong response since the study's inauguration over a decade ago.

Survey responses

Non-response to the invitation to participate was assessed via phone interviews among Panel 1 (2001) nonresponders ($n = 3000$); the main reason cited for not participating was stated as being 'out of the military'. Additional comparisons of medical record data between responders and non-responders have been conducted and showed little bias (Wells et al. 2008a). Finally, statistical assessments of non-response were performed after the 2004 survey cycle (Littman et al. 2010). Continued assessments of the potential impact of non-response to the initial and follow-up surveys are planned.

Linkage with other medical and military data sources

Participant survey data can be linked to a variety of other data sources to achieve a robust evaluation of the service members' health and military experiences. Potential sources of linkage are shown in Table 5.6. All data are confidentially maintained by using participant subject identification numbers and vigorous security measures; databases are protected behind firewalls restricted to local host access, and all user accounts require specific permissions for access.

Examples of available data linkages include both the Standard Ambulatory Data Record (SADR) and the Standard Inpatient Data Record (SIDR), which contain International Classification of Diseases, 9th Edition (ICD-9) codes from both outpatient and inpatient military medical records. Medical diagnoses from civilian facilities paid for using the TRICARE insurance system [Tricare Enrollment Data – Institutional (TEDi) and TRICARE Enrollment Data – Noninstitutional (TEDni) databases] are also utilized. Medication data are available from the Pharmacy Data Transaction System (PDTS), and immunization data are accessible from the DMDC. Pre-service survey data among Marine Corps personnel who completed recruit training at the Marine Corps Recruit Depot in San Diego (via the Recruit Assessment Program) and all births among service members (DoD Birth and Infant Health Registry) can be linked for specific health outcomes; both of these large datasets are maintained at NHRC. Similarly, information can be obtained from the Career History Archival Medical and Personnel System (CHAMPS), a comprehensive database that provides an individually based, longitudinal record of career events and medical events from the date of enlistment until the date of separation or retirement. Additionally, data on deployments (DMDC) and environmental exposures are obtainable.

Table 5.6 Linkages of Millennium Cohort Study data with other sources

Type of Data	Source
Medical record data from military medical facilities worldwide and civilian facilities covered by the DoD insurance system (TRICARE)	Standard Ambulatory Data Record (SADR) and the Standard Inpatient Data Record (SIDR) TRICARE Encounter Data (TED)
Immunization, deployment (location and dates) and contact data	Defense Manpower Data Center (DMDC)
Pharmaceutical data from military medical facilities and civilian pharmacies which medications are paid for by TRICARE	Pharmacy Data Transaction System (PDTS)
Service and medical data from time of enlistment to separation	Career History Archival Medical and Personnel System (CHAMPS)
Injury data from in theater	Joint Theater Trauma Registry (JTTR) and the Navy-Marine Corps Combat Trauma Registry Expeditionary Medical Encounter Database Total Army Injury and Health Outcomes Database (TAIHOD)
Baseline pre-service data on Marine Corps recruits	Recruit Assessment Program (RAP)
Data on pregnancies and birth outcomes (e.g., birth defects)	Birth and Infant Health Registry
Spouse health, behavioral and relationship data; some child outcomes	Millennium Cohort Family Study
Environmental Exposures	US Army Public Health Command
Links occupational codes between the military services and civilian counterparts	Master Crosswalk File from the DoD Occupational Conversion Index Manual
Health symptoms and perception, as well as exposure data	Pre- and Post-Deployment Health Assessments (DD2795 and DD2796)
Medical status and resource utilization	Health Enrollment Assessment Review (HEAR)
Mortality data	Social Security Administration Death Master File, Department of Veterans Affairs (VA) files, Department of Defense Medical Mortality Registry, and National Death Index
Medical benefit eligibility and insurance, dates of service, military occupation and locations, centralized immunization data	Defense Enrollment Eligibility Reporting System (DEERS)
Medical encounters at the Veterans Administration Medical Centers	Veterans Administration*
Blood samples	DoD Serum Repository*

* Linkage not currently available

Linkages with the Veterans Administration Systems are being explored, as an increasing number of participants have separated from the service. Overall, these data complement the survey's subjective measures with objective measures of exposures and health outcomes providing additional methods to capture data on the health of the Cohort.

Value of the Millennium Cohort Study

Nearly two million US troops have been deployed to Afghanistan and Iraq since October 2001, some of whom are returning with an array of mental and physical health complaints (Institute of Medicine 2010). As such, the Millennium Cohort Study is an essential component of the DoD's Force Health Protection strategy. This large study is setting a new standard for prospective evaluation of the potential short- and long-term health consequences of military occupational exposures, among both active military personnel and the growing number of veterans who have separated or retired from military service and entered the civilian population. Unlike data assembled from Gulf War veterans, the Millennium Cohort Study collects pre-deployment information and follows service members over time to allow for the longitudinal assessment of military service experiences, such as deployment, and a variety of mental and physical health outcomes. This study will allow military leaders and researchers to understand the impact of military service and deployments more completely than ever before in US military history. Findings of this study can inform DoD policy, preventive and treatment programs, interventional studies, and military training requirements.

To address public and veteran concerns over the potential impact of military deployments to Iraq and Afghanistan on veterans' health, this longitudinal study allows for the collection of multiple exposures and potentially related outcomes. Further, owing to the prospective study design, the potential for participant recall bias (an issue with many of the Gulf War retrospective studies and registries) is markedly reduced. The survey can also be modified based on new threats to military personnel and newly discovered medical outcomes. Compared with the Framingham Heart Study (Gray et al. 2002), this study may contribute knowledge which can be applied to the prevention or early management of diseases of public health importance among both military and civilian populations. Data from this study have already been used by Office of the Assistant Secretary of Defense for Health Affairs to enhance preventive programs and by the IOM to define military health care needs (Institute of Medicine 2010).

Reserve and National Guard

As Reservists and National Guard members have been called to active duty service at an unprecedented rate over the past decade, understanding health outcomes among these groups is critical. Debate exists over whether or not these groups have unique experiences that influence health outcomes (e.g., PTSD) post-deployment (Vasterling et al. 2010). The Millennium Cohort Study is distinct in its collection of data among both active duty and Reserve/National Guard personnel. To date (Panels 1–3), a total of 54,608 Reserve/National Guardsmen are participants of the Millennium Cohort Study. The current enrollment cycles will enroll additional members from these vital groups.

To date, several of the Millennium Cohort Study papers have examined outcomes among Reserve/National Guard personnel. Of particular note is a study that showed increased alcohol outcomes (including binge drinking, heavy drinking, and alcohol-related problems) among Reserve/Guard personnel deployed with combat exposures. This finding is concerning in light of increased reliance on Reserve/Guard forces supporting the current operations. Possible explanations for increased risk in Reserve/Guard members after deployment include: inadequate training and preparation of civilian soldiers for the added stresses of combat exposures during deployment, increased stress transitioning between military and civilian occupational settings, lack of military unit cohesiveness, and less access to supportive services (Jacobson et al. 2008). Such data are key in informing/influencing DoD policy and preventive strategies. Future research is planned with the Millennium Cohort Study to examine Reserve/National Guard members for a variety of additional health-related outcomes.

Foundational and methodological studies

The Millennium Cohort Study is the first large, longitudinal study of its kind in a US military setting. Initial publications regarding this study included several foundational papers to validate the reliability of the study's design and survey instrument. These studies examined internal reliability between survey responses, validity of responses by comparing survey data with both medical and military record data, potential response bias by comparing responders and non-responders, and differential responses by mail and Internet questionnaires. Overall, these foundational studies established that the Millennium Cohort Study Cohort was representative of US military service personnel and that the survey data were reliable.

The internal consistency of responses on the standardized instruments and concordance of responses in a test-retest setting were evaluated among 76,742 participants and enrollment of a subgroup of 470 participants who submitted an additional survey within six months of their original submission, respectively. The results of this study showed a high internal consistency for 14 of 16 health components, with lower internal consistency found among two alcohol components. Further, the subgroup analysis noted substantial test–retest stability for stationary variables. These results demonstrate the excellent internal consistency and stability of several standard health instruments utilized in the Cohort (Smith TC et al. 2007a).

Additional studies assessed the accuracy of self-reported medical history and deployment data. In the first study, the accuracy of self-reported medical conditions was evaluated, since self-reported diagnoses may differ from medical record diagnoses, due to misunderstanding during clinician–patient communications and/or self-diagnosis of symptoms. Thirty-eight self-reported medical conditions were compared with the electronic medical record data. Using positive and negative agreement statistics for less-prevalent conditions, near-perfect negative agreement and moderate positive agreement were found for the 38 diagnoses (Smith B et al. 2008a). In a second study, self-reported and military deployment data were compared for > 51,000 participants and agreed in 92 percent of cases. Agreement was substantial for deployment status, frequency, and number of deployments (kappa statistics = 0.81, 0.71, and 0.61, respectively) (Smith B et al. 2007c). Reasons for instances of disagreement between self-report and the military records are unknown, but may be due to more recent deployment being reported by participants before military records are updated, deployment occurring at a different time or location, or that the member could not report his/her deployment (e.g., in the case of Special Forces). Overall, deployment timing and duration metrics, which are critical for military epidemiological studies, are valid in the Millennium Cohort Study.

Other studies have compared self-reported anthrax vaccination with electronic vaccine records for 67,018 participants (2001 and 2003) and found greater than substantial agreement (kappa = 0.80): of all participants with electronic documentation of anthrax vaccination, 98 percent self-reported being vaccinated; of all participants with no electronic record of vaccination, 90 percent self-reported not receiving a vaccination (Smith B et al. 2007a). Further agreement between self-reported smallpox vaccination and electronic vaccination records was examined among 54,066 participants. Substantial agreement (kappa = 0.62) was found between self-report and electronic recording of smallpox vaccination: of all participants with an electronic record of smallpox vaccination, 90 percent self-reported being vaccinated; of all participants with no electronic record of vaccination, 82 percent self-reported not receiving a vaccination (LeardMann et al. 2007). In addition, in both of these studies, discordant reporting of anthrax or smallpox vaccination was not associated with substantial differences in health among the participants. Finally, a study was conducted on the concordance between self-reported and electronic occupation codes for female participants and demonstrated that self-reported occupation can be used with confidence (Smith TC et al. 2007b). These foundational studies display the excellent reliability of survey responses and highlight the distinct advantage of the Millennium Cohort Study's ability of obtaining both medical and military data from multiple sources.

Analyses have also been conducted regarding the potential for response bias. One study determined whether health, as measured by healthcare use preceding invitation, influenced responses to the invitation to participate in the Millennium Cohort Study. Inpatient and outpatient diagnoses were identified among more than 68,000 people during a one-year period prior to the invitation to enroll. Response rates were similar over a diverse range of inpatient and outpatient diagnostic categories and number of days assessing healthcare between responders and non-responders (Wells et al. 2008a). A second study examined possible non-response biases by evaluating data from the baseline and first follow-up survey among 76,775 eligible individuals. Similar to other studies (Cunradi et al. 2005; Young et al. 2006), characteristics associated with a greater probability of response included female gender, older age, higher education level, officer rank, active-duty status, and lack of chronic alcohol consumption, history of smoking, or major depressive disorder. There was no difference in response by history of PTSD, panic disorder, or mode of response (i.e., paper vs. the Internet). These findings suggest that the prospective data from this Cohort are not substantially biased by non-response at the first follow-up assessment (Littman et al. 2010).

Finally an analysis of the use of the Internet vs. paper was conducted. Over 50 percent of the 77,047 Panel 1 participants chose the Internet, and as expected, Internet responders were slightly more likely to be male, to be younger, to have a college degree, and to work in information technology. Question completion rates were 98.3 percent on average, for both Internet and paper responders (Smith B et al. 2007b). Since 2001, an increasing number of Millennium Cohort Study participants have responded via the Internet, with ~90 percent participating during the last survey cycle (2007) through this route.

Further methodology work will continue to ensure that the Cohort is representative of the US military population. Methods to encourage non-biased responses and retention in the Cohort are also in place and updated over time.

Health outcomes: findings to date

Mental health and behavioral findings

Given the high risk of mental health problems reported among service members returning from the current operations in Iraq and Afghanistan (Hoge et al. 2004; 2006; Milliken et al. 2007), several publications from the Millennium Cohort Study have focused on these outcomes and provided cutting-edge work in the areas of posttraumatic stress disorder (PTSD), depression, and alcohol and tobacco use among US service members. Because of the collection of pre-deployment data and follow-up longitudinal data, this study can assess the temporal association between exposures and outcomes and evaluate the natural history of symptoms and diseases over time.

In an early study, new-onset and persistent PTSD symptoms were evaluated using initial (July 2001 to June 2003) and follow-up data (June 2004 to February 2006). A positive screen for PTSD was based on the checklist-civilian version using *Diagnostic and Statistical Manual of Mental Disorders*, Fourth Edition (DSM-IV) criteria (at least one intrusion symptom, three avoidance symptoms, and two hyperarousal symptoms at moderate or more extreme levels, and a total score ≥ 50). A positive screen for new-onset PTSD or self-report of a diagnosis from a health care provider were identified in 7.6–8.7 percent of deployers who reported combat exposures between baseline and follow-up, 1.4–2.1 percent of deployers who did not report combat exposures, and 2.3–3.0 percent of non-deployers. Among those with a positive screen for PTSD at baseline, deployment did not affect persistence of symptoms; however, among those with combat exposure, 43 percent continued to screen positive post-deployment. In summary, this work showed that combat deployers had three-fold higher odds of PTSD symptoms, and that specific combat exposures, rather than deployment itself, significantly affect the onset of PTSD (Smith TC et al. 2008a).

Additional work in the area of PTSD evaluated potential vulnerability or resiliency factors. One study found that a positive screen for new-onset PTSD or self-report of a diagnosis from a health care provider was more than two-fold higher in both women and men who reported assault prior to a combat deployment (Smith TC et al. 2008b). This study and others (Iversen et al. 2008) demonstrate that prior assault confers an increased vulnerability for, rather than resilience against, PTSD symptoms among deployed military personnel who experience combat. A second study performed among combat deployers ($n = 5410$) found that 7.3 percent had a positive screen for new-onset PTSD or newly reported diagnosis from a health care provider at follow-up. Individuals whose baseline mental or physical component summary scores were below the 15th percentile had a two to three times risk for PTSD compared with those in the 15th–85th percentile. These data suggest that service members with a history of assault or low mental/physical health status before combat exposure may represent a more vulnerable group that could potentially benefit from interventions targeted to prevent PTSD (LeardMann et al. 2009).

In another study, participants who reported proportionately less physical activity were more likely to screen positive for PTSD. Specifically, those with ≥ 20 minutes of vigorous physical activity twice weekly had significantly decreased odds for new-onset (odds ratio [OR] 0.58, 95% confidence interval [CI] 0.49–0.70) and persistent (OR 0.59, 95% CI 0.42–0.83) PTSD symptoms. These data suggest that physical activity, especially vigorous activity, may be associated with decreased odds of screening positive for PTSD, and that a physical activity component may be valuable to PTSD treatment and prevention programs (LeardMann et al. 2011).

Finally, a recent study using Millennium Cohort Data assessed the relationship of pre-deployment psychiatric status and injury severity with post-deployment PTSD. The study involved participants who completed a baseline questionnaire (from July 2001 through June 2003) and at least one follow-up questionnaire (from June 2004 through February 2006 and from May 2007 through December 2008) and who were deployed in the intervening period. Of 22,630 eligible participants, 8.1 percent screened positive for PTSD at follow-up, and 0.8 percent sustained a deployment-related physical injury. The odds of screening positive for PTSD were 2.52 (95% CI, 2.01–3.16) times greater in those with ≥ 1 baseline mental health disorder and 1.16 (95% CI, 1.01–1.34) greater for every three-unit increase in the Injury Severity Score. Irrespective of injury severity, self-reported preinjury psychiatric status was significantly associated with PTSD at follow-up, suggesting that this group may benefit from interventions targeted to prevent or to ensure early identification and treatment of post-deployment PTSD (Sandweiss et al. 2011).

Depression is also an important mental health outcome that may occur among service members. Using Millennium Cohort data, new-onset depression was studied among service members recently deployed to the wars in Iraq and Afghanistan, and it was found that combat-deployed men and women were at increased risk for screening positive for new-onset depression compared with non-deployed men and women (men: OR 1.32, 95% CI, 1.13–1.54; women: OR 2.13, 95% CI, 1.70–2.65). However, deployers without combat exposures had decreased odds for screening positive for new-onset depression compared with those who did not deploy (men: OR 0.66, 95% CI, 0.53–0.83; women: OR 0.65, 95% CI 0.47–0.89), suggesting a "healthy warrior" effect that persons with underlying mental conditions may not be deployable. These data emphasize the importance of post-deployment mental health screening for US service members exposed to combat (Wells et al. 2010).

Similar to PTSD and depression, high rates of alcohol misuse after combat deployment have been reported among personnel returning from war (Milliken et al. 2007; Richards et al. 1989). Data from the Millennium Cohort Study were utilized to determine whether deployment with combat exposures was associated with new-onset alcohol consumption, binge drinking, and alcohol-related problems. Participants who completed both a baseline (July 2001 to June 2003) and follow-up (June 2004 to February 2006) questionnaire were studied. After exclusion criteria (e.g., excluded due to missing alcohol outcome information at baseline or follow-up, or missing demographic or covariate data) were applied, the analyses included 48,481 participants (active duty, n = 26,613; Reserve or National Guard, n = 21,868). New-onset prevalence of heavy weekly drinking, binge drinking, and alcohol-related problems among Reserve or National Guard personnel who deployed with combat exposures was 8.8 percent, 25.6 percent, and 7.1 percent, respectively. Among active-duty personnel, new-onset rates were 6.0 percent, 26.6 percent, and 4.8 percent, respectively. Analyses revealed that Reserve and National Guard personnel who deployed and reported combat exposures were significantly more likely to experience new-onset heavy weekly drinking (OR 1.63, 95% CI, 1.36–1.96), binge drinking (OR 1.46, 95% CI, 1.24–1.71), and alcohol-related problems (OR 1.63, 95% CI, 1.33–2.01) compared with non-deployed personnel. The youngest members of the cohort were at highest risk for all alcohol-related outcomes. These results suggest that targeted interventions regarding alcohol misuse should be implemented, especially among Reserve and National Guard personnel and younger service members who deploy with reported combat exposures (Jacobson et al. 2008). These data were directly utilized by Office of the Assistant Secretary of Defense for Health Affairs to enhance alcohol-related programs for Reserve and National Guard personnel.

Similarly, the impact of the stress of military deployments and combat may result in other maladaptive behaviors, including tobacco use. Using participants who submitted baseline data (July 2001–June 2003) and follow-up data (June 2004–January 2006), new-onset smoking was identified among baseline never-smokers and smoking recidivism among baseline past-smokers. Smoking initiation was noted in 1.3 percent of non-deployers and 2.3 percent of deployers, and smoking recidivism in 28.7 percent of non-deployers and 39.4 percent of those who deployed. Additionally, deploying for > 9 months and multiple deployments increased smoking recidivism. Since, military deployment was associated with both smoking initiation and recidivism, these data suggested that programs should be implemented during and after deployment to discourage tobacco use (Smith B et al. 2008b). As cigarette use may be prohibited during some deployments (e.g., on the flight deck or in combat situations where the flame may reveal military position) and other forms of tobacco have known negative health effects, additional work examining smokeless tobacco use is currently underway.

Finally, the effect of military deployments and combat environments on disordered eating and weight changes has been studied in the Cohort, since maintaining an ideal weight is important for overall health. Deployment was not significantly associated with new-onset disordered eating in women or men in the adjusted models. However, deployed women who reported combat exposures were 1.78 times (95% CI 1.02–3.11) more likely to report new-onset disordered eating and 2.35 times (95% CI 1.17–4.70) more likely to lose 10 percent or more of their body weight compared with non-combat deployers (Jacobson et al. 2009a).

In summary, these data suggest that combat increases the odds for several mental health outcomes, and that certain military service members have increased odds of developing mental and behavioral conditions after combat deployments. Further work in the area of mental health will focus on specific populations (e.g., women and military augmentees), examine the effect of PTSD symptoms on weight changes and binge eating over time, describe the relationship between dwell time (i.e., time at home between deployments) and mental health outcomes, and assess the occurrence of maternal depression among women who deploy shortly after childbirth. Understanding vulnerable populations and how health outcomes are interrelated in service members can help inform the DoD and VA regarding focused preventive and early management programs.

Physical health findings

In addition to mental health issues, concerns regarding a variety of physical health outcomes have surfaced, including respiratory conditions among returning service members from Iraq and Afghanistan (King et al. 2011). Data from Millennium Cohort Study participants who completed baseline (July 2001–June 2003) and follow-up (June 2004–February 2006) questionnaires were studied for respiratory outcomes. Deployers had a higher rate of newly reported respiratory symptoms (persistent or recurring cough or shortness of breath) than non-deployers (14 percent vs. 10 percent), especially among ground troops (i.e., Army and Marine Corps). Regarding medical diagnoses, there were similar rates of chronic bronchitis or emphysema (1 percent vs. 1 percent) and asthma (1 percent vs. 1 percent) among deployers compared with non-deployers. These data suggest that ground-troop deployments may be associated with increased respiratory symptoms, and that specific exposures rather than deployment in general may be determinants of post-deployment respiratory illness (Smith B et al. 2009). Further studies are planned including assessing the natural history of respiratory symptoms and determining if diagnoses of pulmonary diseases are changing over time.

Hypertension and diabetes mellitus are major causes of cardiovascular disease and impact survival. The role of military experiences on these conditions is largely unknown. For example, stressful situations (e.g., combat deployments) may heighten the risk for these conditions. Among Panel 1 participants, 6.9 percent reported newly diagnosed hypertension between the baseline and follow-up surveys. In the adjusted models, multiple combat exposures was associated with higher odds of hypertension (OR 1.33, 95% CI 1.07–1.65) compared with non-combat deployers, possibly indicating a stress-induced hypertensive effect (Granado et al. 2009). In a second study, the impact of military deployment, combat exposures, and mental health conditions were studied in relationship to newly reported diabetes mellitus. A total of 44,754 participants were studied (median age 36 years at time of baseline survey completion), and the incidence of new-onset diabetes was three cases per 1,000 person-years. After adjustments for covariates (e.g., age, sex, body mass index), screening positive for PTSD was significantly associated with newly reported diabetes (OR 2.07, 95% CI 1.31–3.29). Deployment with or without combat was not significantly associated with diabetes (Boyko et al. 2010). These data suggest that mental and physical health outcomes may be interrelated and that military members with combat experiences and PTSD may benefit from blood pressure and blood sugar measurements, respectively, to ensure the health of service members over time.

The issues of sleep quality and length have increasingly gained attention as the war has lingered into its second decade. Self-reported sleep patterns were studied among Millennium Cohort members who completed baseline (2001–2003) and follow-up (2004–2006) surveys. This study showed deployment significantly influenced sleep quality and quantity in this population, although the effect sizes were modest. Additionally, personnel reporting combat exposures or mental health symptoms were more likely to have trouble sleeping, suggesting that these subgroups may benefit from sleep assessments (Seelig et al. 2010).

The Cohort has also been utilized to study headache disorders, a leading cause of missed days of work. The prevalence of migraines among men and women were 6.9 percent and 20.9 percent, respectively, and recurrent severe headaches, 9.4 percent and 22.3 percent, respectively. Combat deployers were found to have higher odds of any new-onset headache disorder than non-deployers [OR 1.72 (95% CI 1.55–1.90) for men and 1.84 (95% CI 1.55–2.18) for women], while deployers without combat exposure did not. These data suggest that deployed personnel with reported combat exposure are more likely to have headache disorders and provide valuable information on healthcare needs among returning service members (Jankosky et al. 2011).

In addition to medical outcomes, health care utilization has been studied. An early study in the Cohort showed that active duty service members had an increased risk of hospitalization after deployment compared with before deployment, but a lower risk when compared with non-deployers (Smith TC et al. 2009). Recent studies have also examined the use of complementary and alternative medicine (CAM) among members of the US military. A cross-sectional study of participants who completed a survey from 2004 to 2006 found that 30 percent reported using at least one practitioner-assisted CAM therapy and 27 percent reported using at least one self-administered CAM therapy, whereas 59 percent did not report using any CAM therapy. Increasing health conditions and health-related symptoms were associated with CAM use (Jacobson et al. 2009b). In a second study, the number and types of medical visits were compared between CAM and non-CAM users. Those who used CAM had a higher odds ratio for hospitalizations (OR 1.29, 95% CI 1.16–1.43) and more outpatient visits (7.0 days vs. 5.9 days, $p < 0.001$) compared with those not using CAM (White et al. 2011). These data suggest that CAM use is common among military personnel and may be a marker for poorer underlying health.

Finally, Millennium Cohort data have been utilized to examine the impact of vaccinations given prior to deployment, including smallpox (beginning in 2001) and anthrax (beginning in the late 1990s). A study examined 40,472 individuals (8,793 of whom received the smallpox vaccine and 31,679 who did not) and found no significant adverse associations with self-reported health outcomes (Wells et al. 2008b). Future studies in the Millennium Cohort will continue to provide policy makers and health care providers with critical information about the impact of military service on mental and physical health outcomes and healthcare utilization. For example, studies will evaluate a range of other health care issues, such as autoimmune diseases, heart disease, cancers, and mortality, which will be of particular interest as the Cohort ages. As new potential exposures (e.g., open air burn pit exposure) or health care concerns (e.g., traumatic brain injury, suicide, motor vehicle crashes) arise, the Millennium Cohort Study is in a valued position to provide critical information to both the DoD and VA. Finally, given the triennial assessments of health over time, the survey data may detect changes in health, which may be the result of new military experiences or implemented preventive programs.

Future areas of research

In addition to the future work regarding mental and physical health outcomes, the Millennium Cohort can provide valuable data on a range of topics, including the impact of deployment and mental health symptoms on post-service employability and the health care needs of veterans, data which are critical for the development of VA programs. The newly initiated Millennium Cohort Family Study will also provide data on the dyad (both the service member and spouse) and children, and provide information regarding needed programs to support the military family. Moreover, as few longitudinal data exist on the outcomes of service members long after deployment experiences and service separation, this study will continue to provide important information for the next 21+ years. The study is also perfectly poised to collect invaluable data on the impact of future conflicts or exposures that may occur.

Conclusion

In summary, the Millennium Cohort Study has successfully enrolled over 150,000 US service members, with the goal of achieving > 200,000 participants, including military spouses, during the current survey cycle. This is the first comprehensive study to prospectively evaluate the impact of military experiences, together with deployment and combat experiences, on mental and physical health outcomes of US service members. Through its collection of pre-deployment data, longitudinal study design, and linkage with other medical and military data sources, never has such a wealth of data been available regarding long-term health of veterans. Findings from the Millennium Cohort Study have informed DoD policy to strengthen preventive and treatment programs. The success of this longitudinal study sets a new standard for data collection within both military and civilian populations. With a 21-year follow-up period, the Millennium Cohort Study will continue to provide long-term militarily relevant data on health outcomes and public health issues significant to both DoD and VA leaders and healthcare providers.

Note

Conflict of Interest: The author reports no financial or other conflict of interest relative to this work.

The content and views expressed in this publication are the sole responsibility of the author and do not necessarily reflect the views or policies of the Department of Defense or the Departments of the Army, Navy, or Air Force, Department of Veterans Affairs, nor the US Government. Mention of trade names, commercial products, or organizations does not imply endorsement by the US Government.

This work is original and has not been published elsewhere.

Corresponding Author: Dr. Nancy Crum-Cianflone, Naval Health Research Center, 140 Sylvester Road, San Diego CA 92106-3521; phone: 619-553-7335; E-mail: nancy.crum@med.navy.mil.

References

Boyko EJ, Jacobson IJ, Smith B, Ryan MAK, Hooper TI, Amoroso PJ, Gackstetter GD, Barrett-Connor E, & Smith TC, for the Millennium Cohort Study Team 2010, 'Risk of diabetes in US military service members in relation to combat deployment and mental health', *Diabetes Care*, vol. 33, no. 8, pp. 1771–1777.

Committee on Measuring the Health of Gulf War Veterans IoM: Hernandez LM, Durch JS, Blazer DG, & Hoverman IV (eds) 1999, *Gulf War Veterans: Measuring Health*, National Academy Press, Washington DC, Available from http://www.nap.edu/openbook.php?isbn = 0309065801 [October 18, 2011].

Cunradi CB, Moore R, Killoran M, & Ames G 2005, 'Survey nonresponse bias among young adults: the role of alcohol, tobacco, and drugs,' *Substance Use & Misuse*, vol. 40, no. 2, pp. 171–185.

Department of Veterans Affairs, 'Annual Report to Congress: Federally Sponsored Research of Persian Gulf Veterans' Illnesses for 1998. Washington, DC: Department of Veterans Affairs', The Research Working Group of the Persian Gulf Veterans Coordinating Board, 1999. Available from: http://www.research.va.gov/resources/pubs/GulfWarRpt99.cfm [October 26, 2011].

Dillman, DA 1978, *Mail and telephone surveys: The total design method*, Wiley & Sons, New York.

Granado NS, Smith TC, Swanson GM, Harris RB, Shahar E, Smith B, Boyko EJ, Wells TS, & Ryan MAK 2009, for the Millennium Cohort Study Team, 'Newly reported hypertension after military combat deployment in a large population-based study', *Hypertension*, vol. 54, no. 5, pp. 966–973.

Gray GC, Hawksworth AW, Smith TC, Kang HK, Knoke JD, & Gackstetter GD 1998, 'Gulf War Veterans' Health Registries. Who is most likely to seek evaluation?', *American Journal of Epidemiology*, vol. 148, no. 4, pp. 343–349.

Gray GC, Chesbrough KB, Ryan MAK, Amoroso P, Boyko EJ, Gackstetter GD, Hooper TI, & Riddle JR, for the Millennium Cohort Study Group 2002, 'The Millennium Cohort Study: A 21-year prospective cohort study of 140,000 military personnel', *Military Medicine*, vol. 167, no. 6, pp. 483–488.

Hoge CW, Castro CA, Messer SC, McGurk D, Cotting DI, & Koffman RL 2004, 'Combat duty in Iraq and Afghanistan, mental health problems, and barriers to care', *New England Journal of Medicine*, vol. 351, no. 1, pp. 13–22.

Hoge CW, Auchterlonie JL, & Milliken CS 2006, 'Mental health problems, use of mental health services, and attrition from military service after returning from deployment to Iraq or Afghanistan', *Journal of the American Medical Association*, vol. 295, no. 9, pp. 1023–1032.

Institute of Medicine 2010, *Returning Home from Iraq and Afghanistan: Preliminary Assessment of Readjustment Needs of Veterans, Service Members, and Their Families*, National Academic Press, Washington DC. Available from http://www.iom.edu/Reports/2010/Returning-Home-from-Iraq-and-Afghanistan-Preliminary-Assessment.aspx [November 5, 2011].

Iversen AC, Fear NT, Ehlers A, Hacker Hughes J, Hull L, Earnshaw M, Greenberg N, Rona R, Wessely S, & Hotopf M 2008, 'Risk factors for post-traumatic stress disorder among UK Armed Forces personnel', *Psychological Medicine*, vol. 38, no. 4, pp. 511–522.

Jacobson IG, Ryan MAK, Hooper TI, Smith TC, Amoroso PJ, Boyko EJ, Gackstetter GD, Wells TS, & Bell NS, for the Millennium Cohort Study Team 2008, 'Alcohol use and alcohol-related problems before and after military combat deployment', *Journal of the American Medical Association*, vol. 300, no. 6, pp. 663–675.

Jacobson IG, Smith TC, Smith B, Keel PK, Amoroso PJ, Wells TS, Bathalon GP, Boyko EJ, & Ryan MAK for the Millennium Cohort Study Team 2009a, 'Disordered eating and weight changes after deployment: longitudinal assessment of a large US military cohort', *American Journal of Epidemiology*, vol. 169, no. 4, pp. 415–427.

Jacobson IG, White MR, Smith TC, Smith B, Wells TS, Gackstetter GD, & Boyko EJ, for the Millennium Cohort Study Team 2009b, 'Self-reported health symptoms and conditions among complementary and alternative medicine users in a large military cohort', *Annals of Epidemiology*, vol. 19, no. 9, pp. 613–622.

Jankosky C, Hooper TI, Granado NS, Scher A, Gackstetter GD, Boyko EJ, & Smith TC, for the Millennium Cohort Study Team 2011, 'Headache disorders in the Millennium Cohort: epidemiology and relations with combat deployment', *Headache*, vol. 51, no. 7, pp. 1098–1111.

Kang HK, Dalager NA, & Lee KY 1995, *Health Surveillance of Persian Gulf War Veterans: a Review of the Department of Veterans Affairs Persian Gulf Registry and In-Patient Treatment Files*. Washington DC: Environmental Epidemiology Service, Department of Veterans Affairs.

King MS, Eisenberg R, Newman JH, Tolle JJ, Harrell FE Jr, Nian H, Ninan M, Lambright ES, Sheller JR, Johnson JE, & Miller RF 2011, 'Constrictive bronchiolitis in soldiers returning from Iraq and Afghanistan', *New England Journal of Medicine*, vol. 365, no. 3, pp. 222–230.

LeardMann CA, Smith B, Smith TC, Wells TS, & Ryan MAK, for the Millennium Cohort Study Team 2007, 'Smallpox vaccination: comparison of self-reported and electronic vaccine records in the Millennium Cohort Study', *Human Vaccines*, vol. 3, no. 6, pp. 245–251.

LeardMann CA, Smith TC, Smith B, Wells TS, & Ryan MAK, for the Millennium Cohort Study Team 2009, 'Baseline self-reported functional health predicts vulnerability to posttraumatic stress disorder following combat deployment: prospective US military cohort study', *British Medical Journal*, vol. 338, b1273.

LeardMann CA, Kelton ML, Smith B, Littman AJ, Boyko EJ, Wells TS, & Smith TC, for the Millennium Cohort Study Team 2011, 'Prospectively assessed posttraumatic stress disorder and associated physical activity', *Public Health Reports*, vol. 126, no. 3, pp. 371–383.

Littman AJ, Boyko EJ, Jacobson IG, Horton J, Gackstetter GD, Smith B, Hooper TI, Amoroso PJ, & Smith TC, for the Millennium Cohort Study Team 2010, 'Assessing nonresponse bias at follow-up in a large prospective cohort of relatively young and mobile military service member', *BMC Medical Research Methodology*, vol. 10, no. 1, p. 99.

Milliken CS, Auchterlonie JL, & Hoge CW 2007, 'Longitudinal assessment of mental health problems among active and reserve component soldiers returning from the Iraq war', *Journal of the American Medical Association*, vol. 298, no. 18, pp. 2141–2148.

Richards MS, Goldberg J, Rodin MB, & Anderson RJ 1989, 'Alcohol consumption and problem drinking in white male veterans and nonveterans', *American Journal of Public Health*, vol. 79, no. 8, pp. 1011–1015.

Sandweiss DA, Slymen DJ, LeardMann CA, Smith B, White MR, Boyko EJ, Hooper TI, Gackstetter GD, Amoroso PJ, & Smith TC, for the Millennium Cohort Study Team 2011, 'Preinjury psychiatric status, injury severity, and postdeployment posttraumatic stress disorder', *Archives of General Psychiatry*, vol. 68, no. 5, pp. 496–504.

Secretary of Defense: Report to the Committee on National Security. House of Representatives and the Armed Services Committee, 1998. US Senate, on Effectiveness of Medical Research Initiatives Regarding Gulf War Illnesses. Washington DC, Department of Defense.

Seelig AD, Jacobson IJ, Smith B, Hooper TI, Boyko EJ, Gackstetter GD, Gehrman PR, Macera CA, & Smith TC, for the Millennium Cohort Study Team 2010, 'Sleep patterns before, during, and after deployment to Iraq and Afghanistan', *Sleep*, vol. 33, no. 12, pp. 1615–1622.

Smith B, Leard CA, Smith TC, Reed RJ, & Ryan MAK, for the Millennium Cohort Study Team 2007a, 'Anthrax vaccination in the Millennium Cohort: validation and measures of health', *American Journal of Preventive Medicine*, vol. 32, no. 4, pp. 347–353.

Smith B, Smith TC, Gray GC, & Ryan MAK, for the Millennium Cohort Study Team 2007b, 'When epidemiology meets the Internet: Web-based surveys in the Millennium Cohort Study', *American Journal of Epidemiology*, vol. 1345–1354.

Smith B, Wingard DL, Ryan MAK, Macera CA, Patterson TL, & Slymen DJ, for the Millennium Cohort Study Team 2007c, 'US military deployment during 2001–2006: comparison of subjective and objective data sources in a large prospective health study', *Annals of Epidemiology*, vol. 17, no. 12, pp. 976–982.

Smith B, Chu LK, Smith TC, Amoroso PJ, Boyko EJ, Hooper TI, Gackstetter GD, & Ryan MAK, for the Millennium Cohort Study Team 2008a, 'Challenges of self-reported medical conditions and electronic medical records among members of a large military cohort', *BMC Medical Research Methodology*, vol. 8, p. 37.

Smith B, Ryan MAK, Wingard DL, Patterson TL, Slymen DJ, & Macera CA, for the Millennium Cohort Study Team 2008b, 'Cigarette smoking and military deployment: a prospective evaluation', *American Journal of Preventive Medicine*, vol. 35, no. 6, pp. 539–546.

Smith B, Wong CA, Smith TC, Boyko EJ, Gackstetter GD, & Ryan MAK, for the Millennium Cohort Study Team 2009, 'Newly reported respiratory symptoms and conditions among military personnel deployed to Iraq and Afghanistan: a prospective population-based study', *American Journal of Epidemiology*, vol. 170, no. 11, pp. 1433–1442.

Smith TC, Smith B, Jacobson IG, Corbeil TE, & Ryan MAK, for the Millennium Cohort Study Team 2007a, 'Reliability of standard health assessment instruments in a large, population-based cohort study', *Annals of Epidemiology*, vol. 17, no. 7, pp. 525–532.

Smith TC, Jacobson IG, Smith B, Hooper TI, & Ryan MAK, for the Millennium Cohort Study Team 2007b, 'The occupational role of women in military service: validation of occupation and prevalence of exposures in the Millennium Cohort Study', *International Journal of Environmental Health Research*, vol. 17, no. 4, pp. 271–284.

Smith TC, Ryan MAK, Wingard DL, Slymen DJ, Sallis JF, & Kritz-Silverstein D, for the Millennium Cohort Study Team 2008a, 'New onset and persistent symptoms of posttraumatic stress disorder self-reported after deployment and combat exposures: prospective population-based US military cohort study', *British Medical Journal*, vol. 336, no. 7640, pp. 366–371.

Smith TC, Wingard DL, Ryan MAK, Kritz-Silverstein D, Slymen DJ, & Sallis JF, for the Millennium Cohort Study Team 2008b, 'Prior assault and posttraumatic stress disorder after combat deployment', *Epidemiology*, vol. 19, no. 3, pp. 505–512.

Smith TC, Leardmann CA, Smith B, Jacobson IG, & Ryan MA 2009, 'Postdeployment hospitalizations among service members deployed in support of the operations in Iraq and Afghanistan', *Annals of Epidemiology*, vol. 19, no. 9, pp. 603–612.

Strom Thurmond National Defense Authorization Act for Fiscal Year 1999, Conference Report (H. Rpt. 105-736). SEC. 743, Available from http://www.ogc.doc.gov/ogc/contracts/cld/hi/105-261.html [October 18, 2011].

Vasterling JJ, Proctor SP, Friedman MJ, Hoge CW, Heeren T, King LA, & King DW 2010, 'PTSD symptom increases in Iraq-deployed soldiers: comparison with nondeployed soldiers and associations with baseline symptoms, deployment experiences, and postdeployment stress', *Journal of Traumatic Stress*, vol. 23, no. 1, pp. 41–51.

Welch KE, LeardMann CA, Jacobson IG, Speigle SJ, Smith B, Smith TC, & Ryan MA, for the Millennium Cohort Study Team 2009, 'Postcards encourage participant updates', *Epidemiology*, 20, no. 2, pp. 313–314.

Wells TS, Jacobson IG, Smith TC, Spooner CN, Smith B, Reed RJ, Amoroso PJ, & Ryan MAK, for the Millennium Cohort Study Team 2008a, 'Prior health care utilization as a determinant to enrollment in a 22-year prospective study, the Millennium Cohort Study', *European Journal of Epidemiology*, vol. 23, no. 2, pp. 79–87.

Wells TS, LeardMann CA, Smith TC, Smith B, Jacobson IG, Reed RJ, & Ryan MAK, for the Millennium Cohort Study Team 2008b, 'Self-reported adverse health events following smallpox vaccination in a large prospective study of US military service members', *Human Vaccines*, vol. 4, no. 2, pp. 127–133.

Wells TS, LeardMann CA, Fortuna SO, Smith B, Smith TC, Ryan MAK, Boyko EJ, & Blazer D, for the Millennium Cohort Study Team 2010, 'A prospective study of depression following combat deployment in support of the wars in Iraq and Afghanistan', *American Journal of Public Health*, 100, no. 1, pp. 90–99.

White MR, Jacobson IG, Smith B, Wells TS, Gackstetter GD, Boyko EJ, & Smith TC, for the Millennium Cohort Study Team 2011, 'Health care utilization among complementary and alternative medicine users in a large military cohort', *BMC Complementary and Alternative Medicine*, vol. 11, p. 27.

Young AF, Powers JR, & Bell SL 2006, 'Attrition in longitudinal studies: who do you lose?', *Australian and New Zealand Journal of Public Health*, vol. 30, no. 4, pp. 353–361.

6 Screening for mental illness in the armed forces

Roberto J. Rona and Simon Wessely[1]

Background

The profession of arms is an inherently dangerous occupation. Many studies of the military have demonstrated high prevalence of posttraumatic stress disorder (PTSD), depression, alcohol misuse and multiple physical symptoms (MPS) (Fear et al. 2010; Hoge et al. 2004, 2006; Jacobson et al. 2008; Milliken et al. 2007; Hotopf et al. 2006). This is especially so in times of long military operations such as those in Iraq and Afghanistan (Hoge et al. 2004), and particularly so among those performing a combat role (Fear et al. 2010; Hoge et al. 2004). Screening is one of the interventions available to ameliorate the possible consequences of a military occupation on mental injury.

Screening is understood as the application of relatively simple tests to those who have not sought medical help for a disorder, to distinguish between those who probably have a specific disorder which warrants further action from those who do not (Morrison, 1992; Koepsell and Weiss 2003). The purpose of screening is to identify at an early stage those with a disorder so that management of the condition is more likely to be effective than if left until the person experiences a more severe form of the condition or is able to recognize the symptoms of the condition without the use of a screening tool. Screening therefore is about increasing the recognition of disorders that might otherwise be detected later or not at all.

Screening has been used for two purposes in the military: to improve the effectiveness, readiness and hardiness of the armed forces by excluding those who are likely to debilitate the organization; to focus on improving the health status of individuals whether in service or after exiting the services. Both objectives can go hand in hand in some situations, but one perspective may take precedence in different situations. The focus of most programs of screening for mental illness in the twentieth century was at the recruiting or induction stage to exclude from the armed forces in general, or specific operations in particular, individuals who would have a high degree of vulnerability to mental disorders.

Jones et al. (2003) provided a historical perspective of screening based on the experiences of World War 1 (WW1) and WW2, and more recent conflicts. One of the most famous historical examples was the screening program carried out in the United States at the start of American involvement in WW2, which subsequent research has shown did little to prevent neuropsychiatric disorder. Indeed, the psychiatric casualty rate reached its peak of 31,000 admissions per month by August 1943 (Jones et al. 2003). The average neuropsychiatric admission rate for divisions including the reserves was 260 per thousand men per year between June and November 1944, a substantially higher rate than for WW1 (Appel et al. 1946). This despite the fact that nearly 11 percent of those registered for the draft were turned down for neuropsychiatric reasons or because of low intelligence (Jones et al. 2003).

The failure of screening in WW2 was due to the lack of recognition that although there was an association between detection by the psychological tools of the period and vulnerability to future breakdown, the tools did not have sufficient predictive value for use as a screening tool. Indeed, the screening for vulnerability was made before the individuals (most of them young men still at formative stages of their personality) had the opportunity to see action. In a study, most of those who were labeled as vulnerable performed satisfactorily when inducted despite having been rejected initially (Egan et al. 1951). On the other hand, many of those who passed the screening broke down during operations.

Although this was a dramatic and costly (both in economic and personal terms) example of failed mental health screening, this definitely does not mean that mental health screening can never work within the armed forces. Diagnostic instruments, combat conditions, recruitment policies, the cultural background and health of potential recruits, and health care systems were different from those prevailing today. The real lesson from the past is that there must be a clear set of criteria to evaluate the advantages and disadvantages of a prospective screening program before its implementation. The development of agreed criteria for screening among allied forces would benefit from the diversity of experiences and contribute to understanding each other's perspective.

In 1998, the US Department of Defense (DoD) introduced a short pre-deployment questionnaire and a post-deployment questionnaire. The program has progressively been applied to regulars and veterans (Wright et al. 2008; Seal et al. 2008). Following a finding that mental disorders increased between reintegration and 4 months (Bliese et al. 2007), post-deployment assessment happened at reintegration and at 3 to 6 months. A pre-deployment assessment with minimal data collection on mental disorders was also implemented (Nevin 2009). In 2010 the screening program was extended in two ways: the mental health assessment was now applied at four time points (2 months before deployment, between 3 and 6 months post-deployment, 7 to 12 months post-deployment and 16 to 24 months post-deployment); and the options for more detailed assessments of PTSD and depression included the PTSD checklist, PCL, and the patient health questionnaire, PHQ-9, respectively (Office of the Assistant Secretary of Defense, 2010).

The rationale for a screening program for mental disorders of four assessments over two years is unclear. The Australian Defense Force and the Canadian Department of National Defense have also implemented a post-deployment screening program for mental disorders, albeit not as extensive as the United States. Although the UK armed forces has evaluated a program of primary prevention similar to the US Army Battlemind (Adler et al. 2009a,b) and implemented a Trauma Risk Management (TRiM) program designed to detect mental illness via peer recognition (Greenberg et al. 2010), the UK Ministry of Defence has postponed a decision to implement a screening program for mental ill health until a DoD funded study to evaluate the effectiveness of post-deployment screening in UK service personnel reports its results.

Criteria for deciding to introduce a screening program

In their seminal work, Wilson and Jungner (1968) made recommendations on the requirements for a screening program, and considered the standard for appraising the merits of a program. It has been summarized in five main criteria in this article following more recent recommendations (US Preventive Services Task Force Guide, 1996; UK National Screening Committee Criteria 2010; Koepsell and Weiss, 2003) (Table 6.1). These criteria are widely accepted by policy makers, researchers and practitioners. We believe that it is worthwhile to adhere to these criteria when making a decision to implement a screening program because although screening can be beneficial it can also be damaging, expensive and once implemented difficult to stop. In addition it may use resources that could be better used for other activities.

In this chapter we propose to appraise the current evidence for implementing screening for mental ill health in the military using the five criteria in Table 6.1. This overview may overlap in some respects with a previously published commentary (Rona et al. 2005), but the contents and emphasis in this chapter are different. The emphasis will be on current rather than historical issues as others have covered the historical perspective (Jones et al. 2003; Shephard 2002).

Table 6.1 Criteria for initiating a screening program

1	The disease is an important public health problem, in terms of its frequency and/or severity
2	The natural history of the disease presents a suitable opportunity for screening
3	A suitable screening test is available and valid, i.e. able to distinguish between diseased and non-diseased people; inexpensive; safe; easy to administer; acceptable to the population
4	Effective treatment is available within the context of screening, i.e. able to favorably alter the natural history of the disease, and the effectiveness is greater if treatment is started early rather than later in the evolution of the disease
5	There are resources and an organization able to cope with the extra demand for services which screening will stimulate

The disease should be an important public health problem, in terms of its frequency and / or severity

The reasons why it is important to fulfill this criterion are: 1) The prevalence of a condition in a population has an impact in predicting the percentage of subjects correctly identified as having the condition (positive predictive value of a test) at given level of sensitivity and specificity. The fraction of individuals correctly assessed as having a condition will decrease as a function of the prevalence of the condition, a lower fraction corresponding to a lower prevalence; 2) It may be less appropriate to screen for less severe conditions.

There are several candidate conditions for screening for mental ill health in the military. The US DoD includes in its recently implemented program: PTSD, depression, alcohol misuse, significant stressor or significant impairment, and, in a face-to-face interview, questions on suicidal ideation (Office of the Assistant Secretary of Defense, 2010). The US DoD is funding, and the UK MoD is sponsoring, a randomized controlled trial (RCT) to assess the effectiveness of screening for PTSD, depression, alcohol misuse and generalized anxiety. The prevalence of PTSD, psychological distress and alcohol misuse in the UK Forces are 4 percent (7 percent in those with a combat role), 20 percent and 13 percent respectively (Fear et al. 2010). The corresponding rates in the US military vary from 5 percent to 20 percent for PTSD, 5 to 16 percent for depression/anxiety and approximately 9 percent for alcohol misuse (Hoge et al. 2004; Sundin et al. 2010). Only PTSD was measured with the same instrument in the United Kingdom and the United States so direct comparisons of rates are appropriate only for PTSD. However, regardless of the tools even a 4 percent prevalence of PTSD should be considered high (Fear et al. 2010).

Although PTSD, depression and alcohol misuse tend to co-occur and some individuals may have all three conditions or combinations of any two, the percentage with any mental health concern was approximately 19 percent in a study of those deployed to Iraq and 11 percent in those deployed to Afghanistan (Hoge et al. 2006). In another study the percentage of those with depression, anxiety or PTSD varied from 21 to 29 percent when a broad definition was used and from 9 to 17 percent when a strict definition was used (Hoge et al. 2004). In the UK military, 20 percent would have a mental health problem counting cases of psychological distress (GHQ-12 of 4 or over) or PTSD (PCL score 50 or over), rising to 29 percent if alcohol misuse is added (AUDIT score of 16 or over). Thus regardless of the tools, thresholds or method of assessment possible mental illness is a common feature in the military. This is so even without considering estimates of multiple physical symptoms reporting of which is common (Hotopf et al. 2006) and which may represent manifestations of psychological problems in a large proportion of cases (Kroenke et al. 1997; 2010).

The severity of a condition is an important consideration in the context of screening. Conditions of short duration or which are self-limiting are less suitable for screening. There is little literature regarding the severity of cases uncovered by screening programs of mental illness in the military. However, it is safe to predict that a large percentage of those with a possible mental disorder will be at the milder end of the continuum of severity. There are three avenues to explore the severity of mental disorders as assessed in surveys or screening programs: to assess the level of functional impairment at the time of assessment; to assess the percentage of those detected in population studies who subsequently make use of primary and secondary care services; or to assess the trajectory of the condition detected over time. None of these three approaches fully corresponds to severity. Functional impairment reflects symptoms at the time of assessment, but does not have predictive power of the condition (Schnurr et al. 2006). The expectation is that those who access health care services will be those with a more severe mental disorder who would be unable to cope without help. However, in a study to assess the explained variation associated with low perceived need for treatment in young adults, the authors found that only 45 percent of the explained variance was related to illness factors (van Voorhees et al. 2006). The threshold at which people decide to seek professional help may be affected by barriers that are independent of the severity of the condition such as lack of recognition of a problem, stigma, a wish to cope with problems without external help, reluctance to make use of health services, and perceived structural barriers to accessing services (Zamorski, 2011). On the other hand the persistence of symptoms in longitudinal studies only takes into account the duration of symptoms rather than their intensity. In some cases subjects with short but intense episodes of mental illness may be more in need of health care services than those with protracted but less intense symptoms.

Most studies have shown that a low percentage of those with a possible mental disorder access health services for their symptoms (Vogt, 2011). Hoge et al. (2004) found that the percentage seeking professional help in the past year among those who met criteria for depression, generalized anxiety or PTSD was between 23 and 40 percent using an all-inclusive definition of professional help, and between 13 and 27 percent seeking help from mental health professionals. From a different perspective, Hoge et al. (2006) reported that 35 percent of those deployed to Iraq and 22 percent of those deployed to Afghanistan accessed services for mental health problems within the first year post-deployment. However, only a minority (3.2 to 3.5 percent) were diagnosed with a mental health problem. The authors concluded that the mental health screening program had limited utility in predicting the level of mental health services that were needed after deployment.

In a study in the UK military, only 19 percent of those with perceived mental disorders were receiving any form of medical help (Iversen et al. 2010). Non-medical sources of help were more widely accessed, especially "any informal help". This low percentage of receipt of medical help conceals a large variation between conditions, being only 16 percent for alcohol misuse, 31 percent for depressive/anxiety disorder and reaching 54 percent for those with PTSD symptoms. Of the 15 percent with a mental health issue in Canadian Forces, 55 percent did not perceive a need for services and a further 16 percent believed that their needs were not met (Sareen et al. 2007; Zamorski 2011). The percentage of service personnel who do not seek help and who state that this is due to issues around stigma is high (Iversen et al. 2010). However, contrary to expectations, it has been shown that the percentage of military personnel seeking mental health care is unrelated to stigma (Zamorski 2011). This finding can be interpreted in two ways: either when having reached a certain threshold of mental ill health service personnel would be prepared to access services regardless of perceived stigma; alternatively patients whose problems are being managed by health professionals perceive stigma when interacting with the chain of command or peers.

Follow-up studies have shown that between 31 and 68 percent of those with possible PTSD at baseline continue to have PTSD in subsequent surveys (Dohrenwend et al. 2006; Koenen et al. 2003; Blanchard et al. 1996). This topic is revisited under the natural history of disease section.

In summary mental disorders in military personnel are common in most if not all military studies. There is more doubt about the severity of symptoms in those assessed as cases of those studies. An area that needs further research is the evaluation of the proportion of individuals with a possible mental illness who may benefit from professional management of the condition given its severity.

The natural history of the disease presents a suitable opportunity for screening

Natural history refers to the progression of a disease from its biological onset, until the stage at which the individual recovers, becomes permanently disabled or dies. The assumption regarding screening is that the sooner a case of a disease is recognized and treated the higher the chance of recovery. Early recognition is not necessarily synonymous with better prognosis for many conditions. However, there is a generalized view which supports early recognition for mental disorders such as alcohol misuse, PTSD and depression. This conceptualization of screening is clear when we refer to breast cancer or another cancer, as the initial stages of the condition are usually asymptomatic and the condition is expected to deteriorate and its severity increase. But such a course it is not necessarily a feature of common psychiatric disorders. Some individuals indeed follow a severe and protracted course, but there are also those who spontaneously recover and those who are initially well but have a delayed response (Bonanno and Mancini, 2010; Muthen and Muthen, 2000; Jackson and Sher 2006). There are also those who tend to have relapses over time followed by long periods of symptomatic remission (Simon, 2000). Given this lack of homogeneity it is important to have a conceptual paradigm which allows the evaluation of the impact of screening for mental illness from a population perspective.

Most of those with a high PCL score following the traumatic experience of a road traffic accident recovered within one year (Blanchard et al. 1997). A study of Vietnam veterans showed that approximately half of the 22.5 percent with lifetime PTSD had current PTSD 11 years after the end of the war (Dohrenwend et al. 2006). Of those with current PTSD less than half had an impairment at least of moderate difficulty and in those with PTSD in the past less than 10 percent had impairment. This would indicate that approximately a quarter of those with PTSD ever have a severe condition in terms of duration and level of impairment. Studies in the military have shown that a large proportion of subjects with PTSD recover in the first 2 to 3 years (Koenen et al. 2003; Rona et al. 2012). The current evidence would suggest that a large percentage of those with PTSD may have decreased levels of symptoms; and only a fraction of those with persistent PTSD may continue to be impaired at a meaningful level.

We can say much the same about both depression and alcohol. Longitudinal studies on the trajectory of major depression have shown that approximately 45 percent remit over a period of two years and approximately 40 percent have sub-threshold depression following their index episode in primary care (Simon, 2000). Those who do not remit by the third month, but do later, have a greater chance of a relapse. Within the constraints of a study carried out in primary care, management of the condition and adherence to treatment could influence the trajectory of the condition. The large proportion of patients who continue to experience episodes of depression over a long time and the large proportion of relapses are important when considering depression as a candidate condition for screening. Muthen and Muthen (2000) found that four classes best represented heavy drinking in young adults in a US National sample: a large normative class which included 73 percent of the total group characterized by heavy drinking increasing in the early years, but later declining; another two groups comprising 19 percent of the total of early very heavy drinking slowly decreasing but remaining high; and a fourth group representing increasing heavy drinking with age. Trajectories of depression and alcohol misuse can be influenced by factors such as gender, family history, and in the case of alcoholism peer culture. We are unaware of long-term studies of depression or alcoholism in military personnel.

So now we have to consider whether we can identify those who will follow a protracted course, and whether it is worth treating those who follow a short course of the condition. The variability of trajectories of the three conditions frequently considered for screening indicates that a large percentage of those with symptoms will be able to cope in the long term. However, the multi-factorial reasons for such diversity suggest that it is difficult to separate those who will follow a more benign course and those who will follow a protracted and severe course. For example in a recent analysis we assessed our ability to predict a persistent course from all cases of PTSD at baseline. We found that the risk factors with the greatest association of protracted course of PTSD such as age, PTSD checklist score (PCL score), presence of other comorbidities, feeling unsupported and self-reported fair or poor general health were only modest predictors of persistent PTSD (Rona et al. 2012). The complexity in the trajectories of PTSD, depression and alcohol misuse underscore the importance of large studies to assess the effectiveness of population screening. Even if the initial prevalence of common mental disorders is high, the large proportion of cases which may improve without help indicates that the statistical power of any study is of great importance.

Suitability of the screening tests available

The central issue of any screening program is that the tests to assess the condition should be valid, i.e. that the tests measure what they purport to measure. It means that we need gold standards for whatever is the condition of interest. For mental disorders, Mini International Neuropsychiatric Interview (MINI) and Clinician-administered PTSD Scale (CAPS) will represent gold standards (Sheehan et al. 1998; Weathers et al. 2001). The tests which are used in screening studies are also derived from the *Diagnostic and Statistical Manual of Mental Disorders-III-Revised* (DSM-III-R). Thus the gold standard tests and the screening tools originated from the same source and it would therefore be expected that they would be correlated.

There is also another pragmatic approach to the validation of a test. The approach is to use medical practitioners as gold standard and compare the decision they make against the screening test results. So rather than asking the question whether the screening tests are appropriate, the issue is whether medical practitioners reach the same diagnosis as the screening test (Rona et al. 2004).

The validity of a test is usually characterized by its sensitivity and specificity, positive and negative predictive value and the positive and negative likelihood ratio (Table 6.2). Sensitivity and specificity provide an estimate of the ability of the test to correctly identify cases of the condition, measures of the performance of a binary classification test. The positive and negative predictive value of the test represent the likelihood that a person with a positive test has the condition tested or the likelihood that a person with a negative result will not have the condition tested. These estimates are influenced by the prevalence of the condition. The lower the prevalence of the condition, the lower the probability that a positive test will represent a true case of the disease given the same sensitivity and specificity.

The likelihood ratio is another helpful way of assessing the value of the test. It tells us the probability of somebody with a positive test having the condition of interest and the probability of somebody with a negative test result not to having the condition. A sobering point is that although tests may have reasonably high levels of sensitivity and specificity, their corresponding predictive values and likelihood ratios may be just fair.

Table 6.2 Assessing the validity of a test

Test result	Diagnosis of a Disorder using a Gold Standard Measure	
	Yes	No
Positive	*a*	*b*
Negative	*c*	*d*

Sensitivity = $a/(a + c)$
Specificity = $b/(b + d)$
Positive predictive value = $a/(a + b)$
Negative predictive value = $d/(c + d)$
Positive likelihood ratio = Sensitivity/ $(1 - \text{Specificity})$
Negative likelihood ratio = $(1 - \text{Sensitivity})/$ Specificity

Another test of validity frequently used is the receiver operating characteristics (ROC) which plots false positives (1 – specificity) against true positives (sensitivity) and the area under the curve (AUC) which serves as a summary estimate of the plot.

Bliese et al. (2008) assessed the value of the Primary Care Posttraumatic Stress Disorder Screen (PC-PTSD) and the PCL compared with the MINI. For the PC-PTSD, a four-item test, the most reasonable performance was at cut-off of 2 or 3 (range of test 0 to 4) with sensitivity of 85 percent and 76 percent and specificity of 71 percent and 76 percent respectively. The positive predictive value with scores 2 and 3 were 25 percent and 46 percent, and the AUC was 87 percent, all of which reflects a good performance. The authors concluded that the PC-PTSD was as valid as the PCL, a 17-item test, although we lack the 95 percent confidence interval for any of their estimates.

Armed with Bliese's data (2008), the US military and the Veterans Health Administration used the PC-PTSD in their screening programs, but in this situation the percentage of positive cases was much higher than perhaps anticipated. For example, Seal et al. (2008) and Gahm and Lucenko (2007) found that more than 60 percent were identified as possible PTSD cases. This would indicate that the threshold when using the PC-PTSD was set too low.

The probability of true PTSD increases with the PCL score. At a PCL score of 50 the probability of PTSD is around 60 percent and at 40 is around 40 percent (Bliese et al. 2008). Terhakopian et al. (2008) reported weighted average sensitivity and specificity of 62 percent (95% CI 53–71%) and 90 percent (95% CI 87–94%) respectively for cut-off scores of 44 to 45 and 54 percent (95% CI 43–64%) and 93 percent (95% CI 90–96%) for cut-off scores from 48 to 50. If scores from 48 to 50 are used, an approximate estimate of positive likelihood ratio would be around 8 and the negative likelihood ratio would be 0.5. These estimates would indicate that the PCL is a satisfactory tool for screening. The PCL is the instrument which is being used in the newly introduced US screening program as a second-stage assessment and is the instrument used in an RCT to assess the value of screening in the UK military.

The situation is not dissimilar for depression. A systematic review showed that the PHQ-9 has sensitivity which varies from 77 to 88 percent and specificity between 88 and 92 percent (Kroenke et al. 2010). This level of performance would provide a positive likelihood ratio of 8, similar to the PCL for PTSD, and a negative likelihood ratio of 0.2, better than the PCL for PTSD. The validity of shorter versions of the PHQ-9 has also been assessed indicating slightly lower levels of validity (Bliese et al. 2004). The validity of instruments used to assess alcohol misuse has been shown to be high (Bohn et al. 1995; Fiellin et al. 2000; Saunders et al. 1993), particularly for the AUDIT and the CAGE.[2] A systematic review of the AUDIT found a sensitivity of the instrument of 90 percent and a specificity of 80 percent (Saunders et al. 1993).

It can be concluded that there are satisfactory instruments for assessing PTSD, depression and alcohol misuse. We have focused on three instruments, the PCL, PHQ-9 and the AUDIT, because the authors are more familiar with these instruments and they have been used in many military studies, but no doubt there are others.

One argument that sometimes surfaces whenever psychiatric questionnaires are used, whether for screening or research, is that they may trigger unpleasant levels of anxiety. However, there is ample evidence to refute this (Boscarino et al. 2004; French et al. 2009; Iversen et al. 2010).

Effectiveness and efficacy of screening for mental disorders in the military

It is a matter of some regret that there are few studies purposefully designed to assess the effectiveness of screening programs of mental illness in the military, and particularly so given the interest and indeed use of such programs in several contemporary militaries. We are aware of only one study which assessed the effectiveness of screening for mental illness, but even then not using an RCT design, which all the authorities agree must be the best design (Warner et al. 2011). The reality is that screening programs have often been introduced more as a political response to the perceived high prevalence of post-deployment mental disorders (Office of the Chairman, 1998) – the "something must be done" argument. The overwhelming consideration has been that untreated mental illness will be associated with a poorer level of functioning (Gahm and Lucenko 2007; Schonfeld et al. 1997).

The assumption that has permeated decision making is that health services are effective in dealing with common mental disorders such as depression and anxiety, and PTSD. Of course there is no doubt that certain treatments are indeed effective for the treatment of mental health disorders including PTSD in clinical settings (Brady et al. 2000; National Institute for Clinical Excellence, 2005; Connor et al. 1999; Ehlers et al. 2003; Roberts et al. 2010). But one must be careful about extrapolating this to the different context of screening. It is appropriate to distinguish between efficacy and effectiveness of a treatment in the context of screening. Efficacy is the degree to which an intervention benefits a group with a disorder in an ideal setting; effectiveness is the degree to which an intervention achieves in practice the intended benefits expected from efficacy trials. The distinction is not trivial because the organization of health services and resources available may differ between allied forces and the expected benefits from an intervention may also differ.

A systematic review and meta-analysis of early psychological interventions to treat acute traumatic stress symptoms and PTSD concluded that cognitive behavioral interventions (CBT) were more efficacious than a waiting list or supportive counseling at 6 months follow-up (Roberts et al. 2010). However, the overall result was based on considerable heterogeneity in the efficacy of the interventions between studies. This is important because previous research has found an association between poorer methodologies and more favorable results (Moher et al. 1998). In addition the report could not show efficacy of CBT beyond 6 months follow-up, because of dwindling numbers of studies. We need also to consider that these studies were based only in civilian populations.

Systematic reviews and meta-analysis have shown that collaborative care is effective in the management of depression (Gilbody et al. 2006). Brief counseling for the management of alcoholism in primary care is effective, even though there remains heterogeneity between studies (Babor et al. 2001; Kaner et al. 2009). However, it does not follow that screened populations would experience similar benefits. Those identified using screening techniques differ from patients seen in routine clinical care in terms of severity, interest in accessing health services and commitment to treatment. Clinical trials tend to use highly codified treatments with qualified therapists, monitored for quality control and fidelity to the treatment model. Within military screening settings such a degree of control is unlikely to be feasible and therapist effects may have strong influence on the results. In reality many of the RCT studies we have referenced measure efficacy rather than effectiveness. It cannot be assumed that the findings of existing meta-analyses and clinical trials can be extended to a military screening program.

In a recent study Warner et al. (2011) showed that pre-deployment mental health screening was associated with reduction in occupationally impairing mental health problems, medical evacuations from Iraq for mental health reasons, and suicidal ideation. This study was not an RCT and does not correspond in its conception to screening because it used diagnosed psychiatric disorder of those who were receiving treatment and whose illness severity was assessed. This is very different to screening conceived as tests to ascertain a probable disorder in previously unknown subjects. What Warner et al. (2011) describe ought to be part of the preparation for deployment in any well-organized armed force, although there is evidence that this is not always the case (Hodgetts and Greasley, 2003). The results from the study were unexpected in terms of the size of its beneficial effects, but the relevance of the study is difficult to gauge because a cluster design based on brigades as unit of selection was used, the period of assessment corresponded to the first 6 months of a 15-month deployment, the outcomes were not based on mental disorders but proxies (Hsiao-Rei Hicks, 2011) and there was no adjustment for possible confounders in the analysis.

Resources and an organization of services able to cope with the extra demand which a screening program will stimulate

Effectiveness of an intervention in its true sense requires appropriate organization of health systems and welfare services to ensure that efficacious treatments are properly resourced and managed. The management of depression when there is in place a recognized collaborative care approach is effective (Bower et al. 2006). Collaborative care is a complex intervention and it is difficult to differentiate effective from ineffective components. It is unclear whether the relevant component is a case manager in the system, a mechanism to increase liaison between primary care and mental health departments or the introduction of sharing information on the progress of a case (MacMillan et al. 2005). The majority of those who have used the evidence that collaborative care is effective have extrapolated from that to assume that screening for depression would also be effective if linked to collaborative care (US Preventive Services Task Forces 2009). Gilbody and Beck (2010) formally addressed this issue in a meta-analysis showing that there was no significant difference between collaborative care alongside screening and collaborative care without screening. The authors recognized that their analysis is not ideal because of the diversity of approaches in collaborative care and the lack of adjustment for possible confounders between studies. The appropriate design to address this issue would be an RCT to compare a screening group with collaborative care as part of the intervention with a non-screened control group. We are unaware of such a study.

There is a balance to strike in the armed forces between a screening program which is limited to only serious cases and one which aims to "treat" anyone slightly above the advised threshold. Widespread alcohol misuse, at the lower end of the scale of alcohol misuse in the armed forces, would suggest that screening may not be acceptable to a large percentage of personnel staff who are aware of their life style but may not be inclined to seek medical help and change their drinking behavior. It would be more advisable in a setting in which hazardous drinking is common to introduce programs of primary prevention by creating an environment which discourages problem drinking, encouraging commanders to use disciplinary measures when appropriate and introducing measures to control availability and price of alcohol. We found that those with an AUDIT score of 20 or more, who endorse dependence or alcohol-related harm are more likely to perceive functional impairment (Rona et al. 2010). Approximately 11 percent of the UK armed forces have a serious alcohol problem based on these criteria and this group may be more amenable to accept help within a screening program.

A screening program needs as a minimal requirement to be effective that the number of professionals with appropriate expertise is sufficient, professionals are fully informed and aware of the program, collaborative arrangements and coordination systems between professionals are in place and, though difficult to assess, the health service staff are well disposed towards such a program. The organization of the service should be audited in order to detect any deficiencies. However, even if the organization of welfare and health care systems is optimal the results will not be beneficial if service personnel do not wish to seek and make use of the mental health services. Screening is a complex intervention and cannot be conceived as cost neutral.

Conclusions

Screening for mental disorders cannot be considered good or bad per se; context matters. There is no doubting the importance of the problem for contemporary militaries, particularly in respect of those with physical injuries and/or a combat role. The tools to assess mental illness are suitable to separate those who probably have a disorder from those who probably do not. There are many studies showing efficacy of treatments to manage PTSD, depression, anxiety and alcohol misuse. Screening appears an attractive proposition to politicians and the public. However, the factors in favor of screening for mental illness should be weighed against the uncertainties related to screening. These can be summarized as: 1) The natural history of mental health disorders are far from homogenous in their pattern of progression. Resources may be used to detect a large percentage of disorders that may be of short duration and of mild severity. In addition we do not know how to differentiate those who will follow a long protracted course from the rest; 2) The actual screening itself may be acceptable, but we know that a large percentage of those who may have a mental disorder do not wish to make use of health services either because of stigma or a determination to solve the problem without outside intervention; 3) Studies on the effectiveness of screening for mental disorders are not available.

The lack of randomized trial evidence in support of a screening program is critical. If a study based on an RCT were to show that screening is effective, the trajectories of the disorders screened for and issues related to attitudes towards treatment would no longer be relevant for decision making on the merits of screening. On the other hand if studies were to demonstrate a lack of effectiveness of screening further efforts would be necessary to understand the natural history of mental disorders and the reasons service personnel are reluctant to access health services.

Notes

1   Roberto Rona and Simon Wessely work at King's College London, King's Centre for Military Research, Weston Education Centre, London SE5 9RJ.
2   CAGE is an acronym which stands for Cut down (focus of the first question); Annoyed (focus of the second question); Guilty (focus of the third question); Eye opener (focus of the fourth question).

References

Adler AB, Bliese PD, McGurk D, Hoge CW, Castro CA. (2009a) "Battlemind debriefing and battlemind training as early interventions with soldiers returning from Iraq: Randomization by platoon", *Journal Consulting and Clinical Psychology*, 77: 928–40.

Adler AB, Castro CA, McGurk D. (2009b) "Time-driven battlemind psychological debriefing: a group-level early intervention in combat", *Military Medicine*, 172:21–8.

Appel JW, Beebe GW, Hilger DW. (1946) "Comparative incidence of neuropsychiatric casualties in World War I and World War II", *American Journal of Psychiatry*, 103: 196–9.

Babor TF, Higgins-Biddle JC, Saunders JB, Monteiro MG. "AUDIT: The alcohol use disorders identification test. Guidelines for use in primary care", 2nd edn, World Health Organization. Department of Mental Health and Substance Dependence. WHO/MSD/MS/01.6a. 2001.

Blanchard EB, Hickling EJ, Forneris CA, Taylor AE, Buckley TC, Loos WR, Jaccard J (1997) "Prediction of remission of acute stress disorder in motor vehicle accident victims", *Journal of Traumatic Stress*, 10: 215–34.

Bliese P, Wright K, Adler A, Thomas J. (2004) "Research Report 2004–02. Validation of the 90 to 120 day post-deployment psychological short screen", USAREUR Short screen Development Report 2004.

Bliese PD, Wright KM, Adler AB, Thomas JL, Hoge CW. (2007) "Timing of post-combat mental health assessment", *Psychological Services*, 4: 141–8.

Bliese PD, Wright KM, Adler AB, Cabrera O, Castro CA, Hoge CW. (2008) "Validating the primary care posttraumatic stress disorder screen and posttraumatic stress disorder checklist with soldiers returning from combat", *Journal of Consulting and Clinical Psychology*, 76: 272–81.

Bohn MJ, Babor TF, Frankzler HR. (1995) "The Alcohol Use Disorders Identification Test (AUDIT): Validation of a screening instrument for use in medical settings", *Journal of Studies on Alcohol*, 56: 423–32.

Bonanno GA, Mancini AD. (2010) "Beyond resilience and PTSD: mapping the heterogeneity of responses to potential trauma", *Psychological Trauma: Theory, Research, Practice, and Policy*, doi: 10.1037/a0017829.

Boscarino JA, Figley CR, Adams RE, Galea S, Resnick H, Fleischman AR, Bucuvalas M, Gold J. (2004) "Adverse reactions associated with studying persons recently exposed to mass urban disaster", *Journal of Nervous and Mental Disease*, 192: 515–24.

Bower P, Gilbody S, Richards D, Fletcher J, Sutton A. (2006) "Collaborative care for depression in primary care. Making sense of a complex intervention: systematic review and meta-regression", *British Journal of Psychiatry*, 189: 484–93.

Brady K, Pearlstein T, Asnis GM, Baker D, Rothbaum B, Sikes CR, Farfel GM. (2000) "Efficacy and safety of sertraline treatment of posttraumatic stress disorder: a randomized controlled trial", *JAMA*, 283: 1837–44.

Connor KM, Sutherland SM, Tuplaer LA, Malik ML, Davidson JR. (1999) "Fluoxetine in post-traumatic stress disorder: randomised, double-blind study", *British Journal of Psychiatry*, 175: 17–22.

Dohrenwend BP, Turner JB, Turse NA, Adams BG, Koenen KC, Marshall R (2006) "The psychological risks of Vietnam for US veterans: a revisit with new data and methods", *Science*, 313: 979–82.

Egan JR, Jackson L, Eanes RH (1951) "A study of meuropsychiatric rejectees", *JAMA*, 145:466–9.

Ehlers A, Clark D, Hackmann A, McManus F, Fennell M, Herbert C, Mayou RA. (2003) "Randomized controlled trial of cognitive therapy, self-help booklet, and repeated assessments as early interventions of posttraumatic stress disorder", *Archives of General Psychiatry*, 60: 1024–32.

Fear NT, Jones M, Murphy D, Hull L, Iversen A, Coker B, Machell L, Sundin J, Woodhead C, Jones N, Greenberg N, Landau S, Dandeker C, Rona RJ, Hotopf M, Wessely S. (2010) "What are the consequences of deployment to Iraq and Afghanistan on the mental health of the UK armed forces? A cohort study", *Lancet*, 375: 1783–97.

Fiellin DA, Reid C, O'Connor PG. (2000) "Screening for alcohol problems in primary care", *Archives of Internal Medicine*, 160: 1997–89.

French DP, Eborall H, Griffin S, Kinmonth AL, Prevost AT, Sutton S. (2009) "Completing a postal health questionnaire did not affect anxiety or related measures: randomized controlled trial", *Journal of Clinical Epidemiology*, 62: 74–80.

Gahm GA, Lucenko BA. (2007) "Screening soldiers in outpatient care for mental health concerns", *Military Medicine*, 173: 17–24.

Gilbody S, Beck D. (2010) " Implementing screening as part of enhanced care: screening alone is not enough" in Mitchell AJ and Coyne JC (eds) *Screening for depression in clinical practice. An evidence-based guide*, New York: Oxford University.

Gilbody S, Bower P, Fletcher J, Richards D, Sutton AJ. (2006) "Collaborative care for depression. A cumulative meta-analysis and review of longer-term outcomes", *Archives of Internal Medicine*, 2314–21.

Greenberg N, Langston V, Everitt B, Iversen A, Fear NT, Jones N, Wessely S. (2010) "A cluster randomized controlled trial to determine the efficacy of Trauma Risk Management (TRiM) in a military population", *Journal of Trauma Stress*, 23: 430–6.

Hodgetts TJ, Greasley LA. (2003) "Impact of deployment of personnel with chronic conditions to forward areas", *Journal of the Royal Army Med Corps*, 149: 277–83.

Hoge CW, Castro CA, Messer SC, Gurk D, Cotting DI, Koffman RL. (2004) "Combat duty in Iraq and Afghanistan, mental health problems, and barriers to car", *New England Journal of Medicine*, 351: 13–22.

Hoge CW, Auchterlonie JL, Milliken CS. (2006) "Mental health problems, use of mental health services, and attrition from military service after returning from deployment to Iraq or Afghanistan", *JAMA*, 295:1023–32.

Hotopf M, Hull L, Fear NT, Browne T, Horn O, Iversen A, Jones M, Bland D, Earnshaw M, Greenberg N, Hacker Hughes J, Tate AR, Dandeker C, Rona R, Wessely S. (2006) "The health of UK military personnel who deployed to the 2003 Iraq war: a cohort study", *Lancet*, 367:1731–41.

Hsiao-Rei Hicks M. (2011) "Mental health screening and coordination of care for soldiers deployed to Iraq and Afghanistan", *American Journal of Psychiatry*,168: 341–3.

Iversen AC, van Staden L, Browne T, Greenberg N, Hotopf M, Rona RJ, Wessely S, Thornicroft G, Fear NT. (2010) "Help seeking and receipt of treatment in United Kingdom Service Personnel", *British Journal of Psychiatry*, 197: 149–55.

Iversen AC, van Staden L, Hughes JH, Greenberg N, Hotopf M, Rona RJ, Thornicroft G, Wessely S, Fear NT. (2011) "The stigma of mental health problems and other barriers to care in the UK Armed Forces", *BMC Health Services Research*, 11:31.

Jackson KM, Sher KJ. (2006) "Comparison of longitudinal phenotypes based on number and timing of assessment: a systematic comparison of trajectory approaches II", *Psychology of Addictive Behaviors*, 20: 373–84.

Jacobson IG, Ryan MAK, Hooper TI, Smith TC, Amoroso PJ, Boyko EJ, Gackstetter GD, Wells TS. (2008) "Alcohol use and alcohol-related problems before and after military combat deployment", *JAMA*, 300: 663–75.

Jones E, Hyams KC, Wessely S. (2003) "Screening for vulnerability to psychological disorders in the military: an historical survey', *Journal of Medical Screening*, 10: 40–6.

Kaner EF, Dickinson HO, Beyer FR, Campbell F, Schlesinger C, Heather N, Saunders JB, Bernard B, Pienaar ED. (2009) *Effectiveness of brief interventions in primary care populations (Review)*, 2nd issue, The Cochrane Collaboration, Wiley.

Koenen KC, Stellman JM, Stellman SD, Sommer JF (2003) "Risk factors for course of posttraumatic stress disorder among Vietnam: a 14-year follow-up of American Legionnaire". *J Consulting Clin Psychol*, 71:980–6.

Koepsell TD, Weiss NS. (2003) *Epidemiological methods. Studying the occurrence of illness*, Oxford: University Press.

Kroenke K, Jackson JL, Chamberlin J. (1997) "Depressive and anxiety disorders in patients presenting with physical complaints: clinical predictors and outcome", *American Journal of Medicine*, 103: 339–47.

Kroenke K, Spitzer RL, Williams JB, Lowe B. (2010) "The Patient Health Questionnaire somatic, anxiety, and depressive symptom scales: a systematic review", *General Hospital Psychiatry*, 32: 245–59.

MacMillan HL, Pattersson CJS, Wathen CN, and the Canadian Task Force on Preventive Care (2005) "Screening for depression in primary care: recommendation statement from the Canadian Task Force on Preventive Health Care", *CMAJ*, 172: 33–5.

Milliken CS, Auchterlonie JL, Hoge CW. (2007) "Longitudinal assessment of mental health problems among active and reserve component soldiers returning from the Iraq War", *JAMA*, 298: 2141–8.

Moher D, Pham D, Jones A, Cook DJ, Jadad AR, Moher M, Tugwell P, Klassen TP. (1998) "Does quality of reports of randomized trials affect estimates of intervention efficacy in meta-analysis?", *Lancet*, 352: 609–13.

Morrison AS. (1992) *Screening in Chronic Disease*. 2nd edn. New York: Oxford University Press.

Muthen B, Muthen LK. (2000) "Integrating person-centered and variable-centered analyses: growth mixture modelling with latent trajectory classes", *Alcoholism: Clinical Experimental Research*, 24: 882–91.

National Institute for Clinical Excellence (2005) *Post-traumatic stress disorder (PTSD): The management of PTSD in adults and children in primary and secondary care*.

Nevin RL. (2009) "Low validity of self-report in identifying recent mental health diagnosis among US service members completing Pre-Deployment Health Assessment (PreDHA) and deployed to Afghanistan, 2007: a retrospective cohort study", *BMC Public Health*, 9: 376.

Office of the Assistant Secretary of Defense. Department of Defense (July 2010) "Mental health assessment for members of the Armed Forces deployed in connection with contingency operations", Available HTTP: <http://www.health.mil/libraries/HA_Policies_and_Guidelines/10-005.pdf> (accessed September 2011).

Office of the Chairman. The Joint Chiefs of Staff. Dennis C Blair (4 December 1998) "Deployment Health Surveillance and Readiness", Available HTTP: <http://afhsc.mil/viewDocument?file=JCS_PDFs/MCM-251-98 04 DEC 1998.pdf> (accessed 24 November 2011).

Roberts NP, Kitchiner NJ, Kenardy J, Bisson JI. (2010) "Early psychological interventions to treat acute traumatic stress symptoms (Review)", 3rd issue, *Cochrane Database of Systematic Reviews*, Art No.: CD007944. DOI: 10.1002/14651858.CD007944.pub2.

Rona RJ, Hooper R, Jones M, French C, Wessely S.(2004) "Screening for physical and psychological illness in the British Armed Forces: III: The value of a questionnaire to assist a Medical Officer to decide who needs help", *Journal of Medical Screening*, 11:158–61.

Rona RJ, Hyams KC, Wessely S. (2005) "Screening for psychological illness in military personnel", *JAMA*, 293: 1257–60.

Rona RJ, Jones M, Fear NT, Hull L, Hotopf M, Wessely S. (2010) "Alcohol misuse and functional impairment in the UK Armed Forces: a population based study", *Drug Alcohol Dependence*, 108: 37–42.

Rona RJ, Jones M, Sundin J, Goodwin L, Hull L, Wessely S, Fear NT. (2012) "Predicting persistent posttraumatic stress disorder (PTSD) in UK military personnel who served in Iraq: A longitudinal study", *J Psychiatr Res.*, 46: 1191–8.

Sareen J, Cox BJ, Afifi TO, Stein MB, Belik S-L, Meadows G, Asmundson GJG (2007) "Combat and peacekeeping operations in relation to prevalence of mental disorders and perceived need for mental health care", *Archives of General Psychiatry*, 64: 843–52.

Saunders JB, Aasland OG, Babor TF, de la Fuente JR, Grant M. (1993) "Development of Alcohol Use Disorders Identification Test (Audit): WHO collaborative project on early detection of persons with harmful alcohol consumption-II", *Addiction*, 88:791–804.

Schnurr PP, Hayes AF, Lunney CA, McFall M, Uddo M. (2006) "Longitudinal analysis of the relationship between symptoms and quality of life in veterans treated for posttraumatic disorder", *Journal of Consulting Clinical Psychology*, 74: 703–13.

Schonfeld WH, Verboncoeur CJ, Fifer SK, Lipschutz RC, Lubeck DP, Buesching DP (1997) "The functioning and well-being of patients with unrecognized anxiety disorders and major depressive disorder", *Journal of Affective Disorders*, 43: 105–19.

Seal KH, Berthenthal D, Maguen S, Gima K, Chu A, Marmar C. (2008) "Getting beyond 'Don't ask; don't tell': An evaluation of US Veterans Administration Postdeployment mental health screening of veterans returning from Iraq and Afghanistan", *American Journal of Public Health*, 98: 714–20.

Sheehan DV, Lecrubier Y, Sheehan KH et al. (1998) "The Mini-International Neuropsychiatric Interview (M.I.N.I.): the development and validation of a structured diagnostic psychiatric interview for DMS-IV and ICD-10", *Journal of Clinical Psychiatry*, 59: 22–33.

Shephard B. (2002) *A war of nerves. Soldiers and psychiatrists 1914–1994*, London: Pimlico.

Simon GE. (2000) "Long-term prognosis of depression in primary care", *Bulletin of the World Health Organization*, 78: 439–45.

Sundin J, Fear NT, Iversen A, Rona RJ, Wessely S. (2010) "PTSD after deployment to Iraq: conflicting rates, conflicting claims", *Psychology of Medicine*, 40:367–82.

Terhakopian A, Sinaii N, Engle CC, Schnurr PP, Hoge CW. (2008) "Estimating population prevalence of posttraumatic stress disorder: an example using the PTSD checklist", *Journal of Traumatic Stress*, 21: 290–300.

UK National Screening Committee Criteria for appraising the viability, effectiveness and appropriateness of a screening programme. 2010. Available HTTP: <http://www.nsc.nhs.uk/pdfs/criteria.pdf>.

US Preventive Services Task Forces (2009) "Clinical guidelines: Screening for depression in adults: US Preventive Services Task Force recommendation statement", *Annals of Internal Medicine*; 151: 784–92.

US Preventive Services Task Forces Guide to clinical preventive services: Reports of the US Preventive Service Task Force, 1996, 2nd edn, Baltimore: Williams and Wilkins.

Van Voorhees BW, Fogel J, Houston TK, Cooper LA, Wang N-Y, Ford DE. (2006) "Attitudes and illness factors associated with low perceived need for depression treatment among young adults", *Social Psychiatry and Psychiatric Epidemiology*, 41: 746–54.

Vogt D. (2011) "Mental health – related beliefs as a barrier to service use for military personnel and veterans: a review", *Psychiatric Services*, 62: 135–42.

Warner CH, Appenzaller GN, Parker JR, Warner CM, Hoge CW. (2011) "Effectiveness of mental health screening and coordination of in-theatre care prior to deployment to Iraq: a cohort study", *American Journal of Psychiatry*, 168: 378–85.

Weathers FW, Keane TM, Davidson JR. (2001) "Clinician-administered PTSD scale: a review of the first ten years of research", *Depression and Anxiety*, 13: 132–56.

Wilson JMG, Jungner G. (1968) *Principles and practice of screening disease for disease*. Geneva, Switzerland: World Health Organization.

Wright KM, Adler AB, Pliese PD, Eckford RD. (2008) "Structure clinical interview guide for postdeployment psychological screening programs", *Military Medicine*, 173: 411–21.

Zamorski MA. (2011) "Towards a broader conceptualization of need, stigma, and barriers to mental health care in military organizations: Recent research findings from the Canadian Forces", keynote address presented at Mental Health and Wellbeing across the military spectrum NATO/OTAN RTO-MP-HFM-205 in Bergen, April 2011.

7 Ongoing efforts to address the public health problem of military suicide within the United States Department of Defense[1]

Robert Ireland, Marjan Ghahramanlou Holloway, and David G. Brown

In August 2010, the Defense Health Board's Congressionally-mandated *Task Force on the Prevention of Suicide by Members of the Armed Forces* (hereafter referred to as the Task Force) completed its year-long independent review of suicide prevention programs in the Department of Defense (DoD, 2010). Overall, the Task Force "commend[ed] the Armed Forces for the suicide prevention initiatives it has undertaken" and emphasized that "no other employer … has focused as much attention and resources on suicide prevention." Recommendations provided by the Task Force related to four strategic initiatives: (1) Organization and Leadership; (2) Wellness Enhancement and Training; (3) Access to, and Delivery of, Quality Care; and (4) Surveillance, Investigations, and Research. This chapter presents a historical review of DoD suicide prevention efforts targeted at the Armed Forces over the past decade. Emphasis is placed on Service specific as well as interagency collaborations in the areas of surveillance, programmatic initiatives, and research. While coverage of each of the four strategic initiatives put forth by the Task Force is beyond the scope of this chapter, the reader is provided with a foundation of knowledge for better understanding them.

The chapter is organized into several sections. The first section familiarizes the reader with the recent evolution of collaborative efforts among Departments to develop a standardized DoD suicide surveillance and nomenclature methodology. The second section provides examples of Federal interagency suicide prevention and other mental health collaborations. The third section outlines a number of current programmatic research efforts focused on military suicide prevention. A final section of the chapter highlights current DoD and service level suicide prevention initiatives.

Efforts to enhance suicide surveillance and nomenclature methodology within the Department of Defense

Standardized and systematic surveillance serves as a critical foundation for suicide prevention. While surveillance has always been a component of DoD suicide prevention efforts, estimations of suicide rates and determination of associated risk factors were not always standardized across service branches, leaving little that could be said with great accuracy about suicides DoD-wide. More specifically, while each Department collected similar data, variation in precisely what was collected made merging such rich data a challenge. In recent years, collaborative efforts across all service branches have led to the standardization of suicide rates and risk factors (2006 and 2008, respectively) and subsequently resulted in the first meaningful substantive sets of DoD-level data available for analyses. While having service-specific suicide information is important in and of itself, the creation of a larger pooled population database provides the statistical power needed for more reliable analyses.

Unique considerations for DoD suicide surveillance

Suicide is a rare event whose rate is usually expressed as the number of suicides per 100,000 persons per year. As the US military services are small compared with state and national populations, a given service may have up to 40 percent annual variation in suicide rates due to a difference of only a few suicides (Carr et al. 2004). Thus across DoD, interdepartmental size differences dramatically affect military suicide rate variation. For example, if all other factors are equal, the US Marine Corps (USMC) suicide rate for ~200,000 members is expected to vary considerably more than the US Army (USA) rate (~550,000 members), as only a few suicides dramatically affect the USMC annual rate. Therefore, small fluctuations in annual suicide rates, regardless of direction, must be interpreted with great caution by military leaders lest they reactively adjust their programs based only upon (expected) random statistical variations. In fact, suicide trends over several years, instead of annual rates, best inform prevention programs and policies.

DoD suicide rates are also significantly affected by gender composition in the military, as men in the US die by suicide at a higher rate than women (National Center for Injury Prevention and Control, 2011). Services with a higher percentage of males, as the USMC at 94 percent, are expected to have a higher rate of suicide than departments with a lower percentage of males, as the US Air Force (USAF) (80 percent) (DoD, 2010). Suicide rates are further affected by the percentage of persons in certain high risk groups (e.g., 17–24-year-old military males). Thus, Departments with a greater number of members in this group (e.g., USMC) are expected to have a higher suicide rate than those with a lower number of members in the same group. The same logic applies to the racial breakdown of members across Services due to the lower rates of suicide in Black and Hispanic populations. Moreover, consider the fact that enlisted rates of suicide are estimated to be twice the rate of officer suicides. Given this information, the suicide rates for the USMC (with the highest percentage of enlisted) and the USAF (with the lowest percentage of enlisted), for instance, need to be compared carefully.

Finally, a particularly vexing Department-specific challenge is that of shipboard losses in the US Navy (USN). For millennia, sailors have fallen from ships into the sea unintentionally or intentionally, often without witnesses (especially at night), with or without recovery of their bodies. In some of these cases, evidence of intention to die by suicide is insufficient, resulting in an inability to determine suicide as the cause of death. Thus, a fair number of these events may be suicides (versus accidents), but may not be counted as such. Such lack of evidence could be a contributing factor to USN suicide rates generally being lower than rates observed for other Services.

Suicide determinations within the DoD

Both personnel and medical systems within the DoD collect suicide data. Sources of data include: (1) death certificates (often completed prior to official cause of death determinations in order to meet the needs of family member survivors and tracked by the Defense Casualty Information Processing System); (2) law enforcement's Defense Incident Based Reporting System; (3) the DoD Mortality Surveillance Division of the Office of the Armed Forces Medical Examiner (AFME) (which includes a review of civilian medical records, coroner/medical examiner reports, and labs); and (4) the military Departments' Suicide Prevention Program Managers (SPPMs) who coordinate with these and other military and civilian entities.

In cases where cause of death is especially challenging to determine, a psychological autopsy may be performed to better delineate psychological factors at the time of death and circumstances suggesting possible intent to die by self-directed violence. While various agencies' roles determine the extent of their validation processes, for forensic purposes, the final cause of death determination is made by the AFME based upon policies and practices in place at the time of the investigation. This is not to suggest that forensic suicide determinations should be the sole source of suicide data for prevention purposes. After sufficient investigations, counting "suspected suicides" as "suicides" is a realistic prevention policy even in the common context of survivor denial. Thresholds for making such calls may vary between organizations tracking suicides, and vary per personnel rotating through such organizations. Ultimately, potential "over-counting" (counting "suspected suicides" as "suicides" for prevention purposes) is a reasonable approach rather than underestimating the true extent of the problem of suicide (due, for example, to the challenges of surmising intentionality in self-inflicted deaths). In 2006, the efforts to implement standardized practices for counting DoD suicides (as described below) aimed to maximize the accuracy of reported suicide rates.

Standardization efforts within the DoD

Calculation of military suicide rates and public dissemination

In 2005, SPPMs and AFME staff working together on the DoD Suicide Prevention and Risk Reduction Committee (SPARRC) increasingly recognized differences between military Departments' calculations of suicide rates. Variations with regard to which deaths were included in each of the military Departments' reported suicide numbers (numerators) and differences in calculating annual Departments' populations (denominators) influenced rates of suicide (Kennedy and Zillmer 2006). For example, there were Departmental variations with regard to counting or not counting suicides of Service academy cadets, service members on appellate leave, deserters, and reservists. Of greatest statistical significance (± 2 suicides/100,000/year), there was Service variation with regard to counting suspected, but not proven, suicides. These variations made it impossible to accurately compare military Departments' suicide rates as well as merge their data to produce a meaningful DoD suicide rate.

To specifically address these challenges, day-long offsite rate standardization and suicide nomenclature work group meetings were conducted by the SPARRC over 2005–2007 with leading civilian academic subject matter experts[2] participating with the SPPMs of each Service and Coast Guard, as well as AFME, Health Affairs, and Office of the Secretary of Defense/Personnel and Readiness staff. Consensus was reached on two primary issues: (1) the suicides (numerator) that would be counted by each Department and (2) the sampling methodology for determining a Department's population (denominator) year-to-year. One of the most significant reporting changes was the inclusion of suicides of activated Reserve and Guard members, for which a denominator and time on active duty could be accurately calculated.

Consensus recommendations also included suicide rate public dissemination/ reporting intervals, as reporting rates more than once a year was leading to both statistical and public relations credibility problems. The problem was exacerbated by some leaders insisting on monthly or even weekly projections of annual suicide rates, and associated vulnerability to forming conclusions and taking actions regarding suicide prevention programming in response to statistical "noise" (high variability due to short and/or variable time intervals measured). With such variable reporting requirements, Departments could be looking well in one moment and "the sky was falling" in the next. The SPARRC reporting standard for suicide rates was thus established for every calendar year, in line with the Centers for Disease Control and Prevention (CDC).

Consensus regarding reporting numbers of those who died by suicide (not rates) was developed based on the CDC methodology of waiting until 90 percent of cause of death determinations were complete. For the CDC, this process takes 2 to 3 years (producing a 2 to 3 year lag for DoD to CDC civilian suicide comparisons for a given year). As the Mortality Surveillance Division of the AFME usually finalizes 90 percent of cause of death determinations within 90 days, the SPARRC standardization work group recommended providing quarterly numbers of deaths by suicide 90 days after the previous quarter – to include those deaths strongly suspected to be suicides but not proven to be so. This short lag obviated continuous and confusing wide fluxes of suicide numbers being reported prematurely (as "provens" plus many more "suspecteds"). For prevention and SPARRC purposes, SPPMs preserved their discretion to count as suicide those cases which they strongly suspected to be suicide, even if the AFME did not. However, over time, such occurrences were actually rare (1 to 2 deaths/year across DoD) and did not substantially increase suicide rates. Thus in recent years, AFME and SPPM thresholds for counting a suspected suicide as a suicide have appeared to be about the same.

The SPARRC's initial recommendations for the Services to standardize their suicide rates were presented in December 2005 at a meeting of the Assistant Secretary of Defense for Health Affairs (ASD/HA) and the three Surgeon Generals, who unanimously supported the development of consensus recommendations. The Under Secretary of Defense for Personnel and Readiness also concurred with the final SPARRC recommendations and published them in a June 18, 2006 policy memo, "Standardized DoD Suicide Data and Reporting" (http://afspp.afms.mil/idc/groups/public/documents/afms/ctb_056436.pdf). Fortuitously, the SPPMs and AFME staff were able to apply the standardization policy retroactively to suicide data extending back through 2001, making it comparable to current data to which the policy was being applied in 2006. Unfortunately, methodologies for pre-2001 data were so dissimilar as to prevent further retroactive standardization. From a methodological standpoint, 2000 and earlier years' suicide data cannot be accurately compared with 2001 and later data.

Suicide surveillance and the DoD Suicide Event Report (DoDSER)

Several years before the DoD standardization of suicide rates and reporting, each military Department was using a unique database to track risk factors of deaths by suicide. The USA used the *Army Suicide Event Report* (ASER), the USAF the *Suicide Event Surveillance System* (SESS), and USN/USMC the *Department of Navy Suicide Incident Report* (DONSIR). While these databases had served the individual Departments well, the absence of a joint DoD database limited the statistical power and therefore the types of conclusions that could be drawn from the collected data. To address this gap, in 2005, the AFME staff prepared a merged database based on each Service's common data elements. In 2007, the USA completed its draft of a revised ASER. As the SESS and the DONSIR were also "showing their age", the other SPPMs sought and received permission to explore revising their Services' suicide data tracking systems, as well. This serendipitously provided the opportunity for deliberating a common DoD suicide surveillance system. Confident after successes working together to standardize suicide rates and reporting, the SPARRC convened database standardization work group meetings to examine every data element (250+) and to jointly forge consensus for a comprehensive DoD suicide database.

The revised ASER was offered as a possible template for a common DoD database, which was positively embraced by all SPPMs. However, in order to implement a joint DoD database, it was necessary to preserve the latitude and ownership of an individual Department's comprehensive suicide data. In addition, individual Departments required the option to retain data elements that were unique to their Services, such as the Navy's tracking of those missing from ships and likely suicides. Thus, the emerging "DoD Suicide Event Report" would have multiple components: (1) a common database completed by each Service; (2) a unique database option for each Service; and (3) a DoD database merging components of common Service databases.

Instrumental to the final implementation of the emerging DoDSER were further collaborations to address several remaining challenges. The first potential roadblock had to do with all military Departments' highly confidential suicide data residing on a Service-unique platform (Army server for the ASER plus DoDSER). The original ASER was located on servers at Ft Lewis where, as it turns out, the DoD Telehealth and Technology Directorate (T2) of the emerging DoD Centers of Excellence for Psychological Health and Traumatic Brain Injury (DCoE) was located, and eventually named the "National Center for Telehealth and Technology". This new role essentially transformed the designated "Army ASER" (soon to become part of the DoDSER) server to that belonging to a DoD lead agency (T2), removing potential objections for locating all Services' suicide data on one server. Each Department retained complete ownership of its database, while common de-identified components were merged into the DoDSER.

The initial data-collection website for the DoDSER was developed and launched on January 1, 2008. However, incomplete functionality and use-of-site credentialing issues threatened the completion of data entry for 2008. A work-around using paper and pencil datasheets was initiated across the Departments as a backup plan to capture all agreed-upon suicide data for 2008, to be entered into the database as the software matured and as protocols and training for those who entered the data were formalized for implementation over the course of the year. A major software revision was deployed in August 2009 which enabled Common Access Card (CAC) secure log-in with accounts that differ by role of the reporting official, and other account management features. The commitment and persistence demonstrated by the SPPMs and the Ft Lewis team to implement expeditiously this landmark surveillance effort when the consensus iron was hot cannot be overstated.

Currently, the DoDSER provides a mechanism for collecting and tracking objective, subjective, and detailed standardized information including comprehensive event data, as method of death, location, and fatality information. Extensive risk factor data categories include dispositional/personal (as demographics); historical/developmental (as military history); contextual/situational (as firearms in home); and clinical/symptom factors (as diagnoses). Previous to the DoDSER, only the Army was attempting to track non-fatal suicide-related behaviors, known primarily through the medical system surveillance. At the time of this writing, all Departments are preparing to track suicide-related behaviors in the DoDSER, providing important baselines for future surveillance (especially for those at high risk of suicide due to previous suicide attempts), and for those still in the military and those seeking care in the US Department of Veterans Affairs (VA).

DoDSER data sources for suicides may include a review of the following: (1) medical and behavioral health records; (2) personnel and counseling records; (3)

investigative agency records; (4) records related to manner of death as casualty reports, toxicology, autopsy, and suicide notes; and (5) interviews with co-workers and supervisors, responsible investigative agency officers, other involved professionals and family members when appropriate. For surveillance of non-fatal suicide-related behaviors, data sources are patient interviews, medical and behavioral health records review, and interviews of co-workers and supervisors.

Remaining challenges on standardization: Guard and Reserve suicides

SPARRC modifications of suicide surveillance in 2006, to include activated Guard and Reserve suicides, revealed higher rates of suicide among the Reserve Component (RC) members. As a result, Reserve Affairs has undertaken additional surveillance of all RC personnel, to include those who die by suicide when not on active duty. This surveillance effort is complicated by a lack of authorized support from the AFME, with RC installations perhaps having only anecdotal information from family members of an RC member who died by suicide or a suspected suicide; or at best, a cursory report from a coroner or medical examiner if the family so authorized its release. Thus, challenges of standardizing this data and assessing its reliability are formidable.

However, for the first time at least some idea of the scope of deactivated RC member suicides is possible. Hypotheses regarding increased activated RC (and perhaps, deactivated) suicides include: (1) RC members' stressors related to retaining personal businesses or jobs while deployed (economic stress and insecurity); (2) less mental health support and clinical resources than those available to regular members; (3) less preparation of and support for families during long deployment absences (and in some cases, geographical separation of Reserve families); and/or (4) dealing with unanticipated demands of their RC commitment in terms of prolonged and repeated combat deployments.

Finally, gaps in suicide data for non-activated RC members and any service member who dies by suicide in a civilian setting are amenable to potential remedy, such as federal legislation requiring release of sufficient data to DoD medical examiners to adjudicate cause of death determinations to military standards. Standardization across medical examiner and coroner professional communities in terms of thresholds for suicide cause of death determinations could also enhance suicide surveillance of military members who die outside of military jurisdictions. The issue of electing coroners deserves special attention with regard to preserving objective cause of death formulations independently of satisfying a voting constituency.

Efforts to enhance DoD and Federal inter-agency suicide prevention collaborations

Since 2005, the number of levels of DoD and Federal inter-agency collaborations has increased markedly, especially due to the proactive leadership in the VA, the Department of Health and Human Services' Substance Abuse and Mental Health Services Administration (SAMHSA), and the DoD Health Affairs. In 2008, a VA member position was created on the SPARRC allowing monthly coordination and sharing of suicide prevention information in real time between the Departments. SPARRC and VA subject matter experts conducted meetings to explore the co-development of a joint suicide prevention website. Expanding joint efforts, the Annual DoD Suicide Prevention Conference became the DoD/ VA Suicide Prevention Conference in January of 2009 (and henceforth a joint annual conference). Suicide prevention synergy was enhanced by providing a forum for education and sharing of prevention strategies with the Suicide Prevention Coordinators from VA medical facilities (two per facility) and expanding the conference to over 500 attendees. This interface between hundreds of DoD suicide preventionists (including chaplains) and VA Suicide Prevention Coordinators markedly improved mutual understanding of the suicide prevention challenges in both Departments, appreciation of each other's pro-active cultures, and knowledge of respective mental health resources and approaches. The second joint Annual DoD/VA Suicide Prevention Conference was held on January 10–14, 2010, in Washington, DC with approximately 1,000 attendees. In addition to providing a forum for exchange of ideas, the conference highlighted progress and innovations in suicide prevention efforts related to clinical intervention, practical applications and/or tools, research, and a range of other disciplines.

Since 2006, the DoD and the VA have collaborated monthly in several SAMHSA-coordinated Federal Priority Work Groups as leaders or members, including those on Suicide Prevention, co-chaired by SAMHSA and DoD (Air Force and then USMC SPPMs from 2006–2010). Since 2008, collaborations among the DoD, VA, and SAMHSA have occurred via the post-deployment "Reintegration Work Group" co-chaired by DoD and the VA, the "Workgroup on Disaster and Emergency Response" co-chaired by DoD, the "Primary Care/ Mental Health Integration Work Group" with a DoD member, and in 2009, the DoD's National Center for Telehealth and Technology's facilitating of SAMHSA's Federal Partners' "Exploratory Committee on Telemental Health". Each of these work groups has contributed either directly or indirectly to important areas of concern for VA and military suicide prevention. DoD and VA experts co-presented joint DoD/VA seminars on suicide prevention at SAMHSA's "National Paving the Road Home" Conference in 2008, expanding expertise and knowledge to representatives of various states' organizations attempting to meet the post-deployment needs of service members and families, including suicide prevention.

While both DoD and the VA advertise the SAMHSA-coordinated National Suicide Prevention Lifeline (1-800-273-TALK), in July 2007 the VA launched its own suicide hotline, accessible to veterans (as well as military members) who call the National Suicide Prevention Lifeline and use the "Press #1" option for veterans. After three years of operation, the VA hotline was credited with over 10,000 rescues, with many callers being active duty service members. The VA also established a veterans' suicide prevention live chat line via the NSPL website http://www.suicidepreventionlifeline.org/.

SAMHSA developed a comprehensive "crosswalk" of SAMHSA resources potentially useful for DoD in order to address the specific recommendations of the DoD Task Force on Mental Health report released in June 2007. Finally, a number of DoD, VA, and SAMHSA subject matter experts served on both the Congressionally-directed DoD Task Force on Mental Health and the DoD Task Force on the Prevention of Suicide by Members of the Armed Forces, from which many specific recommendations for improving the mental health of service members and their families and reducing suicides were accepted by the Secretary of Defense.

Efforts to enhance military suicide prevention research

Since the onset of Operation Iraqi Freedom (OIF) and Operation Enduring Freedom (OEF), the DoD has paid increasing attention to programmatic research in the area of military suicide prevention. The rise in military suicides since 2007 precipitated significant DoD investments in analysis and research to find a way to reduce suicides. In 2009, the US Army Medical Research and Materiel Command (USAMRMC), under the leadership of Colonel Carl Castro, organized a meeting with DoD and civilian subject matter experts in order to delineate the gaps in the scientific research pertaining to suicide prevention among the Armed Forces. Over the past several years, the DoD funding allocated to such research has significantly increased and scientific collaborations across disciplines and among various academic as well as DoD institutions have been formed to move the science of military suicide prevention forward. Never before has suicide prevention research received so much attention in the US military.

For instance, the RAND National Defense Research Institute (a nonprofit research organization) recently completed a study sponsored by the Office of the Secretary of Defense (OSD). The findings of this study were publicly disseminated in a 2011 report, titled, the *War Within: Preventing Suicide in the U.S. Military* (Ramchand et al. 2011). The objectives of the study were to (1) review the military suicide epidemiology literature; (2) identify best practices in suicide prevention; (3) review and catalog suicide prevention programs across the Services; and (4) utilize this review to inform recommendations for enhancements of current DoD programs. The 229-page summary of the study's findings is available online for free download: http://www.rand.org/pubs/monographs/MG953.html.

In addition to this RAND study, a DoD-funded Army and National Institute of Mental Health (NIMH) collaboration, titled, Army Study to Assess Risk and Resilience in Servicemembers (STARRS) is the largest epidemiologic study of risk and protective factors pertaining to suicide-related behaviors among active Army and the Reserve Components, ever undertaken in the US. The USMC has recently joined the collaboration to examine risk and protective factors among the Marines. The Army STARRS consists of four separate research methodologies: (1) Historical Data Study which involves the examination of de-identified health and administrative records maintained historically by the DoD; (2) All Army Study which assesses psychological and physical health-related factors in soldiers throughout all phases of their Army service; (3) New Soldier Study which will focus on the characteristics of new soldiers entering the Army; and (4) the Soldier Health Outcomes Study which involves two case-control comparison studies that examine the predictors for positive and negative psychological health related outcomes. The interdisciplinary research program is directed by Robert J. Ursano, MD of the Uniformed Services University of the Health Sciences (USUHS) and Murray Stein, MD, MPH of the University of California, San Diego with other key investigators from University of Michigan and Harvard Medical School. The consortium brings together research teams that are internationally known for their expertise and experience in research on military health, behavior/health surveys, epidemiology, and suicide, including genetic and neurobiological factors involved in suicidal behavior. For up-to-date information on preliminary study findings, please visit http://www.armystarrs.org/.

While epidemiologic research is much needed in this area, there is also a significant need for evidence-based assessment and treatment strategies targeting the unique needs of military personnel. A variety of programmatic research efforts in this area have been supported by private and government funding sources – in particular by the USAMRMC, Military Operational Medicine Research Program. Presently, there are a number of randomized controlled trials designed to examine the efficacy and effectiveness of targeted suicide prevention treatments for military personnel. For instance, an evidence-based model of outpatient cognitive treatment for prevention of suicide (Brown et al. 2005) has been adapted for inpatient implementation. The newly adapted intervention, Post-Admission Cognitive Therapy (PACT; Ghahramanlou Holloway et al. 2011), targets the treatment needs of military personnel admitted for inpatient psychiatric care following a suicide attempt; PACT is currently being piloted and refined at the Walter Reed National Military Medical Center. A brief intervention, Safety Planning (Stanley and Brown 2011), is another example of a targeted suicide prevention intervention that is under empirical evaluation within an inpatient military sample, consisting of those who have been psychiatrically hospitalized due to suicide ideation and/or a recent suicide attempt. Collectively, the findings associated with such treatment outcome research will result in innovative and effective assessment and treatment strategies best adapted for military populations.

Summary of current suicide prevention initiatives and programs: Department of Defense

The DoD Health Affairs formed the Suicide Prevention and Risk Reduction Committee to provide a forum for inter-Service and DoD-level coordination and most recently a full partnership with the VA. Originally chaired by the Health Affairs' Program Director for Mental Health Policy, from 2008 through 2011 the SPARRC was chaired by the Resilience and Prevention Directorate staff of the Defense Centers of Excellence for Psychological Health and Traumatic Brain Injury (DCoE). In 2011, by recommendation of the Task Force (DoD, 2010), the SPARRC transitioned to the Office of the Under Secretary of Defense for

Personnel and Readiness, consistent with the concept of suicide prevention as primarily a leadership responsibility rather than a medical problem.

Moreover, in 2011, the Office of the Secretary of Defense for Personnel and Readiness created the Defense Suicide Prevention Oversight Council (DSPOC), to provide senior level governance, oversight, and policy direction to ensure DoD-wide suicide prevention efforts are visible, coordinated, and maximally effective. In addition to the DSPOC, the Suicide Prevention General Officer Steering Committee (SPGOSC) was created to provide a forum to facilitate the review, assessment, integration, and implementation of policy and program actions that have Department-wide applicability to suicide prevention efforts. The third and final tier is the SPARRC which serves as a collaborative forum for suicide prevention issues that have broad implications across the Department of Defense, and as the action arm and principal advisors in support of the Defense Suicide Prevention Oversight Council and the Suicide Prevention General Officer Steering Committee. The primary members of the SPARRC are the SPPMs and Directors of Psychological Health for each Service, and the Army G3, Navy N3, Marines PP & O, and the Air Force A3.

In addition to efforts in the areas of surveillance, nomenclature, and research (as noted earlier in this chapter), the SPARRC has contributed to a number of other areas. For instance, in terms of suicide prevention policy, a DoD instruction was written to provide policy for suicide prevention, data collection, and reporting. The draft version was completed and is in coordination across the Pentagon. A SPARRC website (www.suicideoutreach.org) was launched in October 2010 to serve as a DoD/VA "clearinghouse" for suicide prevention information, contacts, innovative approaches, and tools. The website creates a joint, collaborative space for active duty members and veterans to enhance dissemination and sharing of resources.

Furthermore, to address perceived barriers to care and stigma, the Real Warriors Campaign was established in May 2009 as a public education initiative that encourages health-seeking behaviors. The campaign provides concrete examples of service members who sought care for psychological health issues and are maintaining successful military careers. The website (www.realwarriors. net) includes several features that help educate and connect service members, veterans, and their families to the resources they need to build resilience and access appropriate care or treatment. Finally, a family subcommittee was established by SPARRC to address DoD gaps in suicide prevention initiatives targeted for families and to provide recommendations on the topic to the SPARRC.

Summary of current suicide prevention initiatives and programs: service-specific

In addition to DoD-wide suicide prevention initiatives, each Service has programs and efforts tailored to the unique needs of their members. Overall, emphasis has been placed on the role of leadership, suicide prevention training, enhanced suicide surveillance, community involvement, as well as stigma reduction in the prevention of deaths by suicide. In the sections below, a few of the Services' suicide prevention efforts and initiatives implemented in recent years are very briefly highlighted. Given the scope of this chapter, we have selected several highlights for each Service. Detailed information about each Service's suicide prevention initiatives may be obtained from their respective Suicide Prevention Program Managers whose contact information is provided on each Service's suicide prevention web page.

United States Air Force (USAF)

The USAF suicide prevention program (Knox et al. 2010) has received recognition from the National Registry[3] of Evidence-Based Programs and Practices. To engage and to motivate the community on suicide prevention efforts, messages from the Chief of Staff of the Air Force (CSAF), other senior leaders, and base commanders are sent out regularly. Commanders receive training on how and when to use mental health services and guidance on their role in encouraging early help seeking behavior. In terms of continued education about suicide prevention, annual trainings, tailored to best meet the community needs, are provided for all USAF military and civilian employees. To best prepare continuing education for behavioral health providers, the USAF is currently working with the Laboratory for the Treatment of Suicide-Related Ideation and Behavior at Uniformed Services University of the Health Sciences to update the Air Force's Guide for Managing Suicidal Behaviors. The revised guide will continue to provide systematic guidance to USAF providers on evidence-informed practices for suicide risk assessment, management, and treatment.

Furthermore, the USAF suicide prevention program has fostered a community model for saving lives. For instance, given that the period following an arrest or investigative interview is a high-risk time for suicide, following any investigative interview, the investigator is required to "hand-off" the individual directly to the commander, first sergeant, or supervisor. The unit representative is then responsible for assessing the individual's emotional state and contacting a mental health provider if any question about the possibility of suicide exists. The Trauma Stress Response teams have been established at every base to respond to traumatic incidents such as terrorist attacks, serious accidents, or suicide. These teams provide Wing-level consultation and advice regarding personnel support after traumatic events. Finally, the Integrated Delivery System (IDS) and Community Action Information Board (CAIB) (1) provide a forum for the cross-organizational review and resolution of individual, family, installation, and community issues that impact the readiness of the force and the quality of life for USAF members and their families, and (2) help coordinate the activities of the various base helping agencies to achieve a synergistic effort to reduce community problems.

Most notably, the USAF suicide prevention program has emphasized a need for reducing barriers to care and perceived stigma. For instance, the Limited Privilege Suicide Prevention Program has provided USAF service members undergoing legal action (who are at risk for suicide) increased confidentiality when seen by mental health providers. Additionally, Limited Patient–Psychotherapist Privilege was established in 1999, limiting the release of patient information to legal authorities during Uniformed Code of Military Justice (UCMJ) proceedings (see AFI 44-109 for additional details; http://www.af.mil/shared/media/epubs/AFI44-109.pdf).

United States Army (USA)

Similar to the USAF suicide prevention efforts, the USA has implemented systematic programs to improve suicide surveillance, prevention training, help seeking, and leadership as well as community involvement. Most notably, several key Army Regulations (AR) and Department of the Army Pamphlets (DA PAMs) have been revised. The revised AR 600-63 (http://www.apd.army.mil/pdffiles/r600_63.pdf) and DA PAM 600-24 (http://www.apd.army.mil/pdffiles/p600_24.pdf) provide enhanced guidance and information to help Army leaders, suicide prevention professionals and other key personnel improve programs at the installation level. In addition, the Army's multi-disciplinary Task Force (2010, http://csf.army.mil/downloads/HP-RR-SPReport2010.pdf) was established to make rapid improvements across the full spectrum of health promotion, risk reduction and suicide prevention programs.

To provide some illustrative examples of the types of suicide prevention approaches in the USA, let us mention three specific programs. First, the Confidential Alcohol Treatment and Education Pilot (CATEP), implemented in the summer of 2009, was designed to enhance the self-referral process for Soldiers in the early phase of alcohol abuse, prior to developing problems that hit a trip-wire. The program offers confidential evening and weekend sessions (without mandated command notification) and protection against automatic adverse career consequences. Second, the USA has focused on increasing resources such that funding for the use of "3R" bonuses (recruiting, relocation, and retention) has been provided to hire additional substance abuse and family advocacy program counselors. The Office of the Secretary of Defense has provided the authority to offer permanent health profession bonuses to Clinical Psychologists and Social Workers. These new benefits include incentive pay and accession bonuses for Clinical Psychologists, and replacing the current Critical Skills Retention Bonus and accession bonuses for Social Workers.

Third, in terms of suicide prevention training efforts, approximately 200,000 pocket-sized suicide awareness guidebooks have been distributed for leaders to assist them in preventing suicide and effectively intervening when they see a Soldier at risk. Furthermore, the "Shoulder to Shoulder: No Soldier Stands Alone" video provides statements by Senior Army Leadership to convey the importance of seeking behavioral health care when feeling distressed. The video, "Beyond the Front" which is accompanied by a facilitated discussion to help reduce stigma, allows the viewers to interactively select courses of action to intervene with Soldiers in distress. The Ask, Care, Escort (ACE) Suicide Intervention (ACE-SI) program has been reviewed and accepted by the Suicide Prevention Resource

Center and the American Foundation for Suicide Prevention Best Practices Registry for Suicide Prevention.

United States Navy (USN)

The USN suicide prevention programmatic efforts have also grown over the past decade. For instance, the Suicide Prevention Cross Functional Team was established in February 2009 and included a multidisciplinary team of individuals from Navy Personnel, Fleet Operational Commands, Navy Medicine, Safety, Installations and Family Programs, Public Affairs, Resourcing, and Training. The purpose of the team was to review in-place efforts and to identify gaps and develop a way ahead which de-emphasizes stigma associated with help-seeking. Recommendations to the Chief of Naval Operations, based on the team's efforts, were provided to ensure an informed strategy to suicide prevention. In addition, a review of the USN policies has been initiated to identify potential barriers to seeking appropriate care or successful reintegration to a viable career path following treatment.

In May 2009, a Behavioral Health Quick Poll was administered to obtain a representative sampling of Sailors' stress, coping, expectations, and attitudes; as well as to provide a measure of training compliance, preferences, and retained knowledge related to suicide prevention. In response, the Operational Stress Control (OSC) program (based on the stress continuum model) led by operational leadership and supported by Navy Medicine has been designed to address the psychological health needs of Sailors and their families. To date, more than 84,000 Sailors have received the initial OSC familiarization brief. Formal training curriculum for key points throughout a Sailor's career is now in various stages of development and rollout.

In order to best meet the needs of Navy Reserves, starting in 2008, two coordinators and three outreach team members (all licensed clinical social workers) were provided to each of the five Navy Reserve Regions to engage in training, active outreach, clinical assessment, referral to care and ensure follow-up services for reserve Sailors. Moreover, to best meet the needs of Navy providers who work with suicidal Sailors and Marines, the USN Suicide Prevention Program in collaboration with the Suicide Prevention Resource Center has provided training on Assessing and Managing Suicide Risk to USN providers. A program evaluation component, as recommended by the DoD Task Force was also embedded within this suicide prevention program to best inform future training efforts.

United States Marine Corps (USMC)

The USMC's suicide prevention program has also approached the problem of suicide in a direct and targeted manner. For instance, the USMC has required annual suicide prevention training for all Marines since 1997. Trainings are conducted at the unit level but are also incorporated into a Marine's formal education and professional development. Strong emphasis has been placed on the development and continual adaptations of innovative primary prevention curricula targeted to specific at-risk populations. In fact, focused trainings have been created for USMC recruits in boot camp, drill instructors, and new officers in the Basic School. Trainings are based on current best practices in risk identification, resource awareness, and inculcation of bystander response training. Real-life stigma scenarios are utilized for discussion of how to reduce stigma among these groups. Messages conveyed in such programs, are at times disseminated to the USMC population in rather innovative ways. To illustrate, the USMC Martial Arts Program, which is completed by all Marines, most recently began to incorporate a suicide prevention message into martial arts relevant metaphors, to demonstrate the importance of resilience and emotional as well as physical fitness.

Moreover, the Operational Stress Control and Readiness Extenders (OSCAR Extenders) is a new training on recognizing and responding to signs of combat operational stress. Training offered by the USMC has commenced with those units deploying soonest and will continue in the months to come. Finally, the role of USMC leadership in suicide prevention has been additionally emphasized in recently prepared videos. All first commanding generals and their sergeant majors produced and disseminated a personal suicide prevention message for their Marines. These 3–5 minute personal videos with messages from senior leadership were designed to demonstrate the importance of addressing this tragedy at the most senior level and to reduce the stigma of asking for help. An information paper was distributed to all commands to offer subject matter expert guidance on the development of subject videos.

Similar to the other services, there are additional resources put into suicide prevention. USMC plans to place 23 permanent full time civilian hires as Suicide Prevention Coordinators on USMC Installations and select major commands are currently underway. These individuals will support training and coordination of installation suicide prevention efforts and act as a conduit of information between Headquarters Marine Corps Suicide Prevention Program and unit level suicide prevention programs. In addition, following an evaluation of current program resourcing, three additional full-time civilian staff members were hired to support the Headquarters, Marine Corps Suicide Prevention Program.

Recommendations

The 2010 DoD Task Force report on the prevention of suicide among members of the Armed Forces is a comprehensive document which presents 49 findings and 76 targeted recommendations based on a year-long review of programmatic efforts within the DoD, examination of research based evidence on military mental health and suicide, consultation with subject matter experts, and discussions with service members and their family members. Readers of this chapter are encouraged to refer to the full report made available online to gain a better understanding of the specific recommendations provided. Based on the content presented in this chapter, two specific recommendations are particularly emphasized below. However, it is important to note that enhancing DoD's approach to military suicide prevention will continue to require resources, a sustained and systematic effort, and much compassion from those involved in reducing deaths and injuries associated with suicide-related behaviors.

One notable gap in the DoD's suicide prevention efforts includes the military's relatively non-standardized threshold for conducting a psychological autopsy, such as whenever cause of death is unclear. Military communities are accustomed to accident investigations that involve loss of life or high value military assets, such as multi-million dollar aircraft. Safety investigations are initiated, for example, when a life is lost or damage results in total disability, or damage exceeds one million dollars. Such "Class A" mishaps result in a formal safety board of subject matter experts, including a physician and life support officer, that convenes at the installation related to the mishap for 3–4 or more weeks. (A subsequent board completely independent of the safety board convenes months later to deal with legal and liability issues separately.) This assures the rapid identification of causes of mishaps and communication to the military community the measures that may prevent them in the future. Thus, it makes sense to inquire as to whether or not the death of a service member by suicide does not warrant the same investment to adequately establish why it happened, and how to prevent a similar circumstance in the future.

Similarly, lessons can be learned from military medical incident investigations (MII), including murder-suicides, that can reveal deficits in multiple safety nets across an installation about which clinicians and line leaders may have had no awareness. Most suicides involve a level of mental deterioration, diagnosed or not. While stressful for an installation, a MII related to the clinical care of a struggling service member who dies by suicide can uncover factors whose elimination may prevent an unnecessary death in the future. The threshold for conducting a MII for a patient who dies by suicide is not standardized across DoD, and may represent a potential gap in suicide data. Findings of such investigations result in communities more accurately adjusting their thresholds for intervening when an individual or family demonstrates behaviors of concern.

In addition to standardized nomenclature and investigations of suicide and suicide behaviors, the methodologies assuring compliance across all agencies with established policies is critical for successful execution and reliable data. Current investments by each military Service designating a DoDSER suicide data manager to assure compliance with all data requirements for each suicide will result in high completion rates for each department, and a higher percentage of required data elements for each suicide death and documented suicide attempt.

Conclusion

This chapter has provided a relatively brief overview of recent efforts within the Department of Defense to address the significant public health problem of suicide among military personnel. Given the emotional and economic toll on families, the military community, the healthcare system, and our nation resulting from suicide, much remains to be done. Systematic and well-designed surveillance efforts –

along with a sustained programmatic plan for evidence-informed prevention, intervention, and postvention practices – directly aim to reduce suicide and suicide-related behaviors among the brave men and women of the US military. Promotion of mental fitness in addition to physical fitness may be instrumental in maximizing operational readiness of the Armed Forces and their psychological functioning during military service and beyond.

Appendix: Acronyms

ACE	Ask, Care, Escort
ACE-SI	Ask, Care, Escort – Suicide Intervention Program
AFME	Armed Forces Medical Examiner
AR	Army Regulations
ARFORGEN	Army Force Generation
ASD/HA	Assistant Secretary of Defense for Health Affairs
ASER	Army Suicide Event Report
ASSIST	Applied Suicide Intervention Skills Training
CAC	Common Access Card
CAIB	Community Action Information Board
CATEP	Confidential Alcohol Treatment and Education Pilot
CDC	Centers for Disease Control
CGIP	Commanding General Inspection Program
CSAD	Chief of Staff of the Air Force
DA PAMs	Department of the Army Pamphlets
DCoE	Department of Defense Centers of Excellence for Psychological Health and Traumatic Brain Injury
DoD	Department of Defense
DoDI	DoD Instruction
DoDSER	DoD Suicide Event Report
DONSIR	Department of Navy Suicide Incident Report
DSPOC	Defense Suicide Prevention Oversight Council
IDS	Integrated Delivery System
MCCS	Marine Corps Community Services
MEPRS	Medical Expense and Performance Reporting System
MII	Medical Incident Investigations
mTBI	Mild Traumatic Brain Injury
NCO	Non-Commissioned Officer

NIMH	National Institute of Mental Health
NLMB	Never Leave a Marine Behind
NSPL	National Suicide Prevention Lifeline
OEF	Operation Enduring Freedom
OIF	Operation Iraqi Freedom
OPNAVINST	Office of the Chief of Naval Operations Instructions
OSC	Operational Stress Control
OSCAR	Operational Stress Control and Readiness
PACT	Post-Admission Cognitive Therapy
PTSD	Posttraumatic Stress Disorder
RACE	Recognize, Ask, Care, Escort
SAMSHA	Substance Abuse and Mental Health Services Administration
SESS	Suicide Event Surveillance System
SPARRC	Suicide Prevention and Risk Reduction Committee
SPCs	Suicide Prevention Coordinators
SPGOSC	Suicide Prevention General Officer Steering Committee
SPPM	Suicide Prevention Program Manager
STARRS	Study to Assess Risk and Resilience in Servicemembers
T2	DoD's National Center for Telehealth and Technology
UCMJ	Uniformed Code of Military Justice
USA	United States Army
USAF	United States Air Force
USAMRMC	United States Army Medical Research and Materiel Command
USMC	United States Marine Corps
USN	United States Navy
VA	Department of Veterans Affairs

Notes

1 Disclaimer: The opinions or assertions contained herein are the private views of the authors and are not to be construed as official or as reflecting the views of the Department of Defense.
2 Experts included Drs. Alex Crosby (US Centers for Disease Control), David Jobes (Catholic University of America), Morton Silverman (Suicide Prevention Resource Center), and Barry Wagner (Catholic University of America).
3 The Best Practices Registry addresses specific goals of the National Strategy for Suicide Prevention and has been reviewed by a panel of three suicide prevention experts and found to meet standards of accuracy, safety, and programmatic guidelines.

References

Brown, G.K., Ten Have, T., Henriques, G.R., Xie, S.X., Hollander, J.E., & Beck, A.T., 2005. Cognitive therapy for the prevention of suicide attempts: A randomized controlled trial. *Journal of the American Medical Association*, 294(5), 563–570.

Carr, J.R., Hoge, C.W., Gardner, J., & Potter, R., 2004. Suicide surveillance in the U.S. military – Reporting and classification biases in rate calculations. *Suicide and Life Threatening Behavior*, 34(3), 233–241.

Ghahramanlou-Holloway, M., Cox, D., & Greene, F., 2011. Post-admission cognitive therapy: A brief intervention for psychiatric inpatients admitted after a suicide attempt. *Cognitive and Behavioral Practice*, Epub ahead of print. doi: 10.1016/j.cbpra.2010.11.006.

Kennedy, C.H., & Zillmer, E.A., 2006. *Military psychology: Clinical and operational applications*. New York: Guildford Press.

Knox, K., Pflanz, S., Talcott, G., Campise, R.L., Lavigne, J.E., Bajorska, A., Tu, X., & Caine, E.D., 2010. The US Air Force suicide prevention program: Implications for public health policy. *American Journal of Public Health*, 100(12), 2457–2463.

National Center for Injury Prevention and Control, 2011. WISQARS leading causes of death reports, national and regional, 1999–2008 [online]. Available from: http://webappa.cdc.gov/sasweb/ncipc/leadcaus10_us.html [Accessed May 25, 2011].

Ramchand, R., Acosta, J., Burns, R.M., Jaycox, L.H., & Pernin, C.G., 2011. *The war within: Preventing suicide in the U.S. military*. Monographs: RAND Corporation.

Stanley, B., & Brown, G.K., 2011. Safety planning intervention: A brief intervention to mitigate suicide risk. *Cognitive and Behavioral Practice*, Epub ahead of print. doi: 10.1016/j.cbpra.2011.01.001.

United States Department of Defense, 2010. The challenge and the promise: Strengthening the Force, preventing suicide and saving lives – Final report of the Department of Defense Task Force on the prevention of suicide by members of the Armed Forces [online]. Available from: http://www.health.mil/dhb/downloads/Suicide%20Prevention%20Task%20Force%20 final%20report%208-23-10.pdf [Accessed August 4, 2011].

Part III

Deployment

8 Far forward medical care for US service members

Bryan Fisk

Providing front-line medical care in a combat theater can be one of the most rewarding experiences available to a medical provider at any level of training. There is a unity of purpose among the members of any military unit and the opportunity to utilize one's training to support and provide aid to those brothers and sisters in arms tends to be a very gratifying endeavor. However, it can also be a difficult one with a unique set of challenges and hardships to overcome in order to provide the best care possible in the far forward setting. A few of these include balancing the sometimes competing interests of mission goals versus individual patient needs, limited supplies, professional isolation, and presence of increased threats. This chapter reviews the medical capabilities available to provide medical treatment to the forward-deployed service member (SM), as well as the means by which certain topically relevant issues are addressed by the forward provider (i.e. mild traumatic brain injury and post-traumatic brain injury).

The military health system provides a continuum of care encompassing the forward stabilization on the battlefield to definitive care and rehabilitation at military medical centers in the continental United States. This is a complex system that is separated into five distinct zones of care, designated as Echelons I–V (alternatively, medical treatment facilities within these echelons may sometimes be referred to as Roles 1–5), with each successive level consisting of greater medical capabilities. Echelon I medical care refers to the initial responder care and includes aid provided by combat life-savers and/or the combat line medics, as well as medical care rendered at the battalion aid station (BAS). Echelon II care includes that provided by medical companies and forward surgical teams (FST). Next is Echelon III care which is provided by the combat support hospitals (CSH) in theater. Echelons IV and V refer to fixed medical treatment facilities either outside of or within the continental United States, respectively. The focus of this chapter is care that is rendered at Echelon I.

Overview of Echelon I medical capabilities

Trauma and emergency services

The first medical provider in the continuum of care is the enlisted SM known as the combat medic, also referred to as a Health Care Specialist. These SMs are embedded in the units they support and provide on-site medical care during mission operations. Combat medics receive training in pre-hospital emergency medical trauma care and are certified as emergency medical technicians – basic (EMT-B). However, the training differs from their civilian emergency medical services (EMS) counterparts in that it also incorporates additional skill sets required to manage casualties in the tactical setting. To this end, the combat-relevant trauma protocols of the Tactical Combat Casualty Care (TCCC) guidelines are taught and trained. These guidelines began as an initiative of the US Special Operations Command to address the differences of combat medicine with formalized protocols for tactical care. However, they are now used by all services in the US military and have been credited as a major factor in US forces having the highest casualty survival rate in history, according to the United States Army Institute of Surgical Research. The Committee on TCCC, which is now part of the Defense Health Board, is responsible for making changes and updates to the TCCC program.

Some of the key differences from civilian trauma protocols are the integration of medical care with the need to deal with hostile threats, emphasizing the control of exsanguinating hemorrhage prior to airway control, and an emphasis on the aggressive use of tourniquets. During the Vietnam War, exsanguination from extremity wounds was the leading cause of preventable deaths. This statistic was one of the impetuses for developing the Tactical Combat Casualty Care Guidelines, which call for the aggressive use of tourniquets for the initial control of hemorrhage from an extremity wound in a combat environment. Thus, advanced-design tourniquets are now ubiquitous on the battlefield as well as the BAS. The major argument against the use of tourniquets in civilian trauma systems has been the potential loss of limbs from ischemia. However, a case series from the current conflicts evaluated 232 casualties with tourniquets placed in the field on 309 limbs and found no incidences of limbs loss due to ischemia (Defense and Veteran's Brain Injury Center 2004).

While it may not be apparent at first, another major advance in battlefield care by combat medics has been the attention placed on the prevention of hypothermia. The presence of the "lethal triad" of coagulopathy, hypothermia, and hypovolemia has been shown to be a strong predictor of mortality. Hypovolemia from blood loss impairs the body's ability to maintain normal temperatures, even in hot climates. Hypothermia then results in less effective clotting activity, which results in further blood loss. Significant attention has been placed on preventing hypothermia in order to limit the adverse effects of this triad. New devices and blankets have been designed for this purpose and combat medics have been extensively trained to package casualties at the point of injury (POI) prior to evacuation.

Combat medics practice under the medical direction of the Battalion surgeon and/or the Battalion Physician Assistant (PA). Trauma casualties that occur outside of the BAS area, say at a combat outpost or during a combat patrol, are managed by the medic according to established protocols (i.e. TCCC). There is rarely direct communication with a higher level provider, except during times when there is a prolonged time to medical evacuation. Besides trauma care, medics are also responsible for providing routine care to their fellow unit members. Medical control for non-emergent care is typically provided over radio or computer-based chat.

The BAS, also referred to as the Role 1 medical treatment facility (MTF), is typically located at a forward operating base (FOB) along with the battalion headquarters. Here a physician, designated as the battalion surgeon, along with a physician assistant (PA) and the medics of the treatment squad are trained and equipped to provide advanced trauma management to the battlefield casualty. The providers at this level are trained in both Advanced Trauma Life Support and Tactical Combat Casualty Care protocols. The goals at this level are to stabilize the casualty to the greatest extent that is possible in a pre-hospital setting and evacuate to definitive care without unnecessary delay. A typical BAS will be set up to support two to four trauma beds, depending on both staffing and supplies (Figure 8.1).

The BAS possesses a fairly robust capability to resuscitate and stabilize casualties for evacuation, beginning with hemorrhage control. As noted above, tourniquets are used liberally for exanguinating extremity injuries prior to evacuation to Role 2 or 3. Currently used tourniquets have undergone rigorous head-to-head trials to

Figure 8.1 An example of a typical Battalion aid station with two treatment tables. Trauma supplies are in the hanging bags on the walls. Sick call medications are stocked in the medication chest. © Bryan Fisk

select devices to be the most fail safe in application and efficacious at ceasing blood flow. Another advance is development of hemostatic agents or bandages to temporize the control of bleeding from non-compressible sites such as the groin and axillae. The most common form currently utilized is gauze impregnated with the hemostatic agent kaolin.

The full spectrum of options for airway management is available, from basic nasopharyngeal airways to endotracheal intubation or surgical tracheostomy, with LMAs and combitubes in between. Also, there is an increasing presence of video laryngoscopes at Role 1 providing even more options for management of the difficult airway. Mechanical ventilators are not readily available at the standard Role 1 at this time, so ventilatory support must be provided via bag-valve masks and supplemental oxygen. If a mechanical ventilator is required then it is typically requested within the medical evacuation request. Further capabilities to manage breathing issues include chest seals, needle decompression, and chest tube thoracotomy.

Peripheral intravenous 18-gauge catheters remain the primary choice for vascular access. However, another major advance has been the development of new devices for the insertion of intraosseous catheters. This has greatly improved the ability to achieve vascular access in casualties with vascular collapse due to excessive hemorrhage. Blood products are not an option at Role 1, so fluid resuscitation is limited to either crystalloid fluids or artificial colloid solutions (i.e. hetastarch). The artificial colloids provide an advantage for the combat medics since they can carry less volume of IV fluids in their aid bags compared with crystalloid fluids. Although not yet available, it is hoped that freeze-dried plasma will be available in the near future. This will greatly enhance resuscitation capabilities as the colloid properties will improve intravascular fluid retention while the presence of clotting factors can aid in the achievement of hemostasis.

The ability to effectively monitor a patient's clinical status is of utmost importance at the Role 1 level. A casualty with head or penetrating torso trauma may appear to be stabilized initially only to rapidly deteriorate while awaiting evacuation. Such patients must be identified early in order to maximize good outcomes. However, this becomes an increasingly difficult task as the number of casualties being managed increases. Patient monitoring is assisted by the use of automated vital signs monitors and pulse oximeters, which are indispensable when multiple casualties must be managed by a very limited number of providers. Early detection in changes in clinical parameters can prove to be lifesaving to the casualties. Finally, portable ultrasound units are also becoming more common at Role 1 and proving to be extremely useful diagnostic tools to help guide the management of combat casualties.

Besides advanced trauma support, the BAS is also fully capable of providing advanced cardiac life support, with standard Advanced Cardiac Life Support drugs and defibrillators available. While this is an important capability for the rare occurrence of sudden cardiac death in a soldier, it is of more recent importance, given the increased number of older non-military personnel on the battlefield (i.e. contractors, DoD civilians, non-military federal employees, etc.).

Disease and non-battle injury care (sick call)

Besides trauma and emergency services, Role 1 capabilities also include primary care and sick call services. While trauma care often receives the most visibility, non-battle-related health care is of extreme importance to the success of the military mission. Typically, military units lose more fighting strength over time due to illness and non-battle-related injuries than from injuries on the battlefield. The goal of the medical team is to minimize those losses through preventative medicine measures, ensuring that medical treatment is provided at the lowest level necessary, and overseeing a rapid return to duty when appropriate. Having the capability to treat many types of illnesses at the unit level is a benefit not only to the individual units but also to the medical evacuation system. Avoiding unnecessary medical evacuations reduces risks to both the evacuation assets and to other units that may require their services for more direly needed evacuations.

A BAS will usually have some additional diagnostic equipment above the routine equipment required for a physical exam. Most units will have a defibrillator that has the additional capability of providing a rhythm strip to aid in the diagnosis of dysrythmias. Many are also capable of providing a 12-lead ECG to allow for a more detailed analysis, to include detecting the presence of myocardial ischemia or injury. Portable lab analyzers are also becoming more common at the Role 1 level. These analyzers are capable of providing data on arterial blood gases, serum electrolytes, and hemoglobin levels. Usually, there is no x-ray capability at the Role 1 level. However, as noted before, portable ultrasound devices are becoming more common. Advances in ultrasonographic techniques have allowed these devices to be used to diagnose certain conditions that have required x-rays in the past. These conditions include pneumothoraces and long bone fractures. These advances in diagnostic capabilities at the front-lines often allow the provider to rule out worrisome diagnoses, thus avoiding unnecessary evacuations with their inherent risks.

A BAS will stock a wide range of pharmaceutical supplies for the treatment of sick call patients. By far the most abundant medications are for the treatment of minor aches and pains, diarrhea, and non-infectious respiratory symptoms as these are the majority of sick call complaints. The next most common medications would be oral antibiotics, mostly for the treatment of respiratory, gastrointestinal, and skin and soft tissue infections. More potent intravenous antibiotics are available if needed to stabilize seriously ill patients while awaiting evacuation. A more recent phenomenon is the stocking of a wide array of psychiatric medications, mostly antidepressants which are used for numerous indications besides a diagnosis of depression. These medications are mostly used for refilling of prescriptions but also for initiation of therapy. At the start of the OEF/OIF it was rare to encounter a deployed SM who was on this class of medication but this is no longer the case as obtaining medical waivers for depression is not as easy as it used to be.

Dental complaints are another very common presenting complaint at sick call. Supplies are available to provide minor dental repair or temporizing measures to allow for a delay in the time required for an evaluation by a dentist. This will usually allow for the patient to be transported to the rear, where dental services are available, as part of a routine mission.

A recent change in doctrine that has allowed a significant decrease in the number of evacuations from forward units is the forward placement of physical therapy and behavioral health specialists. Like many advances in military medicine, the forward placement of these specialists is a direct result of lessons learned from special operations forces. Physical therapists have been used in these units for the past decade for early recognition and aggressive management of musculoskeletal injuries on the battlefield and have demonstrated success in impacting unit readiness. Since 2006, an increasing number of US Army Brigades have been creating permanent positions for physical therapists within the units. During deployment, PTs will circulate among the various Battalions' areas of operation (AOs) to provide assistance in the management and rehabilitation of musculoskeletal injuries. This has had a great impact in keeping more soldiers in their respective AOs and keeping them in the fight.

Similarly, Brigades also deploy with a behavioral health officer (BHO) and a non-commissioned behavioral health specialist. SMs displaying behavioral health issues can be evacuated to the rear for evaluation by the BHO or, alternatively, can be evaluated by the BHO in their respective AOs during combat support missions. This has an added benefit of keeping SMs with their units where they are among peers who understand what they have been through and may lead to a better recovery. This capability of forward behavioral health services has a great benefit of decreasing the number of behavioral health evacuations. One study found that having forward BH providers limited the rate of these evacuations to 0.1 percent of the fighting force, proving to be a great force multiplier (Warner et al. 2007).

Evacuation to higher levels of care

When a soldier is injured on the battlefield, initial care is provided at the point of injury (POI) by the combat medic. Then, if a higher level of care is indicated a medical evacuation request is submitted from the POI to the unit's higher headquarters, which is most often the battalion tactical operations center (TOC). Depending on multiple factors, casualties will be evacuated from the POI either by ground to the BAS or straight to a Role 2 (FST) or 3 (CSH) medical treatment facility, usually by rotary wing aircraft. The contributing factors include the severity of the injury, presence of ongoing hostilities, weather conditions, availability of medical air evacuations assets, and the distance by ground from the POI to the BAS. Based on these factors the battalion operations officer, with consultation from the battalion surgeon and medical operations officer will then put the evacuation plan into motion.

Casualties evacuated by ground vehicles may be transported from the POI by either non-medical vehicle, termed casualty evacuation (CASEVAC), or by a dedicated medical vehicle (MEDEVAC). During the early part of the OEF/ OIF, ground MEDEVAC was most often accomplished using high mobility multipurpose wheeled vehicle (HMMWV) ambulances. However, as the roadside

Figure 8.2a A mine resistant ambush protected (MRAP) ambulance. Interior arranged to carry three litter patients. © Bryan Fisk

Figure 8.2b Exterior view of a mine resistant ambush protected (MRAP) ambulance. © Bryan Fisk

improvised explosive device (IED) became more pervasive, newer Mine Resistant Ambush Protected (MRAP) ambulances were designed and are now more commonly used in ground evacuation in the combat theaters. These vehicles have been designed to withstand much greater explosive forces compared with the older HMMWV ambulances (Figures 8.2a, 8.2b). They have a v-shaped hull, which is designed to deflect blasts from underneath away from the vehicle to protect the occupants. They are also more medically advanced than their predecessors, with built-in monitors and oxygen concentrators.

If the casualty is evacuated by air, regardless of whether he is evacuated from the POI or from the BAS, a patient hand-off is made with the flight medic, or occasionally with the flight surgeon if present. Medical care is then continued en route to the higher level medical treatment facility. Mechanical ventilators are available on board the medical evacuation aircraft, representing a capability not present at the Role 1 level.

Casualties with serious injuries will be further stabilized at the Role 3 hospital prior to evacuation from theater. For patients with less serious injury, and who are expected to be able to return to duty within seven days, treatment is provided in theater.

Mild traumatic brain injury (mTBI)

Traumatic brain injury (TBI) is a disruption of function in the brain resulting from a blow or jolt to the head or penetrating head injury and the severity can range from mild (i.e. a concussion) to severe involving an extended period of unconsciousness or amnesia. A signature injury of the OEF/OIF has been TBI secondary to blasts, particularly from IEDs. The diagnosis of a casualty with severe TBI is generally not a difficult one to make. However, the identification of an SM with mild traumatic brain injury (mTBI) can be much more difficult and subjective. One reason that an mTBI can go unnoticed is that the SM may not have visible external injuries and symptoms may not be obvious. An mTBI or concussion may cause changes that include a decreased reaction time, vision and hearing problems, balance problems, memory impairments, headaches, irritability and sleep difficulty. These symptoms may result in a decrease in performance, which is critical to mission effectiveness. Thus, it is important to identify SMs with mTBI, not only for the individual's well being, but also for the good of the entire unit.

Since the onset of the OEF/OIF, there has been a major emphasis on refining the cognitive assessment for service members out of concern that blast exposures, particularly repeated exposures, may be resulting in mTBI that was previously going undiagnosed and could be leading to permanent disability. This increased awareness has led to a substantial increase in the diagnosis of mild TBI. For example, the incidence for severe or penetrating TBI in US Service Members in 2005 was 407 and 9,857 for mTBI. By 2010, the incidence of severe or penetrating TBI had increased slightly to 521 but for mTBI the incidence increased to 25,103 (Figure 8.3). During this same time period, a greater emphasis was placed on prevention of mTBI, with improvements in both personal protective equipment and blast-resistant vehicles. The substantially larger increase in mTBI, therefore, is most likely due to the increased awareness of mTBI among both medical providers and SMs.

Since mTBI from blast exposure most often occurs without objective or outward evidence of injury or with non-specific findings, casualties can be difficult

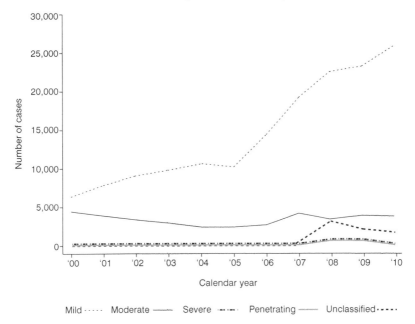

Figure 8.3 DoD numbers for traumatic brain injury. Incidence by severity.

Source: US Government. http://dvbic.org/Totals-at-a-Glance-%282%29.aspx

to identify. Therefore, substantial effort was made to develop standard criteria to screen for the diagnosis on the battlefield. The Military Acute Concussion Evaluation (MACE) is a screening tool that was developed by the Defense and Veterans Brain Injury Center (DVBIC) in 2006. It is a pencil-and-paper exam that can be administered by a trained individual in about 5 minutes. There are three sections: identifying information, event and symptom history, and the examination portion. The tool is used to score measures over four different cognitive domains: orientation, immediate memory, concentration, and memory recall, as well as a brief neurologic assessment. Possible outcomes include no concussion, concussion with no loss of consciousness (LOC), concussion with LOC, and other assessment outcomes. The MACE by itself does not diagnose mTBI and, ultimately, a clinician determines whether an individual has sustained mTBI. However, when combined with other clinical information, it can reveal basic cognitive performance abnormalities and make a diagnosis of mTBI more accurate and can identify those who require further evaluation. Initial screening with the MACE tool is currently being performed by front-line providers and combat medics. Ideally, this screening should occur immediately following the injury event or as soon as operationally feasible. Results can then be used to help guide recommendations including temporary change in duty status or evacuation to a higher level of care.

Those service members with severe symptoms or who have had multiple prior episodes will require medical evacuation from theater. However, the vast majority of SMs who sustain a concussion mTBI will not require evacuation and can expect a spontaneous recovery. These SMs are carefully monitored in theater and, if symptoms persist for longer than two weeks, will then be referred for further work-up and management.

The majority not requiring evacuation will typically be placed on limited or light duty for a short period. A follow-up MACE is obtained after symptoms related to mTBI have abated. If the SM scores within the acceptable range, another MACE is performed after exertion, which can aid in unmasking the presence of residual symptoms. If the exertional MACE is also within the acceptable range, then the SM may be returned to duty. However, it is vital that the SM not be returned to hazardous duty before the symptoms have fully resolved in order to minimize the risk of "second-impact syndrome". This is a rare and potentially fatal complication that results from sustaining another concussion before the symptoms of a prior one have resolved.

Importantly, the diagnosis of mTBI is maintained in the SMs medical record even if he does not require evacuation. This is important not only for identifying potential problems many years later but for keeping visibility on those SMs who may sustain multiple mTBIs during deployments. The risk of multiple mTBIs and their cumulative effects are becoming increasingly evident and thus SMs with multiple mTBIs are important to identify. Each mTBI suffered increases the chance that an individual will suffer an additional mTBI from further exposures (Guskiewicz et al. 2003). So an SM who has had numerous prior events might require a permanent change in his duty assignment.

For SMs who sustain an mTBI while deployed, there is now a means by which changes in neurologic function from their pre-deployment baseline can be identified either in theater or after returning home. Automated Neuropsychological Assessment Metrics (ANAM) is a computer-based tool that was mandated in 2008 and is currently being administered to SMs prior to deployment. It is designed to detect speed and accuracy of attention, memory, and thinking ability. While it is not designed to be utilized as a diagnostic tool, it can be used to identify and monitor changes in function and aid in determining the severity of injury. Laptop computers specific for performing these tests are now deployed in theater and if an SM is injured he can then take a follow-up test, usually under the direction of a deployed psychologist. The results are subsequently compared with the pre-deployment baseline, providing information on the extent of the injury and aiding in developing the best course of treatment.

PTSD and combat and operational stress

Feelings of terror, helplessness, hyper-vigilance, or emotional numbness, both during and immediately after an emotionally traumatic event are considered normal responses to a life-endangering threat. In many individuals, these feelings will abate over time. However, some people will experience a persistence of the initial reactions along with the emergence of others shortly after the trauma. The later reactions include intrusive memories of the event, trauma-related nightmares, troubling thoughts about what the experience means, sleeping difficulty, and avoidance of situations that might provoke memories of the inciting trauma. Post-traumatic stress disorder (PTSD) is considered when these reactions are intense and debilitating, and continue long after the traumatizing event has ended. Exposure to combat obviously increases the chances of traumatic exposures and the risks for developing PTSD. In 2008, the RAND Corporation, Center for Military Health Policy examined the prevalence of PTSD among previously deployed OEF/OIF SMs (Tanielian and Jaycox 2008). Nearly one out of five of the 1,938 participants reported symptoms that were consistent with either PTSD and/or major depression. The prevalence of PTSD was assessed to be 13.8 percent.

Combat poses unique challenges, in part because killing and death are an inherent reality to the required duties of SMs. Thus, in the US military the terms "combat and operational stress", "combat and operational stress reaction" (COSR) and "COSR casualty" are considered more accurate terms for stress stimuli of the battlefield, the stress reactions to battlefield experiences, and those who experience them, respectively. COSR acknowledges the risks of traumatic exposures and the possibility that they may give rise to disturbing and debilitating responses that could become uncontrollable. Labeling someone with PTSD identifies them as abnormal and with a mental disorder. In contrast, identifying an SM as being a COSR casualty tends to normalize the interventions of therapy which are focused on healing and with the expectation of recovery, similar to a physical injury.

Whenever a potentially traumatic event has occurred, the first step in mitigation is typically the leader–led after-action debriefing. This informal debriefing may quickly restore unit cohesion and readiness to return to action. It may also reduce the incidence of long-term stress reactions by sharing and normalizing thoughts, feelings, and reactions related to a potentially traumatic event. It is best to conduct this debriefing as soon as possible once the unit has returned to a relatively safe place and members are no longer in a high state of arousal.

When one or more SMs display symptoms of COSR, an assessment and initial intervention is undertaken by the unit's medical officer and/or chaplain. Unit chaplains, as a result of their responsibilities as counselors and encouragers, play a vital role in the management of COS. They are trained to recognize stress symptoms, provide immediate solace, and recommend further evaluation if indicated. Medical officers will perform a medical evaluation to rule out any underlying physical pathology as well as an initial psychiatric assessment. The management of SMs with complaints that may or may not be due to COSR can be one of the more challenging dilemmas for the forward deployed medical provider. When multiple SMs are exposed to the same traumatic event but only one or a few present with complaints of COSR, this can lead others in the unit to identify them as malingerers, which can lead to disdain and affect unit cohesion. Also, unit leaders do not want SMs evacuated from the AO if not absolutely necessary as this will affect combat strength. Furthermore, there is always the fear that the evacuation of an SM for psychiatric reasons will lead to the spread of similar symptoms among other members of the unit. Thus, it behooves the medical provider to fully assess the SM and attempt local measures if possible.

If the symptoms appear to be affecting the SM's ability to perform or seem likely to pose the risk for progressing to a more serious reaction, the SM is typically referred to the Brigade's behavioral health officer. It is preferred to have the SM with COSR evaluated at or near their respective area of operations as this approach has been demonstrated to improve outcomes and decrease BH evacuations. With each level of evacuation, the military patient becomes more removed from the unit and experience demonstrates that once evacuated from the CSH an SM is unlikely to be returned to combat (Cozza et al. 2004). However, if a unit BHO or specialist is not available or if the SM is likely to require more extensive therapy that precludes an immediate return to duty, he may be referred to a Combat Stress Control team for further evaluation and management. These behavioral health elements are often co-located with or near a Role 2 or 3 MTF. Combat Stress Control units also have small mobile teams that have their own vehicles and can move forward to augment the tactical units or to support combat service support units over a wide area.

In conclusion, the provision of far forward medical care in the combat theater is essential to both mission success and the well-being of individual SMs. Medical teams at the front-lines have been going to extraordinary measures for the past decade to provide the best possible medical care in austere locations. Their dedication, in combination with advances in the medical equipment, protective equipment, and military systems have resulted in lower killed-in-action rates and the highest survivability rate from injuries than during any past conflict. However, the nature of the current conflict, along with increased awareness, is giving rise to an increasing number of SMs suffering from mild traumatic brain injury and post-traumatic stress disorder. Ongoing research and training are underway to prevent, identify, and initiate early treatment for these casualties at the front-lines of conflict.

References

Cozza SJ, Benedek DM, Bradley JC, Grieger TA, Nam TS, Waldrep DA. (2004). Topics Specific to the Psychiatric Treatment of Military Personnel. In: *Iraq War Clinicians Guide*, 2nd Edn. June 2004, Washington, DC: National Center for PTSD and the Department of Veterans Affairs.

Defense and Veteran's Brain Injury Center (2004). http://.dvbic.org. Dismounted Complex Battle Injuries: Report of the DCBI Taskforce. Office of the Surgeon General. U.S. Army. 18 June 2011. *Emergency War Surgery* 3rd U.S. revision. Office of the Surgeon General U.S. Army.

Guskiewicz KM, McCrea M, Marshall SW, Cantu RC, Randolph C, Barr W, Onate JA, Kelly JP. (2003). Cumulative Effects Associated with Recurrent Concussion in Collegiate Football Players: The NCAA concussion study. *JAMA* 290: 2549–2555.

Tactical Combat Casualty Care Guidelines: http://www.naemt.org/Libraries/ PHTLS%20TCCC/TCCC%20Guidelines%20101101.sflb.

Tanielian, T. & Jaycox, L. (Eds.). (2008). *Invisible Wounds of War: Psychological and Cognitive Injuries, Their Consequences, and Services to Assist Recovery*. Santa Monica, CA: RAND Corporation.

Warner CH, MC USA, Breitbach JE, and Appenzeller GN (2007). Division Mental Health in the New Brigade Combat Team Structure: Part I. Predeployment and Deployment. *Military Medicine* 172: 907–911.

9 Evolution in optimal use of Navy hospital ships

Natalie Webb and Anke Richter

In this chapter, we present evidence on the evolution in the use of Navy hospital ships, including an analysis of applicable policy, data on missions for the past 25 years and alternative future configurations and possible uses of the ships. We provide background information, defining levels of military medical care and the roles of the hospital ships including information on their deployments in the past 25 years. We trace relevant historical facts in the use of hospital ships and maritime medicine leading up to today's use of the USNS *Mercy* and USNS *Comfort* as part of modern American Naval medicine. We lay out current policy guidance affecting the ships' current missions and then provide a discussion of goals, desired outcomes and externalities for hospital ship missions. Finally, we outline possible courses of action for the future of the hospital ships and conclude.

Background

Levels of military medical care

Hospital ships fall under the Force Health Protection and Readiness component of the US military health system. As such, they function as part of a military medical hierarchy, part of the structured medical commands and administrative systems that interact with and support deployed combat units. Specifically, hospital ships function like other combat support hospitals (CSHs): they deploy when needed to provide a certain level of health service in support of worldwide military operations.

Levels, also known as "roles," and previously referred to as "echelons" by NATO and ABCA (USA, Britain, Canada and Australia) designate a continuum of care ranging from Level I or initial responder care to Level V or fixed medical treatment facilities inside the continental United States (Borden Institute, 2004, p. 2.1). Levels do not correspond to the American College of Surgeons' use of the same terms in US trauma centers. The military levels focus on the differences in medical capabilities and location of capabilities with respect to the theater of operations. Level I comprises immediate first aid delivered at the scene, in theater. Each subsequent level comprises more advanced care options, more surgical and diagnostic equipment, and more inpatient beds than the ones prior to it; but each also moves further from the theater of operations with a Level IV facility providing definitive medical and surgical care outside the combat zone, yet within the communication zone/Echelon of Care of the theater of operations and a Level V facility being located in CONUS (continental USA) (ibid.).

When an injured military person requires more care than can be provided with immediate first aid delivered at the scene of injury, local personnel submit a medical evaluation request to move the person to a Level II or III facility.[1] The CSHs, Level III facilities, provide stabilization, hospitalization, initial wound surgeries and post-operative treatment for injured personnel evacuated from the battlefield. The Navy hospital ships USNS *Mercy* and USNS *Comfort* are two specific CSHs or Level III facilities. As such, hospital personnel (and CSH personnel at land-based facilities) treat and then return to duty or evacuate injured persons to a Level IV or V facility outside the combat zone. Level III facilities have the capability to treat serious injuries and "represent[s] the highest level of medical care available within the combat zone" (ibid., p. 2.6).

Capabilities of CSHs vary among Level III facilities and by service. Most CSHs are modular and a commander can modify medical responses according to expected demand or need. The army operates two corps-level combat support hospital designs with capacity ranging from approximately 250–300 beds, 24–96 intensive care unit (ICU) beds, and two to eight operating room (OR) tables. The Air Force operates a 25-bed unit with two OR tables. The Navy operates the largest facilities including fleet hospitals with 500 beds, 80 ICU beds and six OR tables and the two hospital ships, each with 1,000 beds, 100-bed ICU capability and 12 OR tables. The Navy also operates multiple Level II facilities on smaller vessels (Society for the History of Navy Medicine, 2010, p. 29).

The role of hospital ships

The two US hospital ships, owned and operated by Military Sealift Command, provide emergency, on-site care for US combatant forces deployed in war or other operations (McGrady & Strauss, 2007). As noted above, hospital ships may be used as CSHs, supporting troops, taking the wounded on board after an engagement and serving as a floating hospital, replacing a hospital on land and giving complete treatment to those taken on board.

The USNS *Mercy* specifies as its primary mission:

> [To provide] rapid, flexible, and mobile acute medical and surgical services to support Marine Corps Air/Ground Task Forces deployed ashore, Army and Air Force units deployed ashore, and naval amphibious task forces and battle forces afloat.
>
> (US Navy, 2011a)[2]

The ships must be ready to deploy to a combat zone within five days of activation (ibid.) and take at least 14 days to reach a continent outside the Americas. While not deployed as combat hospitals, the ships remain in a state of reduced operations.

As Table 9.1 shows, over the past 20 years the hospital ships have deployed only four times for a total of 17 months of combat support (25 months including transit time).[3] The USNS *Comfort* deployed during Operation Desert Shield and Operation Desert Storm and was located in the Persian Gulf for about six months. The USNS *Mercy* also supported Operation Desert Shield and Operation Desert Storm serving for six months in support of multinational allied forces in the Persian Gulf. The *Comfort* deployed in 1994 as part of Operation Uphold Democracy, providing combat support for less than two months in support of contingency operations in Haiti. The *Comfort* again deployed during Operation Iraqi Freedom and served 56 days in the Persian Gulf in early 2003.[4]

When not gearing up or deploying for combat support missions, the hospital ships provide humanitarian assistance and disaster relief (HA/DR) services. The US Navy states the "other mission" for the ships:

> To provide mobile surgical hospital service for use by appropriate U.S. Government agencies in Humanitarian Civic Assistance (HCA), disaster or humanitarian relief or limited humanitarian care incident to these missions or peacetime military operations.
>
> (US Navy, 2011a)

Table 9.2 shows that in support of "other" or secondary missions, the *Comfort* and *Mercy* served approximately 48 months, including transit, since 1987.[5] The *Comfort* deployed in 1994 as part of Operation Sea Signal, serving as a migrant processing center for Haitians. At its peak, the onboard population reached nearly 1,100 migrants. In 2001, she served in response to the terrorist attack on the World Trade Center. She also served in support of recovery efforts after Hurricane Katrina in 2005 and the earthquake in Haiti in 2010. Over the past five years, the *Comfort* participated in the Partnership for the Americas and Operation Continuing Promise missions, providing humanitarian assistance through medical, dental and veterinary care services throughout Latin America. The *Comfort* continues to participate annually in Operation Continuing Promise. The *Mercy* supported victims of the tsunami in South East Asia, including those in the Philippines and Banda Aceh, Indonesia. She participates in the Pacific Partnership missions, alternating years of participation with gray hull vessels, in Southeast Asia and Oceania.

Combatant commanders, acting through and coordinating with a naval component commander, make decisions to deploy the hospital ships for secondary, planned missions. For example, Pacific Fleet in Hawaii plans routine *Mercy* missions, informed by State Department representatives, embassies in-country, ministries of health in-country, and naval leaders. Planning conferences include deploying personnel, NGO personnel and surgeons general of host nations. For other-than-routine missions, combatant commanders coordinate ship deployment with the chief of naval operations.

In sum, despite their multiple capabilities and considerable capacity, the US deploys the hospital ships for combat support much less frequently (not at all in

Table 9.1 Deployments under primary mission (combat support)

Ship	Year	Date	Operation	Location	Measures
Comfort	1990–1991	August–April	Operation Desert Shield; Operation Desert Storm	Persian Gulf	8,000 outpatients, 700 inpatients; 337 complex surgical procedures (not possible on shore)
Mercy	1990–1991	9 August–26 March	Operation Desert Shield	Persian Gulf	690 patients; 300 surgeries
Comfort	1994	September–October	Operation Uphold Democracy	Haiti	Served as a hospital in support of US contingency operations
Comfort	2003	January–June	Operation Iraqi Freedom	Persian Gulf	700 patients (500 US, 200 Iraqi)

Sources:
http://www.med.navy.mil/sites/ustnscomfort/Pages/default.aspx; http://www.defense.gov/news/newsarticle.aspx?id=65236;
http://www.haiticomfort.blogspot.com/;
http://reliefweb.int/node/392551;
http://www.southcom.mil/AppsSC/factfiles.php?id=103;
http://www.southcom.mil/AppsSC/factfiles.php?id=6;
http://www.med.navy.mil/sites/usnsmercy/Commandinfo/Pages/CommandHistory.aspx;
http://navysite.de/ships/mercy.htm;
http://www.c7f.navy.mil/news/2010/08-august/024.htm

almost 10 years) than for HA/DR missions. Perhaps because US leaders no longer expect operations resulting in hundreds of casualties per day, or perhaps due to the specifics of current conflicts, hospital ships provide less attractive assets with which to provide Level III medical support to troops wounded in battle. However, the ships can provide combat support under sea-based and worst-case scenarios and increasingly provide combatant commanders a large asset to deploy for HA/DR missions, two capabilities of considerable importance to navy leaders.

History and evolution of hospital ships

The history of maritime military medicine provides three keys to understanding Navy and other US leaders' views of the role of today's hospital ships. Firstly, medical ships have had a special function and, in the last 100 years, status in providing medical care. As far back as Roman times, medical ships received and provided care for sick, injured and shipwrecked sailors and soldiers. The Athenian Navy's *Therapies*, and the Roman Navy's *Aesculapius*, have names indicating that they were likely medical ships (Convention (II) for the Amelioration of the Condition of Wounded, Sick and Shipwrecked Members of Armed Forces at Sea, 1949, p.154). Recorded missions show that, since the 17th century, naval squadrons "typically were accompanied by special vessels that took in the wounded after each engagement" (Society for the History of Navy Medicine, 2010). During the Crimean War, 1853–1856, England repatriated more than 100,000 sick and wounded personnel on board hospital transports. This reportedly marked the beginning of modern medicine afloat: "no military expedition was ever undertaken without the necessary ships being assigned to evacuate soldiers from the combat area and give them the medical treatment they might require"(Convention (II) for the Amelioration of the Condition of Wounded, Sick and Shipwrecked Members of Armed Forces at Sea, 1949, p.154).

Early American medical ships included the USS *Intrepid*, built in France for Napoleon's use, which in 1804 was employed as a hospital ship; and the USS *Red Rover*, captured by the US Navy from the Confederate States of America, which in the 1860s aided wounded soldiers of both sides during the American Civil War (Riske, 1973).

During the First World War, many medical ships came under attack, with belligerents accusing each other of using the ships as instruments of war rather than medical facilities (Convention (II) for the Amelioration of the Condition of Wounded, Sick and Shipwrecked Members of Armed Forces at Sea, 1949, p. 182). Between 1907 and 1949, hospital ships' legal status increasingly became protected so that today, under the Geneva Convention of 1949, they are exempt from attack as long as they are "innocently employed in their normal role; submit to identification and inspection when required; and do not intentionally hamper the movement of combatants and obey orders to stop or move out of the way when required" (ibid.).

The US has employed various types of naval maritime medical assets including receiving, supply and guard ships; ambulance boats and transports; landing ship

Table 9.2 Deployments under secondary mission (HA/DR)

Ship	Year	Date	Mission and Name of Operation	Location	
Mercy	1987	27 Feb –13 July	Humanitarian	Philippines, South Pacific, 7 ports of call	
Comfort	1994	June - Aug	Operation Sea Signal	Jamaica	
Comfort	2001	14 Sept –1 Oct	Operation Noble Eagle	NYC	
Mercy	2005	Jan (5 months)	Tsunami relief, Operation Unified Assistance	Southeast Asia	
Comfort	2005	Sept –Oct	Humanitarian, Hurricanes Katrina and Rita, Joint Task Force Katrina	US (MI, LA)	
Mercy	2006	April–Sept	Humanitarian	Bangladesh, Philippines, Indonesia (several ports), Timor Leste	
Comfort	2007	June–Oct	Humanitarian, Partnership for the Americas	Central America; Caribbean, 12 countries	
Mercy	2008	22 May, 148 days	Humanitarian Pacific Partnership 2008	Guam, Philippines, Vietnam, Federated States of Micronesia, Papua New Guinea, Timor Leste, {Singapore}, {Australia}	
Comfort	2009	April–July	Humanitarian; Continuing Promise 2009	Central & South America and the Caribbean	
				(Antigua, Colombia, Dominican Republic, El Salvador, Haiti, Nicaragua, and Panama)	

Partners	Measures
Armed Forces of Philippines	62,000 overall, 1,000 inpatient
	Migrant processing center for Haitians
	Meals, housing, psychological and medical services for volunteers and relief workers, 500 mental health consultations, 561 minor medical
	1,500 in Mississippi, 1,956 patients total
5 NGOs (including IRT); military forces of several countries	60,000 patients overall, 1,000+ surgeries, 19,000 immunizations, 16,000 pairs of eyeglasses, hands-on training to more than 6,000 host-nation attendees
Canada, NGOs (Project Hope, Operation Smile, LDS Humanitarian Services, and Atlanta Rotary Club)	98,000 overall; 1,170 surgeries; 32,322 immunizations; 122,245 prescriptions; 24,242 eye glasses; 25,000+ dental patients
Australia, Japan, Canada, New Zealand, Portugal, Republic of Korea, India, Indonesia, Singapore, Chile	Cataract surgery, cleft surgery, dentistry
6 NGOs (East Meets West, International Relief Teams, Operation Smile, Project Hope, University of California San Diego Pre-Dental Society, 3P Foundation)	Micronesia only: 3,000 dental patients; 15,000 medical patients, 200+ surgeries
Brazil, France, Canada, Netherlands	100,000 overall; 1,657 surgeries; 135,000 prescriptions; 15,003 dental patients; 13,000+ animals treated
Personnel: NGOs including Food for the Poor, International Aid, Latter Day Saints Ministries, Operation Smile and Project Hope	
Representatives from the University of California-San Diego Pre-Dental Society, University of Miami	
Donations from: Lions Club, Nour International Relief Aid Foundation, Rotary International, Haitian Resource Development Foundation, Hugs Across America, The Wheelchair Foundation, Rabies Control Partnerships, Institute of the Americas, International Aid, Islamic Relief USA, Agua Viva, and Paul Chester Children's Hope Foundation)	

continued...

Table 9.2 continued

Ship	Year	Date	Mission and Name of Operation	Location	
Comfort	2010	Jan- March	Humanitarian, Operation Unified Response	Haiti	
Mercy	2010	1 May--late Sept	Humanitarian Pacific Partnership 2010	Vietnam, Indonesia, Timor Leste, Cambodia	
Comfort	2011	April–Sept	Continuing Promise 2011	Central & South America and the Caribbean (Colombia, Costa Rica, Ecuador, El Salvador, Guatemala, Haiti, Jamaica, Nicaragua and Peru)	

Sources:
http://www.med.navy.mil/sites/usnscomfort/Pages/default.aspx;   http://www.defense.gov/news/newsarticle.aspx?id=65236;
http://www.haiticomfort.blogspot.com/;
http://reliefweb.int/node/392551;
http://www.southcom.mil/AppsSC/factfiles.php?id=103;
http://www.southcom.mil/AppsSC/factfiles.php?id=6;
http://www.med.navy.mil/sites/usnsmercy/Commandinfo/Pages/CommandHistory.aspx;
http://navysite.de/ships/mercy.htm;
http://www.c7f.navy .mil/news/2010/08-august/024.htm

Partners	Measures
Red Cross	1,000 patients
8 NGOs	101,000 patients overall; cataract surgery, cleft surgery, 1,505 dental patients, 775 surgeries, 58,000 pairs of eyeglasses
(East-Meets West, International Relief Teams, Latter-day Saint Charities, Operation Smile, Project Hope, Hope Worldwide, UCSD Pre-Dental Society, Vets Without Borders, and World Vets)	
10 Partner nations	
(Australia, Canada, Cambodia, France, Japan, New Zealand, Portugal, Republic of Korea, Singapore, and the United Kingdom)	11,000 hours of exchange classes were attended by 2,350 service providers across the four countries
30+ NGOs, 5 partner-nation militaries	70,000 patients

tank hospitals (modified tank landing ships serving in a dual role as interim hospitals for casualty evacuation); rescue ships; and evacuation ships (ships used during WWII, carrying light armament but not meeting the criteria established by the Geneva Conventions for the designation of hospital ship because they carried troops and sometimes arms in combination with injured) (U.S. NAVY, 2011b). During the Vietnam conflict, the US modified barracks ships, originally planned to be riverine hospital ships, but ultimately only refitted one ship for hospital purposes.[6] These ships performed dual roles, such as ferrying injured troops away from combat zones and troops and military supplies into combat zones, again not meeting Geneva Convention designations as hospital ships.

Thus, the first key to understanding today's view of hospital ships draws from understanding the desire of countries to provide maritime medical support to troops near combat zones and the 1949 status accorded to hospital ships as legally protected vessels under the Geneva Convention (Convention (II) for the Amelioration of the Condition of Wounded, Sick and Shipwrecked Members of Armed Forces at Sea, 1949).

The second key comes from recognizing that most medical ships originate from converted passenger and commercial (trade) or combat vessels. As far back as the 17th and 18th centuries, most countries have converted ships for medical use rather than designing and building ships specifically for medical support.[7] For example, in 1798, the British government ordered the HMS *Victory* to be converted to a hospital ship to hold wounded French and Spanish prisoners of war. Even today, the US government uses two converted oil tankers as hospital ships. We found only one instance where the US government constructed a ship specifically as a hospital ship: the Philadelphia Navy Yard manufactured the USS *Relief* (AH-1) in 1917 (commissioned in 1919).

Thirdly, technology plays a key role in today's view of hospital ships. During World War II operations, American forces brought into service higher level medical care in the form of "floating hospitals" in the Pacific since bases were far apart and hospitals on land in short supply (update from: Convention (II) for the Amelioration of the Condition of Wounded, Sick and Shipwrecked Members of Armed Forces at Sea, 1949). At the same time, US military leaders recognized the extent to which helicopters could provide military capabilities, including rapid transport of injured troops to medical support facilities. The Australian Royal Flying Doctor Service, established in 1928, pioneered the use of helicopters for medical transport, flying doctors to patients and patients to hospitals from remote areas of the Australian outback (Royal Flying Doctor Service, 2011). Towards the end of World War II, the US Army built upon this early use of helicopters in the China–Burma–India Theater of World War II, using Sikorsky R-4 helicopters to transport troops from Burma to semi-permanent field hospitals immediately behind the front lines (Weidenburner, 2008). After only a short flight, injured personnel received advanced medical care close to combat areas. The demand for advanced medical support near theater operations linked with advances in aviation technology resulted in today's view that large hospital ships provide superior medical care to American troops nearly anywhere in the world. This key helps to explain why today's leaders express the need for sea-based hospitals capable of providing comprehensive medical and surgical treatment for injured forces (Society for the History of Navy Medicine, 2010).

These three keys together frame the current discussion on the role and characteristics of today's hospital ships: ships provide a necessary and protected component of medical care that can be located all over the world; they tend to be converted ships; they provide services and have capacity similar to a land-based hospital; and they can be easily reached by helicopter. Future plans of policy makers should be informed by these three keys as, to a large extent, they explain Navy and other government leaders' views of hospital ships.

Modern-day hospital ships: USNS Mercy and USNS Comfort

Today, the US, China and Russia are the only countries with navies operating large hospital ships; these are "almost inevitably hulls converted or adapted from other purposes" (ibid.).[8] The US ships, *Mercy* (T-AH 19) and *Comfort* (T-AH 20) are the third ships of the same names, commissioned in 1986 and 1987, respectively. The Navy converted them to service from oil tankers made in 1975 and 1976 (US Navy, 2008).

Just slightly smaller than an aircraft carrier, the hospital ships are the third largest ship in the US Navy. Approximately 900 feet long (the length of three American football fields), the hospital ships measure in height the equivalent of a 10-story building (ibid.), with a distance from the mast to the water line of 124 feet when fully loaded (National Capital Consortium Pediatric Residency Program, 2011). Each ship is painted with nine red crosses, each 27 feet long.

Comfort's propeller weighs 53 tons and is designed to offset a displacement of 39,000 tons of water as the ship moves through the sea. Thirty-five thousand tons of sea water stabilize the ship, weighing more than the ship itself. Size, shape and other ship characteristics make hospital ships stable, permitting most surgical procedures in varying sea conditions. However, the characteristics that make the ship stable also mean less ability to maneuver and a slow steaming speed of just over 17 knots (Global Security, 2011).

Ships are equipped with a helicopter deck capable of landing large military helicopters. Generally, however, the ships do not have dedicated helicopters.[9] Although hospital ships have side ports to take on patients at sea, difficulties in transporting patients during rough weather or while underway commonly prohibit these transfers.

Each ship is designed to receive 200 patients per day and has bed capacity of up to 1,000. Each contains 12 fully-equipped operating rooms, digital radiological services, a medical laboratory, a pharmacy, an optometry lab, a CAT-scan and two oxygen producing plants. Nine elevators carry up to 25 ambulatory patients or six patients on stretchers. Four distilling plants on each ship turn 300,000 gallons of sea water a day into fresh water (National Capital Consortium Pediatric Residency Program, 2011).

Military Sealift Command (MSC) operates the ships, with technical control of the medical treatment facility (MTF) exercised by the chief, Bureau of Medicine and Surgery. Civilian mariners crew the ships and Navy military personnel staff the MTF (US Navy, 2011c). When not activated and in reduced operating status (ROS), the *Mercy* is located in San Diego and the *Comfort* in Baltimore, MD, both within 50 miles of their respective supporting naval medical hospital (Global Security, 2011). When in ROS, 18 mariners and 58 naval medical personnel man the ships. When in full operating status (FOS), 65 mariners and up to 1,215 medical personnel deploy (US Navy, 2008).

Policies affecting hospital ships

US leaders well understand that working towards world peace and security requires different approaches to today's challenges. Policymakers today refer to "smart power," a combination of military force or hard power and diplomacy or soft power (Nye, 2004). Crocker, Hampson and Aall state that smart power "involves the strategic use of diplomacy, persuasion, capacity building, and the projection of power and influence in ways that are cost-effective and have political and social legitimacy" (Crocker, Hampson, & Aall, 2007, p. 13). This vision for improving US and world security suggests that numerous forms of diplomatic and military operations and assets can have value for enhancing peace and stability. Combatant commanders and US leaders view the hospital ships, with their large capacity, great capabilities and symbol of neutrality and stateliness as very valuable assets for these types of missions. Given this wider view of missions and alternatives, government organizations continue to adjust their policies and guidance on civil–military operations, including HA/DR and medical and security cooperation. Although military forces have executed these types of missions for over 100 years, a relatively large number of new or changed policies address the integration of soft and hard power to meet current and future challenges. Many of these policies affect the use of hospital ships.

National Security Presidential Directive 44 (NSPD-44) (Federation of American Scientists, 2005), "Management of Interagency Efforts Concerning Reconstruction and Stabilization" and Title XVI of the 2009 National Defense Authorization require "DoD and other U.S. government agencies to be prepared to work closely together on international stability operations including HA and healthcare reconstruction efforts" (Pueschel, 2011c). These provide the foundation for US agencies to build interagency capabilities and to work to harmonize strategies, goals and execution plans. DoD Directive 3000.05 (US Department of Defense, 2005), issued shortly after NSPD-44, requires DoD organizations to give global health stability and humanitarian operations a comparable priority to combat operations.

In response to DoDD3000.05, DoD leaders created the International Health Division under the Assistant Secretary of Defense for Health Affairs (ASD(HA)). Responsibilities of this division include developing global DoD health policies and providing research to the ASD(HA) on topics including international health stability, security, transition, and reconstruction operations (SSTRO); global HA/DR operations; and foreign medical capacity building missions. In addition, the agency fosters ties among combatant commanders, the ASD(HA), and personnel from the Department of State, NGOs, host nation ministries of health, and other US interagency partners(PUESCHEL, M., 2011c) (Pueschel M. , 2011c).

The Quadrennial Defense Review (QDR) of 2006 translated national defense strategy into additional policies and initiatives. In particular, it stated that the DoD should bring "all the elements of U.S. power to bear to win the long war [...including] foreign aid, humanitarian assistance, post-conflict stabilization and reconstruction" (US Department of Defense, 2009, p.90). Priorities cited include shaping choices of countries at strategic crossroads and suggest that smart power promotes counter-insurgency efforts by permitting intelligence gathering, legitimizing foreign governments through the construction of clinics and clean water facilities, human health provisions, and animal health care (ibid.).

In November of 2007, Secretary of Defense Robert Gates noted, "military success is not sufficient to win [...] providing basic services to the people [...] are essential ingredients to success" (Pueschel, 2011c). A number of instructions and directions flowed from these earlier documents and guidance issued from 2006 to 2011 including DoD Instructions 2205.02 and 6000.16, QDR 2010, and parts of the Navy's "A Cooperative Strategy for 21st Century Seapower".

DoD Instruction 2205.02 issued by the Undersecretary for Defense, Policy (US Department of Defense, 2008), stated that humanitarian and civic assistance (HCA) activities will be conducted in conjunction with authorized military operations of the US armed forces in a foreign country, including deployments for training. The missions must complement, not duplicate, other forms of social or economic assistance provided to the host nation by other US departments or agencies. They are to serve the basic economic and social needs of the people of the host nation. They will promote, as determined by the Secretary of Defense (SECDEF) or secretaries of military departments, activities that serve the security and foreign policy interests of the US and the security interests of the host country.[10]

The Navy's vision for 21st-century seapower includes a section on security, stability and sea-basing, which states that maritime forces are the first line of defense with the ability to deploy quickly and reach difficult locations. The strategy also states that "trust and cooperation cannot be surged. They must be built over time so that the strategic interests of the participants are continuously considered while mutual understanding and respect are promoted" (US Navy, 2007). Navy key maritime strategies include providing humanitarian assistance and disaster response training (Pueschel, 2011b).

The current, 2010 QDR specifically emphasizes building partnership capacity, strengthening DoD support to civilian-led operations and activities, and improving the US's global force posture. One of the policies issued from 2006 and 2010 guidance, DoD Instruction 6000.16 Military Health Support for Stability Operations, May 17, 2010, USD(P&R), "directs the MHS [Military Health System] to prepare to establish and maintain the health sector capacity and capability of other countries when the local population, international or US civilian agencies cannot do so, and to support and collaborate closely with other US departments, foreign governments and security forces, nongovernmental and regional organizations" (Pueschel, 2010). "The new policy elevates the importance of such military health support in stability operations, called Medical Stability Operations (MSOs), to a DoD priority that is comparable with combat operations" (ibid.).

Finally, the National Military Strategy 2011 (NMS) vision states "Our military power is most effective when employed in support and in concert with other elements of power as part of whole-of-nation approaches to foreign policy" (US Department of Defense, 2011).

Across the same time period, organizations outside DoD issued their own policies, reports and instructions based on their own mandates and missions, some of which address or may affect the use of hospital ships. As these interagency missions continue to evolve, policy from organizations outside DoD change, further impacting hospital ship missions. For example, Section 1207 of the FY 2006 National Defense Authorization Act authorized the SECDEF to transfer up to $100 million per year for two years to the Department of State for programs that support security, reconstruction or stabilization. At the same time, the State Department proposed the Civilian Stabilization Initiative (CSI, now renamed the Conflict Stabilization Operations or CSO), which continues to receive funding today. (The FY 2012 budget request includes $92.2 million for CSO.) The Obama administration views CSO capacity as an essential part of the tools of soft power projection, allowing the State Department to focus on diplomacy and permitting the Defense Department to focus on its core military mission responsibilities.[11]

The Congressional Research Service (CRS) Order Code RL34639 discusses the effects of DoD activities on foreign relations and foreign policy goals. While it notes that providing rapid assistance following disasters and other humanitarian emergencies promotes an image of the US as a humanitarian actor, it also notes that the use of military forces may impede progress towards foreign policy goals (ibid., p. 23). For example, one report states that "African publics and governments have already begun to complain that US engagement is increasingly military" (Loftus, 2007). The report further states that using military personnel in state-building activities "may convey mixed signals in activities where the objective is to promote democracy and enhance civilian control" (Congressional Research Service, 2008, p. 24). One study cited in this report found that in crisis situations, civilians provide "the most suitable medical response [...] and water and sanitation" (OECD/DAC, 1998). The same study concluded that using military assets to provide humanitarian assistance in conflict situations is generally more costly than using civilian assets. The CRS report notes that DoD-requested new or expanded authorities relevant to HA for FY 2009 sustain or extend the use of military forces in providing HA. In sum, the report suggests reasons for and against the expansion or continued use of military assets in providing HA/DR, which may be useful context for today's policymakers.

As Stavridis observes "[the] 21st century presents […] unprecedented opportunity to define and shape new means and capabilities that will best achieve US national security objectives in an era of transnational and unconventional threats" (Stavridis, 2010, p. 135). However, this evolving interagency work contributes to incomplete or conflicting strategy and policy guidance for hospital ships (and other organizations) from top levels of the government and military. Because so many policies and organizations come into play in HA/DR situations, and because the nature of medical combat support is also evolving, it is not surprising that government officials do not provide clear goals and objectives for hospital ships, nor do they require clear measures of cost and effectiveness of hospital ship missions.

Goals, desired outcomes and externalities

In this section, we summarize the reasons given (in literature and from discussions with Navy and DoD personnel) for the use of hospital ships in various capacities. Goals for hospital ships vary depending on mission type, location, partners, and a number of other factors, sometimes on a case-by-case basis, and are not often explicitly stated. Many of the reasons given and resultant goals overlap, which in some cases makes distinctions among them difficult. Bearing these commonalities in mind, we hypothesize what the reasons given state or imply about goals and desired outcomes of different types of missions and how the Navy measures activities in support of these reasons. We suggest positive externalities and possible problems or issues that arise as a result of pursuing each goal. Finally, we present a short discussion on the inputs, costs of operations, outputs and, in a very few cases, outcomes of hospital ship missions.

Reasons attributed to and goals for hospital ship missions

Table 9.3 shows eight goals, describing the reasons Navy and US leaders give for different ship missions. Goals 1a and 1b address the hospital ships' primary mission from the aspects of providing US troops with state-of-the-art medical care in a combat zone and providing training opportunities for US medical personnel. Goals 2a–2d focus on planned humanitarian assistance missions. Goal 3 concentrates on providing emergency disaster relief services, and Goal 4 discusses the symbolic neutrality of the hospital ships for HA/DR missions.

Goal 1a: Providing highest level of medical care in a combat area
The declared reason for undertaking the primary mission, Goal 1a, states that the Navy should provide the highest possible level of military medical care in or near a combat area. The Navy's desired outcome is to provide the best possible health and life outcomes for military personnel injured in combat; however, associating hospital ship care with longer-term health outcomes is problematic when injuries require evacuation to a higher-level facility.

Table 9.3 Goals for the use of hospital ships

Goal	Stated or implied reason(s) for mission	Suggested goal(s)	Policy / mission type	Possible desired outcome(s)	
1a	To provide highest level of military medical care in a combat area	Providing best medical care in combat zone	Primary mission: Medical - Combat support	Best health and life outcomes for military personnel injured in combat	
1b	To train medical personnel while providing medical care to host nation(s)	Providing appropriate medical assistance; providing new/ different training situations and opportunities for military medical personnel	HA w/ training in support of primary mission	Best health and life outcomes for military personnel injured in combat; New medical knowledge of deployed medical personnel; Better understanding of Navy/military operations (perhaps by survey of deployed medical personnel)	
2a	To improve health conditions (people and animals)	Providing planned humanitarian / medical assistance in line with host nation, U.S. and possibly international community goals	Smart Power - HA	Meet Millennium Development Goals or those of host nation; Medical and other health or veterinary outcomes; long-term care and health security improvements	
2b	To improve medical training and facilities in-country	Providing planned humanitarian / medical training and construction assistance	Smart Power - HA	Changes (over time and in direct relation to training) in medical outcomes for patients receiving services in-country	

How currently described or measured	Possible positive externalities	Possible problems or issues
Medical services received; timeliness; in some instances, outcomes (returned to duty, medically retired, deceased)	Possible help to other combatants, civilians	Dependent on helo support provided by other organizations; limited helo operations; slow speed, lack of maneuverability; substantial radar signature; staffing and logistics issues
Outputs: services provided (medical, dental, optometry, physical therapy, veterinary procedures performed, medicine dispensed, medical equipment (e.g., glasses, wheel chairs) dispensed); conditions seen	Better services provided for foreign nationals; contacts made for future US deployments	Takes medical personnel from other facilities where they work full time (Bethesda, San Diego, etc.)
Outputs: services provided (medical, dental, optometry, physical therapy, veterinary procedures performed, medicine dispensed, medical equipment (e.g., glasses, wheel chairs) dispensed); in-country personnel trained; Possibly by diagnosis codes, procedures performed compared to what seen in CONUS	Improves host nation's ability to take care of its citizens, improves host nation government's credibility; improves communications and trust; finds common ground, may improve U.S. political situation; attitudes towards Americans	Difficulties in access (helos not provided on Navy ship; difficult to transfer patients by boat; draught of ship too deep to dock close to location where services provided);Lack of proper follow-on care; feelings that selection process is not "fair" or appropriate
Anecdotal experience from ambassadors, State Dept personnel in countries on changed attitudes	Improves host nation's ability to take care of its citizens, improves host nation government's credibility; improves communications and trust; finds common ground, may improve U.S. political situation; attitudes towards Americans	Lack of follow-up on training of local personnel or on maintenance of constructed facilities

continued…

Table 9.3 continued

Goal	Stated or implied reason(s) for mission	Suggested goal(s)	Policy / mission type	Possible desired outcome(s)	
2c	To collaborate / build trust / build partner relationships	Building bridges and relationships; improving interoperability	Smart Power - HA	Change in access to country (for other military assets or other groups); Change in number of work visas granted; Change in time to obtain building and other permits	
2d	To improve attitudes towards Americans and DoD by signaling that we have the resources, desire and capacity to help (Costly signaling)	Winning "hearts and minds"; positive public relations	Smart Power - HA	Change in attitudes over time (as measured by survey); case-by-case reports of changes by US personnel in-country	
3	To show "we care;" Humanitarian concerns	Providing disaster relief services	Smart Power - HA/DR	Change in attitudes over time (as measured by survey); case-by-case reports of changes by US personnel in-country	
4	To provide assistance while maintaining "symbolic neutrality"	Providing any of 2a-3a, planned or unplanned, projecting symbolic neutrality	Smart Power HA/ DR	Survey over time of attitudes towards ship and missions; case-by-case reports of changes by U.S. personnel in-country	

How currently described or measured	Possible positive externalities	Possible problems or issues
Anecdotal experience from ambassadors, State Dept personnel in countries on changed attitudes; one or two studies surveyed individuals and news in receiving countries	Improved communication, trust and common ground (e.g. contacts to provide access, further medical care)	Partner lack of understanding or frustration both on US side (NGOs, other partners) or with foreign governments and individuals
Anecdotal experience from ambassadors, State Dept personnel in countries on changed attitudes; one or two studies surveyed individuals and news in receiving countries	Improves communications and trust; finds common ground, may improve U.S. political situation; attitudes towards Americans	Selection process (or perception of); short- term changes in attitude
Anecdotal experience from ambassadors, State Dept personnel in countries on changed attitudes; one or two studies surveyed individuals and news in receiving countries	Improved communication, trust and common ground; improved political situations if populace likes US better; shows the resources we have ("prestige")	Cannot get there in under a month. "Everyone who was going to die has already died." Carriers and other ships can provide initial services needed.
Not measured	Improved attitudes towards Americans and DoD -- we are willing to work with general population, not just governments	Is a cross (or some other aspect of ships) offensive in some parts of the world or recognized as neutral?

A positive externality of attempting to achieve this goal is that other combatants or civilians in theater may benefit from services provided by the ship's personnel (as seen in Table 9.1). Issues that hinder achievement of Goal 1a include transport bottlenecks to and on the ship (availability of helicopters to transport the injured, difficulties in getting to the ship by sea and limited landing space) (Lawlor et al., 2008; Ward, 2008); slow steaming speed of the ship, making it less flexible to respond to unexpected or sudden conflicts (one month transit time from the US to the Persian Gulf for both the *Mercy* (San Diego, CA) and the *Comfort* (Baltimore, MD); four day travel time from Baltimore, MD, to Haiti); difficulties in preparing the ship to have appropriate staffing, medications, and supplies on board for different situations (Cooperman & Houde, 2008); a large radar signature; and the cost of providing services at sea, particularly when the ship operates well under capacity.

Goal 1b: Providing medical assistance to those in need

One of the reasons used to justify HA/DA missions is the training US medical personnel receive as part of their deployment. We suggest that providing medical assistance to foreign nationals also provides US medical personnel greater exposure and understanding of health conditions, treatments or responses. As such, desired outcomes would not only be better health and life outcomes for foreign nationals, but better health and life outcomes for US military members and their dependents. Other benefits (or outcomes) include better understanding by US medical personnel of the operations and conditions of deployment, and better connections and contacts with foreign medical, non-governmental and government officials, perhaps leading to better relationships and support in the future. What gets measured, however, are services provided (number of patients seen, surgeries provided, etc.). Perhaps comparing diagnosis codes and procedures performed on an HA hospital ship mission with what medical personnel see in CONUS could shed light on whether HA training increases personnel exposure to different health conditions, improving their knowledge of medicine.

A challenging aspect of these deployments results from taking medical personnel from US facilities where they have full-time jobs (from, for example, the National Naval Medical Centers in Bethesda, MD, Portsmouth, VA, and San Diego, CA). This adds to the workload of those not deployed and can have immediate effects on the medical care provided in the US.

Goals 2a–2d: Providing planned humanitarian and medical assistance

Using hospital ships for planned HA missions falls squarely under the policy notion of "smart power." Other phrases justifying these missions include "medical diplomacy," and "winning hearts and minds," a phrase clearly dating back at least as far as US founding father John Adams, who described the American Revolution as being "in the minds and hearts of the people" (Dickinson, 2009). In working towards peace, stability and security in other regions of the world, "medical diplomacy," which policymakers began using as early as the Carter administration, changes people's attitudes about the US (or any country that practices it) (Feinsilver, 2010).[12]

We consider various reasons ascribed to undertaking HA missions using Goals 2a–2d. DoD's general goals for HA missions include (Office of the Assistant Secretary of Defense for Special Operations and Low-Intensity Conflict and the Defense Security Cooperation Agency, 2005):

- Improve DoD visibility
- Improve DoD access to ports and countries
- Generate long-term goodwill and positive public relations
- Promote interoperability
- Coalition building
- Provide experience and functionality for use in disaster relief missions.

Goals 2a and 2b: Improve health conditions and medical training/facilities in country

Goals 2a and 2b, providing planned humanitarian and medical assistance, derive from US officials' stated desire to assist neighboring countries as part of a combatant commanders' (and other US officials') plan to foster security, stability, transition and reconstruction (SSTR) in a country or region. Reasons given for undertaking Goal 2a generally have to do with improving health conditions for people and animals, and mission leaders measure services provided. Desired outcomes include advances in medical and veterinary outcomes, possibly in line with UN Millennium Development Goals (MDG) or host nation goals, and long-term care and health security improvements for foreign nationals, leading to greater "health security." Positive externalities or long-term benefits of providing this help take into account building a foreign government's ability to provide for its own people, increasing its citizens' trust in government, and improving attitudes towards Americans and DoD. However, difficulties in ship access and medical access (understanding the selection process and difficulties in follow-on care) may counter some of the positive effects of undertaking these missions. Some NGOs participating in these types of missions expressed concern that site visits are chosen according to political objectives and provide services according to Navy capabilities rather than serving the populations most in need. In addition, NGO personnel reported being frustrated that some of the patients with the greatest needs did not receive care (Lawlor et al., 2008). Little data exist to support external or long-term benefits – only two follow-up surveys have been conducted to date in Bangladesh and in Indonesia after the deployment of the *Mercy* to these areas (Terror Free Tomorrow, 2006).

Similarly, US leaders reason that improving medical training and facilities (capacity) in-country (Goal 2b) contributes to success of SSTR by improving health conditions, advancing MDGs or host nation goals, improving health security, building the foreign government's capacity and generating goodwill and positive feelings towards Americans and DoD. Measures typically include the number of personnel trained and information about facilities constructed. In this instance, difficulties in ship access have less effect on the success of the missions, but lack of follow-up on performance of trained foreign medical personnel and facilities constructed may result in less benefit to foreign nationals than expected. For example, in the Iraqi medical system, "the US invested $150 million on advanced medical equipment that mostly sits idle because Iraqi doctors are not trained to use it" (McCrummen, 2011). Further, at an American-build maternity hospital, with construction costs of $4 million, Jawad al_Jubouri, a local officer states, "[T]he building is fairly good and the Americans have provided the hospital with a variety of high-tech medical devices, but they did not pay attention to the training of doctors in how to use them" (Williams, 2009).

Goal 2c: Building bridges and relationships

Many commanders and leaders advocate planned HA missions due to their collaborative nature in which the US builds trust and alliances with and increases interoperability among partners and neighbors. These desired outcomes manifest themselves in goals including increased access to the country (for other military units or other groups) or improvements in the way the country does business with the US (work visas granted, number of building permits issued, time to obtain permits or visas, etc.). Achieving these goals depends upon advance planning, cooperation and success with many groups (host nations, local organizations, NGOs, private firms, etc.), and understanding culture, needs, goals and desired outcomes between or among partnering organizations. Improved communications and trust, and finding areas of common ground (such as ways to improve medical care, increased access to decision makers, etc.) can be direct outcomes or positive externalities resulting from pursuing Goal 2c. US officials must take care to understand and work with partners so that lack of understanding and frustration by any partner does not outweigh benefits of the missions.

Goal 2d: Winning "hearts and minds"

Clearly, the phrase "medical diplomacy" encompasses many aspects of the positive feelings foreign nationals have when receiving medical help from another country. "Winning hearts and minds" and "medical diplomacy" imply a public-relations goal, resulting in improved attitudes among local populations and governments towards Americans and US organizations such as the DoD. These improvements result not only from providing medical care, but from showing that the US, with great resources and capacity, is willing to help others. Costly signaling – using an enormous asset operated at great cost – plays a role in winning hearts and minds. "Based on evolutionary and economic theory, within human communities costly signals invoke strong positive feelings within the recipient who may reciprocate indirectly by causing an increase in the prestige of the [...] group sending the signal" (Lawlor et al., 2008). Benefits again include improved communication and trust, and finding common ground, ultimately leading to better political situations involving the US.[13] One of the few extensive polls taken of public opinion (effectiveness measures) after a hospital ship mission comes from Terror

Free Tomorrow, which noted "Indonesians and Bangladeshis overwhelmingly welcomed the US Navy's recent humanitarian mission of the USNS *Mercy* to their shores" (Terror Free Tomorrow, 2006, p. 2). Although no one questions that the hospital ships improve relationships, only a couple of surveys plus anecdotal evidence provided by US and foreign officials substantiate the value of hospital ship HA missions. And while Goals 1b–2d act as "medical diplomacy" or smart power alternatives to building national security, US officials should be wary of how foreign nationals perceive the actions of the US government in its use of hospital ships including the stated and perceived reasons the US provides assistance and other factors related to the appearance and delivery of HA.

Goals 3 and 4: Providing emergency disaster relief and symbolic neutrality

World conditions (natural events or otherwise) sometimes necessitate US involvement in providing basic services and care to foreign nationals in times of emergency. Reasons given for these missions include "how much America cares – as a nation and a people" (US Navy, 2011d) (Goal 3) and that the ships are symbolically neutral (Goal 4). Hospital ships cannot travel quickly enough to provide the first line of response (unless nearby when a disaster occurs), but provide an enormous representation of the resources the US has to help those in need. Desired outcomes for these missions include sustaining life and providing health care resulting in the best life and health outcomes possible. They also have a "costly-signaling" component. Positive externalities may include improving communications and trust, and improving political situations if attitudes of the local population and officials change as a result of the DR mission.

Inputs, costs of operations, outputs and outcomes of hospital ship missions

Input measures such as numbers and types of personnel, numbers of beds, operating rooms, and other descriptive measures are readily available. For primary missions, as we show in Table 9.3, Navy and government leaders can measure effectiveness by following outcomes on the ship's ability to save life and limb, to reduce disease and other non-battle-related injuries, and to return patients to duty quickly and as far forward in theater as possible (Global Security, 2011). Intermediate outcomes such as the ability to stabilize patients for evacuation within operational evacuation guidelines and with minimum delay contribute to the success of longer-term outcomes (ibid.). However, measures of longer-term health outcomes for foreign nationals likely do not exist. Furthermore, attributing improved medical outcomes to experience gained by medical personnel deployed on a particular hospital ship mission in all probability will be impossible to determine.

For HA/DR missions, measuring progress towards MDGs or host nation goals may be possible. As we discussed in the section on goals, however, current procedures generally measure outputs, not outcomes. Tables 9.1 and 9.2 show typical measures of mission success including publically-reported figures on the number of surgeries performed, pairs of eye glasses distributed and number of patients seen. As Goal 2b suggests, counting the number of in-country personnel trained or facilities constructed provide measures of workload or output, but do not translate to measures of effectiveness. Anecdotal evidence from foreign leaders, US ambassadors, State Department personnel in-country and attitudes of other personnel involved in HA/DR missions suggests the missions are effective, but more surveys or studies would provide better evidence on how attitudes, country access and other desired outcomes have been affected over time. Therefore, while the data available provide important information on workload, supplies used, activities and services provided, they generally do not address outcomes, the overall measures of effectiveness for hospital ship deployment.[14]

Cost data for hospital ship missions exist in multiple places. Military Sealift Command has cost estimates on operations, but costs of medicines, other items dispensed and supplies come out of other budgets. Personnel and maintenance costs can be dug out of DoD budgets, but to our knowledge no model summing up the full mission cost of military and civilian personnel, ship operations, supplies, medicines, by mission, exists. To compare the opportunity cost of using the ships for HA/DR with other alternatives, or using the ships in any capacity where an alternative exists, requires better cost data. Articles in the popular press and anecdotal evidence suggest operations costs ranging from $24 million for four months in 2009 to as high as $1 million per day.[15]

The future of Navy hospital ships

We have shown that multiple reasons for hospital ship use drive different types of missions, different goals and desired outcomes, and different external effects. Data reported consist of input, activity, and in some cases, output measures, but generally do not address the desired outcomes.[16] As Pueschel notes, the Navy's humanitarian civic assistance hospital ship missions around the world are evolving (Pueschel, 2011a) and making good decisions about hospital use will increasingly rely on clear goals and measures of effectiveness.

Based on historical perceptions of the roles of the ships, the myriad and sometimes conflicting policies affecting their use, and our assessment of goals and desired outcomes for different missions from Table 9.3, we submit that leaders have not fully developed strategies for optimal use of the hospital ships. Navy and government leaders well understand that the current hospital ships are aging and costly to maintain and operate. Choices for the future of medical care on the seas largely depend on evolving national views and policies on combat support, security, stability and peace, constrained by realities of budgets. In each of the alternative futures we discuss, budget realities may overpower any differing option, thereby relegating the ships to their current or more limited uses. In any case, leaders must be clear about their goals, desired outcomes and measures of success or effectiveness for hospital ship missions so they and the American people get the results they anticipate.

Alternative 1: Buy smaller, more agile ships better suited to current combat support missions

One military view, shared fairly widely in the US and out, holds that smaller, more flexible and more mobile medical units provide a better alternative than sea-based options. If leaders determine the Navy must continue to provide sea-based medical capabilities, smaller, more agile ships represent a good option. As Vice Adm. Michael L. Cowan, the Navy surgeon general and chief of the Bureau of Medicine and Surgery said in 2004, "They're wonderful ships, but they're dinosaurs. They were designed in the '70s, built in the 80s, and frankly, they're obsolete" (Global Security, 2011).

The US, Chinese, British, and German navies increasingly use medical and surgical capabilities built into combat or combat support ships to provide at-sea medical support for operations distant from the home country. Many nations, including Argentina, Denmark and Brazil, operate smaller hospital units (some with flexible configurations allowing use as a mine-layer, mine-clearing operations or medical support ship; Royal Danish Navy, 2011). The US has extensive medical capability in amphibious warfare ships of the LHD, LHA, LPD and LSD classes. Navy leaders are currently studying their options, including trauma treatment spaces on the next generation of amphibious ships.[17]

While smaller ships for combat support may be generally cost-effective to operate, they require procurement, training and new life cycle cost changes, possibly out of reach of current budgets. Retiring the hospital ships may mean fewer training opportunities for medical personnel. More importantly, such a choice puts an end to the ability to provide a large capacity, highly visible, symbolically neutral ship providing medical care to host nations, diminishing public relations, costly signaling, partner-building and other effects listed in Table 9.3.

Alternative 2: Make ship modifications to improve operations

Should military leaders choose to maintain the hospital ships, improvements in flight operations (expansion of the flight deck and dedicated helicopters) would provide greater flexibility in moving patients. Additionally, various Navy components must be clear about roles and responsibility – in a story told to one of the authors by a former MSC commander, the *Comfort* deployed on a disaster relief mission and found that most medications on board were beyond their expiration date. The commander traced this back to a lack of understanding of medical and operational personnel of "who was doing what." Another component to better use of the ships would be to continue Cooperman and Houde's (2008) study on manning, to adequately predict needs for different types of mission. For example, 80 percent of patients treated on the *Comfort* during OIF were Iraqi enemy prisoners of war or civilians. Having to provide unexpected services such as pediatric and obstetric care, and to separate these patients from US troops provided unforeseen challenges for on-board personnel.

Alternative 3: Repurpose the ships for other medical uses

At least one health official has suggested using the *Mercy* to support Guam and the Pacific islands (showing greater US support for the region) and using the *Comfort* to support mainland health care (Lorentzen, 2011). At least one country has set precedence for this – the Spanish Department of Labor operates a large purpose-built hospital ship to serve its fishing and commercial fleets.

Although this option may seem farfetched, one could certainly make the argument that providing medical care to US citizens should be of higher priority than providing free medical care to foreign nationals. In 2009 there were 50.7 million people in the US (16.7 percent of the population) without health insurance (DeNavas-Walt et al., 2010, p. 22). Rather than using the ships during an emergency like Hurricane Katrina or 9/11, perhaps US government officials should facilitate the use of one on a regular basis to provide medical care to needy Americans. A substantial change in mission such as this would require both strategic thinking and resourcing to successfully provide personnel, supplies and other resources required for these new missions.

One advantage of this alternative is that, given proper coordination in staffing, training, supply and strategic thinking, and with some time to change operational status, the ships could be used to support combat or international HA/DR operations on an as-needed basis. An expected downside would be the increased bureaucracy and legal issues inherent in changing the ships to non-traditional, non-military uses.

Alternative 4: Transfer ships to USAID/State Department or other organization

In the long run, the expertise for planning long-term relief and development efforts rests with civilians, and USAID, CSO and other diplomatic personnel likely have better understanding of medical assistance needs throughout the world. Under this scenario, of course, hospital ships would no longer be used for combat support. However, the State Department's severely constrained budget for HA/DR operations, and the current political situation resulting in higher DoD and lower State funding, likely preclude the State's ability to pay for ship operations. A slightly different scenario might result in the lease of smaller commercial ships. Again, however, budget limitations likely prevent this alternative from consideration.

Alternative 5: Sell the ships

Even if a buyer could be found, proceeds from the sale would not pay for a new medical combat support ship. If these missions continue, decision makers have to examine the cost of the new ship, its operating cost and supplies against the proceeds of the sale of the existing ship and the existing ship's operating and supply costs. This is not likely to be a cost-saving endeavor and likely presents a "last resort" option in the event the hospital ships become too outdated to operate.

Conclusions

Today's US Navy hospital ships remain ready to provide emergency, on-site care for deployed US troops. In practical use, however, the ships principally support HA/DR, providing health benefits to foreign nationals and generating smart power in far corners of the world. While this secondary mission provides direct benefits to the US of training military medical personnel and granting access to some areas of the world not permitted in the absence of the HA/DR mission, few studies document direct outcomes such as improved overall health conditions or improved attitudes of non-US citizens. No study substantiates how costs borne by the US Navy accrue to different missions or different outcomes. No definitive research provides cost-benefit or cost-effectiveness analyses of hospital ships relative to other Level III combat support hospitals, and few studies exist that provide information on the cost-effectiveness of HA/DR services delivered.

In this chapter, we examined the use of the hospital ships over time, providing information on the historical view of the role of hospital ships, policies affecting, and goals and desired outcomes for hospital ships missions. We suggested that continued effort towards a whole-of-government strategy will inform Navy planners, combatant commanders and US leaders on the best choices for the use (or non-use) of hospital ships. Without improvements in strategy, these leaders cannot properly task and evaluate whether hospital ships execute missions effectively, efficiently and with the proper staffing and supplies. To gain the best possible effects from hospital ships, strategies must drive clear goals and desired outcomes and inform decision makers on costs. Continued improvement in the alignment of actions and information with policy objectives will better support Navy and US military policies as well as the State Department's public diplomacy priorities.

Notes

1 Multiple factors play into this decision including the severity of the injury, presence of ongoing hostilities, weather conditions, availability of medical air evacuation assets and the distance by ground from the point of injury to the higher-level facility.

2 The US Navy, on its official Navy web site for the USNS *Comfort* "Medical Treatment Facility" states: "Our primary mission […] is to provide a mobile, flexible, and rapidly responsive afloat medical capability for acute medical and surgical care in support of amphibious task forces, Marine Corps, Army and Air Force elements, forward deployed Navy elements of the fleet and fleet activities located in areas where hostilities may be imminent. Operations are governed by the principles of the 'Geneva Convention for the Amelioration of the Wounded, Sick, and Shipwrecked Members of the Armed Forces at Sea' of August 12, 1949."

3 We constructed Tables 9.1 and 9.2 using publicly available data from the following sources: http://www.med.navy.mil/sites/usnscomfort/Pages/default.aspx; http://www.defense. gov/news/newsarticle.aspx?id=65236; http://www.haiticomfort.blogspot.com/; http:// reliefweb.int/node/392551; http://www.southcom.mil/AppsSC/factfiles.php?id=103; http://www.southcom.mil/AppsSC/factfiles.php?id=6; http://www.med.navy.mil/sites/ usnsmercy/Commandinfo/Pages/CommandHistory.aspx; http://navysite.de/ships/ mercy.htm; http://www.c7f.navy.mil/news/2010/08-august/024.htm

4 Hospital ships also participate in training exercises. For example, "the *Mercy* was activated during Kernel Blitz 97, a major amphibious exercise in Southern California" (Global Security, 2011). Using National Guard and Coast Guard Medevac helicopters, "cosmetically prepared" troops played the role of casualties treated by active duty and reserve medical personnel, moving them through five levels of medical care. The *Comfort* participated in Baltic Challenge '98.

5 Data do not provide explicit information on transit time for these missions. The authors' best guess is at least 15.

6 Unofficially called an auxiliary propulsion barracks hospital.

7 During World War II, the British, Australian, New Zealand, Dutch, French and German governments all converted ships to hospital use, and the US Army commissioned 24 hospital ships converted from civilian use (Society for the History of Navy Medicine, 2010).

8 Large hospital ships today belong to the US (*Mercy* class), China (Type 920) and Russia (Project 320 *Ob'* class).

9 CH-47 helicopters can be placed on the ships, relieving ground forces of the burden of having to transport patients onto the deck of the ship, something they do not regularly train to do (Global Security, 2011).

10 Title 10 of the US Code (USC Section 2557, "Excess nonlethal supplies: availability for homeless veteran initiatives and humanitarian relief" and USC Section 2561, "Humanitarian assistance give the authority to U.S. organizations including DoD to conduct HA/DR and emergency response missions and fund transportation programs" (US Government Printing Office, 2011).

11 The original CSI plan called for funding to build, train, equip, and deploy a 4,250-member interagency Civilian Response Corps. Today's down-sized figure is approximately 300 full-time employees with over 1,000 volunteer diplomats.

12 Medical diplomacy options include all kinds of plans for military assets. For example: "Each one of the Department of Defense's five regional combatant commands should have three hospital ships permanently assigned to their respective areas of responsibility. Why so many, you ask? It's so simple that it can be summed up in two words: medical diplomacy" (US Naval Institute, 2008, 2010).

13 In a nationwide poll of Indonesians conducted after the mission, of those who had heard of the *Mercy*'s visit, a remarkable 85 percent had a favorable opinion. In a similar survey throughout Bangladesh, 95 percent of the people of Bangladesh were favorable to the *Mercy*'s mission (Terror Free Tomorrow, 2006).

14 For more on optimal ship manning under different types of mission scenarios, see Cooperman and Houde (2008).

15 In conjunction with MSC personnel, we hope to be able to provide better cost data to help Navy decision makers analyze their alternatives for providing maritime medical care.

16 Several studies have addressed the lack of clarity on goals of and desired outcomes for humanitarian assistance and hospital ship missions. (See, for example, Drifmeyer and Llewellyn (2003), Webb and Richter (2010) and McGrady and Strauss (2007).

17 Global Security notes that, because of the way the ships were converted from oil tankers, patient movement within the ship is severely limited. Lower bulkheads do not have hatches because they were designed to carry oil. Without the hatches, patients must be moved to the top deck to be moved from a lower compartment in one part of the ship to another (Global Security, 2011).

References

Borden Institute. 2004. *Emergency War Surgery, Third United States Revision*. Washington, DC: Borden Institute, Walter Reed Army Medical Center.

Congressional Research Service. 2008a. *Congressional Research Service Report for Congress Order Code RL34639.* [online]. [Accessed 5 October 2011]. Available from: <http://fpc.state.gov/documents/organization/110406.pdf>

Congressional Research Service. 2008b. *The Department of Defense role in foreign assistance: Background, major issues and options for Congress.* [online]. [Accessed 7 October 2011]. Available from: <http://opencrs.com/document/RL34639/>

Convention (II) for the Amelioration of the Condition of Wounded, Sick and Shipwrecked Members of Armed Forces at Sea [1949].

Cooperman, K. & Houde, L. 2008. *A strategic approach to humanitarian medical manpower planning.* Monterey, CA: Naval Postgraduate School Thesis, March.

Crocker, C.A., Hampson, F.O. & Aall, P.R. 2007. *Leashing the dogs of war: Conflict management in a divided world.* Washington, DC: US Institute of Peace Press.

DeNavas-Walt, C., Proctor, B.D. & Smith, J.C. 2010. *Income, poverty and health insurance coverage in the United States: 2009.* [online]. [Accessed 25 October 2011]. Available from: <http://www.census.gov/prod/2010pubs/p60-238.pdf>

Dickinson, E. 2009. *A Bright Shining Slogan.* [online]. [Accessed 11 September 2011]. Available from: <http://www.foreignpolicy.com/articles/2009/08/13/a_bright_shining_slogan>

Drifmeyer, J. & Llewellyn, C. 2003. Overview of overseas humanitarian, disaster and civic aid programs. *Military Medicine*, pp. 975–980.

Federation of American Scientists. 2005. *National Security Presidential Directives.* [online]. [Accessed 30 September 2011]. Available from: <http://www.fas.org/irp/offdocs/nspd/nspd-44.html>

Feinsilver, J. 2010. *Let's have a fleet of 15 hospital ships.* [online]. [Accessed 16 September 2011]. Available from: <http://blog.usni.org/2010/01/21/lets-have-a-fleet-of-15-hospital-ships/>

Global Security. 2011. *T-AH 19 Mercy Class.* [online]. [Accessed 30 September 2011]. Available from: <http://www.globalsecurity.org/military/systems/ship/tah-19.htm>

Lawlor, A., Kraus, A. & Kwast, H. 2008. *Navy-NGO coordination for health-related HCA missions: A suggested planning framework. CRM D0018127.A4/1REV.* Alexandria, VA: Center for Naval Analysis.

Loftus, G. 2007. Speaking out: Expeditionary sidekicks? The military-diplomatic dynamic. *Foreign Service Journal*, December, p. 16.

Lorentzen, Thomas. 2011.

McCrummen, S. 2011. *At Iraq's hospitals, a man-made emergency.* [online]. [Accessed 25 October 2011]. Available from: <http://www.washingtonpost.com/world/middle-east/at-iraqs-hospitals-a-man-made-emergency/2011/04/19/AFFv0PcG_story.html>

McGrady, E.D. & Strauss, D.J. 2007. *USNS Mercy humanitarian deployment: What is the meaning of Naval engagement? CRM DOO 5594.A4/1 Rev. April.* Alexandria, VA: Center for Naval Analysis.

National Capital Consortium Pediatric Residency Program. 2011. *Visit the USNS Comfort.* [online]. [Accessed 30 September 2011]. Available from: <http://www.nccpeds.com/>

Nye, J. 2004. *Soft power: the means to success in world politics.* Cambridge, MA: Public Affairs, Perseus Books Group.

OECD/DAC. 1998. *Civilian and military means of providing and supporting humanitarian assistance during conflict: Comparative advantages and costs.* Paris: OECD.

Office of the Assistant Secretary of Defense for Special Operations and Low-Intensity Conflict and the Defense Security Cooperation Agency. 2005. *Policy and program management direction for FY2005, OHDACA planning and execution, section 3B.* Washington, DC: US Department of Defense.

Pueschel, M. 2010. *New DoD policy outlines military health support in global stability missions.* [online]. [Accessed 20 September 2011]. Available from: <http://home.fhpr.osd. mil/press-newsroom/media_releases/archived_media/10-05-24/New_DoD_Policy_ Outlines_Military_Health_Support_in_Global_Stability_Missions.aspx?id=?id=>

Pueschel, M. 2011a. *Pacific Health Mission Progresses Despite Platform Change.* [online]. [Accessed 5 October 2011]. Available from: <http://fhp.osd.mil/intlhealth/article. jsp?articleID=70>

Pueschel, M. 2011b. *Comfort Mission Shows Renewed MHS Humanitarian Focus.* [online]. [Accessed 30 September 2011]. Available from: <http://fhp.osd.mil/intlhealth/news. jsp?newsID=112>

Pueschel, M. 2011c. *International health stability becoming new DoD priority.* [online]. [Accessed 29 September 2011]. Available from: <http://fhp.osd.mil/intlhealth/news. jsp?newsID=118>

Riske, Milt. 1973. A History of hospital ships. *Sea Classics,* March.

Royal Danish Navy. 2011. *Navy Admiral Danish Fleet.* [online]. [Accessed 29 September 2011]. Available from: <http://forsvaret.dk/SOK/Enheder/ABSL/ABSL_10/ Pages/2010-01-28_absl.aspx>

Society for the History of Navy Medicine. 2010. *Of Ships & Surgeons.* [online]. [Accessed 20 September 2011]. Available from: <http://ofshipssurgeons.wordpress. com/2010/09/29/on-hospitals-in-ships/>

Stavridis, J.G. 2010. *Partnership for the Americas: Western Hemisphere Strategy and U.S. Southern Command.* Washington, DC: National Defense University Press.

Terror Free Tomorrow. 2006. *Unprecedented Terror Free Tomorrow Polls: World's Largest Muslim Countries Welcome US Navy.* [online]. [Accessed 9 October 2011]. Available from: <http:// www.terrorfreetomorrow.org/upimagestft/Final%20Mercy%20Poll%20Report.pdf>

US Department of Defense. 2005. *DoD 3000.05 Military Support for Stability, Security, Transition, and Reconstruction (SSTR).* Washington, DC: Department of Defense.

US Department of Defense. 2008. *DoD Instruction 2205.02 Humanitarian and Civic Assistance (HCA) Activities.* Washington, DC: US DoD, USD(P).

US Department of Defense. 2009. *Quadrennial Roles and Missions Review Report.* [online]. [Accessed 19 September 2011]. Available from: <http://www.defense.gov/news/ Jan2009/QRMFinalReport_v26Jan.pdf>

US Department of Defense. 2011. *The National Military Strategy of the United States of America 2011.* [online]. [Accessed 5 October 2011]. Available from: <http://www.jcs.mil/ content/files/2011-02/020811084800_2011_NMS_-_08_FEB_2011.pdf>

US Government Printing Office. 2011. *United States Code, 2006 Edition, Supplement 4, Title 10 – Armed Forces.* [online]. [Accessed 26 October 2011]. Available from: <http://www.gpo.gov/fdsys/search/pagedetails.action;jsessionid=v9JMT1nCV RvyybF1gxVhwsVTnwqFQC7Xw2BBHcm1Tp1nbdMWQXMH!728675249!- 1958630928?browsePath=Title+10%2FSubtitle+A%2FPart+IV%2FChapter- +152%2FSec.+2561&granuleId=USCODE-2010-title10-subtitleA-partIV-ch>

US Naval Institute. 2008, 2010. *Let's Have a Fleet of 15 Hospital Ships.* [online]. [Accessed 19 September 2011]. Available from: <http://blog.usni.org/2010/01/21/lets-have-a- fleet-of-15-hospital-ships/>

US Navy. 2007. *A Cooperative Strategy for 21st Century Seapower.* [online]. [Accessed 20 September 2011]. Available from: <http://www.navy.mil/maritime/Maritimestrategy. pdf>

US Navy. 2008. *U.S. Navy Factfile.* [online]. [Accessed 19 September 2011]. Available from: <http://www.navy.mil/navydata/fact_display.asp?cid=4400&tid=400&ct=4>

US Navy. 2011a. *USNS Mercy*. [online]. [Accessed 19 September 2011]. Available from: <http://www.med.navy.mil/sites/usnsmercy/Pages/default.aspx>

US Navy. 2011c. *Military Sealift Command*. [online]. [Accessed 30 September 2011]. Available from: <http://www.msc.navy.mil/pm1/>

US Navy. 2011d. *Medical Centers*. [online]. [Accessed 20 September 2011]. Available from: <http://www.navy.com/about/locations/medical-centers.html>

Ward, P. 2008. *Optimizing ship-to-shore movement for hospital ship humanitarian assistance operations*. Monterey: Naval Postgraduate School.

Webb, N.J. & Richter, A. 2010. Strategy at the crossroads: The case of the Navy hospital ships. *Defense & Security Analysis*, pp. 161–179.

Weidenburner, Carl Warren. 2008. *The Hoverfly in CBI*. [online]. [Accessed 29 September 2011]. Available from: <http://cbi-theater-3.home.comcast.net/~cbi-theater-3/hoverfly/hoverfly.html>

Williams, T. 2009. *U.S. Fears Iraqis will not keep up rebuilt projects*. [online]. [Accessed 25 October 2011]. Available from: <http://www.nytimes.com/2009/11/21/world/middleeast/21reconstruct.html?pagewanted=all>

WW2 US Medical Research Centre. 2011. *WW2 Hospital Ships*. [online]. [Accessed 26 September 2011]. Available from: <http://med-dept.com/hosp_ships.php>

Part IV
Post-deployment

10 The history and evolution of traumatic brain injury rehabilitation in military service members and veterans in the United States

*David X. Cifu, Jay P. Granier, Jamie Grimes,
Tammy Crowder, Ajit B. Pai, and Henry L. Lew*

Background

The field of traumatic brain injury (TBI) has evolved since the time of the United States (US) Civil War in response to the needs of patients with injuries and disabilities resulting from war. The Department of Veterans Affairs (VA) and Department of Defense (DoD) through the collaborative efforts of the Defense and Veterans Brain Injury Center (DVBIC) have been in the forefront of the development of the interdisciplinary approach to the rehabilitation of soldiers with TBI, particularly those injured in the recent conflicts in Iraq and Afghanistan. The objectives of this literature review are to examine how the casualties resulting from major wars in the past led to the establishment of the current model of evaluation and treatment of TBI and to review how the field has expanded in response to the growing cohort of young, brain-injured veterans.

Introduction

The essentials of rehabilitation therapies may be traced back nearly two millennia to the ancient Greeks and Romans, who utilized techniques such as massage, electrical currents, heat, and cold to relieve pain (Fialka-Moser, 1999). While deeply rooted in the past, the field of rehabilitation has experienced significant advancements in the past century due to injuries and disability resulting from large-scale wars and the concomitant advances in battlefield medicine that have dramatically increased survival rates. Traumatic brain injury (TBI) rehabilitation has historically lagged behind that of amputation and general orthopedic rehabilitation, but in the last decade there has been a great expansion of TBI services provided to persons serving in the military (Eldar and Jelic, 2003; Hermes, 2002). This literature review examines the influences of major wars on the development of TBI rehabilitation services over the last two centuries, from the US Civil War to the present day conflicts in Iraq and Afghanistan, as well as providing a glimpse into the future of TBI rehabilitation. Building on previous descriptions of the polytrauma and brain injury rehabilitation programs established to provide for the care of combat-injured service members (Schwab et al., 2007; Salazar et al., 2000b; Lew et al., 2007a; Sigford, 2008), this chapter provides an overview of the US Department of Veterans Affairs Polytrauma System of Care.

Historical evolution of TBI rehabilitation in the US military

Prior to the twentieth century, severe TBI was generally considered fatal (Boake, 1989; Walker, 1957). During the US Civil War (1861–1865), gunshot wounds to the head were seen in large numbers, and although accurate statistics for mortality rates are not available, survival was known to be poor (Boake, 1989; Kaufman, 1993). In general, surgeons managed penetrating wounds conservatively in order to avoid introduction of infection, with the exception of removal of foreign material and bone fragments. The lack of qualified surgeons was a practical reason for the prevalence of conservative management. Only one in fifteen doctors was recognized as qualified to operate (Kaufman, 1993).

Despite the high mortality of TBI, a great deal was known about its pathophysiology. Surgical manuals used by physicians on both sides differentiated blunt versus penetrating injuries and described signs and symptoms associated with concussion (primary injury) and compression (secondary injury), including bradycardia, hypertension, labored breathing, and contralateral hemiparesis. Epidural and subdural hematomas were well described, and a Confederate surgeon named John Chisolm discussed the complexities of diffuse axonal injury. Trephination for management of depressed skull fracture was described and the risk of bleeding from the venous sinuses and the middle meningeal artery were recognized (Kaufman, 1993).

Due to the development of improved antiseptic techniques in the later 19th century and more effective neurosurgical techniques, the mortality of a head wound with dural penetration was 35 percent during World War I (1917–1918) (Boake, 1989; Walker, 1957). Also contributing to the increased survival rate of soldiers with penetrating head wounds were the rifles themselves: muzzle velocity was faster and bullets were smaller and more deformable (Lanska, 2009). However, penetrating head wounds still occurred with high frequency due to the insufficient protection to the back of the head afforded by the British "Brodie" helmet and the US Marine Corps Doughboy helmet (Lanska, 2009).

The increased survival rate of individuals with TBI prompted the need for rehabilitation services. Some of the earliest TBI rehabilitation units were established in Germany, the best known of which were directed by Kurt Goldstein in Frankfurt and Walther Poppelreuter in Cologne (Boake, 1989). Poppelreuter emphasized the importance of applying the scientific method in evaluating impairments and the direct remediation of neuropsychological disorders. Goldstein advocated correlation of the results of neuropsychological testing with performance during work activities, simultaneous treatment of cognitive deficits and maladaptive personality traits, and the use of preserved abilities to compensate for deficits (Boake, 1989; Boake and Diller, 2005; Prigatano, 2005). These rehabilitation units were based on providing coordinated services and community reentry in the form of vocational workshops and emphasized the need for systematic, long-term follow up (Boake, 1989; Boake and Diller, 2005). Many patients were followed through World War II, and the programs were largely successful in returning veterans to work after the war. Goldstein reported World War I veterans followed by his unit returning to work at a rate of 73 percent in their pre-injury occupation and 17 percent in a different occupation with only 10 percent failing to return to work (Boake and Diller, 2005).

Early US rehabilitation attempts were closely modeled after the German system. However, TBI rehabilitation in the United States lagged behind due to the country's late entry into WWI and interdisciplinary conflict between orthopedic surgeons and vocational specialists. A system of military rehabilitation hospitals in which all aspects of rehabilitation would be under medical control was proposed at the beginning of the war but never created due to opposition from vocational educators. Rehabilitation services, which often consisted of little more than custodial care, were instead provided within general military hospitals. The only hospital providing specialized TBI rehabilitation was the Hospital for Head Surgery in Cape May, New Jersey, which employed three speech correction teachers and did significant work in aphasia, treating approximately 50 patients from 1918 to 1919 (Boake, 1989).

Unfortunately, by the start of World War II (1941–1945), most of these TBI rehabilitation centers, as well as general rehabilitation hospitals, had closed. Early in the course of WWII, TBI casualties received only physiotherapy for motor difficulties; patients with significant cognitive or behavioral impairments were sent to mental institutions (Eldar and Jelic, 2003). However, with the acute neurosurgical mortality from brain wounds having dropped to 10–13 percent, there was once again a need for specialized TBI centers (Carey et al., 1974). In the United Kingdom, brain injury units were established in Oxford and Edinburgh and produced important research on posttraumatic amnesia, aphasia therapy, and prognostic factors (Boake, 1989). Working in the Soviet Union, Luria developed diagnostic and therapeutic techniques centered upon identifying the specific deficit underlying the dysfunction of overlapping cognitive systems and utilizing unaffected aspects of those systems to perform impaired functions (Prigatano, 2005).

In 1943, a speech disorder unit was established in affiliation with a neurosurgical center at Brooke General Hospital in Fort Sam Houston in San Antonio, Texas, which included an interdisciplinary treatment regimen of physical therapy, physiotherapy, vocational therapy, and occupational therapy; there were thirteen more such units by 1944–1945 (Boake, 1989). A psychiatrist named John Aita asserted that only a small percentage of patients with TBI were incapable of independent living, and established a post-acute head injury rehabilitation program in a military general hospital that utilized the interdisciplinary system of care, in which patients were treated by a team of physical and occupational therapists, psychologists, vocational specialists, a social worker, a physician, and a case manager; the program also incorporated participation from relatives as well as therapeutic trials at home. Aita asserted that the goal of his TBI rehabilitation program was "to restore the experience of usefulness, social acceptance and happiness in any individual long ill and struggling with a residual disturbance of important function" (Aita, 1946). Job therapy was established, which resulted in 60 percent of patients having enrolled in school or returned to work on follow-up.

Aita stressed the importance of adjustment support and long-term follow-up, noting that "it means little to save a life, cover a skull defect, and to give a man veterans' compensation if the adjustment and reintegration of that individual are neglected" (Aita, 1946). His warning went unheeded as, once again, at the conclusion of the war, these rehabilitation programs were shut down (Boake, 1989). However, the efforts of military physicians to provide specialized rehabilitation services for injured soldiers during World War II were the driving force behind the creation of physical medicine and rehabilitation as a medical specialty and the establishment of the American Board of Physical Medicine in 1947 (Opitz et al., 1997). Another consequence of World War II rehabilitation efforts was acceleration in the development of physical therapy, occupational therapy, speech-language pathology, neuropsychology, and vocational rehabilitation as independent rehabilitation disciplines (Boake and Diller, 2005).

During the Korean War (1950–1953), the mortality from head injuries continued to fall. Due to the efforts of Australian-born neurosurgeon Hugh Cairns, helmets had become mandatory (Lanska, 2009). Further, it was recognized that rapid relief of a hematoma was key to reducing mortality (Meirowsky, 1954). Employment of mobile teams at the division level to evacuate hematomas resulted in a drop in the rate of meningiocerebral infections from 42 percent to less than 1 percent over the course of the Korean War (Meirowsky, 1954). By the Vietnam War, it was established that 40 percent of combat fatalities were due to head and neck injuries, and 14 percent of those surviving had TBI (Schwab et al., 2007; 1993). Moreover, survival of these soldiers was improved due to the establishment of air evacuation of the wounded (Ruff, 2005).

At the same time, an increased incidence of high-speed motor vehicle accidents propelled a more rapid development of rehabilitation for TBI in the private sector (Lewin, 1968). In the 1970s, acute head injury rehabilitation units such as the Rancho Los Amigos Hospital near Los Angeles were established in response to increased survival from motor vehicle accidents. The cognitive rehabilitation protocols at these facilities formed the basis of modern rehabilitation and included the introduction of sensory stimulation programs for comatose patients (Boake, 1989). Between 1980 and 1990, TBI rehabilitation was established as a subspecialty of rehabilitation medicine (Cope et al., 2005).

During the Persian Gulf War (1991), brain injuries made up 17 percent of casualties (Dillingham, 2002). In 1992, there were 4,208 admissions for TBI in military medical centers (Ommaya et al., 1996). It was noted that the military population was at higher risk for TBI due to combat, with certain military occupations such as parachuting incurring an even greater risk (Schwab et al., 2007). In order to address the need for TBI rehabilitation, in 1992 the Defense and Veterans Head Injury Program, later renamed the Defense and Veterans

Brain Injury Center (DVBIC), was established as a collaboration between the DoD, the Department of Veterans Affairs (DVA), and civilian partners, with the goal to integrate specialized TBI care, research, and education across the military, veteran, and civilian medical care systems (Schwab et al., 2007; Salazar et al., 2000b).

The DVBIC has established clinical standards and guidelines for TBI. The DVBIC's efforts have included the Military Acute Concussion Evaluation, an in-theater TBI screening tool, a toll-free TBI helpline, an integrated follow-up program, a standardized TBI core evaluation battery, and a standardized TBI screening instrument (Salazar et al., 2000b). The DVBIC also conducted the first large randomized trial of TBI rehabilitation based on casualties from the Persian Gulf war and non-combat injuries in service members and veterans during this time period (mid-1990s) (Salazar et al., 2000a). The significant increase in combat and non-combat service member TBIs that have occurred over the last decade allowed DVBIC to gain significant experience in evaluating and treating various TBI populations which has been applied to help the casualties of the Iraq and Afghanistan conflicts.

Development of innovative rehabilitation services

Operation Enduring Freedom in Afghanistan commenced in October 2001 followed by Operation Iraqi Freedom in May of 2003 (Clark et al., 2007). Nearly two million military personnel have been deployed to Iraq or Afghanistan, and TBI has been labeled the "signature wound" of the current conflicts (Lew et al., 2007a).

The combat operations in Iraq and Afghanistan have resulted in a complex pattern of blast-related injuries from artillery, improvised explosive devices, mines, and rocket-propelled grenades (DVBIC, 2011c). Over 60 percent of blast injuries result in a TBI (Sayer et al., 2008). Injuries to the brain due to blasts can occur by primary blast wave-induced changes in atmospheric pressure, shrapnel or other fragments projected from the blast, or when the individual is thrown as a result of the explosion (Kocsis and Tessler, 2009). There have been 2,288 severe and 36,752 moderate brain injuries suffered by the US Armed Services from 2000 through mid-2011, and it is estimated that up to 20 percent of deployed service members, or more than 169,000 service members (DVBIC, 2011a), may have mild TBI from blast injury. For this reason, although initial rehabilitation treatment efforts were aimed at moderate to severe brain injury, the focus of rehabilitation efforts has shifted to include less severe cases with no radiological evidence of brain injury as well (Samson, 2006). Blast-related mild TBI has been found to be associated with several common concurrent conditions, such as vestibular, auditory, and visual dysfunction, which have been an additional focus of research and novel treatment approaches (Fausti et al., 2009; Lew et al., 2009a).

In response to the large number of returning service members presenting with TBI complicated by multiple concomitant injuries, Congress allocated funding to provide state-of-the-art care and rehabilitation in the VA in 2005 (Lew et al., 2007b) and this funding was utilized to develop the Polytrauma System of Care (PSC). Polytrauma is defined as injury to two or more physical regions or organ systems that occur simultaneously, one or more being life threatening, and frequently includes TBI (Sigford, 2008). The Polytrauma System of Care was designed to balance access with specialized expertise in TBI and is comprised of four components: Polytrauma Rehabilitation Centers (PRC), Polytrauma Network Sites (PNS), Polytrauma Support Clinic Teams (PSCT), and Polytrauma Points of Contact (PPOC). It incorporated the existing expertise of the pre-existing VA Traumatic Brain Injury Lead Centers that had been providing brain injury rehabilitation services to veterans and the military since 1991.

Figure 10.1 summarizes the evolution of the Polytrauma System of Care. The initial four Polytrauma Regional Centers (PRCs) were formally designated in February of 2005 at Veterans Administration Medical Centers (VAMC) in Minneapolis, MN, Palo Alto, CA, Richmond, VA, and Tampa, FL (Sigford, 2008). A fifth polytrauma center was established in October 2011 in San Antonio, TX (Lew et al., 2007a). The PRCs are acute inpatient rehabilitation units with CARF (Commission on the Accreditation of Rehabilitation Facilities; an international, independent, non-profit accreditor of health and human services) accreditation in comprehensive TBI care and specializing in the rehabilitation of the combat-injured polytrauma and TBI patient. These centers also provide residential community reentry services through their Polytrauma Transitional Rehabilitation Programs (PTRP). The PNSs were designated in December of 2005 to provide subacute inpatient rehabilitation as well as outpatient services for polytrauma and TBI patients. They were designated to correspond with existing regional administrative units in VA, the Veterans Integrated Service Networks (VISNs) and were given the additional responsibilities of serving organizational and developmental administrative responsibilities for their respective network. There are currently 23 PNSs providing care to distinct geographical regions (Sigford, 2008), with the San Antonio site opening in October 2011. The PSCTs are outpatient clinic teams dedicated to providing services to polytrauma and TBI patients in their local catchment area. They provide the required follow-up care and case management as long as services are required, which can be for life. As demand grows, new PSCTs are developed and there are currently more than 80 sites. The PPOCs are individuals knowledgeable about polytrauma and TBI patient care and services who serve to direct the care of new referrals to the most appropriate source of care in the system. There is a PPOC at every VAMC that does not serve as one of the other components. In December of 2006, the Veterans Health Administration (VHA) also developed a state-of-the-art Polytrauma Telehealth Network linking VA rehabilitation facilities, resulting in expedited access to care, improved clinical communication, and elimination of unnecessary travel for severely wounded veterans and their families (Darkins et al., 2008).

In addition to providing specialized rehabilitation care, the Polytrauma System of Care (PSC) also developed a cadre of services aimed at easing the transitions from military to civilian life. For example, rehabilitation units were redesigned to

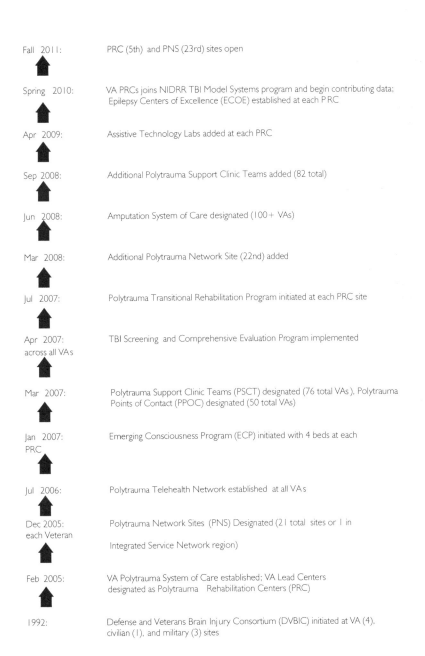

Fall 2011:   PRC (5th) and PNS (23rd) sites open

Spring 2010:   VA PRCs joins NIDRR TBI Model Systems program and begin contributing data; Epilepsy Centers of Excellence (ECOE) established at each PRC

Apr 2009:   Assistive Technology Labs added at each PRC

Sep 2008:   Additional Polytrauma Support Clinic Teams added (82 total)

Jun 2008:   Amputation System of Care designated (100+ VAs)

Mar 2008:   Additional Polytrauma Network Site (22nd) added

Jul 2007:   Polytrauma Transitional Rehabilitation Program initiated at each PRC site

Apr 2007: across all VAs   TBI Screening and Comprehensive Evaluation Program implemented

Mar 2007:   Polytrauma Support Clinic Teams (PSCT) designated (76 total VAs), Polytrauma Points of Contact (PPOC) designated (50 total VAs)

Jan 2007: PRC   Emerging Consciousness Program (ECP) initiated with 4 beds at each

Jul 2006:   Polytrauma Telehealth Network established at all VAs

Dec 2005: each Veteran   Polytrauma Network Sites (PNS) Designated (21 total sites or 1 in Integrated Service Network region)

Feb 2005:   VA Polytrauma System of Care established; VA Lead Centers designated as Polytrauma Rehabilitation Centers (PRC)

1992:   Defense and Veterans Brain Injury Consortium (DVBIC) initiated at VA (4), civilian (1), and military (3) sites

Figure 10.1 Evolution of the polytrauma system of care

promote recognition of the service member's active duty role and commitment and special active duty military liaisons were deployed to VAMCs where care was being provided. In addition, VAMC Social Workers and Rehabilitation Nurses were assigned to the Military Treatment Facilities providing the initial trauma care. Special internet access was provided so that service members could stay in touch with their military comrades, housing for families was provided, and special attention to transitions for the injured service member and their families was made. Each service member was assigned a case manager. These supportive services were an innovation unique to these conflicts. In addition, the development of an organized and integrated system of care allowed broad application of knowledge and best practices to individuals entering the system at any point of care.

As noted above, in addition to service members sustaining moderate to severe TBI, many were returning with mild TBI (mTBI). Some of these individuals were never diagnosed at the time of injury. VHA initiated mandatory screening of all OEF/OIF veterans for TBI in April 2007. If the veteran screened positive for a possible TBI and was still experiencing symptoms, that veteran was then required to be referred to the most appropriate clinical setting in the PSC, if they consented. In this setting, the veteran receives a comprehensive TBI evaluation which includes a detailed history of the injury, a comprehensive physical assessment, and a 22-item post-concussive symptom questionnaire called the Neurobehavioral Symptom Inventory (NSI-22), which helps to direct the plan of care (Cicerone and Kalmar, 1995). The clinics follow the interdisciplinary model and include a physiatrist, a neuropsychologist, a social worker, an occupational therapist, a physical therapist, and a speech-language pathologist (Lew et al., 2007b). In this population of polytrauma patients, treatment is aimed at common post-concussive symptoms such as headache, cognitive problems, and sleep disturbances (Samson, 2006). A written interdisciplinary plan of care is required for all these veterans and each is assigned a case manager. In addition, results of the TBI screen and comprehensive evaluation are entered into the medical record electronically via a specific template that allows standardized recording and later evaluation of additional needs, outcomes, and provision of services at both the individual and system level.

VHA has also funded numerous research initiatives to better understand care and treatment of polytrauma and TBI. Among these is a specialized funding stream named Quality Enhancement Research Initiative (QUERI). QUERI programs are dedicated to implementing best practices across the VHA system. The VHA has funded a Polytrauma/Blast Related Injuries QUERI reflecting the considerable dedication of VHA to understanding and providing effective care to this population of veterans.

Pain in the polytrauma population is currently an area of expanding research and development. Persistent pain has been identified in 42–81 percent of the non-injured military personnel and is nearly universal in polytrauma patients (Gironda et al., 2009). In patients with mTBI, pain was the second most commonly reported impairment after cognitive deficits (Gironda et al., 2009). In a review of patients treated at the Tampa PRC, 96 percent of soldiers had at least one pain problem, 70 percent of those at more than one site (Clark et al., 2007). These pain issues have been addressed with medication, physical and occupational therapy, and to a lesser extent, by use of interventional procedures (Clark et al., 2007).

Psychiatric disorders such as acute stress disorder (ASD) and posttraumatic stress disorder (PTSD) are also often seen co-morbidly with TBI in soldiers, and the relationship between these entities is complex and controversial. The syndrome of psychological and physical impairments resulting from the stress of warfare has been recognized since ancient times and, in the United States, relabeled with each war to reflect various emphases – soldier's heart in the Civil War, shell shock or war neurosis in World Wars I and II, battle fatigue in the Korean War, PTSD in the Vietnam War, Gulf War syndrome in the Persian Gulf War, and post-deployment syndrome in OEF/OIF (Cifu and Blake, 2011). Some researchers have argued that TBI and PTSD are incompatible diagnoses because a patient who has suffered loss of consciousness or amnesia for the injury event cannot re-experience that event, a necessary criterion for the diagnosis of PTSD. Prevailing opinion favors the position that PTSD may co-occur with mild TBI, in which there is an alteration of consciousness without loss of consciousness (Bontke et al., 1996; Bryant, 2001).

The current conflicts in Iraq and Afghanistan have brought this issue to the forefront of military medicine because the widespread use of improvised explosive devices against US forces has resulted in a high incidence of mTBI. In the RAND study of post-Iraqi military deployment, over a third of solders with mTBI were also diagnosed with PTSD or depression (Vanderploeg et al., 2009). Hoge et al. (2008) reported a prevalence of 43.9 percent for PTSD in soldiers with a history of loss of consciousness during deployment. Ongoing research may or may not elucidate the nature of the interaction between the neurologic and psychiatric components of post-deployment syndrome among veterans with traumatic brain injury, but research to this point has underscored the value of early co-treatment of PTSD and TBI, which may prove to be the most important change in TBI rehabilitation to result from OEF/OIF (Vanderploeg et al., 2009).

Posttraumatic seizures are also seen in TBI, ranging in prevalence from 0.7 percent in patients with mTBI to 10 percent in severe TBI, prompting the recent creation of the VA Epilepsy Centers of Excellence (Chen et al., 2009). In response to the host of common issues including pain, epilepsy, and PTSD that are unique to the polytrauma population, the VA is funding polytrauma fellowship programs with the objective of enhancing the skills of clinicians who wish to serve this expanding population of veterans (DVBIC, 2011b).

Innovative research and the future of TBI

With more than 100,000 service members having sustained non-fatal injuries during OEF and OIF as of the beginning of fiscal year 2012, DoD has provided $150 million in funding for research in TBI (Lew et al., 2007a). The United States Congress has approved the Traumatic Brain Injury Reauthorization Bill that expands funding to research at the National Institute of Health, in addition to expanding a range of TBI rehabilitation programs (Meyer et al., 2008), many of these with direct benefits to veterans.

One area of research is in biomarkers, which can be used to define the extent and type of injury as well as to direct therapy (Zafonte, 2006). The University of Florida has identified alpha-II spectrin and survivin as biomarkers of brain injury and is working to develop a palm-sized instrument using these biomarkers to detect axonal debris in the blood, which may be used in the field to determine the extent of brain injury only 2–4 hours after the injury has occurred (Samson, 2006). Oh and colleagues (2007) identified the serum S100 biomarker, which was successfully used to identify patients with CT or MRI positive brain injury. The S100 biomarker as well as serum neuron-specific enolase and myelin protein concentrations have also been found to be biomarkers of TBI by Berger et al. (2005). Biomarkers have potential to serve as a prognostic indicator; in a recent trial by Darwish et al. (2007), poor neurologic outcome has been associated with increased levels of nitrotyrosine in the cerebrospinal fluid.

Little is known about the exact neurological consequences of blast injury, which has sparked the need for innovative research aimed specifically at understanding the mechanism, sequelae, and treatments of blast injuries (Schwab et al., 2007). Chen et al. (2009) have developed an in-vitro TBI model that may be used to study the effects of a blast injury at the molecular and cellular level. Cernak et al. (2001) have examined the effects of blast-induced neurotrauma on memory deficits in rats, and identified that rats with blast injuries had impaired performance on active avoidance tasks for five days post-injury. Long et al. (2009) simulated blast injuries in rats in order to assess the effects of the resultant brain injury on acute cardiovascular homeostasis mechanisms and neurobehavioral functions, as well as to evaluate the protection provided by the Kevlar vest.

The DVBIC is also sponsoring trials aimed at improving the pharmacological treatment of TBI. The most recent of these trials is a randomized study of methylphenidate and its effects on rehabilitation in patients with moderate-to-severe TBI (Schwab et al., 2007). Other agents such as amphetamines and cholinesterase inhibitors have also shown promise as neurostimulants in TBI, but further studies are required (Chew and Zafonte, 2009). Research is also being conducted to assess rehabilitation interventions for TBI patients. The loss of driving skills is associated with disability and is a major obstacle to rehabilitation; therefore, recent studies have utilized a modern driving simulator that approximates real-life activity (Lew et al., 2009b). The driving simulator tests visual-motor speed and accuracy, vigilance, sustained attention, safety, and judgment, and it can be used for both assessment and treatment of patients with driving deficits.

Research is also being done in hopes of improving the inpatient rehabilitation process. A recent study by Vanderploeg et al. (2008) conducted in four Department of Veterans Affairs acute inpatient TBI rehabilitation programs, compared cognitive-didactic and functional-experimental treatments. While there were no differences between the groups in the broad one-year outcome, the cognitive arm seemed to have greater benefit for younger patients and the functional arm was more beneficial for the older patients. The results of studies examining various rehabilitation approaches may be used to better direct treatment of newly brain injured patients.

Given the prevalence of traumatic brain injury among American soldiers involved in current combat operations, there is an urgent need to develop protocols that reliably indicate whether or not a soldier who has suffered a concussion is safe to return to duty. Guidelines for return to play after concussion have been developed and adopted by the governing bodies of national and international amateur and professional athletic associations but they are not directly applicable to combat (McCrory et al., 2009). An effective return to duty protocol would protect brain-injured soldiers and their comrades and enhance the readiness and effectiveness of our forces.

Conclusion

Military activity has consistently spurred advances in the field of Physical Medicine and Rehabilitation. The development of brain injury services for veterans has evolved since the time of the US Civil War to our present-day conflict, in response to the needs of the casualties of war. Due to the circumstances that result in war-related injuries such as blasts and violent trauma, patients with TBI often have co-morbidities such as chronic pain, sensory deficits (auditory, vestibular, visual), in addition to the more obvious cognitive impairments and emotional difficulties. Thus, they will require multi-disciplinary, long-term follow up and care, to ensure the best possible outcome.

The ultimate goal for TBI rehabilitation is community and vocational re-integration. To achieve this goal, there needs to be a concerted effort from clinicians and researchers to provide evidence-based practice for this generation of veterans with TBI. The federal government is continuing to provide funding to improve clinical care and services for this new cohort of veterans. Important efforts have also begun in the VA, NIH, DVBIC, DoD, and Congressionally Directed Medical Research Program (CDMRP) to fund research projects in this area, with the hope that the results will inform clinicians and administrators in improving the diagnosis and functional outcome of patients with TBI and its co-morbidities.

Acknowledgments

The authors wish to thank Dr. Terri K. Pogoda and Barbara Sigford, MD, PhD for their help in the preparation of the manuscript.

Notes

Correspondence: David X. Cifu, MD, Department of PM&R, Virginia Commonwealth University, 1223 East Marshall Street, Richmond, VA 23298-0677. Email: DCIFU@VCU.EDU

Disclosures: Financial disclosure statements have been obtained, and no conflicts of interest have been reported by the authors or by any individuals in control of the content of this chapter.

References

Aita, J.A. (1946) 'Men with brain damage,' *American Journal of Psychiatry,* 103, 205–13.

Berger, R.P., Adelson, P.D., Pierce, M.C., Dulani, T., Cassidy, L.D. & Kochanek, P.M. (2005) 'Serum neuron-specific enolase, S100B, and myelin basic protein concentrations after inflicted and noninflicted traumatic brain injury in children,' *Journal of Neurosurgery,* 103, 61–8.

Boake, C. (1989) 'A history of cognitive rehabilitation of brain-injured patients, 1915–1980,' *Journal of Head Trauma Rehabilitation,* 4, 1–8.

Boake, C. & Diller, L. (2005) 'History of rehabilitation for traumatic brain injury. In High, W., Sander, A., Struchen, M. & Hart, K. (Eds.). *Rehabilitation for traumatic brain injury.* New York, Oxford University Press.

Bontke, C., Rattok, J. & Boake, C. (1996) 'Do patients with mild brain injuries have posttraumatic stress disorder, too?' *Journal of Head Trauma Rehabilitation,* 11, 95–102.

Bryant, R.A. (2001) 'Posttraumatic stress disorder and mild brain injury: controversies, causes and consequences,' *Journal of Clinical Experimental Neuropsychology,* 23, 718–28.

Carey, M.E., Yound, H.F., Rish, B.L. & Mathis, J.L. (1974) 'Follow-up study of 103 American soldiers who sustained a brain wound in Vietnam, *Journal of Neurosurgery,* 41, 542–9.

Cernak, I., Wand, Z., Jiang, J., Bian, X. & Savic, J. (2001) 'Cognitive deficits following blast injury-induced neurotrauma: possible involvement of nitric oxide,' *Brain Injury,* 15, 593–612.

Chen, Y.C., Smith, D.H. & Meaney, D.F. (2009) 'In-vitro approaches for studying blast-induced traumatic brain injury,' *Journal of Neurotrauma,* 26, 861–76.

Chew, E. & Zafonte, R.D. (2009) 'Pharmacological management of neurobehavioral disorders following traumatic brain injury – a state-of-the-art review,' *Journal of Rehabilitation Research and Developemnt,* 46, 851–79.

Cicerone, K. & Kalmar, K. (1995) 'Persistent postconcussion syndrome: the structure of subjective complaints after a mild traumatic brain injury,' *Journal of Head Trauma Rehabilitation,* 10, 1–17.

Cifu, D. & Blake, C. (2011). *Overcoming post-deployment syndrome: A six-step mission to health,* New York, Demos Health.

Clark, M.E., Bair, M.J., Buckenmaier, C.C., 3rd, Gironda, R.J. & Walker, R.L. (2007) 'Pain and combat injuries in soldiers returning from Operations Enduring Freedom and Iraqi Freedom: implications for research and practice,' *Journal of Rehabilitation Research Development,* 44, 179–94.

Cope, D.N., Mayer, N.H. & Cervelli, L. (2005) 'Development of systems of care for persons with traumatic brain injury,' *Journal of Head Trauma Rehabilitation,* 20, 128–42.

Darkins, A., Cruise, C., Armstrong, M., Peters, J. & Finn, M. (2008) 'Enhancing access of combat-wounded veterans to specialist rehabilitation services: the VA Polytrauma Telehealth Network,' *Archives of Physical Medical Rehabilitation,* 89, 182–7.

Darwish, R.S., Amiridze, N. & Aarabi, B. (2007) 'Nitrotyrosine as an oxidative stress marker: evidence for involvement in neurologic outcome in human traumatic brain injury,' *Journal of Trauma,* 63, 439–42.

Dillingham, T.R. (2002) 'Physiatry, physical medicine, and rehabilitation: historical development and military roles,' *Physical Medical Rehabilitation Clinic of North America,* 13, 1–16, v. DVBIC (2011).

DVBIC (2011a) *DoD Worldwide Numbers for TBI.* Available at: http://www.dvbic.org/dod-worldwide-numbers-tbi (accessed 12-2-11).

DVBIC (2011b) *Strategies for Symptom Management*. Available at: http://www.dvbic.org/strategies-symptom-management (accessed 12-2-11).

DVBIC (2011c) *TBI & the Military*. Available at: http://www.dvbic.org/tbi-military (accessed 12-2-11).

Eldar, R. & Jelic, M. (2003) 'The association of rehabilitation and war,' *Disability Rehabilitation*, 25, 1019–23.

Fausti, S.A., Wilmington, D.J., Gallun, F.J., Myers, P.J. & Henry, J.A. (2009) 'Auditory and vestibular dysfunction associated with blast-related traumatic brain injury,' *Journal of Rehabilitation Research Development*, 46, 797–810.

Fialka-Moser, V. (1999) 'Physical medicine and rehabilitation: past – present – future,' *Disability Rehabilitation*, 21, 403–8.

Gironda, R.J., Clark, M.E., Ruff, R.L., Chait, S., Craine, M., Walker, R. & Scholten, J. (2009) 'Traumatic brain injury, polytrauma, and pain: challenges and treatment strategies for the polytrauma rehabilitation,' *Rehabilitation Psychology*, 54, 247–58.

Hermes, L.M. (2002) 'Military lower extremity amputee rehabilitation,' *Physical Medical Rehabilitation Clinics of North America*, 13, 45–66.

Hoge, C.W., Mcgurk, D., Thomas, J.L., Cox, A.L., Engel, C.C. & Castro, C.A. (2008) 'Mild traumatic brain injury in U.S. soldiers returning from Iraq,' *New England Journal of Medicine*, 358, 453–63.

Kaufman, H.H. (1993) 'Treatment of head injuries in the American Civil War,' *Journal of Neurosurgery*, 78, 838–45.

Kocsis, J.D. & Tessler, A. (2009) 'Pathology of blast-related brain injury,' *Journal of Rehabilitation Research Development*, 46, 667–72.

Lanska, D.J. (2009) 'Historical perspective: neurological advances from studies of war injuries and illnesses,' *Annals Neurol*, 66, 444–59.

Lew, H.L., Cifu, D.X., Sigford, B., Scott, S., Sayer, N. & Jaffee, M.S. (2007a) 'Team approach to diagnosis and management of traumatic brain injury and its comorbidities,' *Journal of Rehabilitation Research Development*, 44, vii–xi.

Lew, H.L., Poole, J.H., Vanderploeg, R.D., Goodrich, G.L., Dekekboum, S., Guillory, S.B., Sigford, B. & Cifu, D.X. (2007b) 'Program development and defining characteristics of returning military in a VA Polytrauma Network Site,' *Journal of Rehabilitation Research Development*, 44, 1027–34.

Lew, H.L., Garvert, D.W., Pogoda, T.K., Hsu, P.T., Devine, J.M., White, D.K., Myers, P.J. & Goodrich, G.L. (2009a) 'Auditory and visual impairments in patients with blast-related traumatic brain injury: Effect of dual sensory impairment on Functional Independence Measure,' *Journal of Rehabilitation Research Development*, 46, 819–26.

Lew, H.L., Rosen, P.N., Thomander, D. & Poole, J.H. (2009b) 'The potential utility of driving simulators in the cognitive rehabilitation of combat-returnees with traumatic brain injury,' *Journal of Head Trauma Rehabilitation*, 24, 51–6.

Lewin, W. (1968) 'Rehabilitation after head injury,' *British Medical Journal*, 1, 465–70.

Long, J.B., Bentley, T.L., Wessner, K.A., Cerone, C., Sweeney, S. & Bauman, R.A. (2009) 'Blast overpressure in rats: recreating a battlefield injury in the laboratory,' *Journal of Neurotrauma*, 26, 827–40.

McCrory, P., Meeuwisse, W., Johnston, K., Dvorak, J., Aunry, M., Molloy, M. & Cantu, R. (2009). Consensus statement on concussion in sport – the 3rd International Conference on concussion in sport, held in Zurich, November 2008. *J Clin Neurosci*, 16, 755–63.

Meirowsky, A.M. (1954) 'Penetrating craniocerebral truma: observations in Korean war,' *Journal of the American Medical Association*, 154, 666–9.

Meyer, K., Helmick, K., Doncevic, S. & Park, R. (2008) 'Severe and penetrating traumatic brain injury in the context of war,' *Journal of Trauma Nursing*, 15, 185–9; quiz 190–1.

Oh, E.J., Kim, Y.M., Jegal, D.W., Kahng, J., Park, Y.J. & Han, K. (2007) 'Diagnostic value of Elecsys S100 as a marker of acute brain injury in the emergency department,' *Journal of Clinical Lab Analysis*, 21, 387–92.

Ommaya, A.K., Salazar, A.M., Dannenberg, A.L., Cnervinsky, A.B. & Schwab, K. (1996) 'Outcome after traumatic brain injury in the U.S. military medical system,' *Journal of Trauma*, 41, 972–5.

Opitz, J.L., Folz, T.J., Gelfman, R. & Peters, D.J. (1997) 'The history of physical medicine and rehabilitation as recorded in the diary of Dr. Frank Krusen: Part 1. Gathering momentum (the years before 1942),' *Archives of Physical Medical Rehabilitation*, 78, 442–5.

Prigatano, O.G. (2005) 'A history of cognitive rehabilitation,' in Halligan, P. & Wade, D. (eds). *Effectiveness of rehabilitation for cognitive deficits.* New York, Oxford University Press.

Ruff, R. (2005) 'Two decades of advances in understanding of mild traumatic brain injury,' *Journal of Head Trauma Rehabilitation*, 20, 5–18.

Salazar, A.M., Warden, D.L., Schwab, K., Spector, J., Braverman, S., Walter, J., Cole, R., Rosner, M.M., Martin, E.M., Ecklund, J. & Ellenbogen, R.G. (2000a) 'Cognitive rehabilitation for traumatic brain injury: A randomized trial. Defense and Veterans Head Injury Program (DVHIP). Study Group,' *JAMA*, 283, 3075–81.

Salazar, A.M., Zitnay, G.A., Warden, D.L. & Schwab, K.A. (2000b) 'Defense and Veterans Head Injury Program: background and overview,' *Journal of Head Trauma Rehabilitation*, 15, 1081–91.

Samson, K. (2006) 'Increasing Iraq injuries spur demand for rehab services and high-tech research and development,' *Neurology Today*, 6: 21–2.

Sayer, N.A., Chiros, C.E., Sigford, B., Scott, S., Clothier, B., Pickett, T. & Lew, H.L. (2008) 'Characteristics and rehabilitation outcomes among patients with blast and other injuries sustained during the Global War on Terror,' *Archives of Physical Medical Rehabilitation*, 89, 163–70.

Schwab, K., Grafman, J., Salazar, A.M. & Kraft, J. (1993) 'Residual impairments and work status 15 years after penetrating head injury: report from the Vietnam Head Injury Study,' *Neurology*, 43, 95–103.

Schwab, K.A., Warden, D., Lux, W.E., Shupenk, L.A. & Zitnay, G. (2007) 'Defense and veterans brain injury center: peacetime and wartime missions,' *Journal of Rehabilitation Research and Developemnt*, 44, xiii–xxi.

Sigford, B.J. (2008) '"To care for him who shall have borne the battle and for his widow and his orphan" (Abraham Lincoln): the Department of Veterans Affairs polytrauma system of care'. *Archives of Physical Medical Rehabilitation*, 89, 160–2.

Vanderploeg, R.D., Schwab, K., Walker, W.C., Fraser, J.A., Sigford, B.J., Date, E.S., Scott T, S.G., Curtiss, G., Salazar, A.M. & Warden, D.L. (2008) 'Rehabilitation of traumatic brain injury in active duty military personnel and veterans: Defense and Veterans Brain Injury Center randomized controlled trial of two rehabilitation approaches,' *Archives of Physical Medical Rehabilitation*, 89, 2227–38.

Vanderploeg, R.D., Belanger, H.G. & Curtiss, G. (2009) 'Mild traumatic brain injury and posttraumatic stress disorder and their associations with health symptoms,' *Archives of Physical Medical Rehabilitation*, 90, 1084–93.

Walker, A.E. (1957) 'Prognosis in post-traumatic epilepsy; a ten-year follow-up of craniocerebral injuries of World War II,' *Journal of the American Medical Association*, 164, 1636–41.

Zafonte, R.D. (2006) 'Update on biotechnology for TBI rehabilitation: a look at the future,' *Journal of Head Trauma Rehabilitation*, 21, 403–7.

11 Defense Centers of Excellence for Psychological Health and Traumatic Brain Injury

DoD's response to psychological health (PH) and traumatic brain injury (TBI)

Christopher Robinson, Katherine Helmick, and Jason Guthrie

Introduction

The capacity of military doctors and medical providers to effectively treat battlefield injuries has expanded exponentially since the American Civil War. From the use of improved antiseptics during World War I to the cutting edge trauma and emergency procedures of today, a century and a half of medical research and innovation has dramatically enhanced clinical standards of care, shortened recovery times, improved rehabilitative outcomes, and decreased the rate of fatalities associated with many serious combat injuries. Yet, as we target current and future improvements in the quality of care, the importance of critically evaluating past successes and failures only increases. This chapter rests on the proposition that the wounded soldiers of today are best served, not by blind faith in medical science or the omniscience of doctors, but by the collective willingness of military leaders as well as all those who provide care to service members, veterans and their families to learn from what went before and to effectively apply that knowledge to tackle the biggest defense-related health care challenges of our time.

A "recurrent theme in the history of military psychiatry," historian Eric Dean tells us, "is that the lessons of the last war are almost always ignored in the next war, at least initially" (Dean 1997: 35). This history, Dean suggests, has resulted in a pattern of remembering and forgetting. This chapter examines the ways in which PH and TBI have constituted two categories of injuries for which the ability of medical providers to understand, diagnose and treat has sometimes lagged behind the level of need. As so-called "invisible wounds," PH and TBI have not fit easily into existing military-medical paradigms and often suffered from a paucity of attention, resources, and understanding. History provides a broader context for understanding both current and future reforms: it serves as an important measure of progress in meeting the needs of our service members, demonstrates how similar obstacles to reform were overcome in the past, and assists planning for the future.

From an examination of the historical response to PH and TBI related wounds, the chapter then considers the most recent steps taken to remove these historical impediments and to develop a sustained commitment within the military to improve PH and TBI care. While there is no magic pill that can alleviate the problems and issues encountered by service members and veterans affected by disorders such as PTSD and TBI, we can say that the current Defense Department response benefits from a "high variety" environment. Multiple programs across multiple departments and agencies have maximized the potential for innovation and improved care, but integration and synthesis remain essential to effective communication, education, and dissemination of best practices. The chapter specifically suggests how the Defense Centers of Excellence for Psychological Health and Traumatic Brain Injury can help break the cycle of remembering and forgetting by integrating and disseminating global insights and best practices across the Defense Department.

The US military response to PH and TBI: an historical perspective

Human beings have confronted the costs of war for millennia. Some researchers have speculated about the impact of PTSD, for example, on the behavior of historical figures as diverse as Alexander the Great and Florence Nightingale (Mackowiak & Batten 2008). But as illustrated in Figure 11.1, modern medicine's efforts to distinguish between the physical and mental effects of trauma date to the middle of the nineteenth century. British surgeon John Erichsen's 1867 study of railway accident victims was one of the first attempts to explore the relationship between unexplained physical symptoms and the mental stress produced by traumatic events. Erichsen noted that the "shock" elicited by a railway accident was exceptional for the sheer concussive force that can bombard the body of the victim. Much as "the magnetic force is jarred, shaken, or concussed out" of a magnet if struck with a hammer, he reasoned, "we find that the nervous force is to a certain extent shaken out of the man, and that he has in some way lost nervous power" (Erichsen 1867: 73; Young 1995: 14).

The condition Erichsen described was commonly known as "railway spine," but his observations were not as removed from the concerns of nineteenth-century military doctors and surgeons as they might at first appear. *The Medical and Surgical History of the Rebellion* (published by the US Army Surgeon General's Office after the Civil War) noted for example that, "[i]n movements of large bodies of troops by rail, the men crowded upon platforms and roofs of cars, contusions and lacerations of the scalp, concussions of the brain, and fractures of the skull, were not infrequent" (Surgeon General 1870: 35). Moreover, some Civil War doctors were attuned (as was Erichsen) to possible links between various environmental stressors and the mysterious physical symptoms that afflicted soldiers. For example, Philadelphia-based teacher and clinician Dr. Jacob Mendez Da Costa reported a range of unexplained symptoms among 300 Union Army troops referred to his care, including shortness of breath, heart palpitations, chest pain, fatigue and

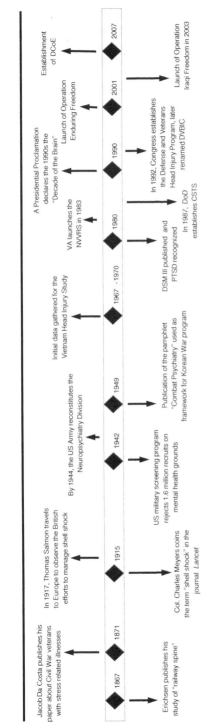

Figure 11.1 Time line of modern medicine's efforts to distinguish between the physical and mental effects of trauma

other ailments with no obvious physical cause. Da Costa concluded that over-stimulated nerves located at the base of the heart were responsible, a condition he labeled "irritable heart" or "soldier's heart" (Hyams et al. 1996: 398).

Despite the efforts of Da Costa and others, during the Civil War the availability of effective treatment for combat stress and traumatic brain injury was extremely limited, if not altogether unavailable.[1] With additional research and the rise of psychiatric medicine in the late nineteenth and early twentieth century, the US military's response to the condition known as "shell shock" was more systematic. After the publication of an article in the British journal *Lancet* in 1915, shell shock became the term most frequently used to describe both blast-related injuries to the head and spine as well as a psychological condition usually related to combat stress. Just as PTSD and TBI have become signature wounds of the current conflicts in Iraq and Afghanistan, shell shock was the signature ailment of the First World War, spreading almost virus-like through the armies of Europe. Medical experts in Britain and on the continent initially related the condition to the concussive effect of exploding mortar shells, but as more and more soldiers who had never entered combat reported and displayed the same symptoms—such as memory loss, change in mental status, blurred vision, hysteria, etc.—medical authorities grew increasingly skeptical that blast etiology alone could explain the phenomenon. Many concluded, as did British army psychiatrist Captain Charles Meyers, that, "[i]n the vast majority of cases the signs of 'shell-shock' appear[ed] traceable to psychic causes," which resembled the symptoms of "peace-time 'hysteria' and 'neurasthenia'" (Shephard 2003: 31).

Before the US committed troops to the fighting in Europe, its doctors, psychiatrists and military leaders were aware of the large numbers of shell shock casualties in the British and French armies and anticipated similar numbers for any American force dispatched to the front. Indeed, it was for this reason that the Army tapped the National Committee for Mental Hygiene (NCMH) to consult on the establishment of a department of neuropsychiatry within the Office of the Surgeon General. Dr. Thomas Salmon was the NCMH's director and, in May 1917, he was dispatched to observe British efforts to contain the shell shock epidemic. His report became the foundation of the US neuropsychiatry program during World War I (Salmon 1917: 509).

The driving concept behind Salmon's plan was, as one of the British sources he interviewed concluded, "that treatment is more satisfactorily carried out and cures more speedily accomplished in hospitals close to the front and where the spirit of army discipline is most felt" (Salmon 1917: 521). Salmon's investigation suggested that soldiers exhibiting symptoms of war neuroses or shell shock were more likely to return to their units if treated quickly, as near the frontlines and their own units as possible, and with the full confidence of a trained psychiatrist that they would be "cured."[2] Even so, Salmon recommended that frontline treatment should be restricted to "those which seem likely to recover within six months" (Salmon 1917: 526). For the most "intractable" cases, he advised that, "no soldier suffering from functional nervous diseases be discharged from the army until at least a year's special treatment has been given" (Salmon 1917: 544). Salmon pointed out that Britain had followed a policy of releasing chronic cases with a full pension, effectively swelling the pension roles and saddling the British government with a heavy financial burden. Financial considerations aside, he also noted that most public hospitals in the US were ill-equipped to provide the kind of care and treatment that would be required by many neuropsychiatric patients.

Given that US military participation in the First World War lasted little more than a year, it is difficult to assess the effectiveness of the program. It has been estimated that of the 4,734,991 Americans who served during World War I approximately 122,000 service members were hospitalized for neuropsychiatric illness—about 34 percent of which were discharged from the military as a result of their condition (Coates 1955: 1). By 1941, federal government expenditures on "disability, compensation, and hospital treatment" for neuropsychiatric cases exceeded $1 billion (Coates 1955: 1). Medical authorities in the US and elsewhere were still unable to draw clear etiological and symptomatological distinctions between shell shock cases involving physical injury (i.e. concussive trauma) and those which constituted what was increasingly labeled "war neuroses" (i.e. psychic or emotional trauma). Greater attention was paid to the psychogenic explanation of neuropsychiatric illness (at least in part) because it provided a greater opportunity to return soldiers to combat. But the question of whether shell shock was primarily psychological or physical in origin had hardly been resolved (Jones et al. 2007b: 1644).[3]

In contrast to the intense planning that preceded US entry into World War I, "there was no comparable effort in the sphere of military psychiatry" at the beginning of World War II (Heaton 1966: 17). Instead, psychiatrist Dr. Harry Stack Sullivan became the central figure of a campaign to eliminate the problem of war neuroses and combat breakdown through the psychiatric profession's ostensible ability to identify mental "weakness." Although Thomas Salmon had also emphasized the need for more thorough screening, unlike Sullivan he never intimated that such a move would or could eliminate psychiatric casualties altogether. Salmon's plan had emphasized a continuum of care for those casualties which, he implied, would inevitably arise from war. In contrast, Sullivan imposed rigid psychological screening as a de facto panacea. The screening process implemented by Sullivan was used to weed out individuals identified as "degenerate" and to bar from service those "thought to have a predisposition to mental disease" (Shephard 2003: 199). In all, 1.6 million potential recruits were rejected on mental health grounds (a rate 7.6 times greater than during the First World War). When the more stringent screening process did not reduce the number of breakdowns, another 438,000 soldiers were discharged because of psychological health concerns. Facing a potential manpower crisis as a result of these policies, by 1944 the Army implemented a midcourse correction. The Surgeon General's Office reconstituted the Neuropsychiatry Division that had been dissolved at the end of World War I and began deploying mental health specialists to forward operating medical units, as had been done under Salmon's plan 24 years before (Dean 1997: 35).

With the Army's recommitment to forward psychiatry, military doctors experimented with a variety of new and old treatment modalities. Instead of a uniform standard of diagnoses and treatment, a variety of methods were tried by doctors operating in the different staging areas and theaters of war. American psychiatrists Roy Grinker and John Spiegel began pioneering a new chemical abreaction therapy using Pentothal, also known as thiopental sodium, during the Tunisia campaign. In contrast, neurologist Frederick R. Hanson rejected the use of Pentothal in favor of a simpler regime. Operating from the perspective that most breakdown cases suffered from sheer exhaustion, Hanson's methods harkened back to the experiences of World War I, in which rest, strengthening group identification, and persistent persuasion at forward medical centers were found to be effective means of returning soldiers to combat quickly. Other doctors, such as Ralph Kaufman, rejected barbiturate treatment and the use of social pressure applied by Hanson in favor of hypnosis.[4]

Perhaps the most important aspect of the military's response during World War II was a change in the way many military doctors perceived neuropsychiatric illnesses (and especially combat stress), from a view that soldiers could be separated into groups of weak and strong to one in which "every man has his breaking point" (Shephard 2003: 326). When the psychogenic explanation of "war neuroses" had initially taken hold, a soldier's vulnerability to psychic disturbance and his susceptibility to a full-blown mental breakdown were generally interpreted as evidence of an inherent flaw in his character. But as Army doctor Fred Hanson wrote in a 1949 bulletin entitled "Combat Psychiatry," medical practitioners had learned that, "a man whose emotional stability is normal, or even superior, before entering combat, may become a psychiatric casualty, usually as the result of a series of cataclysmic event [sic] or prolonged exposure to the dangers of battle" (Hanson 1949: viii). Although the idea itself was not new, the degree to which a portion of the medical profession embraced the "every man has his breaking point" thesis was highly significant and suggested the possibility of both an acute and chronic post-stress response.

The new orientation of many military doctors would have important implications for resilience and prevention as well as treatment. First and foremost, if psychological breakdown was:

> precipitated by a soldiers' inability to control his environment, a situation that over time could "wear away [his] resolution and confidence," then Army psychiatrists found that good morale offered a strong defense in times of trouble. As one Army doctor put it, "[w]here the morale of a unit and its officer–man relationships are good—i.e., good welfare, good leadership, good discipline, there you will find very much less tendency to break down under battle stress."
>
> (Weinberg 1946: 474)

This and other lessons learned during World War II served as a model for the Korean War, with generally positive results. Although military medical authorities encountered resource and logistical delays at the beginning of the conflict, by 1952 psychiatric casualties among US forces had been reduced from 250 per thousand per annum to 37 per thousand per annum, with a return to duty rate consistently reported at between 65 and 80 percent (Hanson 1949: viii).

At the same time, the Army Medical Office reported that brain and head injuries, including skull depression and concussions, accounted for 8.1 percent of all combat injuries resulting in hospital admission (Reister 1973: 9). Approximately one third of all non-battle deaths were the result of head injuries, but accurate statistics for combat deaths resulting from head injury were not consistently recorded and are unavailable for the Korean War.[5] Changes on the battlefield had contributed to an overall reduction in casualty rates for both head/brain and combat stress related casualties. Nevertheless, the success that military psychiatrists experienced returning soldiers to their units in Korea meant that psychiatry would become a distinctive and permanent element of the Defense Department's approach to maintaining force health (Shephard 2003: 342).

In the superheated political climate of the late 1960s and early 1970s, the health and care of soldiers and veterans became part of the broader public debate that engulfed the Vietnam War. US military psychiatrists, for example, were attacked for acting to "conserve [...] fighting strength" rather than (their critics alleged) doing what was in the best interest of their patients (Shephard 2003: 348). At the same time, many within the psychiatric profession spoke out about an emerging "Post-Vietnam Syndrome" affecting some veterans. Despite the acrimony of public discourse, the Vietnam era would result in several important milestones. In 1978, Dr. Charles Figley, a psychiatrist and researcher at Purdue University and himself a Vietnam veteran, published the influential study *Stress Disorders among Vietnam Veterans*. Figley's book was representative of increasing concern within the psychiatric community about the long-term effects of combat stress. That same year a Presidential commission on mental health in the United States concluded that the needs of Vietnam veterans were not being adequately met. The commission's findings focused attention on the broader public health and wellness concerns that affected the families and communities of returning veterans, as well as veterans themselves. A year later, in 1979, Congress passed the Veteran's Health Care Amendment Act creating a series of Vet Centers to assist Vietnam veterans, followed in 1980 by the publication of a new, updated version of the Diagnostic and Statistical Manual of Mental Disorders by the American Psychiatric Association (DSM III). In the DSM III, Post-Vietnam Syndrome became Post Traumatic Disorder (PTSD) and part of the official APA nosology of mental disorders.

Besides the events described above, which contributed to official recognition of PTSD in 1980, the immediate post-Vietnam era was significant for the initiation of several landmark head trauma studies conducted by the National Institutes of Health (NIH) as well as new research into the impact of PTSD. The Vietnam Head Injury Study (VHIS) was the product of collaboration between the Defense Department, the Department of Veterans Affairs, the NIH, and the American Red Cross. The project was initiated by Dr. William F. Caveness, who had been responsible for compiling similar data on head injury during the Korean War. Caveness sought to develop a registry of head injuries for Vietnam, gathered from combat field hospitals between 1967 and 1970 (Sweeny & Smutok 1983; Raymont et al. 2011). The registry included information on 2,000 cases and subsequent efforts yielded complete military and VA records for 1,221 Vietnam veterans who sustained head injuries (Raymont et al. 2011: 1). The study has so far consisted of four phases, covering a 40+-year period after the initial injuries, and has provided valuable information to researchers and clinicians about the health impacts of TBI.

In 1983, an equally ambitious study was initiated by the Department of Veterans Affairs to examine the presence and effects of PTSD among Vietnam veterans. With signs of growing need on the part of Vietnam veterans for services to address PTSD symptoms and related impairments, Congress required the VA to examine the prevalence of PTSD. Working with an independent group, the Triangle Research Institute, the VA completed the National Vietnam Veterans Readjustment Study (NVVRS). At the time the study was conducted in the 1980s, the VA reported that 15.2 percent of males who had served in the Vietnam Theater currently had symptoms that could be diagnosed as PTSD using the DSM III criteria. Over their lifetimes, the study suggested approximately 30 percent of veterans developed PTSD symptoms.[6] Given these results, in 1987 the Defense Department created the Center for the Study of Traumatic Stress or CSTS to address concerns about the long-term effects of traumatic stress.

The legacy of the Vietnam conflict and the subsequent studies of Vietnam veterans continue to shape the Defense Department's response to PTSD and TBI.[7] The experiences of the Vietnam generation demonstrated the need for additional research as well as better treatment and rehabilitative services.

In the case of the First Gulf War, researchers have suggested that service members who served in the Gulf region are 2–3 times more likely than colleagues who served in other regions during the same period to suffer from PTSD and depression. Gulf War veterans also have experienced higher rates of co-morbidity with other psychiatric illnesses (Institute of Medicine Committee on Gulf War and Health 2006).[8] In addition to the possible psychological health impacts of service in the Gulf region, continued concern about the impact of head injuries on military and civilian populations has led to action by policymakers.[9] For example, a July 1990 Presidential Proclamation identifying the 1990s as the "Decade of the Brain" promoted increased awareness and support of brain research. Likewise, in 1991, Congress provided for the establishment of the Defense and Veterans Head Injury Program (DVHIP, later renamed the Defense and Veterans Brain Injury Center or DVBIC) to improve understanding and treatment of brain injuries incurred by US military service members.[10]

More recently, the launch of Operation Enduring Freedom (OEF) and Operation Iraqi Freedom (OIF), and especially the widespread use of IEDs (improvised explosive devices) by the insurgencies in both conflicts, has necessitated a recalibration of the Defense Department response to PTSD and TBI. In February 2007, the *Washington Post* published a series of articles that documented gaps in the quality of care received by some wounded warriors at Walter Reed Army Medical Center (WRAMC), the nation's largest army hospital. The *Post* investigation yielded evidence of a substantial deterioration in the physical conditions at some WRAMC outpatient facilities, especially those serving patients discharged from the hospital's psychiatric ward. Equally troubling, the newspaper claimed that many wounded warriors were left on their own to navigate "a messy bureaucratic battlefield nearly as chaotic as the real battlefields they faced overseas" (Priest & Hull 2007).

Defense Department officials up and down the chain of command answered these accusations with swift action. In May 2007, Secretary of Defense Robert Gates, together with the Secretary of Veterans Affairs R. James Nicholson, announced the creation of a DoD/VA Wounded, Ill, and Injured Senior Oversight Committee (WII SOC) to coordinate the Defense Department response. By September 2007, several governmental commissions, committees, task forces and independent review groups began to publish their findings about the state of the Military Health System (MHS). Investigators presented hundreds of different recommendations for how to improve the quality of care. To manage the variety of changes contemplated, SOC officials disaggregated the list of recommendations into eight "Lines of Action" (LOAs) and disseminated responsibility for each to eight teams of military and civilian experts. One of those teams, known as LOA 2 or the "Red Cell," was given responsibility for psychological health and traumatic brain injury, which alone accounted for about 75 percent of the total number of recommendations that fell within the SOC's purview.[11]

Before it stood down in February 2008, the Red Cell had completed an evaluation of the 400 plus PH and TBI recommendations assigned to it by the WII SOC and had begun to specify which activities would fall to a new Defense Center of Excellence for Psychological Health and Traumatic Brain Injury (DCoE). In addition, the National Defense Authorization Act (NDAA) issued a mandate and spelled out general responsibilities for DCoE and dedicated its budget from a portion of $900 million in new funding allocated for Defense Department PH and TBI programs. The NDAA defined DCoE's overarching purpose as leading DoD efforts regarding prevention, diagnosis, mitigation, treatment, and rehabilitation of psychological health and traumatic brain injuries. A memo from Principal Deputy Under Secretary of Defense for Personnel and Readiness Michael Dominguez coordinated the establishment of DCoE within the Department of Defense.

DCoE exists to help providers leverage the strengths of all the Defense Department's psychological health and TBI programs, to promote continued refinements, to eliminate redundancies, and to consolidate and amplify best practices across the "continuum of care" (Figure 11.2) from prevention to reintegration after deployment.

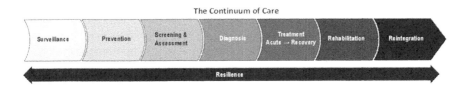

The Continuum of Care

Surveillance | Prevention | Screening & Assessment | Diagnosis | Treatment Acute → Recovery | Rehabilitation | Reintegration

Resilience

Figure 11.2 The continuum of care

The continuum of care constitutes the underlying framework for the Defense Department's holistic, comprehensive response to psychological health and TBI. It is a public health model that builds on more than a century of advancements in medical understanding and encompasses a variety of approaches and programs, each of which can be benchmarked for its effectiveness in addressing the needs of our wounded service members. DCoE's program and product portfolio seeks to drive innovation across the continuum of care by identifying treatment pathways and other clinical and research modalities that deliver superior outcomes. To be clear, the goal is not to create a single "one size fits all" psychological health and TBI program—diversity is one of the greatest assets of the current Defense Department response—but to institute a process of constant improvement that results in the best care for America's service men and women, wherever they are and whenever they need it.

PH programs and policy

Today, DCoE represents the "tip of the spear" of the Defense Department's response to treating traumatic brain injury and the various acute and chronic conditions found under the category of psychological health. However, when Congress launched the Defense Centers of Excellence in 2007 there was a flurry of activity to determine how this important body should be organized. A decision was made to build a structural dichotomy based on the two main categories of disorders, PH and TBI. Within DCoE, subject matter expertise was obtained from TBI and PH experts, each focused exclusively on their respective areas. In addition, a subgroup of PH specialists focused specifically on resilience and prevention. As a result of this organizational structure and division of labor, one of the innovations DCoE embodied was the fact that the two groups were now conjoined and co-located in a single organization to facilitate collaboration as needed and to build-out the integrated network necessary to tackle PH and TBI in a focused, comprehensive fashion.

As the work began of trying to implement the various committee and task force recommendations as well as the broader mission defined for DCoE by Congress, it became clear that rapid and effective change would not come easily. Consider the following facts. There are 231,000 behavioral health outpatient appointments per week in the Military Health System and 4.5 million behavioral health outpatient visits per year for active duty service members and their families. The Military Health System supports a population of 9.6 million beneficiaries across the uniformed services and, since 2005, funding for all psychological health programs in DoD has increased from approximately $1.1 billion to $2.5 billion. Unlike civilian mental health, military psychological health involves interacting and collaborating with commanders and leadership, paying attention to the members' readiness, being sensitive to the community at large, as well as focusing on more traditional medical diagnostic issues. Indeed, developing programs to address the unique circumstances of the respective Services would require intense cooperation and planning as well as careful calibration of resources (TRICARE 2011).

Table 11.1 Incident PTSD cases*, US armed forces, active and reserve components

Year	Incident Cases (Not Previously Deployed	Incident Cases Among OIF/OEF Deployers**
2000	1,618	—
2001	1,709	—
2002	1,721	133
2003	1,538	1,166
2004	1,588	3,915
2005	1,661	6,821
2006	1,725	7,843
2007	2,057	11,793
2008	2,406	14,474
2009	2,476	14,119
2010	2,617	15,107
2011	1,959	10,964
Total	23,075	86,335

* PTSD case defined as either (2) outpatient encounters on different days with ICD9 diagnostic code (any position) of 309.81; OR inpatient encounter with ICD9 diagnostic code (any position) of 309.81.
** Deployment to OEF/OIF lasting longer than 30 days
Prepared by Armed Forces Health Surveillance Center (AFHSC): 07NOV2011
Data Source: Defencse Medical Surveillance System (DMSS)

As the DCoE PH subject matter expert community divided itself into two groups, one focusing on clinical standards of care and the other on resilience and prevention, it also became clear that PH diagnoses required more emphasis. A quick review of the literature demonstrated that three categories of disorders— PTSD, major depression, and substance abuse disorders—accounted for most of the incident cases (Armed Forces Health Surveillance Center 2010), and the frequency of these disorders in the OEF and OIF active duty and veterans populations clearly correlated with service member deployments. Between 2000 and 2010, the incident cases of PTSD for active duty and reserve component OIF/OEF deployers were over three times higher than active duty and reserve component members who had not previously deployed (Table 11.1). The highest incident cases occurred among combat exposed troops and medical workers.

Treatment-seeking service members actually diagnosed by a provider with post-deployment PTSD appeared at first glance to be rather low, equaling just 2.4 percent of deployed service members (DMDC CTS Roster). However, since 2007 many studies have found between 10 percent and 17 percent of service members anonymously self-report symptoms consistent with PTSD. This statistical discrepancy lends credence to the notion that, although the true prevalence of PTSD among OEF/OIF deployers is unknown, it is likely higher than indicated by the number of officially diagnosed cases. The most significant cause of under- or unreported cases is now well-documented and largely associated with the stigma that still surrounds the reporting of mental health symptoms. Indeed, recent studies have demonstrated that a PTSD diagnosis is a significant predictor of punitive discharge, increased risk of demotion, and delayed promotion (Highfill-McRoy et al. 2010).

The costs specifically associated with PTSD are difficult to discern, either from aggregate estimates of war-related expenditures or the overall costs associated with mental health issues. However, the projected costs associated with PTSD and major depression among service members and veterans have been estimated at $4.0–6.2 billion for two years, with even higher estimates for direct medical care and lost productivity (Tanielian & Jaycox 2008). These estimates illustrate the need for a comprehensive approach that combines diagnosis and treatment with resilience and prevention. The significant funding allocations required to effectively treat PTSD and related disorders make it increasingly vital for DoD to identify and promulgate the most effective programs while reducing or eliminating those that are less so.

While PTSD has tended to garner more attention, the incidence rates of depression are comparable or somewhat lower than those for PTSD. In anonymous self-reported surveys, 3–15 percent of the service member population report symptoms consistent with depression. But it is important to note that post-deployment problems are much wider and far-reaching than these diagnoses alone. Suicide, adjustment problems, relationship and family problems, divorce, risky behaviors, demotions, and punitive discharges have also been observed post-deployment and are all complicating factors that may accompany or exist apart from symptoms of depression.

Suicide rates among current active duty members that served in OEF/OIF have doubled since 2001 (MHAT V 2008), and the Institute of Medicine (IOM 2008) reported that there is growing evidence of a link between deployment to a war zone and increased risk for suicide subsequent to that deployment. Researchers have found that veterans diagnosed with PTSD are more likely to die from suicide than those with no PTSD diagnosis (Bullman & Kang 1994). Additionally, Kang and Bullman (2008) reported that OEF/OIF veterans diagnosed with psychological disorders committed suicide at significantly higher rates than the national average.

At the time DCoE was created in 2007, it was clear that OEF and OIF service members and veterans were not immune to the same sorts of psychological health concerns that affected previous generations. It was evident, in other words, that psychological health problems existed in our military population and that they needed to be addressed. Although every war and every conflict in which US forces are deployed is unique, historically combat operations have had a way of exposing gaps in the existing system of care and of emphasizing the need to bring new approaches and treatments to the fore. With the need for action clear, DoD moved quickly to launch new programs and make available new resources.

For example, the DCoE Outreach Center was established in January 2009 and provides information and appropriate support from health professionals related to psychological health and traumatic brain injury to the community at large—24 hours a day, seven days a week. The DCoE Resource Library supports and enhances the work of the Outreach Center by providing credible and relevant content through a searchable online repository of PH and TBI resources. Another tremendously successful initiative is the Real Warriors Campaign. This is a national public awareness campaign designed to impact knowledge, beliefs, attitudes, and behaviors about seeking care for, and dispelling stigma about, psychological health for service members and their families. Specifically, these public outreach activities promote and normalize resilience, recovery, and reintegration activities for returning service members, veterans, and their families, through public service announcements, videos, pod casting, radio spots, outreach materials, advertisements, web-accessible materials, website activities (e.g., blogs, MySpace, Facebook, YouTube), speaking engagements, conference attendance, and marketing campaigns.

In addition to these efforts, in January 2010 DCoE launched a program (*in Transition*) to facilitate continuation of care for service members who receive or have received mental health treatment and are a facing a major life transition, such as call to active duty, relocation, or retirement. This non-medical counseling and information program provides coaching support services that bridge potential gaps in mental health support and which studies have shown often lead people to disengage from treatment entirely. As a complement to these support mechanisms, several mobile applications have been designed and launched that use smart phones and smart phone applications to put valuable health information and coping tools directly in the hands of patients and other consumers of mental health information. Finally, clinical standards for care have become more systematized across the Defense Department as a result of projects such as the DoD-VA PTSD and Major Depression Disorder Clinical Practice Guidelines and toolkits, the creation of a Substance Abuse Disorder toolkit, and the issuance of DoD Instruction (DODI) 6490.07 addressing fitness for duty and ensuring that service members were medically (and psychologically) able to accomplish their duties in deployed environments.

These efforts constitute a strong beginning and have generated increased communication and a historically unprecedented level of transorganizational collaboration. DCoE has worked to build and maintain strong collaborative relationships with the individual Services and, where appropriate, has sought to connect the Defense Department's PH experts with specialists at the VA, in academia, and with private health care providers. At the same time, the unique challenges associated with treating PTSD in the military suggest the need for continued focus on diagnosis and treatment, as well as resilience and prevention. For example, both the disorder itself and the nature of military service limit access to such protective factors as safe environments and close support of family/ friends. Specifically, Brewin, Andrews and Valentine (2000) found that PTSD is frequently associated with the onset of social problems. Since social support has been identified as a significant PTSD protective factor (Ozer, Best, Lipsey & Weiss 2003), the symptoms of the disorder and the culture of the military itself interact to create a situation in which deployed service members are potentially pushed away from a very valuable resilience and recovery resource.

Research has shown that supportive relationships enhance the likelihood that military personnel with PTSD will seek mental health treatment (Meis, Barry, Kehle, Erbes, & Polusny 2010). The inverse suggests that more socially isolated or withdrawn members will be less likely to seek assistance. For these reasons, DCoE has also tried to improve information and services to service members' family members. Because of the unique features of PTSD in the military, the Defense Department has also adopted an aggressive stance in support of early education and training, stepped-up surveillance and screening, combat stress interventions, and, for those who need it, treatment occurring both in deployed and in garrison settings for the full spectrum of trauma-related conditions (e.g., PTSD and acute stress) as well as other frequently co-occurring psychological health problems (e.g., depression, substance use disorders).

Today, the focus of the Defense Department response to psychological health is to ensure that service members are supported across the continuum of care. This commitment is an expansion and extension of the lessons learned during previous conflicts and an expression of the willingness of today's military leaders to prioritize psychological health as an aspect of total force fitness. In the past there was a lack of long-term, consistent focus on the psychological health issues affecting service members and veterans, regardless of the various diagnostic labels used to identify specific problems or disorders. One of the main advances represented by the current Defense Department response to psychological health is that a network of organizations now exists within the Department of Defense to help coordinate improvements in care and to disseminate information about clinical best practices and cutting-edge technologies between the services and across programs and agencies.

TBI programs and policy

As suggested above, historically and from the perspective of more recent events, TBI encompasses a spectrum of injuries that have a significant effect on force health. More particularly, as a result of combat operations in OEF and OIF, the prevalence of TBI has increased steadily for the last 10 years. Indeed, this troubling trend compelled the nation and Congress to invest in the development of policies and programs that support evidence-based care for the full TBI continuum—from mild or mTBI, otherwise known as concussion, to severe and penetrating brain injuries. Although the Defense Department has made great strides in the area of TBI clinical care, education and research, there remains a tremendous need and an opportunity to leverage scientific, policy and clinical advancement to maximize the care available to injured service members, veterans and their families.

The Defense Department first developed a consensus definition of TBI in an October 2007 policy memo (Office of Assistant Secretary of State (Health Affairs) 2007a). This definition is consistent with others proposed by the Centers for Disease Control and Prevention, the World Health Organization and the American Academy of Neurology. Originally defined as a "traumatically induced structural injury or physiological disruption of brain function as a result of external force to the head," this definition is currently being re-evaluated to take account of more recent research into the definitional aspects of TBI. A concussion definition consortium has been established to address the need for revisions.

Once the Defense Department had identified a common definition for TBI, the next great hurdle was how to quantify and measure the scope of the problem. As suggested by the historical analysis presented above, we have traditionally lacked accurate measures of TBI casualties. The source of this lacuna was definitional, diagnostic, technological, and also cultural. So as an important second step, three key surveillance functions had to be installed before worldwide TBI numbers could be obtained and aggregated. First, there were challenges related to International Statistical Classification of Diseases and Related Health Problems (ICD-9) codes. In the ICD-9, there is no code for TBI but rather descriptive codes related to the pathology of brain injury, in addition to separate concussion codes. Therefore, the Defense Department had to standardize the codes that would be used for TBI diagnoses. Second, a strong educational initiative was implemented to ensure proper coding. Finally, data systems had to be adjusted to automate the supply of this information to stakeholders. As a result of these measures, the current TBI incident diagnoses statistics for active duty, guard and reserve component service members are available on the Military Health System website (www.health.mil) or the Defense and Veterans Brain Injury Center website (www.dvbic.org). These numbers capture all severities of brain injury and can be evaluated by Service and severity. Since 2000, there have been 220,430 service members diagnosed with a TBI (through 30 June 2011), the vast majority (75–90 percent) of which are mTBIs (otherwise known as concussion). As illustrated in Figure 11.3, the explanation for the increase in TBI diagnosis since 2005 relates (at least in part) to the Department's response to TBI. The deployment of screening programs throughout the Defense Department has raised awareness and reduced the number of injuries that previously escaped detection.

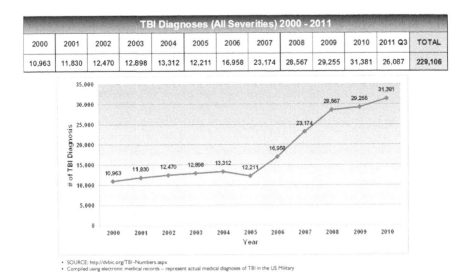

TBI Diagnoses (All Severities) 2000 - 2011												
2000	2001	2002	2003	2004	2005	2006	2007	2008	2009	2010	2011 Q3	TOTAL
10,963	11,830	12,470	12,898	13,312	12,211	16,958	23,174	28,567	29,255	31,381	26,087	229,106

• SOURCE: http://dvbic.org/TBI-Numbers.aspx
• Compiled using electronic medical records – represent actual medical diagnoses of TBI in the US Military

Figure 11.3 TBI diagnoses (all severities) 2000–2011

TBI screening programs

The cornerstone of the Department's response to TBI has been based on the tenet of early detection, thus early treatment. The Department has instituted deliberate screening programs at three stages of the treatment and/or deployment cycle: point of injury, before medical evacuation to continental US (CONUS) facilities and upon redeployment.

Point of injury

Battlefield screening of mTBI is outlined in the recently released Directive-Type Memorandum (DTM) 09-033 (2010), entitled "Policy Guidance for the Management of Concussion/Mild Traumatic Brain Injury in the Deployed Setting." This mandate ensures point of injury screening and has influenced care in many ways: (1) decreased issues associated with seeking out concussion care while in battle; (2) required mandatory documentation of the injury event, screening results and diagnosis; and (3) standardized treatment paradigms and patient movement if treatment is refractory. This policy has helped to eliminate concerns related to seeking medical care during combat since all service members are screened and treated as necessary. In addition, significant data collection processes are outlined in the policy to help analyze trends, assess current needs and inform future efforts. Finally, standardizing the approach to concussion care in theater supports rendering state-of-the-science care to wounded service members. The deployed guidelines for concussion care are currently on their fourth revision, signifying the commitment to revise as more data becomes available.

Medical evacuation

If a service member is medically evacuated to Landstuhl Regional Medical Center in Germany, they are screened for TBI regardless of the reason for the evacuation. This is another screening program that has been instituted since 2006 to ensure that mTBI is detected and treated.

Redeployment

After returning home from a deployment, all service members undergo a post-deployment health assessment (PDHA) and then 90 to 120 days later, a post-deployment health reassessment (PDHRA). During both of these processes, particular survey questions have been added to screen for TBI. Upon review of the self-reported answers to questions about injury events and changes of mental status during those injury events, a clinician will determine if further evaluation is necessary. Currently these questions are undergoing revision to allow for greater sensitivity with a follow-up diagnostic evaluation to ensure specificity.

Neurocognitive programs and policy

Neurocognitive sequelae after TBI are well documented in the literature (Cooper et al. 2011; Belanger et al. 2009). The cognitive domains affected after TBI include attention, memory, social pragmatics and executive function. In fact, attention and memory complaints are the third most reported symptom in returning combat veterans. After a concussion has been diagnosed, the further evaluation of cognitive deficits is necessary to inform clinical decision making with regards to return to duty (RTD) or to help with creating a treatment plan. For those who are on the battlefield and sustain a concussion, RTD determinations can be challenging. Most of the data collected during an assessment for concussion is subjective. DoD instituted a policy in May 2008 to mandate pre-deployment cognitive baseline testing to be performed on all service members scheduled to deploy.

The intent of this policy was to utilize a computerized neurocognitive assessment tool (NCAT) to provide baseline scores for certain cognitive domains most likely affected by concussion. Pre-deployment (and presumably) pre-injury scores could serve as a service member's own control scores should they be injured in theater. A clinician could re-test a service member with the tool and compare those tests with the pre-deployment scores. Because this is the only piece of objective, non-biased data of ongoing cognitive deficits, the NCAT represents an important new arrow in the TBI clinical management quiver, and it directly informs RTD decisions. Currently over 1 million service members have cognitive baseline scores reported. Utilizing these scores in theater is now commonplace in many of the theater concussion care centers. NCATs are also utilized to document cognitive deficits after TBI as well as to track progress and recovery after treatments, namely, cognitive rehabilitation, are completed.

Clinical practice guidelines and effective treatments

Deploying effective treatments for TBI have been more successful for severe TBI than what is available for mTBI, however the development of clinical guidance for mTBI continues to advance. The VA/DoD evidence-based working group released mTBI evidence-based clinical practice guidelines in 2009. In addition, there has been further clinical guidance developed to include the following:

a   Guidelines for the Field Management of Combat Related Head Trauma (2006)
b   Neurobehavioral Evidence Based Guidelines for the Treatment in TBI (2006)
c   Acute Management of Concussion in the Deployed Setting (2007, 2008, 2010, pending)
d   Cognitive Rehabilitation for Mild TBI (2009)
e   Driving Assessments after TBI (2009)
f   mTBI and Co-occurring Psychological Health Disorders Tool Kit (2011)
g   Neurocognitive Clinical Recommendations (2011).

In addition, the following clinical guidance packages are in development and anticipated to be disseminated to the military health system by the end of 2012:

a   Clinical Recommendation (CR) for the Detection and Referral of Visual Dysfunction Following TBI
b   CR for the Detection and Treatment of Vestibular Dysfunction Following TBI
c   CR for the Detection and Treatment of Neuroendocrine Dysfunction in mTBI
d   CR to inform the Evaluation and Treatment Approach to Sleep Disturbances Associated with TBI.

DoD is also focused on identifying effective treatments for mTBI which may include assessing several potential therapies that are currently FDA approved for other indications as well as investigations into the role and effectiveness of complementary and alternative medicines as part of an integrative health approach model for TBI. Developing and validating more effective, technology-enhanced cognitive and behavioral rehabilitation tools are also being explored.

Comorbidities

In an article published shortly after the end of World War II, Army psychiatrist Samuel Kirson related the story of a soldier who was exposed to a shell blast but had no visible physical injuries. Kirson's patient explained his feeling, after the blast, of being "all washed up":

> You can't get your mind on anything any more. You get so damn mixed up. There are a dozen things bothering you. You get angry at yourself. You don't want to quit. You want to keep going. But you know, you just aren't any good any more.
>
> (Weinberg 1946: 473)

For Weinberg, his patient's "breakdown" had a physiological and a psychological basis, which together had "[worn] away [his] resolution and confidence" (Weinberg 1946: 473). Although impossible to confirm, given the circumstances of the injury and Weinberg's description, it seems highly probable that this soldier suffered from some combination of TBI and PTSD. Today, the co-occurrence of mTBI and PTSD (termed the "signature injuries" of the current conflicts in OIF and OEF) has received much attention in the extant clinical literature. A VA Evidence Based Synthesis report found seven studies of the co-occurrence of mTBI and PTSD in VA and military populations. None of these utilized large, representative populations and the prevalence of comorbid TBI and PTSD varied widely across the populations studied. However, the three largest, most representative studies included in the VA cohort reported TBI/PTSD prevalence at between 5 and 7 percent (Carlson, Kehle, Meis, Green, MacDonald, Rutks & Wilt 2009).

Elsewhere, the issue of comorbidities appears more pronounced in populations with an existing diagnosis of a traumatic brain injury. For example, among service members with a history of mTBI, two large studies found PTSD prevalence at 33 to 39 percent of service members. Lew and co-workers (2009) found that in a treatment-seeking sample of 340 VA eligible service members, 81.5 percent reported chronic pain symptoms, 68.2 percent reported PTSD symptoms, 66.8 percent reported TBI symptoms and 42.1 percent reported symptoms of all three. These are now known as the triad of co-occurring conditions with mTBI. Additional symptoms included sleep disorders, substance abuse, psychiatric illness, vestibular disorders, visual disorders, and cognitive disorders.

This comorbidity of PTSD with a history of mTBI, chronic pain and substance abuse is common in the military and complicates recovery from any single condition. In OEF/OIF service members, the primary causes of TBI are blasts, blast plus motor vehicle crashes (MVCs), MVCs alone, and gunshot wounds. Exposure to blasts is unlike other causes of mTBI and may produce different symptoms and course of illness. This is why the DCoE developed, published, and disseminated the Co-occurring Conditions Toolkit: Mild Traumatic Brain Injury and Psychological Health in 2010, with the 2nd edition developed and disseminated in 2011. This resource is available on the DCoE website (www.dcoe.health.mil). Likewise, the patient-centered medical home model (PCMH) was developed to improve access to care, outcomes, wellness, prevention and satisfaction while ensuring a uniform patient care experience for all beneficiaries. A well-coordinated care experience is a high priority for PCMH and involves an integrated care approach for physical, cognitive, and behavioral health symptoms. For example, mental health treatment now becomes routine in primary care. This increases treatment reach and reduces stigma, especially when dealing with patients with comorbid symptoms. PCMH directly addresses overlapping and comorbid conditions and corrects problems often linked to poly-pharmacy, involvement of multiple specialty care providers, and misattribution of symptoms to medical symptoms only. Since combat deployment is strongly associated with PTSD, depression, and generalized physical health problems, this approach is even more useful.

Evaluating the defense department response and the way ahead

DoD has made great strides in understanding PTSD and TBI, but the need remains for a strategic approach capable of effectively harnessing all the work being done to advance the fields of PH and TBI care. As both history and evidence from the current conflicts in Afghanistan and Iraq suggest, the clinical issues associated with PH and TBI are not likely to simply go away. Quite the contrary, PH and TBI represent a serious threat to the health and wellness of service members and civilians in both war and peace time. As suggested above, the core of the current Defense Department response encompasses several key factors: a focus on promoting early detection, thus early treatment; ensuring force readiness and addressing cultural barriers to care; improving collaborations with the Department of Veterans Affairs

(VA), other federal agencies and academic and civilian organizations; improving deployment-related assessments; deploying effective treatments based on the most up-to-date clinical standards; and conducting military-relevant research and enhancing information technology systems to promote data sharing and tracking. Each of these areas requires a coordinated approach to be effectively addressed for the benefit of service members, veterans, and their families.

In an era where cutting-edge research and the application of new technologies have been essential to improvements in the quality of care, the variety entailed by the current Defense Department response is an asset. Nevertheless, advances in PH and TBI care should not be measured simply by the number of programs, each of which may represent a piece of the puzzle but individually lack the ability to formulate a complete picture. The Service branches must have the ability to systematically learn from each other and to access applicable research and medical knowledge generated by civilian organizations and non-military assets. At the same time, we must increase the focus within DoD on those programs and procedures that have been proven most effective, while scaling back or eliminating those that are not. When it comes to executing a comprehensive response to PH and TBI, all those who have a stake in the quality of care provided to US military service members increasingly recognize that collaboration is not just desirable, but essential to the goal of maintaining a healthy and highly effective military.

Increasing collaboration to accomplish the mission, this is the perspective reflected in two new Defense Department initiatives focusing on mental and physical health: Total Force Fitness (TFF) and the Integrated Mental Health Strategy (IMHS). In the CJCS Guidance for 2011, the Chairman of the Joint Chiefs of Staff, Adm. Michael Mullen (Chairman of the Joint Chiefs of Staff 2011), highlighted the need for a new and improved vision regarding fitness and emphasized that the traditional approach of just focusing on physical conditioning covers only a fraction of the overall needs of our service members, who now face even greater psychological and physical demands. The TFF Action Plan can be considered a direct product and consequence of the CJCS Guidance for 2011 and the foundation of a new direction in how the military evaluates the fitness of all service members. The aim of TFF is to restore the balance between readiness and well-being, and encompasses eight domains that determine the overall fitness of a service member: (1) social, (2) physical, (3) environmental, (4) medical, (5) spiritual, (6) nutritional, (7) psychological, and (8) behavioral (Figure 11.4).

The IMHS came about as a result of a Defense Department/VA Joint Mental Health Summit, held in October 2009 to address the mental health needs of military personnel, veterans and their families. These discussions and the work of the WII SOC created to investigate the care and services provided to wounded, ill and injured service members led to the request for a Defense Department/ VA mental health strategy in January 2010 and the development of the IMHS in November 2010. As part of the IMHS, four strategic goals are subdivided into 28 strategic actions or SAs (Figure 11.5), which provide defined end-states based on a public health model. According to the IMHS, each of the goals is expected to be achieved within three years from initiation of strategic efforts.

Figure 11.4 Overall fitness of a service member

IMHS Strategic Goals & Associated Actions			
Strategic Goal #1:	**Strategic Goal #2:**	**Strategic Goal #3:**	**Strategic Goal #4:**
Expand access to behavioral health care in DoD and VA	Ensure quality and continuity of care across the departments for Service members, Veterans and their families	Advance care through community partnerships, education, and successful public communication	Promote resilience and build a better behavioral health care system for tomorrow
Strategic Actions:	**Strategic Actions:**	**Strategic Actions:**	**Strategic Actions:**
•SA 01 – Screening Policies •SA 02 – Primary Care •SA 03 – Vet Center •SA 04 – Mobile Vet Centers •SA 05 – Sharing Mental Health Staff •SA 06 – Telemental Health •SA 07 – Rural Area Providers •SA 08 – Mental Health Provider Gap	•SA 09 – Evidence-based Psychotherapies •SA 10 – Quality Measures •SA 11 – Impact of Caregivers •SA 12 – Patient Outcomes •SA 13 – inTransition •SA 14 – Clinical Info Sharing	•SA 17 – Family Members' Roles •SA 18 – Community Partnership •SA 19 – Mental Health Message •SA 20 – Web-based Self Help Strategies •SA 21 – Access to Web Technologies •SA 25 – Military Culture Training	•SA 15 – Suicide Risk and Prevention •SA 16 – Family Resilience •SA 22 – Mental Health Justice Outreach Pilot •SA 23 – Chaplains Role •SA 24 – Resilience Programs •SA 26 – Translation of Mental Health Research •SA 27 – Review of Pilots •SA 28 – Gender Differences

Figure 11.5 IMHS strategic goals and associated actions

Psychological health and traumatic brain injuries are of particular concern to US service members and their families, military commanders, clinical providers and civilian leaders. In addition, the Defense Department collaborates with our NATO partners and other international allies to find solutions to PH and TBI wounds that impact force health and readiness. Any military command structure that ignores or underestimates the effects of acute and chronic stress, as well as TBI, does so at great risk to the wellbeing and effectiveness of its forces. Because this is a risk we cannot accept, the collaborative efforts currently underway represent a foundation to be strengthened and extended. In short, continued cooperation to advance PH and TBI policies and programs is vital to the collective security interests of the United States, its global allies and regional partners.

Propelled by the conflicts in Afghanistan and Iraq, PH and TBI have received unprecedented attention and resources, which in the US have been and continue to be leveraged to raise the standard of care across the MHS. There is still much work to do, but in collaboration with other federal agencies, academia and international partners, the Defense Department is leading the way toward advances in evaluation and treatment for PH and TBI related illnesses. In future, the continued effectiveness of the DoD's response will depend on the ability to access new clinical information and cutting-edge research, to anticipate problems and identify improvements to care that can be promulgated throughout the military health system, and, when necessary, to adjust existing policies and processes to ensure the best possible care for service members, veterans, and their families.

Notes

1 During the Civil War, fatalities from penetrating head injury exceeded 70 percent and mental health discharges on any grounds were exceedingly rare. Given the harsh conditions that confronted the average soldier and the limited availability of treatment, it seems likely (as historian Eric Dean suggests) that a good number of the over 300,000 documented Union deserters "suffer[ed] from some sort of what we would regard today as a stress disorder" (Dean 1997: 19).

2 Salmon is sometimes credited with developing the PIE (Proximity, Immediacy, and Expectancy) model of forward military psychiatry. As has been indicated elsewhere, he did not, in fact, originate the PIE acronym, which was not formally articulated until the 1960s (Artiss 1963; Jones et al. 2007a).

3 Efforts to build on the knowledge acquired from the war were partially stymied by what happened in its aftermath. With the cessation of hostilities, the study of "traumatic neuroses" and other related mental disorders were pushed to the margins. Following a reorganization of the US Army Surgeon General's Office in January 1918, the Division of Neuropsychiatry that had implemented Salmon's plan "ceased to exist" (Bailey 1929: 10). In 1921, Congress created the Veterans Bureau, which consolidated the services provided to military veterans by several existing federal agencies and developed a system of regional Veterans Hospitals. As of 1919, approximately 38 percent of hospitalized US World War I veterans were reported as neuropsychiatric cases. However, only one facility (located in Cape May, New Jersey) specialized in neuropsychiatric care, providing rehabilitation services for head injury victims (Shephard 2003: 153).

4 Kaufman demonstrated his approach in the Pacific Theater, where some of the fiercest battles of the war occurred, and claimed that hypnosis could achieve the same results as drugs like Pentothal without the side effects (Shephard 2003: 225).

5 Those service members killed in action were not routinely measured by medical personnel. Less than half had a cause of death recorded and head trauma was not one of the reported categories (Reister 1973: 16).

6 These numbers were controversial from the date they were first published. However, in 2006 a new group of researchers reexamined the numbers and the conclusions

of the NVVRS study and generally agreed with its assessments, despite revising downward the PTSD estimates to 9.1 percent "current" and 18.7 percent "lifetime." The study's authors' wrote that, "the message from the NVVRS has been that the Vietnam War took a severe psychological toll on US veterans. Our results provide compelling reasons to take this message seriously" (Dohrenwend et al. 2006).

7 In 2000, Congress mandated that the VA conduct a follow-up study of the NVVRS known as the National Vietnam Veterans Longitudinal Study. After several delays, the VA expects to release the NVVLS results by 2013 (United States Government Accountability Office 2010).

8 An assessment of the First Gulf War's impact on service members is complicated by the controversy surrounding "Gulf War Syndrome." Shortly after service members began returning from deployments to the Persian Gulf, some reported experiencing strange symptoms (chest pain, fatigue, shortness of breath, skin rashes, muscle and joint pain, etc.) with no verifiable cause. In 1998, Congress mandated a comprehensive review of the literature on Gulf War illnesses (including "Gulf War Syndrome") by the VA. The National Academy of Sciences' Institute of Medicine (IOM) was responsible for completing this request, which resulted in several studies of the long-term health effects of Gulf War service. Recent studies have concluded that "Gulf War illness is not the result of combat or other stressors and that Gulf War veterans have lower rates of posttraumatic stress disorder than veterans of other wars." To date, roughly 25 percent of the 697,000 soldiers deployed in the 1990–1991 Persian Gulf War have been affected by "Gulf War Syndrome" or "Gulf War Illness" (Research Advisory Committee on Gulf War Veterans' Illnesses 2008: 13).

9 The relatively brief Gulf War resulted in few battlefield casualties, but about 20 percent of those soldiers treated for combat injuries had head injuries (Schwab 2007).

10 In one study conducted in 1992, soldiers hospitalized for TBI were later found to have "several times the rates of behavioral discharges (early release because of misconduct, behavior disorder, motivation problems, etc.), criminal convictions, substance abuse problems, and medical disability as the total discharge population." In response to the growing need for standardized traumatic brain injury research, education, as well as treatment and rehabilitative services, Congress created DVBIC (Schwab 2007, xiv).

11 Office of Assistant Secretary of Defense (Health Affairs) memorandum, "Traumatic Brain Injury and Psychological Health: A Comprehensive Report on the Activities of the Health Affairs Red Cell, Transition and Sustainment Plan," December 2007.

References

Armed Forces Health Surveillance Center. (2010) *Medical Surveillance Monthly Report*, 17 (11), November 2010. Online. Available at: HTTP://afhsc.mil/viewMSMR?file=2010/ v17_n11.pdf > (accessed 21 November 2011).

Artiss, L. (1963) 'Human behavior under stress: from combat to social psychiatry', *Military Medicine* 128: 1011–1015.

Bailey, Col. P.M.C., Williams, Lieut. Col. F.E., M.C., Komora, Sgt. P.O., Salmon, Col. T.W., and Fenton, Sgt. N. (1929) *The Medical Department of the United States Army in the World War. Volume X: Neuropsychiatry*, Washington: US Government Printing Office.

Belanger, H.G., Kretzmer, T., Yoash-Gantz, R., Pickett, T. and Tupler, L.A. (2009) 'Cognitive sequelae of blast-related versus other mechanisms of brain trauma', *Journal of the International Neuropsychological Society*, 15: 1–8.

Brewin, C.R., Andrews, B. and Valentine, J.D. (2000) 'Meta-analysis of risk factors for posttraumatic stress disorder in trauma-exposed adults', *Journal of Consulting and Clinical Psychology*, 68: 748–766.

Bullman, T.A., and Kang, H.K. (1994) 'Posttraumatic stress disorder and the risk of traumatic deaths among Vietnam veterans', *Journal of Nervous and Mental Disease*,182: 604–610.

Carlson, K., Kehle, S., Meis, L., Green, N., MacDonald, R., Rutks, I., and Wilt, T., (2009) *The Assessment and Treatment of Individuals with History of Traumatic Brain Injury and Post-Traumatic Stress Disorder: A Systematic Review of the Evidence*, Washington: Department of Veterans Affairs, Veterans Health Administration, Health Services Research & Development Services. Online. Available at HTTP://www.hsrd.research.va.gov/publications/esp/tbiptsd.cfm.

Chairman of the Joint Chiefs of Staff. (2011) 'CJCS Annual Guidance for 2011', JCS. Online. Available at: http://www.jcs.mil/content/files/2011-01/011011165132_CJCS_Annual_Guidance_2011.pdf (accessed 212 November 2011).

Coates, Col. J.B. Jr., Hoff, E.C., and Hoff, P.M. (eds) (1955) *Preventative Medicine in World War II: Volume 3, Personal Health Measures and Immunization*, Washington: Office of the Surgeon General, Department of the Army.

Cooper, D.B., Kennedy, J.E., Cullen, M.A., Critchfield, E., Amador, R.R., and Bowles, A.O. (2011) 'Association between combat stress and post-concussive symptom reporting in OEF/OIF service members with mild traumatic brain injuries', *Brain Injury*, 25: 1–7.

Dean, E.T. Jr. (1997) *Shook Over Hell: Post-Traumatic Stress, Vietnam, and the Civil War*, Cambridge, MA: Harvard University Press.

Defense Manpower Data Center (DMDC). 'CTS Roster.' Unpublished.

Directive-Type Memorandum (DTM) (2010) 09-033 'Policy guidance for management of concussion/mild traumatic brain injury in the deployed setting', Signed by Deputy Secretary of Defense, 21 June 2010.

Dohrenwend, B.P., Turner, J.B., Turse, N.A., Adams, B.G., Koenen, K.C., and Marshall, R. (2006) 'The psychological risks of Vietnam for US veterans: a revisit with new data and methods', *Science* 313: 979–982.

Erichsen, J.E. (1867) *On Railway and other Injuries of the Nervous System*, Philadelphia, PA: Henry C. Lea.

Figley, C. (ed.) (1978) *Stress Disorders among Vietnam Veterans: Theory, Research, and Treatment*, New York: Routledge.

Hanson, Col. F.R. (1949) 'Combat psychiatry: experiences in the North African and Mediterranean theaters of operation, American ground forces, World War II', *Bulletin of the U.S. Army Medical Department*, Washington: US Government Printing Office.

Heaton, L.D. (ed.) (1966) *Neuropsychiatry in World War II, Volume I: Zone of the Interior*,Washington: Office of the Surgeon General, Dept. of the Army.

Highfill-McRoy, R.M., Larson, G.E., Booth-Kewley,S., and Garland, C.F. (2010) 'Psychiatric diagnoses and punishment for misconduct: the effects of PTSD in combat deployed Marines', *BMC Psychiatr.* Online. Available at: <http://www.ncbi.nlm.nih.gov/pmc/articles/PMC3020681/?tool=pubmed> (accessed 21 November 2011).

Hyams, K.C., Wignall, F.S., and Roswell, R. (1996) 'War syndromes and their evaluation: from the US Civil War to the Persian Gulf War', *Annals of Internal Medicine*, 125: 398–405.

Institute of Medicine of the National Academies (IOM). (2008). *Gulf War and Health: Volume 6. Physiologic, Psychological, and Psychosocial Effects of Deployment-Related Stress*. Washington: National Academies Press.

Jones, E., Thomas, A., and Ironside, S. (2007a) 'Shell shock: an outcome study of a First World War "PIE" unit', *Psychological Medicine* 37: 215–233.

Jones, E., Fear, N.T., and Wessely, S. (2007b) 'Shell shock and mild traumatic brain injury: a historical review', *American Journal of Psychiatry* 164: 1641–1645.

Kang, H.K., and Bullman, T.A. (2008) 'Risk of suicide among US veterans after returning from the Iraq or Afghanistan war zones', *Journal of the American Medical Association*, 300: 652–653.

Lew, H.L., Otis, J.D., Tun, C., Kerns, R.D., Clark, M.E., and Cifu, D.X. (2009) 'Prevalence of chronic pain, posttraumatic stress disorder, and persistent postconcussive symptoms in OIF/OEF veterans: Polytrauma clinical triad', *Journal of Rehabilitation Research and Development*, 46: 697–702.

Mackowiak, P.A. and Batten, S.V. (2008) 'Post-traumatic stress reactions before the advent of post-traumatic stress disorder: potential effects on the lives and legacies of Alexander the Great, Captain James Cook, Emily Dickinson, and Florence Nightingale', *Military Medicine*, 173: 1158–1163.

Meis, L.A., Barry, R.A., Kehle, S.M., Erbes, C.R., and Polusny, M.A. (2010) 'Relationship adjustment, PTSD symptoms, and treatment utilization among coupled national guard soldiers deployed to Iraq', *Journal of Family Psychology*, 24: 560–567.

Mental Health Advisory Team (MHAT) V. (2008) 'Operation Iraqi Freedom 06–08: Iraq Operation Enduring Freedom 8: Afghanistan, 14 February, 2008'. Online. Available at: <http://www.armymedicine.army.mil/reports/mhat/mhat_v/MHAT_V_OIFandOEF-Redacted.pdf > (accessed 21 November 2011).

Office of Assistant Secretary of Defense (Health Affairs) Memorandum. (2007a) 'Consolidation of traumatic brain injury initiatives in the Department of Defense', 23 March 2007.

Office of Assistant Secretary of Defense (Health Affairs) Memorandum. (2007b) 'Traumatic brain injury: definition and reporting', 1 October 2007.

Office of Assistant Secretary of Defense (Health Affairs) Memorandum (2007c) 'Traumatic brain injury and psychological health: a comprehensive report on the activities of the Health Affairs Red Cell, transition and sustainment plan', December 2007.

Ozer, E.J., Best, S.R., Lipsey, T.L., and Weiss, D.S. (2003) 'Predictors of posttraumatic stress disorder and symptoms in adults: a meta-analysis,' *Psychological Bulletin*, 129: 52–73.

Priest, D. and Hull, A. (2007) 'Soldiers face neglect, frustration at Army's top medical facility,' *Washington Post*, February 18.

Raymont, V., Salazar, A.M., Krueger, F., and Grafman, J. (2011) '"Studying injured minds" – the Vietnam Head Injury Study and 40 years of brain injury research', *Frontiers in Neurology*, 2: 1–13.

Reister, F.A. (1973) *Battle Casualties and Medical Statistics US Army Experience in the Korea War, Volume I*, Washington: Surgeon General, Department of the Army.

Research Advisory Committee on Gulf War Veterans' Illnesses (2008) *Gulf War Illness and the Health of Gulf War Veterans: Scientific Findings and Recommendations*, Washington: US Government Printing Office.

Salmon, T.W. (1917) 'The care and treatment of mental diseases and war neuroses ("shell shock") in the British Army', *Mental Hygiene* I: 509–547.

Schwab, K. (2007) 'Defense and Veterans Brain Injury Center: peacetime and wartime Missions', *JRRD*, 44: xiii–xxi.

Shephard, B. (2003) *A War of Nerves: Soldiers and Psychiatrists in the Twentieth Century*, Cambridge, MA: Harvard University Press.

Surgeon General's Office of the United States Army. (1870) *The Medical and Surgical History of the War of the Rebellion (1861–1865). Part I, Volume 2: Surgical History*, Washington: US Army Printing Office.

Sweeny, J.K. and Smutok, M.A. (1983) 'Vietnam Head Injury Study: preliminary analysis of the functional and anatomical sequelae of penetrating head trauma,' *Physical Therapy*, 63: 2018–2025.

Tanielian, T. and Jaycox, L.H. (eds) (2008) *Invisible Wounds of War: Psychological and Cognitive Injuries, Their Consequences, and Services to Assist Recovery*, Washington: RAND Corporation.

TRICARE. (2011) *2011 MHS Stakeholder's Report*. Online. Available at: <http://mhs.osd. mil/Libraries/Documents_Word_PDF_PPT_etc/2011_MHS_Stakeholders_Report. pdf> (accessed 21 November 2011).

United States Government Accountability Office. (2010) 'VA health care: progress and challenges in conducting the National Vietnam Veterans Longitudinal Study', Testimony Before the Committee on Veterans' Affairs, House of Representatives, May 5.

Weinberg, K.S. (1946) 'The combat neuroses', *American Journal of Sociology* 51: 466–478.

Young, A. (1995) *The Harmony of Illusions: Inventing Post-Traumatic Stress Disorder*, Princeton, NJ: Princeton University Press.

12 Department of Veterans Affairs response to risk of suicide for veterans

Tim A. Bullman and Han K. Kang

Introduction

Among the casualties of war are so-called "hidden casualties". This contemporary term is sometimes used to describe the physical or mental harm not directly inflicted by an armed enemy. One prominent example of "hidden casualties" are suicides among former military personnel. After the Vietnam War there were accounts in the popular media of an excessive number of suicides among Vietnam veterans. Estimates reported at the time ranged from 58,000 to 100,000 Vietnam veteran suicides (Langone 1985; CBS News 1987). However, subsequent research conducted by the Centers for Disease Control (CDC) estimated that the real number of Vietnam veteran suicides was only 9,000 through the end of 1983 (Pollock et al. 1990). In a 30-year follow-up of a cohort of Vietnam veterans, CDC reported that the risk of suicide among Vietnam veterans was no greater than that observed for the US general population or for veterans who served in the military during the Vietnam War but did not serve in Vietnam (Boehmer et al. 2004).

Recently, media attention has again focused on suicides among both those currently serving in the military and those who have separated from the military. Citing suicide numbers supplied by the US Army, both the *New York Times* and NBC News reported that between 2004 and 2008 the number of suicides among active duty Army personnel had steadily increased (Alvarez 2009; Kube & Johnson 2009). Much of this recent interest in suicide among the military has focused on those who are serving or have served in Afghanistan as part of Operation Enduring Freedom (OEF), or in Iraq as part of Operation Iraqi Freedom (OIF). In a study initiated and subsequently reported by CBS on November 13, 2007, OEF/OIF veterans were reported to have a suicide rate that was twice that of the US general population. In fact, the headline for this report was "Suicide Epidemic Among Veterans" (Keteyian 2007).

The effects of media accounts of suicide among former military personnel is perhaps evidenced by the "Veterans Suicide Study Act" which was introduced into legislation on November 15, 2007, only two days following the CBS story (S. 2899 2007). This bill stated that suicide was a serious problem among veterans and that there was a lack of information on the number of veteran suicides. The bill, which was never enacted, would have directed the Secretary of Veterans

Affairs (VA) to conduct a study of suicide among veterans. While the VA already monitored suicides among veterans and had suicide prevention measures in place, the heightened media interest led to increased efforts to determine the extent of suicides among veterans and to provide additional resources for suicide prevention.

This chapter will first examine legislation that directed VA's responses to veteran suicides. Veteran-related suicide legislation generally falls within two general categories, prevention and research, including enumeration of veteran suicides. Secondly, this chapter will outline VA's efforts to meet its legislated mandates. Previous accounts of VA's responses to veteran suicides have also described its suicide prevention efforts in the context of its legislative mandates. However, this current account provides not only the legislative context, but also the public health context, i.e. it examines the results of epidemiologic studies of suicides among veterans. These studies not only provide historical and current estimates of veteran suicides, but also suggest risk factors that should be addressed in any suicide prevention efforts.

Legislative mandates

The first major piece of legislation that was passed regarding the issue of veteran suicide was the Joshua Omvig Veterans Suicide Prevention Act (PL 110-110) (S. 479 2007). Passed in 2007 this legislation, named for an OIF veteran who committed suicide following his service in Iraq, directed the Secretary of Veterans Affairs to develop and implement a comprehensive program to reduce the incidence of suicide among veterans. This law provided a conceptual and practical framework for VA's future response to veteran suicides. Specifically, the VA was instructed to: 1) provide for staff education, including training staff to recognize suicide risk factors, prepare proper protocols for responding to crisis situations involving veterans who may be at risk for suicide, and be aware of best practices for suicide prevention; 2) assess mental health of all veterans who come to VA for care and make appropriate referrals for veterans who show signs of mental health problems; 3) designate Suicide Prevention Counselors at all VA medical facilities; 4) collaborate with other relevant agencies in conducting research on the best practices for suicide prevention; 5) conduct sexual trauma research; 6) provide 24-hour mental health care; 7) provide veterans a toll-free hotline staffed by trained mental health professionals; 8) provide outreach and education for veterans and their families; and 9) provide peer support counseling.

The next piece of relevant suicide legislation passed was the National Defense Authorization Act for Fiscal Year 2008 (PL 110-181) (HR 4986 2008). Signed into law in January 2008, this law directed both the Secretaries of the Department of Defense (DoD) and VA to enter into an agreement with the National Academy of Sciences (NAS) for the study of the mental and physical health and readjustment needs of current and former members of the military who were deployed as part of OEF or OIF. The NAS is a private nonprofit group of scientists, chartered by Congress to advise the government on scientific and technical matters.

The most recently passed legislation that either directly or indirectly relates to suicides among veterans is the Caregivers and Veterans Omnibus Health Services Act of 2010 (S. 1963 2010). Signed into law in May of 2010, one requirement of this legislation mandated that VA conduct a study to determine the number of veterans who committed suicide between 1999 and the date this law was enacted. This law also had provisions regarding the eligibility of OEF/OIF veterans for mental health counseling and services through VA's Readjustment Counseling Service.

In addition to the various bills introduced and laws enacted addressing veteran suicide, there have also been several congressional hearings assessing VA's response to preventing veteran suicides and VA's effort to enumerate the number of veteran suicides. In December 2007, the House Veterans Affairs Committee (HVAC) conducted a hearing entitled "Stopping Suicides: Mental Health Challenges within the US Department of Veterans Affairs" (HVAC 2007). Among the many witnesses were VA officials, who were questioned about VA's suicide prevention efforts and about the extent of suicide among veteran groups, including OEF/OIF veterans. The HVAC cited the earlier report by CBS news alleging a "suicide epidemic" among OEF/OIF veterans (Keteyian 2007). In May 2008, HVAC held another suicide-related hearing, entitled "The Truth About Suicides" (HVAC 2008). As they did in the 2007 hearing, the VA provided information related to its efforts to reduce veteran suicides, including a suicide prevention hotline for veterans and the designation of suicide prevention counselors. This hearing also sought to clear up what the HVAC perceived to be discrepancies between the extent of veteran suicides reported by VA and that being reported in the media.

VA suicide prevention overview

Several programs address the VA's efforts to prevent suicide among OEF/OIF veterans specifically and all veterans in general. These ongoing, or in some cases proposed, programs involve enumerating the problem, identifying suicide risk factors, and educating veterans, VA employees and the general public about all available suicide intervention related resources. By knowing the extent of the problem, i.e. enumerating the number of veteran suicides, the VA feels it can better allocate suicide prevention resources and evaluate the effectiveness of its suicide prevention programs. By identifying at-risk individuals through formal or informal assessment, the VA or anyone who encounters a veteran at risk might be able to provide some sort of effective and timely intervention and ensure proper follow-up. By informing veterans, their families and their caregivers about VA's suicide prevention resources, the VA hopes to provide the tools necessary to facilitate and encourage suicide intervention, either on the part of the veterans or by someone in contact with the veteran.

Prior to the 2007 media and congressional scrutiny into veteran suicides, the VA was already focusing on the issue of suicides among veterans. In 2004, the VA developed its 2004 Comprehensive Mental Health Strategic Plan (MHSP) (DVA 2004). The MHSP set forth the VA's mental health care strategies, initiatives, and goals for the next five years. While all initiatives of the MHSP dealt with mental health issues in general, many of them specifically targeted veteran suicide risk. One of the stated goals of the MHSP was to prevent suicide among veterans. To achieve this goal the VA adopted strategies and objectives as set forth in the National Strategy for Suicide Prevention (HHS 2001) and in IOM's report "Reducing Suicide: A National Imperative" (Goldsmith et al. 2002).

The office charged with implementing VA's suicide-related program specified in the 2004 MHSP is the Office of Suicide Prevention located within the Office of Mental Health Services. Many other VA services and centers participate in VA's suicide prevention efforts, each with a specific research or prevention-related mandate. Among these are: the Mental Health Strategic Healthcare Group (MHSHG), responsible for maintaining and improving the mental health of veterans, through health care, social services, education, and research (DVA 2011a); the Health Services Research and Development Service (HSR&D), which encourages, oversees and supports research, including the topic areas of mental health and suicide (DVA, 2011b); the Serious Mental Illness Treatment Resource and Evaluation Center (SMITREC), located at the VA Center for Practice Management and Outcomes Resource in Ann Arbor, Michigan, a special evaluation field program for MHSHG (DVA 2011c); and the Mental Illness Research, Education and Clinical Centers (MIRECCs), tasked with researching the causes and treatment of mental disorders and using education to improve VA clinical care of mental disorders, including those related to suicide. The mission of the MIRECC located in VA Integrated Service Network 19 (VISN) is to conduct clinical studies with the goal of reducing suicidal tendencies among veterans (DVA 2012). The Northeast Program Evaluation Center (NEPEC), located on the West Haven campus of the VA Connecticut Healthcare System, designs, implements, and evaluates VA mental health related programs (DVA 2011d). The Office of Suicide Prevention along with the aforementioned VA offices were tasked with implementing the following suicide prevention tasks as originally set forth in the 2004 MHSP: 1) developing a national systematic program for suicide prevention; 2) developing methods for tracking veterans with suicide risk factors; 3) evaluating VA suicide prevention efforts; 4) developing training material for VA health care providers to assist them in identifying at-risk veterans and responding in such a manner as to reduce risk; 5) developing a plan to provide 24-hour mental health care through VHA; 6) providing protocols for all first contact personnel specifying appropriate responses to veterans who may be at risk for suicide; and 7) developing a national suicide prevention database.

Outreach

One of the major components of VA's suicide prevention efforts are its outreach programs. These programs were designed to inform both veterans and the public about VA's suicide prevention resources and about possible warning signs of suicide. To ensure the widest dissemination of this information, the VA embarked on a large campaign using various media, including print media and internet sites.

For example, VA has made available three Public Service Announcements (PSAs) that provide information regarding the Veterans Crisis Line and encourage at-risk veterans or those who may know of an at-risk veteran to seek help. These videos are available online at the VA mental health suicide prevention website (DVA 2011e) and as YouTube videos, sponsored by VHA (DVA 2011f).

A printed poster campaign advertises the Veterans Crisis Line on the public transportation systems of at least ten large metro areas where the veteran suicide rate is higher than the national average. Other printed media include brochures and informational sheets available either online via the VA's mental health website (DVA 2011e) or at VA facilities. One such document lists suicide warning signs and veteran-specific suicide risk factors. Another is a pocket guide to assess suicide risk and provide information about available resources, including the Veterans Crisis Line. Another printed guide provides information that is part of the VA's ACE program. ACE, an acronym for Ask, Care, Escort, summarizes the steps to actively prevent suicide (DVA 2010a). Another resource available on the VA's suicide prevention website is a suicide risk assessment guide for VA clinicians (DVA 2008a). All of the aforementioned resources and other suicide-related brochures and information sheets for both veterans and their caregivers are available on the VA Mental Health website, and are also linked to other websites that are related to suicide research and prevention.

At the forefront of VA's suicide prevention efforts is the Office of Suicide Prevention co-located at the VA medical center in Canandaigua, NY within the VISN 2 Center of Excellence (CoE) for Suicide Prevention (DVA 2010b). This office serves as the VA's primary source of new initiatives and guidelines for suicide prevention among veterans. This office along with the CoE provides training resource material for VA personnel, such as Operation SAVE, which summarizes the steps to be taken in preventing suicide. The acronym provides a mnemonic to four important steps personnel can take to assure an active role in suicide prevention: be aware of Signs of suicidal thinking; Ask questions; Validate the person's experience; and Encourage treatment and expedite getting help (DVA 2010c).

Additional VA suicide prevention efforts include: 1) establishment of an annual Veteran Suicide Prevention Awareness Day, to focus attention on VA suicide prevention resources material; 2) flagging the medical records of veteran patients who have been identified as being at risk for suicide to influence future treatment decisions and follow-up (DVA 2008b); and 3) providing mobile health care clinics in buses sent out to rural areas to provide counseling and suicide prevention material to veterans and their families (DVA 2008c).

Counseling/crisis intervention

A primary provision of the Joshua Omvig Veterans Suicide Prevention Act was VA counseling for veterans. To comply with this mandate the VA provides a suicide prevention coordinator, often supported by a trained team, for each of its medical centers. The suicide prevention coordinator is responsible for: 1) promoting suicide prevention awareness at VA; 2) providing training for staff; 3) identifying high risk veterans and assuring their careful and continued monitoring and treatment; and 4) receiving consults from the Veteran Crisis Line to ensure that at-risk veterans seeking assistance receive all appropriate services (Karlin 2008). The VA has also provided for access to counseling for at risk veterans using a 24-hour online veteran chat service that can be accessed by going to the VA mental health suicide prevention website and clicking on the veteran chat link or directly through the suicide prevention lifeline website (DVA 2011g). Perhaps the focal point of the VA's crisis intervention and counseling efforts is the Veterans Crisis Line, formerly called the National Veterans Suicide Prevention Hotline, which can be accessed via the National Suicide Hotline (1-800-273-TALK (8255), then pressing 1 to access the Veterans Crisis Line). This hotline is staffed by trained personnel at the Canandaigua VA Medical Center. In addition to providing immediate assistance to veteran callers, the hotline staff coordinates treatment and further assistance with the VA Suicide Prevention Coordinator closest to the veteran.

Assessing VA suicide prevention efforts

Since the implementation of VA's suicide prevention programs and initiatives there have been several internally (VA) and externally (congressional) ordered evaluations of these efforts. The first took place in 2007 and was conducted by the VA Office of Inspector General (DVA, OIG, Report # 0603706 2007). In its 2007 report, the VA OIG concluded that the VA was making significant progress to meet the goals and initiatives set forth in the 2004 MHSP. Among the recommendations in this report were: 1) ensure all medical facilities can provide 24-hour mental health care, including the availability of a mental health care professional either in person or by phone; 2) provide training relative to handling crises to all staff, including first contact personnel, who might interact with at risk veterans; 3) educate all health care providers regarding suicide risk factors and risk reduction; 4) ensure that sustained sobriety does not prevent a veteran from receiving specialized mental health treatment; 5) exchange information with DoD on at-risk veterans coming to VA from DoD and those veterans who may be redeploying; and 6) conduct a centralized review of VA suicide prevention programs and ensure a single VHA standard of suicide prevention excellence.

In May of 2008, the Congressional Research Service (CRS), a component of the Library of Congress, reviewed VA suicide prevention efforts (CRS 2008). The CRS's primary criticism was that the VA did not currently have a national surveillance system for suicide among veterans. While the VA was able to provide limited findings based on subgroups of veterans, there was no single national accounting of veteran suicides that could be used to determine the success of VA suicide prevention efforts. CRS felt that if the VA could provide a baseline number of veteran suicides, this number could be tracked over time to determine what effect if any VA suicide prevention efforts were having.

As part of the VA's efforts to monitor and if necessary improve its current suicide-related research and prevention programs, the VA Secretary established a Blue Ribbon Work Group on Suicide Prevention in the Veteran Population in May 2008 (DVA 2008d). Among the recommendations of the panel were: 1) the VA should conduct ongoing evaluation of the roles and workloads of the suicide prevention coordinators; 2) the VA should expand its suicide-related outreach efforts, especially those that target veteran family members; and 3) the VA should provide clearer guidelines for flagging a veteran as being at risk for suicide.

In 2009, at the request of VHA, the VA IG again evaluated VA's suicide prevention efforts and initiatives (DVA 2009). This IG review reported that VHA facilities had generally met the requirements of the 2004 MHSP. The report also recommended: 1) greater collaboration between suicide prevention coordinators and mental health providers; 2) development of comprehensive and timely safety plans by mental health providers; and 3) placement of full-time suicide prevention coordinators at large Community-Based Outpatient Clinics.

Another approach to evaluating the success of VA's suicide prevention efforts is to examine the extent to which these resources are utilized. As of July 2011, the Suicide Prevention hotline had received 462,854 calls from veterans, family and friends of veterans (DVA 2011h).

Enumerating/monitoring veteran suicides

A component of the legislative mandate for VA regarding veteran suicides is research. Under this very broad heading are two components: 1) enumerating veteran suicides, not only overall numbers, but rates that can be compared with those for non-veterans; and 2) identifying at-risk groups that could be targeted for prevention/intervention efforts. To address the former issue, especially for comparing suicide rates among veterans with those of the US general population, it is vital that factors related to both military service and suicide risk be addressed. To achieve this it is necessary to first examine the demographics and psycho/social characteristics of all suicides, and then characterize all veterans relative to those characteristics.

Suicide among US general population

United States rates of suicide differ widely by demographic and clinical characteristics (CDC WISQARS 2010). Given the same age group, the annual suicide rate is several times higher among men than women [white males (WM), 25–29 years old: 22 suicides/100,000; white females (WF), 25–29 years old: 5.1/100,000]; within the same gender, the rate is substantially higher among older people than younger people (WM 80–84: 38/100,000; WM 25–29: 22/100,000). Within the same gender and age group, Whites are more likely to die from suicide than Blacks (WM 25–29: 22/100,000; BM 25–29: 14.1/100,000). Individuals with mental disorders, such as a depressive disorder, are at much higher risk of suicide than the general population.

Overview of all US veterans

According to the 2010 US Census, an estimated 23 million US veterans are alive, encompassing a full range of adult age groups of men and women who served during one or more time periods including the World War II era (2.2 million), the Korean War era (2.6 million), the Vietnam War era (7.6 million), the Gulf War to 2009 (5.5 million) and Peacetime only (5.6 million). Approximately 41 percent of all veterans living in the US in 2010 were over 65 years old; 25 percent were 55 to 64 years old; 26 percent were 35 to 54 years old; and 8 percent were 18 to 34 years old. Women made up 8 percent of the total veterans: 16 percent of the Gulf War era veterans; 5 percent of WWII era veterans; and less than 3 percent of Vietnam War era veterans. More veterans were classified as Whites than US civilian adults (85 percent vs. 76 percent) (US Census 2003).

In general, the composition of a group of US veterans does not mirror that of the US general population with respect to gender, age and race. As previously stated all of these characteristics are related to risk of suicide. Therefore, without careful characterization of veterans being studied and appropriate adjustment for differences in these characteristics, the resulting suicide rate of a veteran group, or the estimated relative risk compared with the US general population could be misleading and/or erroneous. A general question of whether or not veterans have an increased risk of suicide is unlikely to yield useful information without careful characterization of the veterans being studied.

The military experience of veterans also varies widely: some were involved in combat and were wounded and many served in an area away from the combat theatre; some were deployed overseas and some served only in the US; some were drafted and some volunteered. According to the 2001 National Veteran Survey, only about 25 percent of veterans have used VA healthcare services (DVA 2001).

Veteran suicide studies

All veterans

To date, multiple studies have assessed risk and rates of suicide among veterans in general, as well as for specific groups of veterans. Brief descriptions and summaries for these studies are presented in Table 12.1. The first two studies assessed suicide risk among all veterans and reported conflicting results. Kaplan et al. (2007) studied a large number of men who participated in the US National Health Interview Surveys 1986–1994 ($n = 320,890$) and linked them to the National Death Index (NDI) for cause of death information through 1997, a 12-year mortality follow-up study. Veteran status was determined by a self-report during the survey. It was reported that "Veterans represented 15.7 percent of the NHIS sample but accounted for 34.1 percent of the suicides."

It is not clear what "this NHIS sample" includes. If it includes both genders, then the statement is very misleading because while 96 percent of self-reported veterans are male, only 38 percent of the non-veteran survey participants are male. Men are

Table 12.1 Risk of suicide among veterans

Authors (Year)	Description	Results, Suicide
Kaplan et al. (2007)	320,890 National Health Interview Survey participants Veteran status – self-report Suicide outcome – NDI Follow-up – 12 years	Veterans were twice as likely to have died of suicide as US men: HR, 2.04; 95% CI, 1.10–3.80.
Miller et al. (2009)	499,356 Cancer Prevention Study II participants Veteran status – self-report Suicide outcome – NDI Follow-up – 12 years	The suicide risk did not differ by veteran status: HR, 1.01; 95% CI, 0.91–1.12.
Boehmer et al. (2004)	18,000 Army Vietnam era veterans Veteran status – military service records Suicide outcome – NDI Follow-up – 30 years	All cause mortality was lower among veterans compared with US men: Vietnam veterans: SMR, 0.93 (0.86–1.0); non-Vietnam veterans SMR, 0.86 (0.80–0.93).
Watanabe & Kang (1995)	20,000 Marine Vietnam era veterans Veteran status – military service records Suicide outcome – death certificates Follow-up – 24 years	All cause mortality and suicide risk were lower among veterans compared with US men. All causes – Vietnam veterans: SMR, 0.87 (0.81–0.94); non-Vietnam veterans SMR, 0.79 (0.72–0.86). Suicide – Vietnam veterans: SMR, 0.91 (0.67–1.21); non-Vietnam veterans: SMR, 0.79 (0.56–1.09).
Kang & Bullman (1996)	1.5 million Gulf War era veterans. Veteran status – military service records Suicide outcome – NDI Follow-up – < 3 years	All cause mortality and suicide risk were lower among veterans compared with US population. All causes – Gulf veterans: SMR, 0.44 (0.42–0.47); non-Gulf veterans SMR, 0.38 (0.36–0.40). Suicide – Gulf veterans: SMR, 0.69 (0.61–0.77); non-Gulf veterans: SMR, 0.73 (0.65–0.82).
Rothberg et al. (1990)	All US Army soldiers on active duty in 1986. Veteran status – military service records Suicide outcome – NDI Follow-up – < 1 year	The suicide mortality risk is lower among the soldiers than among the US general population: SMR, 0.69 (0.56–0.82).

Table 12.1 continued

Authors (Year)	Description	Results, Suicide
McCarthy et al. (2009)	4.7 million VA patients in FY 2000–2001. Veteran status – military service records Suicide outcome – NDI Follow-up – < 7 years	The suicide mortality risk is higher among the veteran patients than the US general population: SMR, 1.66 (1.58–1.75).
Zivin et al. (2007)	807,694 VA patients on the National Registry for Depression (1999–2004). Veteran status – military service records Suicide outcome – NDI Follow-up – 5 years	The rates (per 100,000) of suicide among the depressed VA patients were 7–8 times higher than the general population: veteran patients, 88.3; US population, 13.5.
Bullman and Kang (1994)	4,247 Vietnam veterans with PTSD and 12,010 Vietnam veteran control patients on the VA Agent Orange Registry. Veteran status – military service records Suicide outcome – death certificates Follow-up – < 10 years	The suicide mortality risk is almost 7 times higher among the Vietnam veterans with PTSD and about 70% higher among other Vietnam veteran patients compared with the US general population. PTSD patients – SMR, 6.74 (4.40–9.87); other patients – SMR, 1.67 (1.05–2.53).

many times more likely to die of suicide than women. If the NHIS sample is limited to men for both groups, then the statement is inconsistent with the reported numbers of male veterans (104,026) and male non-veterans (216,864) and corresponding numbers of suicides from each group (veteran suicides, 197; non-veteran suicides, 311). The correct statement according to these published figures should be "Veterans represented 32 percent of the male NHIS sample but accounted for 39 percent of the suicides." This detail shows the difficulty of accurately reporting suicide statistics and does not begin to take account of differences in age or race. The authors did report on the suicide risk among male veterans compared with male non-veterans adjusting for various demographic variables using the Cox proportional hazards model: HR = 2.04 (95% CI, 1.10–3.80).

The second prospective study in Table 12.1, which included a large number of men who participated in the Cancer Prevention Study II (n = 499,356), reached a different conclusion than that reported by Kaplan (Miller et al. 2009). Miller et al. reported that the risk of suicide among US men is independent of veteran status. The suicide risk among male veterans compared with male non-veterans adjusting for various demographic variables using the Cox proportional hazards model was about the same (HR, 1.04; 95% CI, 0.93–1.15). Age-adjusted analyses stratified by branch of service and by period of service also failed to find significant differences in the incidence of suicides by veteran status. The two studies are very similar to each other in materials and methods. The authors of this study speculate that Kaplan et al. "may have found higher rates of suicide among veterans in part because of incomplete adjustment for difference in the age distributions of their veteran and non-veteran participants."

Deployed veterans

Almost all deployment-specific veteran studies published to date do not support a finding of universal increase in suicide risk among all veterans. These studies have reported that the risk of suicide among deployed veterans in general is not higher than age-, sex-, and race-matched non-veterans in the US general population. In fact, most of the studies show that the risk is significantly lower among the veterans than the comparable members of the US general population. Prior to the current conflicts in Iraq and Afghanistan, active duty military personnel and individuals who were recently separated from active duty had a suicide rate that was 30–60 percent lower than the comparable US general population (Kang & Bullman 1996; Writer et al. 1996; Rothberg et al. 1990).

It is generally accepted that a selection bias known as the Healthy Soldier Effect may have contributed to the lower risk among the military personnel and veterans (McLaughlin et al. 2008). Men and women who joined the military and completed military service are generally healthier than other US men and women and they may have better access to healthcare during and after their military service. The veteran mortality rates gradually approached those of the general population over time, but the Healthy Soldier Effect seems to persist for some time, even two or more decades after the date of separation (Watanabe & Kang 1995; Seltzer & Jablon 1974; Boehmer et al. 2004). Because a significant proportion of the US adult male population would include veterans whose suicide rates are much lower than other males, had a group of veterans under study been compared with a reference population excluding veterans, the relative risk would have been even lower than what was reported. Many of these standardized mortality ratio (SMR) studies used the US general population as a reference population.

At-risk veterans

While veterans in general did not have an increased risk of suicide compared with the US general population, sub-groups of veterans who experienced a war-related illness and/or injury may be at increased risk of suicide. The risk of suicide could be elevated among those veterans who experienced prolonged deployment or who survived traumatic injuries that may have resulted in a subsequent mental disorder such as depression or PTSD. To date, multiple studies seem to support the contention that select groups of veterans are at increased risk for suicide. Vietnam veterans who were hospitalized because of a combat wound or were wounded more than once had a statistically significant increased risk of suicide compared with the US general population, when adjusted for covariates (Bullman & Kang 1996). Vietnam veterans who were diagnosed with PTSD, when compared with the general population, had an almost seven-fold statistically significant increased risk of suicide (SMR, 6.74; 95% CI, 4.4–9.9) (Bullman & Kang 1994). Veterans who were treated at a VA medical facility had a higher risk of suicide than the US general population (SMR, 1.66; 95% CI, 1.58–1.75) (McCarthy et al. 2009), and the rates of suicide among those who were treated at VA facilities for depression were seven to eight times higher than among the general population (Zivin et al. 2007). A psychiatric disorder, especially depressive disorder is a well known risk factor for suicide and higher rates of suicide were reported among patients who have been hospitalized for depression (Cornelius et al. 1995; Harris & Barraclough 1997; Bostwick & Pankratz 2000; Simon & VonKorff 1998).

Suicide among OEF/OEF veterans

Monitoring and enumerating suicides among veterans of the current conflicts, Operations Enduring Freedom/Iraqi Freedom (OEF/OIF), has become easier than for prior war veterans due to the availability of troop rosters and the National Death Index Plus. The DoD Defense Manpower Data Center (DMDC) has assembled a roster of all military personnel who have been deployed for OEF/OIF and the roster is continuously updated. For those who were separated from active duty and became eligible for VA benefits, DMDC transfers the roster with appropriate military service information to VA via a secured electronic data transfer mechanism on a monthly basis. Therefore, VA investigators can readily characterize and profile veterans by their demographic and military characteristics. This ever-growing OEF/OIF deployment roster helps VA to monitor their VA health care and benefit utilization. The same type of roster has not been available for WWII veterans, Korean War veterans, or Vietnam War veterans.

The death of OEF/OIF veterans is ascertained through matching the veteran identities with the Social Security Administration Death Master Files, VA Beneficiary Identification Records Locator Subsystem (BIRLS) Death file and CDC's National Death Index (NDI). Their cause of death can be ascertained through the NDI Plus. CDC's National Center for Health Statistics (NCHS) maintains a US national file of all decedents, beginning in 1979, from computer files submitted by vital statistics offices from all states. Death records are added to the NDI file annually, approximately 12 months after the end of a particular calendar year. NCHS provides the underlying, contributing, and all other causes of death coded to the International Classification of Diseases, 9th Revision (ICD-9) or 10th Revision (ICD-10).

In contrast, for a mortality study of WWII veterans, Korean War veterans, and Vietnam War veterans, an investigator has to assemble a study cohort, usually from paper records, determine vital status and ascertain causes of deaths through copies of death certificates obtained from state vital statistics offices for the deaths that occurred prior to 1979. It is a very time consuming and expensive data collection process. In recent years, it became even more time consuming with added review and approval processes imposed by state institutional review boards (IRBs) for the protection of human research subjects.

An unknown fraction of suicides among veterans, less than 10 percent may have been under-recorded on death certificates for various reasons (Kleck 1988). However, because the available rates of suicide among US men and women and among veteran groups are also based on death certificate information, potential bias from the misclassification is expected to be non-differential. Therefore, information on death certificates has been generally accepted as a valid source for epidemiologic research on suicide (Phillips & Ruth 1993). In 2007, VA investigators studied suicide risk among 490,346 veterans who served in OEF/OIF and separated from active duty between October 2001 and December 2005 (Kang & Bullman 2008). Suicide risk among all OEF/OIF veterans and subgroups was assessed by a standardized mortality ratio (SMR) using the life table analysis system software provided by the National Institute for Occupational Safety and Health. The SMR is the ratio of observed number of suicides among veterans to expected number of suicides based on the US general population suicide rates, adjusted for age at entry to follow-up, race, sex and year of death. Veterans on the OEF/OIF deployment roster from the DMDC were matched to the NDI for cause of deaths through 2005.

As expected from previous studies of active duty personnel and recently discharged veterans (Healthy Soldier Effect), OEF/OIF veterans have a significantly lower risk of all causes of mortality than the general population of comparable age, gender, and race composition. The overall mortality of OEF/OIF veterans was half that of the expected (SMR, 0.56; 95% CI, 0.52–0.60). In contrast, the risk of suicide among all veterans was equal to or greater than that of the US general population (SMR, 1.15; 95% CI, 0.97–1.35) suggesting that the suicide risk has increased among these veterans who have returned from the combat theatre. The suicide risk was higher among veterans from former active component units (SMR, 1.33; 95% CI, 1.03–1.69). Moreover, veterans who were diagnosed with a mental disorder had a suicide risk almost twice as high as the rate expected from the US population (SMR, 1.77; 95% CI, 1.01–2.87). The suicide rate for all OEF/OIF veterans was 21.9 per 100,000 veterans.

More recent suicide data among active duty Army soldiers revealed a similar trend for increasing suicides among the soldiers. The annual suicide rate in 2008 among all active duty soldiers has risen to 20.2 per 100,000 compared with 19.5 per 100,000 civilians with similar demographics (Kuehn 2009).

Risk factors among OEF/OEF veterans

Among recent war veterans, traumatic brain injury (TBI) depressive disorders and PTSD are recognized as significant war-related suicide risk factors. For example, individuals with TBI have an increased risk of suicide, suicide attempts and suicidal ideation compared with the general population (Teasdale & Engberg 2001; Anstey et al. 2004). Individuals with severe TBI are four times more likely to die of suicide and individuals with mild injuries also have three times higher risk of suicide than the general population after adjusting for sex and age (Teasdale & Engberg 2001). The types of TBI and injury severity as measured by the length of an individual's hospital stay have been linked to the risk of a subsequent suicide (Teasdale & Engberg 2001). Surveys of veterans returning from deployment to the Persian Gulf and Iraq and Afghanistan indicate prevalence of PTSD ranging from 8–16 percent (Kang et al. 2003; 2009; Schneiderman et al. 2008). Many military personnel serving in Afghanistan and Iraq have experienced TBI (Warden 2006). TBI caused by explosion or blast injury is the most common type of physical injury sustained by combat soldiers in Afghanistan and Iraq (Warden 2006). Several surveys of OEF/OIF veterans show the TBI prevalence rates ranging from 5 to 23 percent (Hoge et al. 2008; Tanielian & Jaycox, 2008; Schneiderman et al. 2008; Terrio et al. 2009). Among the veterans seeking health care from a VA facility, 7.5 percent were evaluated or treated for a condition possibly related to a TBI (VA internal report).

Published studies do not suggest that the risk of suicide among veterans of the Vietnam War or the 1991 Gulf War, as a whole, is significantly higher than non-deployed veterans or than the US general population. However, since historically the rates of suicide among veterans in general have been lower than that of the US population, the recent reports of suicide rates among OEF/OIF veterans rising to equal or be above the rates among civilians with similar demographics should warrant careful consideration for the factors that alone or in concert with others may contribute to or protect against the risk of suicide.

The extent to which returning OEF/OEF veterans have any of the aforementioned suicide risk factors, has implications for allocation of suicide prevention resources and suggests a high risk group to target and monitor closely. Any suicide is a tragic outcome, and efforts to identify a factor(s) that makes a veteran vulnerable to suicide should continue, thereby enabling preventive interventions which might reduce the risk of suicide among veterans. Given the high percentage of returning veterans screening positive for one or more of the known risk factors for suicide, such as a depressive disorder, PTSD and TBI, monitoring and enumerating as well as providing preventive interventions is well warranted.

Summary

Responding to congressional mandates and public interest, the VA has increased its efforts to monitor and prevent veteran suicides. Many prevention efforts involve media campaigns to inform veterans and their caretakers about possible warning signs that might precede suicide behavior and about the various suicide prevention resources available. Additional prevention endeavors include adding personnel to more closely monitor, track, and provide counseling to veterans at risk for suicide. Internal and external reviews of VA's efforts to respond to the reported increase in veteran suicides report that the VA is making progress in complying with its suicide prevention mandates.

The legislated mission of providing suicide rates for all veterans has still not been realized. The difficulty with enumerating all veteran suicides is primarily related to the difficulty of identifying all veterans. The VA has data on all who entered the military since 1977. For those who entered the military prior to 1977, the VA has data only for those who were eligible for VA benefits. While the VA can provide accurate rates for OEF/OIF veteran suicides, it cannot provide real-time rates, i.e. the suicide rates reported by VA are 2 years behind the current calendar year because NDI's collection of cause of death data from the states lags two years. While the VA could request cause of death data directly from state vital statistics offices, this process, due to the restrictions imposed by states and the time it would take to receive and process the data from states, would probably be at least 6 months to a year behind the date of the current calendar year.

While the VA may currently be unable to provide real-time, i.e. up-to-date, suicide numbers and rates for all veterans, or even OEF/OIF veterans, its efforts to identify risk factors such as TBI and PTSD have met with more success. Regarding suicide prevention, the VA has either met or is progressing towards meeting its obligations relative to providing resources to prevent veteran suicides. Perhaps the most important remaining question is the extent to which VA's suicide prevention efforts have been successful. While the VA does have up-to-date counts of calls to its suicide prevention hotline and some follow-up data, to better address the effectiveness of its prevention programs it must first be better able to quantify all veteran suicides.

References

Alvarez L. (2009) Suicides of soldiers reach high of nearly 3 decades. [online] Available at: http://www.nytimes.com/2009/01/30/us.30suicide (accessed August 23, 2010).

Anstey KJ, Butterworth P, Jorm AF, Christensen H, Rodgers B, Windsor TD. (2004) A population survey found an association between self-reports of traumatic brain injury and increased psychiatric symptoms. *J Clin Epidemiol* 57, pp. 1202–1209.

Boehmer T, Flanders D et al. (2004) Post-service mortality in Vietnam veterans: 30 year follow-up. *Archives of Internal Medicine*, 164, pp. 1908–1916.

Bostwick JM, Pankratz VS. (2000) Affective disorders and suicide risk: a reexamination. *Am J Psychiatry*, 157, pp. 1925–1932.

Bullman TA, Kang HK. (1994) Posttraumatic Stress Disorder and the risk of traumatic deaths among Vietnam veterans. *J Nerv Ment Dis*, 182, pp. 604–610.

Bullman TA, Kang HK. (1996) The risk of suicide among wounded Vietnam veterans. *Am J Public Health*, 86, pp. 662–667.

CBS News. (1987) 60 Minutes. Vietnam 101. New York: October 4, 1987. Transcript.

Center for Disease Control and Prevention (CDC). (2010) Web-based Injury Query and Reporting System (WISQARS) [online] Available at: www.cdc.gov/ncipc/wisqars. (accessed July 10, 2010).

Congressional Research Service (CRS). (2008) CRS Report for Congress RL34471, Suicide Prevention Among Veterans. Sundararaman R, Panangala S, Lister S. May 5, 2008.

Cornelius JR, Salloum IM, Mezzich J et al. (1995) Disproportionate suicidality in patients with comorbid major depression and alcoholism. *Am J Psychiatry*, 152, pp. 358–364.

Department of Veterans Affairs (DVA) National Center for Veterans Analysis and Statistics. (2001) 2001 National Survey of Veterans; Final Report. [online] Available at: http://www.va.gov/VETDATA/SurveysAndStudies/Final_Report.asp (accessed on September 14, 2011).

Department of Veterans Affairs (DVA) (2004) Report to the Secretary, A Comprehensive VHA Strategic Plan for Mental Health Services-Revised, Veterans Health Administration, Mental

Health Strategic Plan Workgroup, Mental Health Strategic Care Group, Office of the Assistant Deputy Under Secretary for Health, July 9, 2004. [online] Available at: http://veterans.house.gov/Media/File/110/5-6-08/MHstrategicplan2004.htm (accessed on August 23, 2010).

Department of Veterans Affairs (DVA) (2007) Office of Inspector General. Implementing VHA's Mental Health Strategic Plan Initiatives for Suicide Prevention (Report No 06-03706-126).

Department of Veterans Affairs (DVA) (2008a) Office of Mental Health Services [online] Available at: http://vaww.mentalhealth.va.gov/files/suicideprevention/SuicideRisk Guide.doc (accessed February 16, 2012).

Department of Veterans Affairs (DVA) (2008b) Veterans Health Administration [online] Available at: http://www1.va.gov/vhapublications/ViewPublication.asp?pub_ID=1719 (accessed February 16, 2012).

Department of Veterans Affairs (DVA) (2008c) Office of Public and Intergovernmental Affairs [online] Available at: http://www1.va.gov/opa/pressrel/pressrelease.cfm?id=1552 (accessed February 16, 2012).

Department of Veterans Affairs (DVA) (2008d) Office of Mental Health Services. [online] Available at: http://www.mentalhealth.va.gov/suicide_prevention/Blue_Ribbon_Report-FINAL_June-30-08.pdf (accessed February 16, 2012).

Department of Veterans Affairs (DVA) (2009) Office of Inspector General. Healthcare Inspection: Evaluation of Suicide Prevention Program Implementation in Veterans Health Administration Facilities January–June 2009 (Report No. 09-00326-223).

Department of Veterans Affairs (DVA) (2010a) Office of Mental Health Services [online] Available at: http://www.mentalhealth.va.gov/docs/VA_ACE_CARD_8_6_2009_final_version.pdf (accessed February 16, 2012).

Department of Veterans Affairs (DVA) (2010b) Department of Veterans Affairs Center of Excellence. Canandaigua VA Medical Center, Canandaigua NY. [online] Available at: http://www.canandaigua.va.gov/about/ (accessed February 16, 2012).

Department of Veterans Affairs (DVA) (2010c). Operation S.A.V.E. [online] Available at: http://www.dcoe.health.mil/DCoEV2/Content/navigation/documents/SPC2010/Jan12/1545-1715/Kemp%20-%20Operation%20S.A.V.E.%20-%20Suicide%20Prevention%20Training%20for%20Frontline%20Veterans%20Affairs%20Staff.pdf (accessed February 16, 2012).

Department of Veterans Affairs (DVA) (2011a) Mental Health Strategic Healthcare Group. Department of Veterans, Veterans Health Administration. [online] Available at: http://www.mentalhealth.va.gov/VAMentalHealthGroup.asp (accessed February 16, 2012).

Department of Veterans Affairs (DVA), (2011b) Health Services Research and Development Service. [online] Available at: http://www.hsrd.research.va.gov/ (accessed February 16, 2012).

Department of Veterans Affairs (DVA) (2011c) Serious Mental Illness treatment Resource and Evaluation Center. Department of Veterans Affairs. [online] Available at: http://www.annarbor.hsrd.research.va.gov/SMITREC.asp (accessed February 16, 2012).

Department of Veterans Affairs (DVA) (2011d) Northeast Program Evaluation Center. West Haven Connecticut, VA Connecticut Healthcare System. [online] Available at: http://vaww.nepec.mentalhealth.va.gov/index.htm (accessed February 16, 2012).

Department of Veterans Affairs (DVA) (2011e) Office of Mental Health Services [online] Available at: http://www.mentalhealth.va.gov/suicide_prevention/index.asp (accessed February 16, 2012).

Department of Veterans Affairs (DVA) (2011f) Veterans Health Administration Channel [online] Available at: http://youtube.com/watch?v=xtwkcg5vq_k (accessed September 12, 2011).

Department of Veterans Affairs (DVA) (2011g) [online] Available at: http://suicidepreventionlifeline.org/Veterans/Default.aspx (accessed February 16, 2012).

Department of Veterans Affairs (DVA) Office of Mental Health Services, Suicide Prevention, Patient Care Services (2011h) VA National Suicide Prevention Hotline Call Report 2011 Totals YTD. Internal Report.

Department of Veterans Affairs (DVA) (2012) Mental Illness Research, Education, and Clinical Centers. [online] Available at: http://www.mirecc.va.gov/ (accessed February 16, 2012).

Goldsmith SK, Pellmar TC, Kleinman AM, Bunney WE. (eds). (2002) *Reducing Suicide: A National Imperative*. Institute of Medicine. The National Academies Press, Washington, DC.

Harris EC, Barraclough B. (1997) Suicide as an outcome for mental disorders: a meta-analysis. *Br J Psychiatry*, 170, pp. 205–228.

Health and Human Services (HHS) (2001) National Strategy for Suicide Prevention: Goals and Objectives for Action. US Department of Health and Human Services, Public Health Service, Rockville, MD. [online] Available at: http://www.sprc.org/library/nssp.pdf. (accessed September 14, 2011).

Hoge CW, McGurk D, Thomas JL. et al. (2008) Mild traumatic brain injury in US soldiers returning from Iraq. *N Engl J Med*, 358, pp. 453–463.

House Veterans Affairs Committee (HVAC) (2007) Stopping Suicides: Mental Health Challenges Within The US Department of Veterans Affairs. Hearing Before The Committee On Veterans Affairs US House of Representatives, 110th Congress, 1st sess., December 12, 2007.

House Veterans Affairs Committee (HVAC) (2008) The Truth About Veterans' Suicide. Hearing Before The Committee On Veterans Affairs US House of Representatives, 110th Congress, 2nd sess., May 6, 2008.

HR 4986, 110th Cong., PL. 110-181. National Defense Authorization Act for Fiscal Year 2009. (2008).

Kang HK, Bullman TA. (1996) Mortality among US veterans of the Persian Gulf War. *N Eng J Med*, 335, pp. 1498–1504.

Kang HK, Bullman TA. (2008) The risk of suicide among US veterans after returning from Iraq or Afghanistan war zones. *JAMA*, 300. pp. 652–653.

Kang HK, Natelson BH, Mahan CM, Lee KY et al. (2003) Post-traumatic stress disorder and chronic fatigue syndrome-like illness among Gulf War veterans: A population based survey of 30,000 veterans. *Am J Epidemiol*, 157, pp. 141–148.

Kang HK, Li B, Mahan CM, Eisen SA, Engel CC. (2009) Health of US veterans of 1991 Gulf War: a follow-up survey in 10 years. *J Occup Environ Med*, 51, pp. 401–410.

Kaplan MS, Huguet N, McFarland BH et al. (2007) Suicide among male veterans: a prospective population-based study. *J Epidemiol Community Health*, 61, pp. 619–624.

Karlin B (2008) Suicide prevention in the Department of Veterans Affairs. Presented at the 2008 Conference of the Association of VA Psychologist Leaders. http://www.avapl.org/pub/2008Conference/Suicide%20Prevention%20B.%20Karlin.pdf (accessed November 2012)

Keteyian A. (2007) Suicide Epidemic Among Veterans. http://www.cbsnews.com/stories/2007/11/13/cbsnews_investigates/main3496471.shtml (accessed March 26, 2008).

Kleck G. (1988) Miscounting suicides. *Suicide Life Threat Behav*, 18, pp. 219–236.

Kube C, Johnson A. (2009) Suicides continue alarming rise in military. January 29, 2009. [online] Available at: http://www/msnbc,msn.com/id/28895624 (accessed August 23, 2010).

Kuehn BM. (2009) Soldier suicide rates continue to rise. Military, scientists work to stem the tide. *JAMA*, 301, pp. 1111–1113.

Langone J. (1985) The war that has no ending. *Discover.* June 1985, pp. 44–45.

McCarthy JF, Valenstein M, Kim HM, Ilgen M, Zivin K, Blow FC. (2009) Suicide mortality among patients receiving care in the Veterans Health Administration health system. *Am J Epidemiol*, 169, pp. 1033–1038.

McLaughlin R, Nielsen L, Walter M. (2008) An evaluation of the effect of military service on mortality: quantifying the health soldier effect. *Ann Epidemiol*, 18, pp. 928–936.

Miller M, Barber C, Azrael D, Calle EE, Lawler E, Mukamal KJ. (2009) Suicide among US veterans: a prospective study of 500,000 middle-aged and elderly men. *Am J Epidemiol*, 170, pp. 494–500.

Phillips DP, Ruth TE. (1993) Adequacy of official suicide statistics for scientific research and public policy. *Suicide Life Threat Behav*, 23, pp. 307–319.

Pollock DA, Rhodes P, Boyle CA, et al. (1990) Estimating the number of suicides among Vietnam veterans. *Am J Psychiatry*, 147, pp. 772–776.

Rothberg JM, Bartone PT, Holloway HC. (1990) Life and death in the US Army: in corpore sano. *JAMA*, 264, pp. 2241–2244.

S. 479, 110th Cong., PL. 10-110. Joshua Omvig Veterans Suicide Prevention Act. 1 (2007).

S. 1963, 111th Cong., PL 111-163. Caregivers and Veterans Omnibus Health Services Act of 2010. (2010).

S. 2899, 110th Cong., Veterans Suicide Study Act. (2007).

Schneiderman AI, Braver ER, Kang HK. (2008) Understanding sequele of injury mechanisms and mild traumatic brain injury incurred during the conflicts in Iraq and Afghanistan: Persistent post concussive symptoms and posttraumatic stress disorder. *Am J Epidemiol*, 358, pp. 453–463.

Seltzer CL, Jablon S. (1974) Effects of selection on mortality. *Am J Epidemiol*, 100, pp. 367–372.

Simon GE, VonKorff M (1998) Suicide mortality among patients treated for depression in an insured population. *Am J Epidemiol,* 147, pp. 155–160.

Tanielian T, Jaycox (eds) (2008) *The Invisible Wounds of War: Psychological and cognitive injuries, their consequences, and service to assist recovery.* Santa Monica, CA, Rand.

Teasdale TW, Engberg AW. (2001) Suicide after traumatic brain injury: a population study. *J Neurol Neurosurg Psychiatry*, 71, pp. 436–440.

Terrio H, Brenner LA, Ivins BJ et al. (2009) Traumatic brain injury screening: preliminary findings in a US Army brigade combat team. *J Head Trauma Rehabil*, 24, pp. 14–23.

US Census, (2003) Veterans: 2000. Census 2000 brief. [online] Available at: (www.census. gov/prod/2003pubs/c2kbr-22.pdf) (accessed November 18, 2010).

Warden D. (2006) Military TBI during the Iraq and Afghanistan wars. *J Head Trauma Rehabilitation*, 21, pp. 398–402.

Watanabe KK, Kang HK. (1995) Military service in Vietnam and the risk of death from trauma and selected cancers. *Ann Epidemiol*, 5, pp. 407–412.

Writer JW, DeFraites RF, Brundage JF. (1996) Comparative mortality among US military personnel in the Persian gulf region and world wide during Operations Desert Shield and Desert Storm. *JAMA*, 275, pp. 118–121.

Zivin K, Kim M, McCarthy JF, Austin KL, Hoggatt KJ, Walters H, Valenstein M. (2007) Suicide mortality among individuals receiving treatment for depression in the Veterans Affairs health system: association with patient and treatment setting characteristics. *Am J Public Health*, 97, pp. 2193–2198.

13 An overview of toxicant exposures in veteran cohorts from Vietnam to Iraq

Kimberly Sullivan, Maxine Krengel,
Patricia Janulewicz Lloyd, and
Jonviea Chamberlain

An overview of chemical (toxicant) exposures in military deployments is relevant for clinicians, researchers and laypeople given the many potential post-exposure medical, psychosocial and long-term consequences. These exposures have been linked to altered cognition, ill-health (including development of cancers) and decreased long-term military readiness within and between conflicts. Therefore, the potential safety of troops deployed in the future is also of concern. To our knowledge, the impact of toxicology on military health has not been reviewed in detail. The critical link between military health and toxicology will be the focus of this chapter, which includes an overview of several toxicants and likely health effects across three eras of conflict: Vietnam, Persian Gulf War (GW), Afghanistan (OEF) and Iraq (OIF). These conflicts provide examples of exposure effects given the numerous research studies documenting toxicants in the first two conflicts and the recency of the last two. Although all military occupations have environmental exposures requiring careful prevention and mitigation strategies, the risk for exposure increases exponentially in certain occupational categories described below.

Toxicant exposures have been a hindrance to military health and readiness since WWI (i.e., mustard gas) and throughout subsequent conflicts (e.g., herbicides, pesticides, anti-nerve gas pills, sarin, smoke from oil well fires, burn pits, and diesel fuels). Relevant toxicant exposures can be the result of chemical weapons, accidental overuse or human error. In addition, exposures may occur with single chemicals or mixtures from levels below permissible exposure limits (PEL) to near lethal limits and may occur in the context of stressors, including but not limited to extreme temperatures, fatigue or fear stress (Rossi et al., 2000). Exposures may occur through dermal, inhalation and oral routes (food and water contamination), and it has been determined that some chemical compounds may go directly into the brain through the olfactory system and that physiological stressors may alter the permeability of the blood brain barrier making exposure levels significantly higher. These mechanisms of exposure can cause multiple health effects that may be seen during and well into post-deployment and the range of effects can vary by individual susceptibility. We will discuss both immediate and long-term effects of such agents as a result of acute or chronic exposure and will reference the additive or synergistic effects.

Historically, it was believed that exposure to particular neurotoxicants caused acute behavioral effects and once individuals were removed from the exposure, they would improve greatly and were no longer expected to have long-term health effects. Over the years however, it has become clear that this was not always the case and some lower level chronic exposures can cause long-term health and behavioral changes (Baker et al., 1985, Ray and Richards, 2001). Additionally, the importance of the interaction or synergistic effects of toxicant exposure, physical stressors and emotional trauma are becoming increasingly well understood (Abdel-Rahman et al., 2004b).

In this chapter, we first review the known toxicants from each of the aforementioned conflicts and provide an overview of presumed and/or documented health effects by using a model of known exposure groups in each conflict. This consists of Ranch Hands and Flyswatters from Vietnam, pesticide applicators from the GW and hazardous waste and disposal personnel from Iraq and Afghanistan. We review the literature on health symptom reports, psychological factors and neurocognitive correlates, which are commonly used as indicators of brain and health functioning in exposed individuals (White and Proctor, 1992).

Vietnam War

The aftereffects of the Vietnam War are well documented in several reviews of the emotional traumatization on deployed troops and the resultant post-traumatic stress disorder (PTSD) (Goldberg et al., 1990, Snow et al., 1988, Bullman et al., 1991). It was not until several years after the war that the effects from environmental toxicants and the links to increased cancer rates were studied. Environmental exposures of concern for Vietnam era military personnel include the tactical herbicides (the most common of which was Agent Orange) commonly used in combat as a means of removing foliage, which provided cover for the enemy. This approach not only improved visibility in enemy controlled areas, but also resulted in exposure of military personnel, from those transporting and spraying to the front-line ground troops. Those with the most significant exposures, the Ranch Hands, have been commonly studied in relationship to physical symptoms, including lung and other forms of cancer (Clapp, 1997). Less commonly studied are the cognitive and affective effects from exposure to insecticides and herbicides used in combat areas (Young and Cecil, 2011). This section of the chapter will focus on toxicant exposures known to be prevalent in theatre and the resulting physical health, emotional, and cognitive effects.

The US military herbicide program in South Vietnam took place between 1962 and 1971. The Department of Veterans Affairs has identified the heavily sprayed areas, including the inland and mangrove forests (http://www.publichealth. va.gov/exposures/agentorange/index.asp). Two groups of Vietnam veterans have been identified as having risk for high exposure to Agent Orange: 1) Air Force personnel involved in Operation Ranch Hand and 2) members of the US Army Chemical Corps (IOM, 2009). Presumed exposure to herbicides during the Vietnam War is recognized by the Department of Veterans Affairs (VA) for two circumstances: 1) exposure on land in Vietnam or on a ship operating on the inland waterways of Vietnam between January 9, 1962 and May 7, 1975 and 2) exposure along the demilitarized zone in Korea between April 1, 1968 and August 31, 1971 (http://www.publichealth.va.gov/exposures/agentorange/index.asp). The following three circumstances are not presumed to have been exposed but are regarded as "possibly exposed": 1) exposure to Blue Water veterans on open sea ships off the shore of Vietnam during the Vietnam War, 2) exposure on or near the perimeters of military bases between February 28, 1961 and May 7, 1975, and 3) exposure due to herbicide tests and storage at military bases in the United States and locations in other countries (http://www.publichealth.va.gov/exposures/agentorange/index.asp).

The majority (95 percent) of tactical herbicides sprayed during the Vietnam War was done under the code name Operation Ranch Hand as noted above, which began in 1962 and concluded in 1971. The spraying program was termed the Rainbow Herbicide Program based on sticker colors placed on the side of 55-gallon drums containing the herbicides. Each color designated a different herbicide selected for a specific purpose: i.e., Orange, general defoliation; White, forest defoliation and long-term control; Blue, rapid defoliation and grassy plant control as well as rice destruction. These herbicides contained chemicals of concern for human health. Agent Orange was the most widely used of the herbicides, 11 of the total 19 million gallons of herbicides used during the war (Young, 1984). Agent Orange is a compound mixture of tetrachlorodibenzo-p-dioxin (TCDD, dioxin), which is a lipophilic, or fat soluble, substance that may bioaccumulate. The compounds readily enter the body, do not readily degrade in the environment or body and biomagnify up the food chain. Dioxin contamination levels in Vietnam were much higher than what was deemed appropriate for use in the United States and could have been 1,000 times higher than the level of dioxin in herbicides used domestically (NAS, 1974).

The majority of epidemiological data on the Vietnam veteran cohort exists from the Air Force Health Study of Ranch Hands, which started in 1979 and was part of a federal effort to examine the association between Agent Orange exposure and ill health in this population. Initial studies documented that the median body burden of dioxin in these veterans in 1992 was significant (12.5 ppt: 7.7 ppt for officers, 17.8 ppt for flyers, 24.0 ppt for ground crew and 4.1 ppt for the veteran comparison group: 4.4 for officers, 4.0 for flyers, 4.0 for ground crew) (AFHS, 1991b). Health symptom results from this 20-year study suggest Agent Orange exposure is associated with increased risk of developing diabetes mellitus (Henriksen et al., 1997, Michalek et al., 2001, Michalek and Pavuk, 2008), peripheral neuropathy (Michalek et al., 2001) and having significantly increased levels of thyroid stimulating hormone (Pavuk et al., 2003) although no association with thyroid disease was found (Barrett et al., 2001). Due to the relatively small sample size and the possibility of exposure misclassification, it was difficult to detect small to moderate increases in risks of rare diseases in this population resulting in inconsistent findings on reproductive (Michalek et al., 1998, Wolfe et al., 1995) and cancer outcomes (Akhtar et al., 2004, Ketchum et al., 1999, Pavuk et al., 2006, 2005). However, when comparing the cancer rates in highly exposed veterans to national rates, Akhtar and colleagues (Akhtar et al., 2004) found two or more years of service in Vietnam was associated with increased risk of cancer at all sites.

A handful of studies were conducted on other groups of Vietnam veterans with high exposure risk jobs, including members of the US Army Chemical Corp. These studies have found no association with a surrogate measure of Agent Orange exposure (occupation) and non-Hodgkin's lymphoma (Dalager et al., 1991), Hodgkin's disease (Dalager et al., 1995) or lung cancer (Mahan et al., 1997). However, Kang et al. (2006) did find an increased risk for diabetes, heart disease, hypertension and chronic respiratory conditions with these veterans. Studies conducted by Boston University researchers on Massachusetts Vietnam veterans exposed to Agent Orange found an association between exposure and soft tissue sarcoma, non-Hodgkin's lymphoma, Hodgkin's disease, oral cavity and pharynx cancers (Clapp, 1997, Clapp et al., 1991). One study conducted with Vietnam veterans residing in California found an increased risk of developing prostate cancer (Chamie et al., 2008). The VA, one of the only entities to focus on the 4,140 women who served in Vietnam and the ill-health effects these women and their offspring suffered following Agent Orange exposure, found an increased risk for moderate to severe birth defects in the offspring (Kang et al., 2000a) but no increased risk of miscarriage, low birth weight or preterm delivery. Kang et al. (2000b) also found no increased risk for gynecological cancers in these female Vietnam veterans.

Enacted in 1991, the Agent Orange Act required the VA to request the National Academy of Sciences to review and evaluate all information on exposure to Agent Orange and other herbicides used in Vietnam as well as other compounds with similar chemical properties in exposed veteran populations and relevant occupational and environmental exposures. Pursuant to this Act the National Academy of Sciences' Institute of Medicine (IOM) has published their findings every two years since 1994. The latest IOM report (IOM, 2009) concluded that there were five diseases with sufficient evidence and 15 with limited but suggestive evidence of a link between Agent Orange exposure and disease (see Table 13.1).

The VA has compensation allowances, including health care benefits and disability compensation, for Vietnam veterans exposed to Agent Orange diagnosed with a disease that has been deemed to have sufficient or limited but suggestive evidence in the latest IOM report (IOM, 2009). Compensation is based on service-related disability or death. The 2010 Annual Budget Report (VA, 2010) for the VA states that 1,095,473 Vietnam era veterans are receiving benefits, costing over $16 million in 2010 ($16,153,679). Over 100,000 Vietnam veteran survivors were collecting benefits in 2010 (164,039), costing over $2 million ($2,363,096). Over 1,178 children of Vietnam veterans were collecting benefits for transgenerational effects of Agent Orange exposure, costing nearly $20 thousand ($19,678).

Very few studies have been completed to date documenting the neurocognitive deficits associated with herbicide exposure in Vietnam veterans. One such study evaluated neurocognitive functioning on standardized neuropsychological tests

Table 13.1 Institute of Medicine's list of health outcomes associated with Agent Orange exposure

Weight of the evidence	Disease
Sufficient evidence	soft-tissue sarcoma (including heart), non-Hodgkin's lymphoma, chronic lymphocytic leukemia (including hairy cell leukemia and other chronic B-cell leukemias), Hodgkin's disease, chloracne
Limited but suggestive evidence	laryngeal cancer, cancer of the lung, bronchus, or trachea, prostate cancer, multiple myeloma, AL amyloidosis, early-onset transient peripheral neuropathy, Parkinson's disease, Porphyria cutanea tarda, hypertension, ischemic heart disease, type 2 diabetes (mellitus), and spina bifida in offspring of exposed people
Inadequate/Insufficient evidence	cancers of the oral cavity, pharynx, nasal cavity; cancers of the pleura, mediastinum, and other unspecified sites within the respiratory system and intrathoracic organs; esophageal cancer; stomach cancer; colorectal cancer; hepatobiliary cancers; pancreatic cancer; bone and joint cancer; melanoma; non-melanoma skin cancer; breast cancer; cancers of reproductive organs; urinary bladder cancer; renal cancer; cancers of brain and nervous system; endocrine cancer; cancers at other and unspecified sites; neurobehavioral disorders (cognitive and neuropsychiatric); movement disorders (including amyotrophic lateral sclerosis (ALS) but excluding Parkinson's disease); chronic peripheral nervous system disorders; respiratory disorders; gastrointestinal, metabolic, and digestive disorders; immune system disorders; circulatory disorders (other than hypertension or ischemic heart disease); endometriosis; effects on thyroid homeostasis and certain reproductive effects, i.e., infertility, spontaneous abortion, neonatal or infant death and stillbirth in offspring of exposed people, low birth weight in offspring of exposed people, birth defects (other than spina bifida) in offspring of exposed people, and childhood cancer (including acute myelogenous leukemia) in offspring of exposed people

Source: Institute of Medicine (IOM, 2009)

of motor, memory, academic achievement and general intelligence. Barrett et al. (2001) found the highly exposed Ranch Hand veterans had a significant reduction in performance on fine and gross motor tasks (finger tapping and grip strength) with both dominant and non-dominant hands as well as reduced immediate and delayed memory abilities on the Wechsler Memory Scales (WMS) logical memory subtest. As expected, no differences were found on general mental abilities, premorbid cognitive abilities (Wechsler Adult Intelligence Scale – Revised) or achievement tests (Wide Range Achievement Test). These findings of diminishment in motor functioning are consistent with what would be expected as a long-term consequence of neurotoxicant overexposure (Sullivan et al., 2003, White and Proctor, 1992).

A limited number of researchers have continued to follow Vietnam veterans through middle and advanced age or have assessed the impact of Agent Orange exposure on the aging process. Surprisingly, there are sparse dose–effect relationship studies with Agent Orange and development of age-related diseases including dementia or other neurodegenerative processes. Further studies on this topic could help elucidate if Vietnam veterans are showing accelerated aging patterns including neuroinflammation and other markers of neurodegenerative disease (Barrientos et al., 2010).

Mortality studies have also been used to assess the long-term health impact of Agent Orange exposure. The mortality for 1,262 Ranch Hand veterans to December 31, 1999 was contrasted with that for 19,078 comparison veterans. The relative risk (RR) for all-cause death was borderline significantly increased (RR = 1.15; 95% confidence interval, 1.0–1.3; $p = 0.06$). The risk of death caused by cancer was not increased (RR = 1.0), but the risk of death caused by circulatory system diseases was significantly increased among enlisted ground crew workers (RR = 1.7; 95% confidence interval, 1.2–2.4; $p = 0.001$). Results for Ranch Hand all-cause death differed from previous reports, with the RR now exceeding 1.0. The risk of death attributable to circulatory system diseases continues to be increased, especially for enlisted ground crew, a subgroup with relatively high skin exposure to herbicides (Ketchum and Michalek, 2005).

Although Agent Orange was the most widely known exposure during the Vietnam War, other relevant exposures included operations to reduce malaria-carrying mosquito populations by spraying the insecticide malathion from helicopters and then aircraft previously used to spray Agent Orange. This insecticide spraying operation lasted from 1966 to 1972 and was called Operation FLYSWATTER (Cecil and Young, 2008). During this time, 1.7 million liters of malathion concentrate was sprayed and spraying occurred on average every 9 days. A recent review of thousands of pesticides as part of the Food Quality Protection Act by the Environmental Protection Agency (EPA) has resulted in the re-evaluation of the safety of some organophosphate pesticides, causing recommendations for the restricted use or banning of several of the most commonly used chemicals including malathion. Part of the reason for malathion to be included in this list was that malathion exposure was reported to affect thyroid functioning and to be associated with thyroid tumors in this report (www.epa.gov/pesticides/cumulative/rra-op). As with Agent Orange, there has been a dearth of information regarding long-term effects of exposure to malathion in this group in terms of cognitive and health outcomes, but as stated below the effects of this exposure in other veteran populations have been shown to include diminished motor, cognitive and mood functioning.

Gulf War

Nearly 700,000 US veterans were deployed to the Persian Gulf to secure Kuwait from an Iraqi invasion during the 1990–1991 GW. In this section, we provide an overview of the unique environmental exposures during this deployment and illustrate where combination exposures to neurotoxicants likely resulted in chronic health effects. Although many researchers have studied the ill-health effects of veterans deployed to the GW, we use our well-developed cohorts as examples of specific deployment related health outcomes that have come to be associated with this deployment.

Shortly after return from deployment, many GW veterans reported experiencing multiple health symptoms that could not be explained by any one syndrome or known etiology (RAC, 2004). Initially termed Gulf War Syndrome and later Gulf War Illness, these terms were initially believed to include cognitive, emotional and physical ailments, including but not limited to skin rash, fatigue, muscle aches, and gastrointestinal problems. In addition, cognitive symptoms such as poor attention, diminished concentration and impaired short-term memory were also noted. It became clear relatively early after the war that GW veterans were showing an increase in health symptom reporting in multiple body systems relative to their non-deployed peers. These nonspecific symptoms have been termed chronic multisymptom illness (CMI) or Gulf War multisymptom illness (Fukuda et al., 1998, Steele, 2000).

Studies have found that health symptoms occur concurrently in GW veterans in multiple domains at excess rates and with greater severity than in non-deployed veterans (Barth et al., 2009). These findings were documented in GW veterans from the United States, Britain, Denmark and Canada (Barrett et al., 2002). This documentation was a leading reason cited for the IOM's recent conclusion that there was sufficient evidence of an association between GW deployment and multisymptom illness (IOM, 2010) (see Table 13.2). It was also suspected early on that these health effects were related to environmental exposures during the Gulf War, however, unlike DDT from Vietnam that could be measured years after exposure and compared with increased health effects, pesticides used during the GW are not detectable years after exposure and require study of known exposed populations to study potential exposure-related health effects.

Initial studies comparing the health of GW veterans with specific environmental exposures from pesticides, anti-nerve gas pills (pyridostigmine bromide), low level nerve gas (sarin/cyclosarin), and oil well fires have largely relied on self-report of exposures and results have shown diminished health relative to individuals without such exposures. These effects are documented from individual and, importantly, combined exposures to these environmental toxicants. In their 2008 report, the Research Advisory Committee on Gulf War Veterans' Illnesses (RAC), concluded that combination exposures to pesticides and the anti-nerve gas pill pyridostigmine bromide (PB), was the likely cause of chronic health symptoms in ill GW veterans (RAC, 2008). This report cited several studies showing significant correlations between exposures to pesticides and PB and chronic health effects in GW veterans. This conclusion was further validated by a recent report indicating that GW veterans with personal pesticide and PB use during the war had a significantly higher risk of developing GW multisymptom illness (Steele et al., 2012). One example of a study conducted by our research team is an analysis of GW veterans with high and low pesticide

Table 13.2 Institute of Medicine's Evidence on Gulf War and Health

Weight of the evidence	Disease
Sufficient evidence	Multisymptom Illness, chronic fatigue syndrome, gastrointestinal symptoms consistent with functional gastrointestinal disorders such as irritable bowel syndrome and functional dyspepsia, PTSD and other psychiatric disorders, including generalized anxiety disorders, depression, and substance abuse, especially alcohol abuse
Limited but suggestive evidence	ALS, fibromyalgia and chronic widespread pain, self-reported sexual difficulties, mortality from external causes primarily motor-vehicle accidents, in the early years after deployment
Inadequate/insufficient evidence	Any cancer, diseases of the blood and blood forming organs, endocrine, nutritional, and metabolic diseases, neurocognitive and neurobehavioral performance, multiple sclerosis, other neurological outcomes such as Parkinson's disease, dementia, and Alzheimer's disease, incidence of cardiovascular disease, respiratory diseases, structural gastrointestinal diseases, skin diseases, musculoskeletal system diseases, specific conditions of the genitourinary system, specific birth defects, adverse pregnancy outcomes such as miscarriage, stillbirth, preterm birth and low birth weight, fertility problems
Limited/suggestive evidence of no association	Peripheral neuropathy, mortality from cardiovascular disease in the first 10 years after the war, decreased lung function in the first 10 years after the war, hospitalization for genitourinary diseases

Source: Institute of Medicine (IOM, 2010)

exposures; significantly more of the group with high exposure reported chronic health symptoms years after their initial exposures suggesting a link between environmental exposures during their deployment and chronic health symptoms (Table 13.3).

As stated above, environmental exposures have been documented as a likely cause for the continuation of and worsening of health symptoms in GW veterans (RAC, 2008). Those toxicants of concern for GW-era military personnel include the organophosphate and carbamate insecticides commonly used to protect soldiers from exposure to disease-causing insects including sand flies, mosquitos, fleas and ticks. During the Gulf War, pesticides were used in areas where soldiers worked, slept, and ate; at any given day, it is estimated that, soldiers could have been exposed to 15 different pesticides containing 12 different active ingredients and those applying the pesticides were likely to have been exposed to even higher doses (Table 13.4). An Environmental Exposure Report commissioned by the US Dept of Defense, based on health risk assessment dose-estimates, found it likely that 41,000 general military personnel could have had over-exposure to pesticides during the Gulf War (Winkenwerder, 2003). The Armed Forces Pesticide Management Board (AFPMB) reports that 1 million pounds of pesticides were used during the time of the Gulf

Table 13.3 Prominent health symptoms in GWI Veterans by pesticide exposure

Health Symptom	Pesticide High Exposure % reporting n = 103	Pesticide Low Exposure % reporting n = 41	Chi-Square X2 (p-value)	Odds Ratio OR
Diarrhea	21	5	.02	5.1
Upset stomach	30	12	.02	3.2
Skin rash	25	5	.007	6.3
Weakness	37	10	.001	5.4
Muscle pain	53	34	.05	2.1
Confusion	23	7	.02	3.9
Word finding difficulty	41	20	.02	2.8
Sleep problems	64	34	.001	3.5
Breathing trouble	17	2	.02	8.0
Body tingling	46	20	.003	3.5
General aches and pains	69	39	.001	3.5
Twitching	34	17	.04	2.5
Forgetfulness	49	29	.03	2.3
Rapid heart rate	18	5	.04	4.4
Trouble concentrating	44	25	.04	2.4
Moodiness	42	24	.05	2.2

*   Only statistically significant results presented (16 of 34 total symptoms).

War and through the mid-1990s (www.afpmb.org). Although organophosphates appeared safer (because of their lower bioavailability and relatively short half-life) when compared with prior pesticides such as DDT, it is now clearer that there can be lasting consequences of these exposures and a higher risk for health effects when combined together. This can result in additive and/or synergistic effects in animals and humans (Laetz et al., 2009).

Pesticides such as organophosphates (OP) and carbamates are known to produce chronic neurological and cognitive symptoms with sufficient exposure in agricultural workers, jet pilots and professional pesticide applicators resulting in decreased information processing speed and increased mood complaints (Stephens et al., 1995, Steenland et al., 1994, Bazylewicz-Walczak et al., 1999, Roldan-Tapi et al., 2005, Mackenzie Ross et al., 2010), with chronic low-level exposures as well as with acute poisoning (Golomb, 2008, Sullivan et al., 2003, RAC, 2008). We assessed pesticide exposures during the GW in a uniquely knowledgeable group of veterans whose job responsibility it was to order, administer and dispose of all pesticides used during the GW deployment and compared them with preventative

Table 13.4 Pesticide use and application overview

Use	Designation	Purpose	POPCs, Active Ingredient	Application Method	User or Applicator
General Use Pesticides	Repellents	Repel flies and mosquitoes	DEET 33% cream/stick	By hand to skin	Individuals
			DEET 75% Liquid	By hand to skin, uniforms or netting	
			Permethrin 0.5% (P) Spray	Sprayed on uniforms	
	Area Spray	Knock down spray, kill flies and mosquitoes	d-Phenothrin 0.2% (P) Aerosol	Sprayed in area	Individuals, Field Sanitation Teams, Certified Applicators
	Fly Baits	Attract and kill flies	Methomyl 1% (C) Crystals	Placed in pans outside of latrines, sleeping tents	
			Azamethiphos 1% (OP) Crystals		
	Pest Strip	Attract and kill mosquitoes	Dichlorvos 20% (OP) Pest Strip	Hung in sleeping tents, working areas, dumpsters	
Field Use Pesticides	Sprayed Liquids (emulsifiable concentrates, ECs)	Kill flies, mosquitoes, crawling insects	Chlorpyrifos 45% (OP) Liquid	Sprayed in corners, cracks, crevices	Field Sanitation Teams or Certified Applicators
			Diazinon 48% (OP) Liquid		
			Malathion 57% (OP) Liquid		
			Propoxur 14.7% (C) Liquid	Sprayed in corners, cracks, crevices	Certified Applicators
	Sprayed Powder (wettable powder, WP)	Kill flies, mosquitoes, crawling insects	Bendiocarb 76% (C) Solid		
	Fogs (Ultra-Low Volume Fogs, ULVs)	Kill flies, mosquitoes	Chlorpyrifos 19% (OP) Liquid	Large area fogging	Certified Applicators
			Malathion 91% (OP) Liquid		
Delousing Pesticide	Delousing Pesticide	Kill lice	Lindane 1% (OC) Powder	Dusted on EPWs, also available for personal use	Certified Applicator, Military Police, Medical Personnel

Table 13.5 Pesticides of potential concern

Repellents	Pyrethroids	Organophosphates	Carbamates	Organochlorines
DEET	Permethrin	Azamethiphos*	Methomyl	Lindane*
	D-Phenothrin	Chlorpyrifos*	Propoxur	
		Diazinon*	Bendiocarb*	
		Dichlorvos*		
		Malathion*		

* Current use restricted or banned by EPA as part of the Food Quality Protection Act pesticides review. Source: Environmental Exposure Report – pesticides (Winkenwerder, 2003).

medicine personnel, who were less exposed. This cohort is described below after a brief description of the pesticide and other relevant exposures from the GW.

The pesticides of potential concern used by US military personnel during the GW can be divided into five major classes or categories (Table 13.5). These include: 1) organophosphorus pesticides, such as dichlorvos, malathion, and chlorpyrifos; 2) carbamate pesticides, such as bendiocarb; 3) the organochlorine, lindane; 4) pyrethroid pesticides, such as permethrin; and 5) the insect repellent DEET. For a more thorough description of the classes of toxicants used during the GW, the reader is referred to Cecchine et al. (2000).

Pyridostigmine bromide (PB) is a chemical in the carbamate class that reversibly blocks the enzyme acetylcholinesterase (AChE). During the GW, pyridostigmine bromide was given prophylactically to military personnel in pill form to protect them from poisoning from exposure to the nerve gas soman (which irreversibly binds AChE). Thirty milligram tablets were given in packets of 12 for troops to self-administer when directed by their supervisor or when they deemed that a threat was imminent (Sullivan et al., 2003). This was the first time that PB tablets were used during a US military deployment due to fears that Iraq would use chemical weapons during the war as it had done during the Iran–Iraq war.

During the cease-fire in March 1991, US Engineering Battalion troops destroyed a large munitions storage complex at Khamisiyah, Iraq. This munitions complex was believed to have contained warheads with a mixture of sarin and cyclosarin (DoD, 2002). Troops who were potentially exposed were later notified by the DoD about the possible ill effects from these exposures. Roughly 100,000 veterans were notified of potential sarin exposure and advised to obtain a GW registry examination at their local VA hospital.

It was estimated that 600 Kuwaiti oil wells were on fire at the end of the GW, creating massive black smoke and oil plumes. Although few chronic health effects have been correlated directly with exposure to the oil well fires, studies of brain cancer mortality risk in GW veterans have shown an almost 3-fold risk in GW veterans who were exposed to low level sarin from the Khamisiyah weapons depot detonations and to oil well fires. Specifically, the veterans who were exposed to the Khamisiyah weapons depot detonations for two or more days were almost three times more likely to die from brain cancer than those not exposed. GW veterans exposed to oil well fire smoke were almost twice as likely to die from brain cancer than those not exposed. There was no interaction effect of combined exposures but both exposures remained significantly associated with brain cancer mortality when included in the same statistical model (Barth et al., 2009).

A review of research studies conducted by Boston researchers serves as examples of the gradual understanding of the contribution of AChE inhibiting pesticides, pyridostigmine bromide (PB) and nerve gas (sarin/cyclosarin) exposures and chronic health effects in GW veterans (Proctor et al., 1998, White et al., 2001, Wolfe et al., 2002, Sullivan et al., 2003). For a more thorough review of all GW literature, the reader is referred to RAC (2008).

A unique sample of GW deployed veterans (n = 2,949) that came back from deployment in 1990–1991 through Ft. Devens, MA was surveyed within five days of their return (originally known as the Ft. Devens ODS cohort) at the Boston Environmental Hazard Center (BEHC), a joint Boston University–VA Boston Healthcare System research center. Originally responding to questions pertaining to their psychosocial and family adjustment, the sample was surveyed again at 18–24 months after return from deployment (n = 2,313) and responded to questionnaires pertaining to health symptoms, stress variables, potential environmental exposures, vaccinations and medical interventions during deployment in order to better understand the reason for health symptom complaints. As mentioned above, the most commonly reported chronic health symptoms included joint pain, headaches, memory and attention difficulties, skin rash, gastrointestinal difficulties and sleep problems.

Several follow-up studies with this cohort have documented that the health symptoms reported by GW veterans are chronic in nature and that 90 percent of veterans who had previously been identified as showing signs of chronic health effects continued to meet defining criteria for CMI two years later with the most significant symptoms (including fatigue, joint pains and forgetfulness) experienced by over 50 percent of those surveyed (Proctor et al., 1998). Even after controlling for covariates, including PTSD and major depression, GW deployed groups reported significantly higher individual rates of health symptoms.

Assessment of potential exposure variables found that low-level nerve agent exposure (from Khamisiyah weapons arsenal) was associated with mood complaints and diminished executive system cognitive functioning in GW veterans (White et al., 2001). More recent studies reported diminished performance in the motor and visuospatial domains (Proctor et al., 2006) when sarin exposure was assessed in a dose-dependent manner and motor slowing in a large national cohort of GW veterans (Toomey et al., 2009).

In addition to the Devens Cohort, BEHC investigators examined a treatment-seeking group of GW deployed veterans compared with a treatment-seeking group of GW-era veterans in order to assess the impact of treatment seeking on the characterization of GW Illness and to assess the health effects of specific environmental exposures during the war. These individuals were initially referred for health symptom and cognitive concerns through medical clinics at the VA Boston Healthcare System and through the Gulf War registry. The results of this study suggested that GW veterans were not simply displaying cognitive patterns indicative of treatment seekers in general but that they showed a distinct profile separate from the GW-era deployed treatment seekers (Sullivan et al., 2003). Correspondingly, results of self-reported exposure to taking PB pills during the war showed a significant relationship between PB use and diminished frontal-executive system functioning in the exposed GW veterans (Sullivan et al., 2003).

A follow-up longitudinal assessment of health symptoms and neuropsychological variables 5–7 years after the initial assessment assessed the chronic nature of GW health and cognitive symptoms (Krengel et al., 2002). A 34-item health symptom checklist was given to participants at both Time 1 and Time 2 (5 years later) that evaluated the number of dichotomous (yes/no) responses for each health symptom variable. Comparisons of change scores in health symptom reporting between GW-deployed veterans and GW-era controls showed significant differences for the symptoms of aches and pains and joint pain with GW veterans reporting higher percentage of change than the non-deployed treatment-seeking veterans (White, 2003). These results suggested that GW veterans were not simply displaying symptoms that happen after every deployment but rather a more specific type of chronic illness.

For example, Table 13.6 shows the average percentage of GW-deployed and era veterans experiencing each of the major categories of symptoms. Controls did not reach the level of the GW-deployed groups, even at Time 1.

In order to more fully understand the contribution of pesticide and other AChE inhibitor exposures during the GW, former BEHC investigators were able to identify and study a subsample of 159 veterans of a cohort of pesticide applicators and preventative medicine personnel from the Gulf War who had originally been interviewed by the Force Health Protection and Readiness office of the Department of Defense (DoD) (Winkenwerder, 2003). These individuals were assessed with a battery of neuropsychological tests, health symptom questionnaires and exposure interviews. Health symptom findings from the 34-

Table 13.6 Changes in report of health symptoms from time 1 to time 2

Symptom	GW (n = 90)			Controls (n = 21)			GW vs. Control p-value
	Time 1	Time 2	Change	Time 1	Time 2	Change	
Aches and pains	45%	77%	+32%	21%	36%	+15%	.029
Joint pain	54%	88%	+34%	31%	29%	−2%	.024
Headaches	68%	78%	+10%	64%	43%	−21%	.281
Skin rash	48%	62%	+14%	15%	21%	+7%	.142
Fatigue	72%	88%	+16%	36%	64%	+28%	.069
Nausea	48%	59%	+11%	21%	31%	+10%	.310
Forgetfulness	72%	81%	+9%	44%	58%	+14%	.576
Concentration	54%	74%	+20%	43%	57%	+14%	.979
Confusion	33%	55%	+22%	25%	23%	−2%	.649

item health symptom checklist showed over 50 percent reporting rates of joint pain, sleep difficulties, and muscle pain, forgetfulness, poor concentration, body tingling, word finding problems and weakness similar to reports from the Ft. Devens cohort (Proctor et al., 1998, Sullivan et al., 2003). Pesticide applying personnel in the higher pesticide exposure group reported significantly more chronic health symptoms than the low pesticide exposure group such that the mean number of health symptom reported by the higher exposure group was 11.8 symptoms and that of the lower exposure group was 7.4 symptoms. This was statistically significant at the $p < .05$ level. In addition, results from this study suggest that specific pesticides may have been particularly influential with respect to continued mood-related complaints (methomyl, lindane) and worse information processing speeds (dichlorvos) (Krengel and Sullivan, 2008). Results also support findings of deficits in response speed and efficient set switching ability in subgroups of GW-deployed veterans that have been reported previously (Lange et al., 2001, Toomey et al., 2009, Krengel and Sullivan, 2008).

As shown above, evidence from studies conducted at the former VA BEHC and elsewhere has consistently identified elevated health symptom reporting in GW veterans when compared with many types of control groups, including non-deployed GW-era veterans and military personnel deployed to other conflicts. Furthermore, the symptom complaints of GW veterans appear to persist to the present time and have increasingly been associated with AChE inhibitor environmental exposures including pesticides, PB, and low level sarin/cyclosarin (White et al., 2001, Sullivan et al., 2003, RAC, 2008, Golomb, 2008, Steele et al., 2012, Heaton et al., 2007).

In an attempt to correlate neuropsychological and mood functioning with objective structural brain imaging, MRI studies were completed on the previously mentioned BEHC cohorts as well. Brain white matter has been found to be sensitive to chemical exposures in several studies of neurotoxicant poisonings and has in some cases been linked to development of chronic neurological deficits called toxicant encephalopathy (Filley, 2001). Correspondingly, an early study of neuroimaging of veterans through the BEHC found that sarin-exposed veterans showed significantly lower brain white matter volumes in a dose-dependent manner (Heaton et al., 2007). Another study with Boston cohorts comparing high and low health symptom reporters found that GW veterans with lower brain white matter volumes were twice as likely to be in the high health symptom reporting group (> 10 symptoms) than in the low symptom reporting group (Sullivan et al., under review).

A subsample of 24 veterans from the pesticide cohort mentioned above underwent neuroimaging 2–3 years after the original cognitive evaluations. The specific aims of this project were to identify the relationships between pesticide exposure, differences in brain volumetrics, and health symptoms. Veterans categorized as having high exposure to pesticides had lower brain white matter volumes, reported more health symptoms and performed less well on cognitive testing than veterans with low pesticide exposure. Pesticide exposed veterans reporting more health symptoms showed significantly lower brain white matter volumes (Table 13.7).

Table 13.7 White matter and health symptom correlations

		White matter	*Health symptom*
White matter	Pearson Correlation	1	−.505
	Sig. (2-tailed)		.012
	N	24	24
Health symptom	Pearson Correlation	−.505	1
	Sig. (2-tailed)	.012	
	N	24	24

Table 13.8 Brain volumetric comparisons by lindane and dichlorvos exposure groups

Brain Volume	*Non-exposed Group Mean*	*Dichlorvos × Lindane Group Mean*	*p-value*
% White matter	34	33	.03
% Gray matter	33	27	.008
% Cerebellum white matter	1.9	1.75	.03

When individuals with pesticide exposures that had shown significant independent differences in the pesticide cognition study were compared with respect to white matter volumes, there was significant between-group difference for the interaction effect of specific pesticides (dichlorvos (pest-strips) and lindane exposures; $p = .03$). When gray matter volumes were compared between individual pesticide exposures, there were significantly lower volumes between high and low exposed dichlorvos groups ($p = .01$). In addition, there was a significant interaction effect for the group with high lindane (delouser) and dichlorvos (pest-strips) exposure ($p = .008$) (Table 13.8).

Due to recent reports of neuronal cell death particularly in the hippocampus (which is involved in memory functions) in animals exposed to combinations of DEET, PB and/or other relevant pesticides (malathion or permethrin) (Abdel-Rahman et al., 2004a, 2002), initial comparisons were performed comparing malathion and DEET exposure on hippocampal volumes. Results showed significant interaction effects in the DEET and PB exposed group with lower hippocampal volumes when compared with the non-exposed or individually exposed groups (DEET only or PB only) and when adjusted for individual head size using percentage of total intracranial volume. Sample sizes for the current comparisons were small and were not adjusted for multiple comparisons, but they suggest the need for further study of these combined exposures in larger groups to further validate these findings.

Additional analyses compared individuals with combinations of high and low DEET separately and with malathion or PB with respect to memory functioning. Analyses performed comparing the visual memory domain showed a significant

Table 13.9 Hippocampal volumetric and cognitive comparisons by exposure group

Brain Volume	DEET Mean	PB Mean	DEET × PB Mean	DEET × PB p-value
R-hippocampus	.30	.31	.25	.004
L-hippocampus	.30	.30	.25	.005
Cognitive domain				
Verbal memory	84	78	81	.92
Visual memory	49	44	35	.02
Rey-O immed. recall	24.3	23.8	17.7	.01
Rey-O delay recall	24.9	20.1	17.4	.04
Visuospatial domain	61.2	57.2	54.6	.03
Rey-O copy	32.5	30.9	27.5	.04

Mean hippocampal volumes adjusted for age and gender and presented as % intracranial volume. $N = 24$ total subjects.

interaction effect between the groups ($p = .02$) with the DEET and PB group performing significantly worse than the separately exposed or non-exposed groups (Table 13.9). These findings suggest that a structure and functional relationship exists between these exposures and lower brain volumes and cognitive functioning in these pesticide exposed veterans.

Since the Gulf War, significant efforts have been made by the Armed Forces Pesticide Management Board (AFPMB) to significantly reduce total pesticide usage by two-thirds by instituting integrated pest management (IPM) practices (www.afpmb.org) and emphasizing the use of individual insect repellent systems. Thus current exposure levels of soldiers in Iraq and Afghanistan are quite different from those for the 1990–1991 Gulf War soldier. There now exists a compilation of research findings to suggest that the particular combinations of environmental exposures (pesticides, nerve agents and PB) from the time of the 1990–1991 GW may in fact have resulted in chronic multisymptom illness or a chronic subclinical encephalopathy (White and Proctor, 1992) in roughly one quarter of all GW veterans.

The health care costs associated with GW deployment are difficult to determine given that many reports also include costs related to post 9/11/01 Iraq deployment (OIF). However, according to the last Gulf War veterans health utilization report (Gulf War veterans Information System report), the estimated cumulative cost per 1990–1991 GW patient within the VA system in 2009 was $5,379 with 110,487 service connected veterans receiving care. This report breaks down health care costs by reporting that 26,521 service members receive VA benefits and health care associated with Khamisiyah and another 14,749 receive health care for undiagnosed illnesses. Further, 214,343 veterans have service connected disability status related to the 1990–1991 GW deployment; 45,891 for Khamisiyah exposure and another 20,069 for undiagnosed illnesses (http://www.vba.va.gov/REPORTS/gwvis/historical/index.asp).

Afghanistan/Iraq Wars

Following the World Trade Center terrorist attacks on September 11, 2001, US troops invaded Afghanistan and, in 2003, Iraq resulting in two ongoing wars, Operation Enduring Freedom (OEF) and Operation Iraqi Freedom (OIF). The third and final era of conflict that will be discussed in this chapter involves these two military operations.

Many of the veterans from these most recent deployments had significant exposures to blast explosions from improvised explosive devices (IEDs) and resulting physical and psychological trauma including PTSD, major depression and mild Traumatic Brain Injury (mTBI). The rates of PTSD and mTBI in these cohorts are discussed at length in other chapters in this book and will not be discussed in this section. In addition to psychological and physical trauma, there are also important toxicant exposures from these deployments that warrant careful follow-up over time to document any development of chronic health effects. The toxicant exposures relevant to OEF and OIF have a fair amount of overlap with each other and include burn pits, depleted uranium, CARC paint and chromium from the Qarmat Ali water treatment facility. Each exposure will be described and the known and suspected human health effects will be discussed.

In Iraq and Afghanistan, open-air burn pits were used on military sites to dispose of chemicals, paint, medical/human waste, metal/aluminum cans, munitions, petroleum/lubricant products, wood, rubber, plastics/Styrofoam, and discarded food (http://www.publichealth.va.gov/exposures/burnpits/index.asp). These waste materials have the potential to produce smoke containing toxins such as dioxins, particulate matter, polycyclic aromatic hydrocarbons (PAHs), volatile organic compounds (VOCs), carbon monoxide, hexachlorobenzene, and ash. In 2010 the United States Central Command estimated that there were 251 burn pits in Afghanistan and 22 in Iraq (http://www.publichealth.va.gov/exposures/burnpits/index.asp). No pit burns exactly the same materials, and so veterans have a wide range of varying exposures that are affected by factors such as types of products burnt in the pit, duration of exposure, proximity to burn pit, and individual biological susceptibility; all of which add to the difficulty of conducting epidemiological studies to examine the connection between exposure and outcome. Correspondingly, the Institute of Medicine recently reported that more research is necessary to conclude whether chronic respiratory problems and specific cancers are associated with burn pit exposures (IOM, 2011).

Short-term health effects that have been shown to resolve after removal from burn pit exposure include coughing/throat irritation, skin itching/rashes, eye irritation/burning, and breathing difficulties (http://www.publichealth.va.gov/exposures/burnpits/index.asp). A survey conducted in 2005 (Sanders et al., 2005) found that 69.1 percent of the 15,000 military personnel deployed to OEF/OIF reported experiencing respiratory illnesses, with 17 percent of them requiring medical care. This was true for both asthmatics (5 percent of deployed personnel) and non-asthmatics (Roop et al., 2007). Long-term health effects have not yet been reported for this military population, although the VA is currently conducting a prospective study involving 30,000 veterans from OEF and OIF, examining the connections between burn pit exposure and adverse health outcomes (http://www.publichealth.va.gov/exposures/burnpits/index.asp). Based on epidemiologic studies of populations with similar exposures to those compounds released from the burn pits, one can postulate which organ systems and possible disease types the veterans will present with following their exposure. Dioxin exposure has been linked to a number of adverse health effects as mentioned above in the Vietnam War section of this chapter.

The majority of the epidemiologic studies on air pollution and human health have focused on particulate matter. Chronic exposure to particulate matter has been shown to be associated with an increased risk of lung cancer (Turner et al., 2011, Peters et al., 2011), decreased cardiac function (Weichenthal et al., 2011, Shrey et al., 2011, Williams R et al., 2011) and death due to cardiac arrest (Breitner et al., 2011, Laden et al., 2000), decreased respiratory function (Leitte et al., 2011, Alfaro-Moreno et al., 2007) as well as decreased immune system function (Williams L et al., 2011, Inoue and Takano, 2011). Health effects seen in these epidemiological studies of PM exposure are dependent upon the size of the particle, frequency and duration of exposure and the general health status of the population. Polycyclic aromatic hydrocarbons, volatile organic compounds and hexachlorobenzene have been shown to be carcinogenic (Hirano et al., 2011, McClean et al., 2011, Wang et al., 2011, Lee et al., 2010, Daniel et al., 2011, Reed et al., 2007, Grant, 2009), respiratory irritants (Rosa et al., 2011, Kumar et al., 2008, Wichmann et al., 2009, Mendes et al., 2011) and immune system dysregulators (Selgrade and Gilmour, 2010, Detmar and Jurisicova, 2010, Emara et al., 2010, Hertz-Picciotto et al., 2008). Fly ash has been linked to development of bronchiolitis (Boswell and McCunney, 1995). The burn pit exposures experienced by the OEF and OIF veterans were so variable and complex that none of the studies above can act as a surrogate for their exposure, but they do present important information about the adverse health effects of each of the component compounds.

Exposure to hexavalent chromium is specific to particular military and civilian personnel who served in Iraq. The Iraqi oil industry was hard hit by the war due to military operations, desertion of workers and looting. In 2003, following combat operations the US Army Corps of Engineers contracted with a US-based company, Kellogg, Brown and Root (KBR), to restore the infrastructure of the oil industry in Iraq. This restoration included work on several hundred sites (DoD, 2010).

Part of the infrastructure was the Qarmat Ali Industrial Water Treatment Plant, where water from the Tigris River was treated and then used in the production of oil. Sodium dichromate is a corrosion suppression agent that was used in the water treatment process, and contains hexavalent chromium, a known carcinogen. The soil in and around the plant was heavily contaminated with the orange colored substance (DoD, 2010) when the personnel arrived, resulting in exposure for hundreds of individuals. As of September 2010, 972 living military and civilian personnel were identified as having worked at the site and considered to have probable exposure to hexavalent chromium (DoD, 2010). The contractor, KBR, admits first awareness of the contamination several months following initial work at the site (DoD, 2010). Immediate remediation began with initial covering of the contaminated soil with uncontaminated soil from outside the plant to reduce the amount of direct contact with the hexavalent chromium. Personnel were required to wear personal protective equipment when on site. Following soil and air testing confirming chromium contamination, the contaminated soil was encapsulated with asphalt.

The DoD and the VA have attempted to contact all individuals with probable exposure to hexavalent chromium at the Qarmat Ali water treatment plant and provide them with access to medical care, although no acute toxicity was apparent in this population. The VA has set up the Qarmat Ali Medical Surveillance Program to follow the health of exposed individuals over time at no expense to veterans. The veterans who enroll receive an initial health examination including a full physical exam, chest X-ray and tests of pulmonary function with an additional health exam one year later and a chest X-ray every 5 years. If any abnormalities are found, the individual is sent to a specialist (http://www.publichealth.va.gov/exposures/occupational_environmental/chromium.asp).

Hexavalent chromium has been studied in other populations, mostly occupations such as welders and those working in the electroplating industry. Chronic exposure has been shown to cause shortness of breath, coughing and wheezing, bronchitis and asthma (WHO, 1988, EPA, 1998). Occupational studies of hexavalent chromium exposure have shown chronic injury and inflammation to the lung and lung cancer (Langard et al., 1990, Langard, 1990, Hayes, 1997, Beaver et al., 2009a, 2009b, Halasova et al., 2009) and increased DNA damage (Zhang et al., 2011, Sellappa et al., 2010). An ecologic study conducted in Greece found an increased rate of cancer mortality in populations with hexavalent chromium exposure (Linos et al., 2011). Other research has labeled hexavalent chromium an environmental immunological stressor (Mignini et al., 2009). In vivo studies have reported human DNA and lung tissue damage following exposure to hexavalent chromium (Caglieri et al., 2008, Myers and Myers, 2009, Xie et al., 2009). The EPA has reported that chromium is a human carcinogen when it is breathed in, but ingestion through food or water cannot yet be causally linked to cancer; ingestion of contaminated water was not a concern for the Quarmat Ali exposure since it was determined that it did not provide a source for drinking water.

Other exposures during the Iraq war included a case study that was reported in 2004 of an Army explosive ordnance disposal sergeant who put an improvised explosive device (IED) in his vehicle to defuse in a safer place when he became confused, had a severe headache, blurred vision and experienced difficulty breathing (Loh et al., 2010). He was taken to the medic and was found to have significantly reduced cholinesterase levels and required hospitalization for several days and an additional two weeks recuperation before he was able to return to duty. Studies of the IED showed a clear liquid was present and was confirmed to contain weaponized sarin. This soldier appeared to have recovered from the exposure after returning to duty, but two months later he started to complain of cognitive difficulties and balance problems. Eight months later, he was evaluated at an Army hospital. Neuroimaging studies appeared normal to visual inspection, but neuropsychological assessments documented reduced speed of information processing, attentional difficulties for focused and divided attention tasks, and motor function testing (Loh et al., 2010). This case report was significant for documenting chronic health effects from weaponized sarin as a war casualty. Although this appeared to be an isolated incident, it does suggest that Iraq was in possession of at least some weaponized sarin stores that were denied before the US invasion in 2003.

Conclusions

This chapter provides a brief overview of the toxicant exposures experienced by veterans during three eras of military conflict. Environmental exposures during deployment have been encountered since the earliest conflicts and will continue to be an important issue in future deployments. Determining the appropriate levels of interventional chemicals (e.g. insecticides, herbicides, prophylactic medications) to reduce the risk of disease from pests and possible chemical warfare agent exposures while at the same time decreasing the likelihood of negative effects from the chemical toxicant exposures themselves is a difficult yet crucial task. These exposures will be an ongoing concern in future deployments. The ideal practice would protect troops from disease and exposure but not cause adverse health outcomes in our troops at the same time. In clinical medicine, causing harm through the use of interventional therapies or medicines that were designed to improve health is referred to as iatrogenic medicine. This idea is rooted in the Hippocratic Oath taken by physicians that roughly translates to "first do no harm." In the future, deployed troops will likely be exposed to the various toxicants mentioned above (or others not yet identified), so it will be necessary to continue to study them over much longer time periods to assess long-term and chronic effects. This approach could help avoid future episodes of Agent Orange chronic sequelae or Gulf War multisymptom illness or cancer incidence as a result of hexavalent chromium exposures. In addition it may also help answer the questions that remain including, "what is the impact of genetic factors interacting with exposures on resultant health symptom concerns?", "what are the effects on an aging population with prior exposures?" and "are there potential treatments to diminish the multiple medical, neuropsychological and psychological effects of these exposures?"

It is widely known that with significant exposures, toxicants impact the central nervous system directly. Additionally, there are long-term or chronic impacts on health symptoms, which can then lead to brain/behavior relationship concerns. Lessons learned from military occupational exposures can have direct applicability to other occupationally exposed groups and vice versa.

For example, enough research regarding the potential adverse and chronic health effects from pyridostigmine bromide pill usage should be heeded by those who would suggest that PB be used prophylactically by agricultural workers and pesticide applicators (Sullivan et al., 2003, Golomb, 2008, Henderson et al., 2012). Correspondingly, treatments identified as potentially therapeutic in civilian agricultural workers with pesticide overexposures could also be used for pesticide-induced military encephalopathies (Soltaninejad and Abdollahi, 2009). These treatments could include antioxidants and anti-inflammatory medications (quercetin, luteolin, Co-Q10) as well as newly employed cognitive enhancers including intranasal insulin (Craft et al., 2012).

In conclusion, military preventative medicine has a difficult task to ensure the health of deployed troops and must take steps to make sure that insect-borne illness is minimized. Control strategies including integrated pest management should be carefully considered along with what types and amounts of insecticides or herbicides are absolutely necessary for disease vector control. This type of careful consideration could prevent the long-term health effects described in this chapter and ensure military health and readiness in future deployments.

References

Abdel-Rahman, A., Shetty, A.K. & Abou-Donia, M.B. 2002. Acute exposure to sarin increases blood brain barrier permeability and induces neuropathological changes in the rat brain: dose–response relationships. *Neuroscience*, 113, 721–41.

Abdel-Rahman, A., Abou-Donia, S., El-Masry, E., Shetty, A. & Abou-Donia, M. 2004a. Stress and combined exposure to low doses of pyridostigmine bromide, DEET, and permethrin produce neurochemical and neuropathological alterations in cerebral cortex, hippocampus, and cerebellum. *J Toxicol Environ Health A*, 67, 163–92.

Abdel-Rahman, A., Dechkovskaia, A.M., Goldstein, L.B., Bullman, S.H., Khan, W., El-Masry, E.M. & Abou-Donia, M.B. 2004b. Neurological deficits induced by malathion, DEET, and permethrin, alone or in combination in adult rats. *J Toxicol Environ Health A*, 67, 331–56.

AFHS 1991b. *Epidemiologic Investigation of Health Effects in Air Force Personnel Following Exposure to Herbicides. Serum Dioxin Analysis of 1987 Examination Results*. Brooks, AFB, TX: USAF School of Aerospace Medicine.

Akhtar, F.Z., Garabrant, D.H., Ketchum, N.S. & Michalek, J.E. 2004. Cancer in US Air Force veterans of the Vietnam War. *J Occup Environ Med*, 46, 123–36.

Alfaro-Moreno, E., Nawrot, T.S., Nemmar, A. & Nemery, B. 2007. Particulate matter in the environment: pulmonary and cardiovascular effects. *Curr Opin Pulm Med*, 13, 98–106.

Baker, E.L., White, R.F., & Murawaski, B.J. 1985. Clinical evaluation of neurobehavioral effects of occupational exposure to organic solvents and lead. *Int J Med Health*, 14, 135–58.

Barrett, D.H., Morris, R.D., Akhtar, F.Z. & Michalek, J.E. 2001. Serum dioxin and cognitive functioning among veterans of Operation Ranch Hand. *Neurotoxicology*, 22, 491–502.

Barrett, D.H., Gray, G.C., Doebbeling, B.N., Clauw, D.J. & Reeves, W.C. 2002. Prevalence of symptoms and symptom-based conditions among Gulf War veterans: current status of research findings. *Epidemiol Rev*, 24, 218–27.

Barrientos, R.M., Frank, M.G., Watkins, L.R. & Maier, S.F. 2010. Memory impairments in healthy aging: Role of aging-induced microglial sensitization. *Aging Dis*, 1, 212–31.

Barth, S.K., Kang, H.K., Bullman, T.A. & Wallin, M.T. 2009. Neurological mortality among U.S. veterans of the Persian Gulf War: 13-year follow-up. *Am J Ind Med*, 52, 663–70.

Bazylewicz-Walczak, B., Majczakowa, W. & Szymczak, M. 1999. Behavioral effects of occupational exposure to organophosphorous pesticides in female greenhouse planting workers. *Neurotoxicology,* 20, 819–26.

Beaver, L.M., Stemmy, E.J., Constant, S.L., Schwartz, A., Little, L.G., Gigley, J.P., Chun, G., Sugden, K.D., Ceryak, S.M. & Patierno, S.R. 2009a. Lung injury, inflammation and Akt signaling following inhalation of particulate hexavalent chromium. *Toxicol Appl Pharmacol,* 235, 47–56.

Beaver, L.M., Stemmy, E.J., Schwartz, A.M., Damsker, J.M., Constant, S.L., Ceryak, S.M. & Patierno, S.R. 2009b. Lung inflammation, injury, and proliferative response after repetitive particulate hexavalent chromium exposure. *Environ Health Perspect,* 117, 1896–902.

Boswell, R.T. & McCunney, R.J. 1995. Bronchiolitis obliterans from exposure to incinerator fly ash. *J Occup Environ Med,* 37, 850–5.

Breitner, S., Liu, L., Cyrys, J., Bruske, I., Franck, U., Schlink, U., Leitte, A.M., Herbarth, O., Wiedensohler, A., Wehner, B., Hu, M., Pan, X.C., Wichmann, H.E. & Peters, A. 2011. Sub-micrometer particulate air pollution and cardiovascular mortality in Beijing, China. *Sci Total Environ,* 409, 5196–204.

Bullman, T.A., Kang, H.K. & Thomas, T.L. 1991. Posttraumatic stress disorder among Vietnam veterans on the Agent Orange Registry. A case-control analysis. *Ann Epidemiol,* 1, 505–12.

Caglieri, A., Goldoni, M., De Palma, G., Mozzoni, P., Gemma, S., Vichi, S., Testai, E., Panico, F., Corradi, M., Tagliaferri, S. & Costa, L.G. 2008. Exposure to low levels of hexavalent chromium: target doses and comparative effects on two human pulmonary cell lines. *Acta Biomed,* 79 Suppl 1, 104–15.

Cecchine G.G.B., Hilborne Lh, Spektor D, & Anthony C.R. 2000. *A Review of the Scientific Literature As It Pertains to Gulf War Illnesses: Pesticides.* Arlington, VA: National Defense Research Institute (RAND).

Cecil, P.F., Sr. & Young, A.L. 2008. Operation FLYSWATTER: a war within a war. *Environ Sci Pollut Res Int,* 15, 3–7.

Chamie, K., Devere White, R.W., Lee, D., Ok, J.H. & Ellison, L.M. 2008. Agent Orange exposure, Vietnam War veterans, and the risk of prostate cancer. *Cancer,* 113, 2464–70.

Clapp, R.W. 1997. Update of cancer surveillance of veterans in Massachusetts, USA. *Int J Epidemiol,* 26, 679–81.

Clapp, R.W., Cupples, L.A., Colton, T. & Ozonoff, D.M. 1991. Cancer surveillance of Veterans in Massachusetts, USA, 1982–1988. *Int J Epidemiol,* 20, 7–12.

Craft, S., Baker, L.D., Montine, T.J., Minoshima, S., Watson, G.S., Claxton, A., Arbuckle, M., Callaghan, M., Tsai, E., Plymate, S.R., Green, P.S., Leverenz, J., Cross, D. & Gerton, B. 2012. Intranasal insulin therapy for Alzheimer disease and amnestic mild cognitive impairment: a pilot clinical trial. *Arch Neurol,* 69, 29–38.

Dalager, N.A., Kang, H.K., Burt, V.L. & Weatherbee, L. 1991. Non-Hodgkin's lymphoma among Vietnam veterans. *J Occup Med,* 33, 774–9.

Dalager, N.A., Kang, H.K., Burt, V.L. & Weatherbee, L. 1995. Hodgkin's disease and Vietnam service. *Ann Epidemiol,* 5, 400–6.

Daniel, C.R., Schwartz, K.L., Colt, J.S., Dong, L.M., Ruterbusch, J.J., Purdue, M.P., Cross, A.J., Rothman, N., Davis, F.G., Wacholder, S., Graubard, B.I., Chow, W.H. & Sinha, R. 2011. Meat-cooking mutagens and risk of renal cell carcinoma. *Br J Cancer,* 105, 1096–104.

Detmar, J. & Jurisicova, A. 2010. Embryonic resorption and polycyclic aromatic hydrocarbons: putative immune-mediated mechanisms. *Syst Biol Reprod Med,* 56, 3–17.

DoD 2002. Technical Report: Modeling Gulf War Illness and the Health of Gulf War Veterans and Risk Characterization of U.S. Demolition Operations at the Khamisiyah Pit. Washington, DC: Office of the Special Assistant to the Undersecretary of Defense (Personnel and Readiness) for Gulf War Illnesses Medical Readiness and Military Deployments.

DoD 2010. *Exposure to Sodium Dichromate at Qarmat Ali Iraq in 2003: Part I – Evaluation of Efforts to Identify, Contact, and Provide Access to Care for Personnel.* Washington, DC: United States Department of Defense.

Emara, A.M., Abo El-Noor, M.M., Hassan, N.A. & Wagih, A.A. 2010. Immunotoxicity and hematotoxicity induced by tetrachloroethylene in Egyptian dry cleaning workers. *Inhal Toxicol*, 22, 117–24.

EPA 1998. *Toxicological Review of Trivalent Chromium.* Washington, DC: National Center for Environmental Assessment, Office of Research and Development, Environmental Protection Agency.

Filley, C. 2001. *The Behavioral Neurology of White Matter*, Oxford University Press.

Fukuda, K., Nisenbaum, R., Stewart, G., Thompson, W.W., Robin, L., Washko, R.M., Noah, D.L., Barrett, D.H., Randall, B., Herwaldt, B.L., Mawle, A.C. & Reeves, W.C. 1998. Chronic multisymptom illness affecting Air Force veterans of the Gulf War. *JAMA*, 280, 981–8.

Goldberg, J., True, W.R., Eisen, S.A. & Henderson, W.G. 1990. A twin study of the effects of the Vietnam War on posttraumatic stress disorder. *JAMA*, 263, 1227–32.

Golomb, B.A. 2008. Acetylcholinesterase inhibitors and Gulf War illnesses. *Proc Natl Acad Sci USA*, 105, 4295–300.

Grant, W.B. 2009. Air pollution in relation to U.S. cancer mortality rates: an ecological study; likely role of carbonaceous aerosols and polycyclic aromatic hydrocarbons. *Anticancer Res*, 29, 3537–45.

Gulf War Veterans: Information System Report, www.vba.va.gov/reports/gwvis/2008/Feb_2008.pdf

Halasova, E., Matakova, T., Kavcova, E., Musak, L., Letkova, L., Adamkov, M., Ondrusova, M., Bukovska, E. & Singliar, A. 2009. Human lung cancer and hexavalent chromium exposure. *Neuro Endocrinol Lett*, 30 Suppl 1, 182–5.

Hayes, R.B. 1997. The carcinogenicity of metals in humans. *Cancer Causes Control*, 8, 371–85.

Heaton, K.J., Palumbo, C.L., Proctor, S.P., Killiany, R.J., Yurgelun-Todd, D.A. & White, R.F. 2007. Quantitative magnetic resonance brain imaging in US army veterans of the 1991 Gulf War potentially exposed to sarin and cyclosarin. *Neurotoxicology*, 28, 761–9.

Henderson, J.D., Glucksman, G., Leong, B., Tigyi, A., Ankirskaia, A., Siddique, I., Lam, H., Depeters, E. & Wilson, B.W. 2012. Pyridostigmine bromide protection against acetylcholinesterase inhibition by pesticides. *J Biochem Mol Toxicol*, 26, 31–4.

Henriksen, G.L., Ketchum, N.S., Michalek, J.E. & Swaby, J.A. 1997. Serum dioxin and diabetes mellitus in veterans of Operation Ranch Hand. *Epidemiology*, 8, 252–8.

Hertz-Picciotto, I., Park, H.Y., Dostal, M., Kocan, A., Trnovec, T. & Sram, R. 2008. Prenatal exposures to persistent and non-persistent organic compounds and effects on immune system development. *Basic Clin Pharmacol Toxicol*, 102, 146–54.

Hirano, M., Tanaka, S. & Asami, O. 2011. Classification of polycyclic aromatic hydrocarbons based on mutagenicity in lung tissue through DNA microarray. *Environ Toxicol* 2011: 1–8.

Inoue, K. & Takano, H. 2011. Particulate matter-induced hypersusceptibility to infection. *J Allergy Clin Immunol*, 128, 906.

IOM 2009. *Veterans and Agent Orange: Update 2008*. Washington, DC: National Academy Press.

IOM 2010. *Gulf War and Health: Health Effects of Serving in the Gulf War*. Washington, DC: National Academies Press.

IOM 2011. *Long-Term Health Consequences of Exposure to Burn Pits in Iraq and Afghanistan*. Washington, DC: National Academies Press.

Kang, H.K., Mahan, C.M., Lee, K.Y., Magee, C.A., Mather, S.H. & Matanoski, G. 2000a. Pregnancy outcomes among U.S. women Vietnam veterans. *Am J Ind Med*, 38, 447–54.

Kang, H.K., Mahan, C.M., Lee, K.Y., Magee, C.A. & Selvin, S. 2000b. Prevalence of gynecologic cancers among female Vietnam veterans. *J Occup Environ Med*, 42, 1121–7.

Kang, H.K., Dalager, N.A., Needham, L.L., Patterson, D.G., Jr., Lees, P.S., Yates, K. & Matanoski, G.M. 2006. Health status of Army Chemical Corps Vietnam veterans who sprayed defoliant in Vietnam. *Am J Ind Med*, 49, 875–84.

Ketchum, N.S. & Michalek, J.E. 2005. Postservice mortality of Air Force veterans occupationally exposed to herbicides during the Vietnam War: 20-year follow-up results. *Mil Med*, 170, 406–13.

Ketchum, N.S., Michalek, J.E. & Burton, J.E. 1999. Serum dioxin and cancer in veterans of Operation Ranch Hand. *Am J Epidemiol*, 149, 630–9.

Krengel, M. & Sullivan, K. 2008. *Neuropsychological Functioning in Gulf War Veterans Exposed to Pesticides and Pyridostigmine Bromide*. Fort Detrick, MD: U.S. Army Medical Research and Materiel Command.

Krengel, M., Sullivan, K., White, R.F., Honn, V., & Proctor, S.P. 2002. Self-reported health symptoms of Gulf War-era veterans: how have they changed? *Arch Clin Neuropsychol*, 17, 754.

Kumar, R., Nagar, J.K., Raj, N., Kumar, P., Kushwah, A.S., Meena, M. & Gaur, S.N. 2008. Impact of domestic air pollution from cooking fuel on respiratory allergies in children in India. *Asian Pac J Allergy Immunol*, 26, 213–22.

Laden, F., Neas, L.M., Dockery, D.W. & Schwartz, J. 2000. Association of fine particulate matter from different sources with daily mortality in six U.S. cities. *Environ Health Perspect*, 108, 941–7.

Laetz, C.A., Baldwin, D.H., Collier, T.K., Hebert, V., Stark, J.D. & Scholz, N.L. 2009. The synergistic toxicity of pesticide mixtures: implications for risk assessment and the conservation of endangered Pacific salmon. *Environ Health Perspect*, 117, 348–53.

Langard, S. 1990. One hundred years of chromium and cancer: a review of epidemiological evidence and selected case reports. *Am J Ind Med*, 17, 189–215.

Langard, S., Andersen, A. & Ravnestad, J. 1990. Incidence of cancer among ferrochromium and ferrosilicon workers: an extended observation period. *Br J Ind Med*, 47, 14–19.

Lange, G., Tiersky, L.A., Scharer, J.B., Policastro, T., Fiedler, N., Morgan, T.E. & Natelson, B.H. 2001. Cognitive functioning in Gulf War Illness. *J Clin Exp Neuropsychol*, 23, 240–9.

Lee, K.H., Shu, X.O., Gao, Y.T., Ji, B.T., Yang, G., Blair, A., Rothman, N., Zheng, W., Chow, W.H. & Kang, D. 2010. Breast cancer and urinary biomarkers of polycyclic aromatic hydrocarbon and oxidative stress in the Shanghai Women's Health Study. *Cancer Epidemiol Biomarkers Prev*, 19, 877–83.

Leitte, A.M., Schlink, U., Herbarth, O., Wiedensohler, A., Pan, X.C., Hu, M., Wehner, B., Breitner, S., Peters, A., Wichmann, H.E. & Franck, U. 2011. Associations between size-segregated particle number concentrations and respiratory mortality in Beijing, China. *Int J Environ Health Res*, 22(2): 119–33.

Linos, A., Petralias, A., Christophi, C.A., Christoforidou, E., Kouroutou, P., Stoltidis, M., Veloudaki, A., Tzala, E., Makris, K.C. & Karagas, M.R. 2011. Oral ingestion of hexavalent chromium through drinking water and cancer mortality in an industrial area of Greece – an ecological study. *Environ Health,* 10, 50.

Loh, Y., Swanberg, M.M., Ingram, M.V. & Newmark, J. 2010. Case report: Long-term cognitive sequelae of sarin exposure. *Neurotoxicology,* 31, 244–6.

Mackenzie Ross, S.J., Brewin, C.R., Curran, H.V., Furlong, C.E., Abraham-Smith, K.M. & Harrison, V. 2010. Neuropsychological and psychiatric functioning in sheep farmers exposed to low levels of organophosphate pesticides. *Neurotoxicol Teratol,* 32, 452–9.

Mahan, C.M., Bullman, T.A., Kang, H.K. & Selvin, S. 1997. A case-control study of lung cancer among Vietnam veterans. *J Occup Environ Med,* 39, 740–7.

McClean, M.D., Kelsey, K.T., Sison, J.D., Quesenberry, C.P., Jr., Wrensch, M.R. & Wiencke, J.K. 2011. A case-control study of asphalt and tar exposure and lung cancer in minorities. *Am J Ind Med,* 54, 811–8.

Mendes, A., Madureira, J., Neves, P., Carvalhais, C., Laffon, B. & Teixeira, J.P. 2011. Chemical exposure and occupational symptoms among Portuguese hairdressers. *J Toxicol Environ Health A,* 74, 993–1000.

Michalek, J.E. & Pavuk, M. 2008. Diabetes and cancer in veterans of Operation Ranch Hand after adjustment for calendar period, days of spraying, and time spent in Southeast Asia. *J Occup Environ Med,* 50, 330–40.

Michalek, J.E., Rahe, A.J. & Boyle, C.A. 1998. Paternal dioxin, preterm birth, intrauterine growth retardation, and infant death. *Epidemiology,* 9, 161–7.

Michalek, J.E., Akhtar, F.Z., Arezzo, J.C., Garabrant, D.H. & Albers, J.W. 2001. Serum dioxin and peripheral neuropathy in veterans of Operation Ranch Hand. *Neurotoxicology,* 22, 479–90.

Mignini, F., Tomassoni, D., Traini, E., Vitali, M., Scuri, S., Baldoni, E., Grappasonni, I. & Cocchioni, M. 2009. Immunological pattern alteration in shoe, hide, and leather industry workers exposed to hexavalent chromium. *Environ Toxicol,* 24, 594–602.

Myers, J.M. & Myers, C.R. 2009. The effects of hexavalent chromium on thioredoxin reductase and peroxiredoxins in human bronchial epithelial cells. *Free Radic Biol Med,* 47, 1477–85.

NAS 1974. *The Effects of Herbicides in South Vietnam.* Washington, DC: National Research Council.

Pavuk, M., Schecter, A.J., Akhtar, F.Z. & Michalek, J.E. 2003. Serum 2,3,7,8-tetrachlorodibenzo-p-dioxin (TCDD) levels and thyroid function in Air Force veterans of the Vietnam War. *Ann Epidemiol,* 13, 335–43.

Pavuk, M., Michalek, J.E., Schecter, A., Ketchum, N.S., Akhtar, F.Z. & Fox, K.A. 2005. Did TCDD exposure or service in Southeast Asia increase the risk of cancer in air force Vietnam veterans who did not spray agent orange? *J Occup Environ Med,* 47, 335–42.

Pavuk, M., Michalek, J.E. & Ketchum, N.S. 2006. Prostate cancer in US Air Force veterans of the Vietnam war. *J Expo Sci Environ Epidemiol,* 16, 184–90.

Peters, S., Kromhout, H., Olsson, A.C., Wichmann, H.E., Bruske, I., Consonni, D., Landi, M.T., Caporaso, N., Siemiatycki, J., Richiardi, L., Mirabelli, D., Simonato, L., Gustavsson, P., Plato, N., Jockel, K.H., Ahrens, W., Pohlabeln, H., Boffetta, P., Brennan, P., Zaridze, D., Cassidy, A., Lissowska, J., Szeszenia-Dabrowska, N., Rudnai, P., Fabianova, E., Forastiere, F., Bencko, V., Foretova, L., Janout, V., Stucker, I., Dumitru, R.S., Benhamou, S., Bueno-De-Mesquita, B., Kendzia, B., Pesch, B., Straif, K., Bruning, T. & Vermeulen, R. 2011. Occupational exposure to organic dust increases lung cancer risk in the general population. *Thorax* Feb 67(2): 111–16.

Proctor, S.P., Heeren, T., White, R.F., Wolfe, J., Borgos, M.S., Davis, J.D., Pepper, L., Clapp, R., Sutker, P.B., Vasterling, J.J. & Ozonoff, D. 1998. Health status of Persian Gulf War veterans: self-reported symptoms, environmental exposures and the effect of stress. *Int J Epidemiol*, 27, 1000–10.

Proctor, S.P., Heaton, K.J., Heeren, T. & White, R.F. 2006. Effects of sarin and cyclosarin exposure during the 1991 Gulf War on neurobehavioral functioning in US army veterans. *Neurotoxicology*, 27, 931–9.

RAC 2004. *Scientific Progress in Understanding Gulf War Veterans' Illnesses: Report and Recommendations*. Washington, DC: US Goverment Printing Office; GPO 2004-657-077.

RAC 2008. *Gulf War illness and the Health of Gulf War Veterans: Scientific Findings and Recommendations*. Washington, DC: US Government Printing Office.

Ray, D.E. & Richards, P.G. 2001. The potential for toxic effects of chronic, low-dose exposure to organophosphates. *Toxicol Lett*, 120, 343–51.

Reed, L., Buchner, V. & Tchounwou, P.B. 2007. Environmental toxicology and health effects associated with hexachlorobenzene exposure. *Rev Environ Health*, 22, 213–43.

Roldan-Tapi, L., Leyva, A., Laynez, F. & Santed, F.S. 2005. Chronic neuropsychological sequelae of cholinesterase inhibitors in the absence of structural brain damage: two cases of acute poisoning. *Environ Health Perspect*, 113, 762–6.

Roop, S.A., Niven, A.S., Calvin, B.E., Bader, J. & Zacher, L.L. 2007. The prevalence and impact of respiratory symptoms in asthmatics and nonasthmatics during deployment. *Mil Med*, 172, 1264–9.

Rosa, M.J., Jung, K.H., Perzanowski, M.S., Kelvin, E.A., Darling, K.W., Camann, D.E., Chillrud, S.N., Whyatt, R.M., Kinney, P.L., Perera, F.P. & Miller, R.L. 2011. Prenatal exposure to polycyclic aromatic hydrocarbons, environmental tobacco smoke and asthma. *Respir Med*, 105, 869–76.

Rossi, J., 3rd, Ritchie, G.D., Nordholm, A.F., Knechtges, P.L., Wilson, C.L., Lin, J., Alexander, W.K. & Still, K.R. 2000. Application of neurobehavioral toxicology methods to the military deployment toxicology assessment program. *Drug Chem Toxicol*, 23, 113–38.

Sanders, J.W., Putnam, S.D., Frankart, C., Frenck, R.W., Monteville, M.R., Riddle, M.S., Rockabrand, D.M., Sharp, T.W. & Tribble, D.R. 2005. Impact of illness and non-combat injury during Operations Iraqi Freedom and Enduring Freedom (Afghanistan). *Am J Trop Med Hyg*, 73, 713–9.

Selgrade, M.K. & Gilmour, M.I. 2010. Suppression of pulmonary host defenses and enhanced susceptibility to respiratory bacterial infection in mice following inhalation exposure to trichloroethylene and chloroform. *J Immunotoxicol*, 7, 350–6.

Sellappa, S., Prathyumnan, S., Keyan, K.S., Joseph, S., Vasudevan, B.S. & Sasikala, K. 2010. Evaluation of DNA damage induction and repair inhibition in welders exposed to hexavalent chromium. *Asian Pac J Cancer Prev*, 11, 95–100.

Shrey, K., Suchit, A., Deepika, D., Shruti, K. & Vibha, R. 2011. Air pollutants: the key stages in the pathway towards the development of cardiovascular disorders. *Environ Toxicol Pharmacol*, 31, 1–9.

Snow, B.R., Stellman, J.M., Stellman, S.D. & Sommer, J.F., Jr. 1988. Post-traumatic stress disorder among American Legionnaires in relation to combat experience in Vietnam: associated and contributing factors. *Environ Res*, 47, 175–92.

Soltaninejad, K. & Abdollahi, M. 2009. Current opinion on the science of organophosphate pesticides and toxic stress: a systematic review. *Med Sci Monit*, 15, RA75–90.

Steele, L. 2000. Prevalence and patterns of Gulf War illness in Kansas veterans: association of symptoms with characteristics of person, place, and time of military service. *Am J Epidemiol*, 152, 992–1002.

Steele, L., Sastre, A., Gerkovich, M.M. & Cook, M.R. 2012. Complex factors in the etiology of Gulf War illness: wartime exposures and risk factors in veteran subgroups. *Environ Health Perspect*, 120, 112–8.

Steenland, K., Jenkins, B., Ames, R.G., O'Malley, M., Chrislip, D. & Russo, J. 1994. Chronic neurological sequelae to organophosphate pesticide poisoning. *Am J Public Health*, 84, 731–6.

Stephens, R., Spurgeon, A., Calvert, I.A., Beach, J., Levy, L.S., Berry, H. & Harrington, J.M. 1995. Neuropsychological effects of long-term exposure to organophosphates in sheep dip. *Lancet*, 345, 1135–9.

Sullivan, K., Killiany, R., Powell, F., Krengel M., Pinto., L., Proctor, S.P., Heeren, T. & White, RF. Under review. Objective Biomarkers of GWI: Structural MRI and Diffusion Tensor Imaging, *Neurotoxicology and Teratology*, submitted.

Sullivan, K., Krengel, M., Proctor, S.P., Devine, S., Heeren, T., & White, R.F. 2003. Cognitive functioning in treatment-seeking Gulf War veterans: pyridostigmne bromide use and PTSD. *J Psychopathol Behav Assess*, 25, 95–103.

Toomey, R., Alpern, R., Vasterling, J.J., Baker, D.G., Reda, D.J., Lyons, M.J., Henderson, W.G., Kang, H.K., Eisen, S.A. & Murphy, F.M. 2009. Neuropsychological functioning of U.S. Gulf War veterans 10 years after the war. *J Int Neuropsychol Soc*, 15, 717–29.

Turner, M.C., Krewski, D., Pope III, C.A., Chen, Y., Gapstur, S.M. & Thun, M.J. 2011. Long-Term Ambient Fine Particulate Matter Air Pollution and Lung Cancer in a Large Cohort of Never Smokers. *Am J Respir Crit Care Med*, Dec 184(12): 1374–81.

VA 2010. Annual Benefits Reports—Veterans Benefits Administration Reports. Available at www.vba.va.gov/REPORTS/abr/index.asp

Wang, Y., Yang, H., Li, L., Wang, H., Xia, X. & Zhang, C. 2011. Biomarkers of chromosomal damage in peripheral blood lymphocytes induced by polycyclic aromatic hydrocarbons: a meta-analysis. *Int Arch Occup Environ Health*, 85(1): 13–25.

Weichenthal, S., Kulka, R., Dubeau, A., Martin, C., Wang, D. & Dales, R. 2011. Traffic-related air pollution and acute changes in heart rate variability and respiratory function in urban cyclists. *Environ Health Perspect*, 119, 1373–8.

White, R.F. 2003. *A Re-examination of Neuropsychological Functioning in Persian Gulf War Era Veterans*. Fort Detrick, MD: US Army Research and Materiel Command.

White, R.F. & Proctor, S.P. 1992. Research and clinical criteria for development of neurobehavioral test batteries. *J Occup Med*, 34, 140–8.

White, R.F., Proctor, S.P., Heeren, T., Wolfe, J., Krengel, M., Vasterling, J., Lindem, K., Heaton, K.J., Sutker, P. & Ozonoff, D.M. 2001. Neuropsychological function in Gulf War veterans: relationships to self-reported toxicant exposures. *Am J Ind Med*, 40, 42–54.

WHO 1988. *Chromium Environmental Health Criteria*. Geneva, Switzerland: World Health Organization.

Wichmann, F.A., Muller, A., Busi, L.E., Cianni, N., Massolo, L., Schlink, U., Porta, A. & Sly, P.D. 2009. Increased asthma and respiratory symptoms in children exposed to petrochemical pollution. *J Allergy Clin Immunol*, 123, 632–8.

Williams, L., Ulrich, C.M., Larson, T., Wener, M.H., Wood, B., Chen-Levy, Z., Campbell, P.T., Potter, J., Mctiernan, A. & De Roos, A.J. 2011. Fine particulate matter (PM(2.5)) air pollution and immune status among women in the Seattle area. *Arch Environ Occup Health*, 66, 155–65.

Williams, R., Brook, R., Bard, R., Conner, T., Shin, H. & Burnett, R. 2011. Impact of personal and ambient-level exposures to nitrogen dioxide and particulate matter on cardiovascular function. *Int J Environ Health Res*, 22(1): 71–91.

Winkenwerder, W. 2003. *Environmental Exposure Report: Pesticides Final Report.* Washington, DC: U.S. Department of Defense, Office of the Special Assistant to the Undersecretary of Defense (Personnel and Readiness) for Gulf War Illnesses Medical Readiness and Military Deployments.

Wolfe, J., Proctor, S.P., Erickson, D.J. & Hu, H. 2002. Risk factors for multisymptom illness in US Army veterans of the Gulf War. *J Occup Environ Med*, 44, 271–81.

Wolfe, W.H., Michalek, J.E., Miner, J.C., Rahe, A.J., Moore, C.A., Needham, L.L. & Patterson, D.G., Jr. 1995. Paternal serum dioxin and reproductive outcomes among veterans of Operation Ranch Hand. *Epidemiology*, 6, 17–22.

Xie, H., Holmes, A.L., Young, J.L., Qin, Q., Joyce, K., Pelsue, S.C., Peng, C., Wise, S.S., Jeevarajan, A.S., Wallace, W.T., Hammond, D. & Wise, J.P., Sr. 2009. Zinc chromate induces chromosome instability and DNA double strand breaks in human lung cells. *Toxicol Appl Pharmacol*, 234, 293–9.

Young, A.L. 1984. Determination and measurement of human exposure to the dibenzo-p-dioxins. *Bull Environ Contam Toxicol*, 33, 702–9.

Young, A.L. & Cecil, P.F., Sr. 2011. Agent Orange exposure and attributed health effects in Vietnam veterans. *Mil Med*, 176, 29–34.

Zhang, X.H., Zhang, X., Wang, X.C., Jin, L.F., Yang, Z.P., Jiang, C.X., Chen, Q., Ren, X.B., Cao, J.Z., Wang, Q & Zhu, Y.M. 2011. Chronic occupational exposure to hexavalent chromium causes DNA damage in electroplating workers. *BMC Public Health*, 11, 224.

14 VHA health care in response to a new generation of female veterans

Rachel Kimerling, Sally Haskell, Shira Maguen, Kristin Mattocks, Stacy Garrett-Ray, Laure Veet, and Susan McCutcheon

Over the past decade, the number of women veterans using Veterans Health Administration (VHA) care has nearly doubled, and numbers are continuing to rise. Women veterans of Operation Enduring Freedom, Operation Iraqi Freedom, and Operation New Dawn (OEF/OIF/OND) are substantially more likely to seek VHA health care than women from previous eras. This influx of new women veterans represents a changing face of women in VHA. With more than two-thirds of the OEF/OIF/OND cohort in reproductive age groups, there is a projected need for enhanced services across many domains. There is a growing need for reproductive health care, including attention to the issues of contraception and childbirth. These age groups also represent the peak years for utilization of mental health services among women. As such, there is a need for increased attention to access for mental health services, including treatment of war-zone exposures, and attention to couples and family issues that are especially relevant to women's adjustment.

The health care system has responded with new programs, policies, and initiatives for comprehensive health care for women veterans in an effort to provide the highest quality of patient-centered care to this newest generation of veterans. In this chapter, we review the changing demographics of female veterans and the expanded role of women in the war zone. We then review the literature on gender issues in the health care of OEF/OIF/OND veterans using VHA. After we highlight key VHA programs and policies that are helping VHA provide health care services tailored to the needs of this new generation of women veterans, we conclude with ongoing initiatives that will help VHA continue to meet the needs of future generations of women.

Changing demographics of female veterans

Women are one of the fastest growing segments of the US military population, comprising 14.5 percent of all active duty military, 18 percent of all National Guard and Reserves, and 8 percent of the total veteran population. Within the veteran population there are 1.9 million women, of which 6 percent are VHA health care users (*VetPop National Tables*, 2007). In the last decade, the number of women veterans utilizing VHA has nearly doubled from 159,000 in FY2000 to over 315,000 in FY2010 (Frayne et al., 2010). Service-connected status of VHA enrollees indicates an injury or illness was incurred or aggravated during military service, with an assigned disability severity rating from 0 to 100 percent. The proportion of women veteran VHA patients with a service-connected disability rating of 50 percent or more has increased over the past ten years. Over 50 percent of women veterans in VHA now carry some service-connected disability rating, making them eligible for lifelong VHA care for their service-connected conditions (Frayne et al., 2010).

Women veterans are, on average, younger than male veterans, because they are overwhelmingly members of the more recent cohorts of veterans, while the older cohorts (e.g., for World War II, Vietnam, Korea) were almost entirely male (96.5 percent). In FY2009, the average age of VHA users was 48 years old for women and 63 years old for men (Frayne et al., 2010). Among women veterans returning from OEF/OIF/OND, 79 percent are age 40 or below and 50 percent are 30 or younger. The representation of racial and ethnic minority women veterans is also increasing with more than 40 percent of OEF/OIF women veterans being racial/ethnic minorities (Veterans Health Administration, 2011). Of the various eras of women veterans, OEF/OIF/OND veterans have utilized VHA care at the highest rates. Currently 53.7 percent of female OEF/OIF/OND veterans have received VHA health care. Of this group, 88.5 percent have used VHA health care services more than once; 51 percent have used VHA health care 11 or more times (Frayne et al., 2010). These figures suggest that VHA health care is an especially important resource to women veterans of this cohort.

Over the past ten years, the OEF/OIF/OND cohort has contributed to an overall shift in the age distribution in women veterans utilizing the VHA. In FY2000, there was a bimodal age distribution with the tallest of two peaks at age 44 and the second at age 76. At nearly 45 percent, women veterans between the ages of 45 to 64 are currently still the largest sub-population of women VHA health care users. However, the growing numbers of OEF/OIF/OND women veterans who are seeking care from VHA has quickly led to a trimodal age distribution. In FY2009 the largest subpopulation of women veterans using VHA still centered around age 47, with the second largest subpopulation clustering around age 85, but with a new substantial group of younger women users centered around age 27 (Frayne et al., 2010). This new age distribution emphasizes the importance of comprehensive VHA health care for women across the life span, including a new emphasis on care for younger women.

Women in the war zone

While women have long served in war zones, women's greater numbers and expanded roles in OEF/OIF/OND have brought increased attention to their experiences of combat and their unique issues in post-deployment adjustment. This newest generation of female veterans reports higher levels of combat exposure than women veterans of prior wars, at rates more commensurate with the experiences of men. Among recently deployed veterans, approximately 45 percent of female and 50 percent of male veterans report some level of combat exposure (Jacobson et al., 2008). More broadly, combat stress can be conceptualized in four factors (King et al., 2003): combat experiences, exposure to the aftermath of battle, perceived threat, and difficult living and working environments. The factor of combat experiences receives the greatest degree of attention in research with veterans, and includes distinctive war-zone experiences such as firing a weapon, being fired upon, or witnessing injury or death. Exposure to the aftermath of battle refers to experiences such as handling human remains or other exposure to casualties, or interacting with refugees or detainees. A third factor is perceived threat, or concerns for safety and survival. The fourth factor includes the difficult living and working environments of combat, such as uncomfortable climate, unsanitary conditions, or lack of rest and privacy, often referred to as malevolent environment.

In a detailed assessment of combat stress among a national sample of OEF/OIF/OND veterans, significant gender differences emerged in the degree of combat stress, with men experiencing significantly higher levels of combat exposure, exposure to the aftermath of battle, and difficult living and working environment. Effect sizes were small, however, suggesting that both men and women experienced significant levels of combat-related stress during deployment (Vogt, Vaughn et al., 2011). Interestingly, no gender differences emerged in the relationship of these factors to post-deployment mental health, suggesting similar levels of resilience between women and men.

While men and women may respond similarly to combat stress, research has identified gender-specific factors that impact post-deployment adjustment. In particular, post-deployment social support appears to have a significantly stronger relationship to post-deployment PTSD among women as compared with men (Vogt, Smith et al., 2011). Relationship concerns during deployment also seem to play a unique role in women's post-deployment PTSD, an effect mediated by post-deployment stressors and post-deployment social support. The authors hypothesize that less social support may be available to returning women because of the relationship problems experienced during deployment (Vogt, Smith et al., 2011). More research is needed to explore the ways in which deployment may disrupt relationship or family functioning, particularly among women. For example, we have little research thus far on families with young children and issues of attachment and parenting, which may be particularly salient for women. Similarly, there is little data on the impact of multiple deployments and extended separation from family. Exposure to sexual harassment and assault is also a deployment-related stressor that emerged as particularly common to women, and is associated with poorer post-deployment mental health (Vogt, Vaughn et al., 2011).

Health of OEF/OIF/OND veterans in VHA

Medical conditions

The most common medical conditions that women veterans of OEF/OIF were treated for in VHA within the first year after deployment were back problems, joint disorders, PTSD, depression, musculoskeletal disorders, adjustment disorders, skin disorders, major depression, ear and sense organ disorders, and reproductive health conditions. Compared with men veterans, women veterans were more likely to be diagnosed with depression, musculoskeletal disorders, adjustment disorders, and skin disorders (Haskell et al., 2011).

Women veterans are at high risk for musculoskeletal injury, which has been hypothesized to stem in part from physical stresses of military service, such as the differential effects of wearing and carrying heavy gear or packs while working. In further analysis of the rates of musculoskeletal conditions in women compared with men veterans in the first seven years after deployment, women veterans had higher rates of back problems, musculoskeletal conditions, and joint problems than men veterans. From one year after deployment to seven years after deployment, the rates of these conditions increased for both men and women, but the odds of having a painful musculoskeletal condition increased each year for women compared with men in years 1–7 after deployment (Haskell et al., 2012).

Women's expanded roles in the combat theater have left them increasingly vulnerable to blast injury and traumatic brain injury (TBI), often referred to as the "signature wound" of these conflicts. In a study of 327,633 OEF/OIF veterans screened for TBI 654 women and 11,951 men had confirmed deployment related TBI. Women with TBI were more likely than men to report neurobehavioral symptoms such as affective, somatosensory, cognitive, or vestibular disorders (Iverson et al., 2011).

Because a substantial majority of this cohort of women veterans is 45 years old or younger, reproductive health issues are common. Many of these women are sexually active and seek contraceptive management (Yano et al., 2011). Approximately one third of OEF/OIF/OND women in VHA care have been treated for a sexually transmitted infection, the most common of which are HPV and pelvic inflammatory disorder (Turchik et al., in press). Another recent study of OEF/OIF/OND women veterans in VHA care (Mattocks et al., 2010) found that approximately 7 percent had been pregnant, and over 30 percent of these pregnant veterans had been diagnosed with at least one mental health condition prior to or during pregnancy. To date, no studies have examined maternal child health outcomes among combat-exposed women. Approximately one percent of OEF/OIF/OND women in VHA have sought treatment for infertility, and 85 percent of this care was provided by VHA providers (Mattocks et al., in review).

Mental health conditions

Approximately one half of both women (49.7 percent) and men (51.9 percent) OEF/OIF/OND veterans seen by VHA have been diagnosed with a mental health condition. Adjustment reactions (including PTSD), depression, and other anxiety disorders are among the most common conditions (Veterans Health Administration, 2011). Recent studies have found some gender differences in the prevalence of mental health conditions. For example, female veterans may be more likely than male veterans to be diagnosed with depression (23 percent vs. 17

percent), and less likely to be diagnosed with PTSD (17 percent vs. 22 percent) and alcohol use disorders (3 percent vs. 8 percent) (Maguen et al., 2010). The gender differences in the diagnoses of depression and alcohol misuse are consistent with findings among the general population of OEF/OIF/OND veterans, while some studies have not found gender differences in the prevalence of PTSD diagnoses or symptoms (Vogt, Vaughn et al., 2011). PTSD is associated with substantial medical comorbidity among both male and female veterans in this cohort, and some evidence suggests that the PTSD-related medical comorbidity is substantially greater among women as compared with men (Frayne et al., 2011).

Gender differences in mental health conditions are also found among OEF/OIF veterans in VHA care who have experienced TBI (Iverson et al., 2011). Among this population, PTSD is the most common mental health diagnosis for both men and women, but is significantly more common among men. Women with TBI were twice as likely as men to receive depression diagnoses and also significantly more likely to be diagnosed with another anxiety disorder.

Exposure to sexual assault or sexual harassment during military service has also received increasing attention among this cohort. These experiences are termed military sexual trauma (MST) in the context of VHA care. As of 2010, the VHA surveillance data indicates that 18.5 percent of women and 0.8 percent men that served in OEF/OIF/OND reported MST. Among those veterans who report MST, 58.4 percent of women and 48.3 percent of men received MST-related mental health treatment (Military Sexual Trauma Support Team, 2011). While PTSD is the most common mental health condition associated with MST, these experiences are also linked to increased risk for other anxiety disorders, depression, and substance use disorders (Kimerling et al., 2010). Among women OEF/OIF/OND veterans diagnosed with PTSD, 31 percent report MST (Maguen et al., 2012). These women are diagnosed with a greater number of mental health conditions comorbid to PTSD as compared women diagnosed with PTSD but who did not report MST.

Utilization and cost

Women veterans of OEF/OIF/OND who utilize VHA care appear to engage with primary care and mental health services. Among those who used any VHA care in the first year after deployment, 87 percent of females and 80 percent of males had at least one visit with primary care. Forty-two percent of women and 43 percent of men had at least one visit with mental health care. Among those who used primary care and mental health services, women made more visits to both primary care and mental health care than men (Haskell et al., 2011). However, some studies of both men and women OEF/OIF/OND veterans utilizing mental health care suggest that substantial proportions of these veterans are not receiving an adequate treatment dose (i.e. a sufficient number of visits to achieve meaningful clinical change).

Both women and men diagnosed with PTSD were seen for a median of about three mental health outpatient visits per year, which is lower than expected, particularly given that nine or more visits are recommended for evidence-based PTSD treatment (Seal et al., 2010). This suggests that although veterans diagnosed with PTSD are coming into mental health clinics, they may not be getting an optimal dose of mental health treatment. However, these figures echo those found in the general US population, where only approximately one third of patients with psychiatric disorders receive a minimally adequate dose of treatment (Wang et al., 2005). In both veterans and the general population, women are somewhat more likely than men to receive an adequate dose of mental health treatment (Seal et al., 2010; Wang et al., 2005). Both women and men with mental health conditions comorbid to PTSD utilize more services than those without comorbid conditions, with depression being an especially common comorbid condition. Among OEF/OIF/OND veterans with comorbid PTSD and depression, women are twice as likely to receive residential or inpatient mental health treatment as compared with men (Maguen et al., in press).

In an analysis of the costs of care in the first year after returning from service in Iraq and Afghanistan, a slightly greater proportion of women than men were found to have a service connected disability (20.7 percent versus 19.8 percent). After adjusting for demographic differences in the population, there were no significant differences in the cost of care by gender within the first year after deployment, however there were significant differences in inpatient and outpatient care. While men veterans had higher inpatients costs, women veterans had higher outpatient and pharmacy costs (Leslie et al., 2011).

Overall, OEF/OIF/OND women veterans seem to utilize VHA primary care and outpatient services at slightly higher rates than their male counterparts, and demonstrate concomitant higher outpatient cost of care. Access to mental health care is an issue that merits continued attention for both men and women. Some evidence suggests that after adjusting for comorbidity and demographic characteristics, OEF/OIF/OND veterans are actually receiving more mental health care compared with veterans from other cohorts (Harpaz-Rotem & Rosenheck, 2011).

The changing face of VHA: new programs and policies

VHA has a long history of providing health care to women veterans. Ongoing monitoring of health care quality reveals high satisfaction ratings of VHA care among both women and men (Wright et al., 2006). Studies of women veterans have found that comprehensive health care, including the availability of reproductive health care, emerges as an important factor in the extent to which women use VHA services (Bean-Mayberry et al., 2004). Research also indicates that women who receive gender-specific services are more satisfied with their VHA care (Bean-Mayberry et al., 2003). These services are especially relevant for the younger, reproductive-aged OEF/OIF/OND cohort.

The type of gender-specific care provided within each VHA facility varies depending on the women's health delivery model and the complexity of reproductive health services provided within the facility. All VHA healthcare systems offer basic gender-specific services such as cervical cancer screening, menstrual disorder diagnosis, and hormonal contraception treatment and management. Availability of advanced gynecologic services, such as endometrial biopsy, intrauterine device (IUD) insertion, infertility treatment, and general gynecologic surgery varies considerably across VHA sites (Seelig et al., 2008; Washington et al., 2003).

When gender-specific care is not available at a VHA facility, federal law allows veterans to receive care at outside facilities via contract or fee-basis care arrangements. Fee-basis care arrangements are those in which community providers are reimbursed by the VHA for each individual service rendered to veterans. In contrast, contract care is provided by non-VHA physicians under a capitated payment system (Liu et al., 2010). Recent evidence suggests that the proportion of gender-specific care provided by fee-basis providers has increased substantially over the past ten years (Mattocks et al., under review).

The Veteran's Health Care Eligibility Reform Act of 1996 established a VHA maternity benefit program for female veterans, in which female veterans receive pre-natal, intra-partum and post-partum care from fee-basis providers in their communities. In addition, the Caregivers and Veterans Omnibus Health Services Act of 2010 allows the VHA to pay for care of newborn children of veterans when the veterans are receiving maternity care furnished by VHA. VHA provides infertility services for eligible women veterans, including assessment of reproductive capacity and treatment or correction of some fertility-related problems, such as endometriosis. In addition, surgical reversal of tubal ligation is a covered benefit for treatment of infertility. However, in vitro fertilization is not a covered benefit in the VHA. Preventive screening programs for women veterans include screening for cervical, breast, and colon cancer. Breast and cervical cancer screenings are monitored on a regular basis as quality indicators. Cervical cancer screening rates in VHA consistently exceed 90 percent (Goldzweig et al., 2004; VHA Performance Measurement, 2011).

Despite this wide range of services, women veterans using VHA services are often unaware of the full extent of VHA gender-specific and reproductive health services, especially services related to infertility and prenatal care (Mattocks et al., 2011). Many of the new initiatives in women's health care focus on service delivery models that make these services more accessible to women veterans.

Comprehensive health care for women veterans

In response to the growing population of women veterans, in 2008, the Under Secretary for Health convened a work group to evaluate the provision of primary care to women veterans. The work group found that VHA care for women was often fragmented with general primary care needs and gender-specific primary care needs handled by different types of providers in different settings. This multi-visit primary care delivery model was felt to interfere with continuity and increase barriers to care (*Report of the Under Secretary for Health Workgroup on Provision of Primary Care to Women Veterans*, 2008). In addition, although quality of care in VHA often exceeds that in the private sector, there were disparities identified in several areas in terms of clinical prevention performance indicators for women compared with men within the VHA. Cholesterol control, diabetes care, and measures such as vaccination rates, colorectal cancer screening, and mental health screenings were all lower for women compared with men (*Gender Report*, 2008).

The work group reviewed VHA research showing that access and wait times were better at sites where gender-specific services were available in a "one-stop shopping model," i.e., one appointment to receive all primary care including general primary care and gender-specific services (*Report of the Under Secretary for Health Workgroup on Provision of Primary Care to Women Veterans*, 2008) and that women veterans preferred to receive general and women's health care from the same provider or clinic (Washington et al., 2006). In addition, the work group examined evidence from the private sector on the Department of Health and Human Services, Office of Women's Health designated National Centers of Excellence (CoE) in Comprehensive Primary Care Women's Health that showed that women served in CoEs were more likely than women in national and community comparison samples to receive a range of age-appropriate screening services and counseling, and reported higher patient satisfaction (Anderson et al., 2002). Based on the research literature, the work group recommended that the VHA adopt a model of Comprehensive Primary Care. They proposed a consensus definition of Comprehensive Primary Care for Women Veterans (*Report of the Under Secretary for Health Workgroup on Provision of Primary Care to Women Veterans*, 2008, p. 4):

> Comprehensive Primary Care for women Veterans is defined as the availability of complete primary care from one primary care provider at one site. The primary care provider should, in the context of a longitudinal relationship, fulfill all primary care needs, including acute and chronic illness, gender-specific, preventive, and mental health care.

In 2009 the VHA Women Veterans Health Strategic Health Care Group rolled out the national implementation of Comprehensive Women's Health requiring that all facilities develop a Women's Comprehensive Health Implementation Plan (WCHIP). This was followed in 2010 by VHA Policy, "Health Care Services for Women Veterans" (Veterans Health Administration, 2010) that outlines specific services to be provided at VHA hospitals and community-based outpatient clinics. The policy not only defines comprehensive primary care for women veterans, but also requires that women veteran patients be assigned "Designated Women's Health Providers." Designated Women's Health Providers must be trained or experienced in women's health and have a large enough proportion of women in their patient panels (at least 10 percent) to maintain competency in women's health.

The policy also defines three different models of care for women veterans. Women's primary care within VHA can now be provided in any of these models: Model 1 where comprehensive primary care is delivered by a designated women's health provider in a gender-neutral primary care clinic; Model 2 where comprehensive primary care is offered by a designated women's health provider in a separate but shared space that may be located adjacent to or near primary care; and Model 3 where comprehensive primary care is delivered in a comprehensive women's clinic in an exclusive, separate space, that co-locates primary care, gynecology, mental health and other services for women veterans.

The transformation of Women's Health within VHA includes many other initiatives that support the implementation of Comprehensive Primary Care. Among these are a national focus on reducing gender disparities and eliminating deficiencies in privacy and environment of care for women veterans. Other projects are supporting improved care coordination through development of a national breast cancer tracking and registry, a system for alerting providers who prescribe potentially teratogenic (causing birth defects) drugs to women of childbearing age, and a national survey of emergency care for women veterans. The Women Veterans Health Program has adopted a mission statement "to ensure that all women veterans receive equitable high-quality and comprehensive health care services in a sensitive and safe environment in all VHA facilities; and to be a national leader in the provision of health care for women veterans, thereby raising the standard of care for all women."

Provider education and training initiatives in women's health

The increasing numbers of women veterans along with VHA's goal of providing comprehensive primary care by one provider and team at its more than 900 sites of care has led to the need for training (or re-training) of providers in primary care women's health. The VHA has launched major education initiatives to meet this need. The VHA "Mini-Residency Program on Primary Health Care for Women Veterans" was created to prepare providers to care for the growing population of women veterans—particularly women of child-bearing age—and the program was subsequently expanded to include topics relevant to women in older age groups. The full program consists of two 2.5-day women's health courses ("Part 1" and "Part 2"). To date, over 1,200 VHA primary care providers have been trained in "Part 1" which was launched in 2008 and over 500 in "Part 2", launched in 2010.

Highlights of the program include hands-on instruction on pelvic and breast exams using trained, standardized patients; didactic lectures by expert faculty; large-group discussions; and small-group facilitated instruction. Other unique aspects of the program include seating participants from the same geographic area together to facilitate networking and collaboration; a "show and tell" display table containing Pap smear equipment, endometrial biopsy equipment, intrauterine devices and other items; and a facilitated session during which participants develop individual action plans to improve one aspect of care at the individual's site. Examples of actions undertaken successfully include streamlined referrals and communication between women's health primary care and military sexual trauma, substance abuse and other mental health professionals; same-day mammography; and increased availability for simple gynecologic procedures and vaccines at individual clinics. The program also includes participation by a clinical pharmacist experienced in women's health medication issues. This individual is onsite during the training and available to address participants' questions on issues related to prescribing in women. Additional hands-on training opportunities utilizing pelvic and breast simulation equipment as part of a "task trainer lab" were added in 2011.

Topics covered in Women's Health Mini-Residency Program, "Part 1" include cervical cancer screening, uterine bleeding, contraception, and post-deployment/reintegration issues and military sexual trauma. Topics covered in Women's Health Mini-Residency Program, "Part 2," include osteoporosis, menopause, cardiovascular disease, and sexual dysfunction. Results of participant surveys from the national program indicate significant improvements in participant pre- and post-training evaluation scores in the 14 areas queried. Course evaluations reveal that 100 percent of participants in "Part 1" and 97 percent of participants in "Part 2" would recommend the training to others.

In addition to the mini-residency program, VHA has several other ongoing educational initiatives including monthly audio-conferences, women's health research cyber-seminars, and women's health fellowship programs. VHA will also soon release a virtual course for women's emergency care geared toward emergency medicine providers and women's health nursing curricula, among others. As the influx of women veterans continues, VHA expects to continue to evaluate, adapt, develop, and deploy training programs to help maintain clinical staff proficiencies to meet the health care needs of our veterans.

Military sexual trauma

VA's definition of military sexual trauma (MST) comes from Title 38 US Code 1720D and is "physical assault of a sexual nature, battery of a sexual nature, or sexual harassment."

VHA efforts to detect and treat MST were first authorized in 1992 by US Code and corresponding VHA Directives. While these initiatives are not new, the OEF/OIF/OND cohort represents the first generation to return from a large-scale conflict to what currently represents one of the most comprehensive approaches to the detection and treatment of sexual trauma in a healthcare setting. There is universal screening of men and women for MST in all VHA health care settings. All inpatient, outpatient, and pharmaceutical care for mental and physical health conditions related to MST is provided free of charge. Every VHA facility has a designated MST Coordinator who helps veterans access the services they need, and facilitates staff education and training and outreach to veterans. Every VHA facility provides specialized medical and mental health care for conditions related to MST. Specialized residential or inpatient MST-related care is available in every geographic region. Evidence-based mental health care is available to all veterans diagnosed with mental health conditions related to MST. Facilities are also encouraged to accommodate veterans' requests for a provider of a particular gender.

Seeing a provider of the same gender is often a concern among women who have experienced sexual trauma. Among women who seek MST treatment in VHA, a recent evaluation conducted by the VHA Office of Mental Health Services (OMHS) indicates that the majority of female veterans (84.7 percent) who received MST-related mental health care received that care from a female provider for one or more encounters. Among women who saw a female provider at least once, the large majority of their MST-related mental health encounters (80.5 percent) were with a female provider.

Though some research suggests that women exposed to interpersonal violence are less satisfied with health care services, research suggests that veterans who have experienced MST are as satisfied with their VHA care as veterans who have not experienced MST (Kimerling et al., 2011). The positive feelings about quality of care among women, including those who have experienced MST, are likely due to the extensive efforts VHA has made to ensure the availability of services targeting women's specific needs and to address environmental issues so that women veterans are comfortable receiving care in VHA settings. As a part of ongoing efforts to promote best practices throughout the system, the VHA Office of Mental Health Services engages in ongoing provider training and educational initiatives for the treatment of conditions related to MST. The office also engages in ongoing monitoring of MST screening and treatment at each VHA facility, including annual reports on MST among OEF/OIF/OND veterans.

Dissemination of evidence-based psychotherapy

Several initiatives are underway in the VHA Office of Mental Health Services to increase the availability and fidelity of evidence-based psychotherapies across the VHA health care system. These initiatives map well to the most commonly occurring mental health conditions among women, and all utilize treatments with a good evidence base for efficacy with women. Specialized outpatient mental health treatment is available throughout the system, and every VHA facility has a specialized PTSD Clinical Team or a PTSD specialist. Specialized providers are also available at each facility to coordinate treatment or patients with PTSD and comorbid substance use disorders. Over one third of VHA medical centers have designated women's mental health providers or clinics, while nearly half have at least some gender-specific mental health programming (Oishi et al., 2011), and these proportions are increasing over time.

There are currently ongoing dissemination programs for evidence-based treatments for PTSD, depression, and serious mental illness (SMI). The structure of these programs is similar. The goal is to use intensive competency-based training efforts to develop decentralized training capacity within each geographic region, or Veterans Integrated Service Network (VISN). This "train the trainer" model is intended to maintain the capacity of trained mental health professionals and coordinate care within the region's facilities. Training efforts are accompanied by a number of top-down and bottom-up implementation efforts to enhance collaboration with local facility leadership, create a culture that supports the adoption of new evidence-based treatments, and, when needed, modify systems and processes of care that support the implementation of these treatments. Evidence-Based Psychotherapy coordinators have been established at each medical center to facilitate this structure. There is also outreach to veterans including educational awareness campaigns and psycho-educational information through videos and websites that provide information about each of the evidence-based treatments. It is VHA policy that all OEF/OIF/OND veterans diagnosed with PTSD, depression or SMI are offered treatment with one of the empirically supported psychotherapies.

Dissemination initiatives for PTSD began in 2006 and are among the most developed and far-reaching of the dissemination initiatives. For detailed descriptions of these dissemination programs, see Karlin et al. (2011). Two psychotherapies for PTSD were selected for dissemination following landmark studies that supported their effectiveness with veteran populations. Cognitive Processing Therapy (CPT) (Resick & Schnicke, 1992) has an extensive evidence base, having been conducted with women who have experienced interpersonal violence, but has also demonstrated efficacy with veterans (Monson et al., 2006). Similarly, Prolonged Exposure (PE) (Foa et al., 2007) also has an extensive evidence base including many studies with women and interpersonal violence, and has demonstrated efficacy in a large study of women veterans (Schnurr et al., 2007).

Training for both treatments began in collaboration with the original developers, but with special materials adapted for VHA. All training materials include case examples for women patients, and also include materials related to military sexual trauma. Information about the unique clinical issues of the OEF/OIF/OND cohort is included. In addition to intensive three- and four-day seminars that incorporate techniques such as video examples of therapy techniques and role-playing, regular case consultation from VHA experts is required as newly trained therapists apply these therapies. Communication and collaboration with local staff and leadership in PTSD specialty clinics have helped to share best practices in clinic design and other ways to restructure clinical services to support routine delivery of these services. As early as 2009, CPT or PE was available at 96 percent of all VHA facilities, representing a substantial increase in access since the dissemination initiatives began (Karlin et al., 2011).

Family services

OMHS commitment to disseminate evidence-based psychotherapy (EBP) described earlier also extends to family services. Research with women OEF/OIF/OND veterans suggests that family concerns may be especially important factors in women's post-deployment adjustment (Vogt, Smith et al., 2011). VHA is disseminating a marriage and family evidence-based psychotherapy, Integrative Behavioral Couples Therapy (IBCT) (Jacobson et al., 2000). This treatment incorporates behavioral couples therapy with acceptance-based strategies. The overarching goals of IBCT are to reduce couples' distress and strengthen family relationships. This initiative also includes training in basic parenting skills and assessment of domestic violence as part of the IBCT marriage and family psychotherapy workshop, both of which are especially relevant to the needs of reproductive-age OEF/OIF/OND women.

The OMHS is also disseminating evidence-based family psychotherapy for individuals with serious mental illness and their families, which is known as Family Psychoeducation (FPE). Two models of FPE have been selected for dissemination: Behavioral Family Therapy (BFT) (Mueser & Glynn, 1995) for use with a single family, and Multiple Family Group Therapy (McFarlane, 2002) which can be used in a multi-family group format. These treatments focus on supporting the well-being and current functioning of that individual, but improved family well-being is also an important intermediate and additional benefit. FPE provides families with current information about their family member's illness and develops coping skills for handling problems posed by mental illness in one member of the family. These treatments also include communication skills training and instruction in problem solving. The broad goal of FPE is for the veteran, family and clinician to all work together in a partnership to support recovery.

Conclusions

As increasing numbers of women enter the military and serve in new and critical roles, the VHA health care system is challenged to address the myriad ways that military service can impact women's lives (Hayes, 2011). Continued research on women's health in VHA is an essential component of the health care system's continuing evolution to provide high quality, veteran-centered care. The policies and programs described in this chapter have benefitted from a strong tradition of VHA research with women veterans.

Recently, the VHA Office of Health Services Research and Development (HSR&D) invested in a national Women's Health Research Consortium, which builds the capacity for women's health research through ongoing training, technical assistance, and dissemination of research results. Despite women's increasing numbers in VHA, women are still a small minority at most VHA medical centers, creating challenges for women-focused studies. To address this issue, HSR&D has launched a women's health Practice-Based Research Network (PBRN), a network of researchers and clinicians across the system that will collaborate to provide needed infrastructure for health care research with women (Lipson & Eisen, 2011).

Systematic reviews (Bean-Mayberry et al., 2011) and system-wide agenda setting activities continue to accelerate research progress. Furthermore, because VHA is a nationwide, integrated system, strategic communication and collaboration between researchers and policy-makers allows for efficient implementation of new research results and focused research efforts to address key health issues. For example, the VHA Women Veteran's Health Strategic Health Care Group supports the Women's Health Evaluation Initiative, researchers devoted to providing leadership with clinically and policy relevant data for planning and implementation of women's health programs (Frayne et al., 2010). Similarly, the Office of Mental Health Services supports the MST Support Team, a group of researchers devoted to evaluation of VHA MST services and provision of policy-relevant data for use by mental health leadership. Partnerships with research initiatives and resources has helped VHA move forward with a strong evidence base to care for women veterans (Yano et al., 2011).

In summary, the increasing numbers of women serving in widespread critical roles in the OEF/OIF/OND war zones has resulted in a new generation of women veterans who are seeking VHA care in historic proportions. Research that investigates the health of women veterans, and the organization and implementation of health care services to women, will continue to inform the expansion of services for women and further tailor VHA programs to women's needs. A great number of new policies and initiatives are underway within VHA that serve to increase the availability of health and mental health care that meets the needs of OEF/OIF/OND women. In addition to augmenting services for comprehensive women's health, there is increased attention to sexual trauma, effects of war-zone exposure among women, and family services. As VHA works to continue to deliver the "best care anywhere" (Longman, 2007), a focus on OEF/OIF/OND women will continue.

References

Anderson, R.T., Weisman, C.S., Scholle, S.H., Henderson, J.T., Oldendick, R., & Camacho, F. (2002). Evaluation of the quality of care in the clinical care centers of the National Centers of Excellence in Women's Health. *Womens Health Issues, 12*(6), 309–326.

Bean-Mayberry, B.A., Chang, C.-C.H., McNeil, M.A., Whittle, J., Hayes, P.M., & Scholle, S.H. (2003). Patient satisfaction in women's clinics versus traditional primary care clinics in the Veterans Administration. *Journal of General Internal Medicine, 18*(3), 175–181.

Bean-Mayberry, B., Chang, C.C., McNeil, M., Hayes, P., & Scholle, S.H. (2004). Comprehensive care for women veterans: Indicators of dual use of VA and non-VA providers. *Journal of the American Medical Women's Association, 59*(3), 192–197.

Bean-Mayberry, B., Yano, E.M., Washington, D.L., Goldzweig, C., Batuman, F., Huang, C. et al. (2011). Systematic Review of Women Veterans' Health: Update on Successes and Gaps. *Women's Health Issues, 21*(4, Supplement), S84–S97.

Foa, E.B., Hembree, E.A., & Rothbaum, B. (2007). *Prolonged Exposure Therapy for PTSD: Emotional processing of traumatic experiences.* Oxford: Oxford University Press.

Frayne, S.M., Phibbs, C.S., Friedman, S.A., Berg, E.A., Ananth, L., Iqbal, S. et al. (2010). *Sociodemographic Characteristics and Use of VHA Care.* Washington, DC: Women Veterans Health Strategic Health Care Group, Department of Veterans Affairs.

Frayne, S.M., Chiu, V.Y., Iqbal, S., Berg, E.A., Laungani, K.J., Cronkite, R.C. et al. (2011). Medical care needs of returning veterans with PTSD: their other burden. *J Gen Intern Med, 26*(1), 33–39.

Gender Report (2008). Department of Veteran Affairs.

Goldzweig, C.L., Parkerton, P.H., Washington, D.L., Lanto, A.B., & Yano, E.M. (2004). Primary care practice and facility quality orientation: Influence on breast and cervical cancer screening rates. *American Journal of Managed Care, 10*(4), 265–272.

Harpaz-Rotem, I., & Rosenheck, R.A. (2011). Serving those who served: retention of newly returning veterans from Iraq and Afghanistan in mental health treatment. *Psychiatr Serv, 62*(1), 22–27.

Haskell, S., Mattocks, K., Goulet, J., Krebs, E., Skanderson, M., Leslie, D. et al. (2011). The Burden of Illness in the First Year Home. Do Male and Female VA Users Differ in Health Conditions and Healthcare Utilization? *Women's Health Issues, 21*(1), 92–97.

Haskell, S., Ning, Y., Krebs, E., Goulet, J., Mattocks, K., Kerns, R. et al. (2012). The prevalence of painful musculoskeletal conditions in female and male veterans in 7 years after return from deployment in Operation Enduring Freedom/Operation Iraqi Freedom. *Clinical Journal of Pain,* 28(2) 163–7.

Hayes, P.M. (2011). Leading the nation in women's health: the important role of research. *Women's Health Issues, 21*(4S), S70–S72.

Iverson, K.M., Hendricks, A.M., Kimerling, R., Krengel, M., Meterko, M., Stolzmann, K.L. et al. (2011). Psychiatric Diagnoses and Neurobehavioral Symptom Severity among OEF/OIF VA Patients with Deployment-Related Traumatic Brain Injury. A Gender Comparison. *Women's Health Issues, 21*(4s), S 210–217.

Jacobson, N.S., Christensen, A., Prince, S.E., Cordova, J., & Eldridge, K. (2000). Integrative behavioral couple therapy: an acceptance-based, promising new treatment for couple discord. *J Consult Clin Psychol, 68*(2), 351–355.

Jacobson, I.G., Ryan, M.A.K., Hooper, T.I., Smith, T.C., Amoroso, P.J., Boyko, E.J. et al. (2008). Alcohol use and alcohol-related problems before and after military combat deployment. *Journal of the American Medical Association, 300*(6), 663–675.

Karlin, B.E., Ruzek, J.I., Chard, K.M., Eftekhari, A., Monson, C.M., Hembree, E. et al. (2011). Dissemination of evidence-based psychological treatments for posttraumatic stress disorder in the Veterans Health Administration. *Journal of Traumatic Stress, 23*(6), 663–673.

Kimerling, R., Street, A.E., Pavao, J., Smith, M., Cronkite, R., Holmes, T.H. et al. (2010). Military-related sexual trauma among Veterans Health Administration patients returning from Afghanistan and Iraq. *American Journal of Public Health, 100*(8), 1409–1412.

Kimerling, R., Pavao, J., Valdez, C., Mark, H., Hyun, J., & Saweikis, M. (2011). Military sexual trauma and patient perceptions of Veteran Health Administration health care quality. *Women's Health Issues, 21*(4 Suppl), S145–S151.

King, D.W., King, L.A., & Vogt, D.S. (2003). *Manual for the Deployment Risk and Resilience Inventory (DRRI): A Collection of Measures for Studying Deployment-Related Experiences of Military Veterans.* Boston, MA: National Center for Posttraumatic Stress Disorder.

Leslie, D., Goulet, J., Skanderson, M., Mattocks, K., Haskell, S., & Brandt, C. (2011). VA health care utilization and costs among male and female Veterans in the first year after service in Afghanistan and Iraq. *Military Medicine, 176*(3), 265–269.

Lipson, L., & Eisen, S. (2011). VA Research: Committed to women who have "Borne the Battle" and beyond. *Women's Health Issues, 21*(4S), S67–S69.

Liu, C.F., Chapko, M., Bryson, C.L., Burgess, J.F., Jr., Fortney, J.C., Perkins, M. et al. (2010). Use of outpatient care in Veterans Health Administration and Medicare among veterans receiving primary care in community-based and hospital outpatient clinics. *Health Serv Res, 45*(5 Pt 1), 1268–1286.

Longman, P. (2007). *Best Care Anywhere: Why VA health care is better than yours.* Sausalito: Polipoint Press.

Maguen, S., Ren, L., Bosch, J.O., Marmar, C.R., & Seal, K.H. (2010). Gender differences in mental health diagnoses among Iraq and Afghanistan veterans enrolled in veterans affairs health care. *Am J Public Health, 100*(12), 2450–2456.

Maguen, S., Cohen, B., Ren, L., Bosch, J., Kimerling, R., & Seal, K. (2012). Gender Differences in Military Sexual Trauma and Mental Health Diagnoses Among Iraq and Afghanistan Veterans With Posttraumatic Stress Disorder. *Womens Health Issues, 22*(1): e61–6.

Maguen, S. Cohen, B., Cohen, G., Madden, E., Bertenthal, D., & Seal, K. (in press). Gender differences in health service utilization among Iraq and Afghanistan Veterans with posttraumatic stress disorder. *Journal of Women's Health.*

Mattocks K.M., Nikolajski C., Haskell S., Brandt C., McCall-Hosenfeld J., Yano E., Pham T., & Borrero S. (2011) Women veterans' reproductive health preferences and experiences: a focus group analysis. *Womens Health Issues* 21(2): 124–9.

Mattocks, K.M., Skanderson, M., Goulet, J.L., Brandt, C., Womack, J., Krebs, E. et al. (2010). Pregnancy and mental health among women veterans returning from Iraq and Afghanistan. *J Womens Health (Larchmt), 19*(12), 2159–2166.

Mattocks, K.M., Zephyrin, L., Herrera, L., Haskell, S., Frayne, S., Yano, E. et al. (in review). Dual sources of care for gender-specific conditions among OEF/OIF women veterans. *Health Services Research.*

McFarlane, W.R. (2002). *Multifamily groups in the treatment of severe psychiatric disorders.* New York: Guilford Press.

Military Sexual Trauma Support Team (2011). *Special Report of Operation Enduring Freedom / Operation Iraqi Freedom / Operation New Dawn (OEF/OIF/OND) Veterans.* Washington, DC: Department of Veterans Affairs, Office of Mental Health Services.

Monson, C.M., Schnurr, P.P., Resick, P.A., Friedman, M.J., Young-Xu, Y., & Stevens, S.P. (2006). Cognitive processing therapy for veterans with military-related posttraumatic stress disorder. *Journal of Consulting and Clinical Psychology, 74*(5), 898–907.

Mueser, K., & Glynn, S. (1995). *Behavioral family therapy for psychiatric disorders.* Needham Heights, MA: Allyn & Bacon.

Oishi, S.M., Rose, D.E., Washington, D.L., MacGregor, C., Bean-Mayberry, B., & Yano, E.M. (2011). National variations in VA mental health care for women veterans. *Womens Health Issues, 21*(4 Suppl), S130–137.

Report of the Under Secretary for Health Workgroup on Provision of Primary Care to Women Veterans (2008). Department of Veteran Affairs.

Resick, P.A., & Schnicke, M.K. (1992). Cognitive processing therapy for sexual assault victims. *Journal of Consulting & Clinical Psychology, 60*(5), 748–756.

Schnurr, P.P., Friedman, M.J., Engel, C.C., Foa, E.B., Shea, M.T., Chow, B.K. et al. (2007). Cognitive behavioral therapy for posttraumatic stress disorder in women: A randomized controlled trial. *Journal of the American Medical Association, 297*(8), 820–830.

Seal, K.H., Maguen, S., Cohen, B., Gima, K.S., Metzler, T.J., Ren, L. et al. (2010). VA mental health services utilization in Iraq and Afghanistan veterans in the first year of receiving new mental health diagnoses. *J Trauma Stress, 23*(1), 5–16.

Seelig, M.D., Yano, E.M., Bean-Mayberry, B., Lanto, A.B., & Washington, D.L. (2008). Availability of gynecologic services in the department of veterans affairs. *Womens Health Issues, 18*(3), 167–173.

Turchik, J.A., Pavao, J.R., Nazarian, D., Iqbal, S., McLean, C., & Kimerling, R. (in press). Sexually transmitted infections and sexual dysfunctions among newly returned veterans with and without military sexual trauma. *International Journal of Sexual Health.*

Veterans Health Administration (2010). Healthcare Services for Women Veterans (Vol. VHA Policy 1330.01).

Veterans Health Administration (2011). VA Health Care Utilization (Inpatient and Outpatient) Among 156,317 Female and 1,197,310 Male Operation Enduring Freedom (OEF), Operation Iraqi Freedom (OIF), and Operation New Dawn (OND) Veterans through 3rd quarter FY 2011. Environmental Epidemiology Service, Office of Public Health.

VetPop National Tables (2007). Department of Veteran Affairs.

VHA Performance Measurement (2011). Retrieved 10/17/2011, from Department of Veteran Affairs, Veteran Health Administration, Office of Quality and Performance: <http://vaww.oqp.med.va.gov/programs/pm/pmReports.aspx>.

Vogt, D., Smith, B., Elwy, R., Martin, J., Schultz, M., Drainoni, M. et al. (2011). Predeployment, deployment, and postdeployment risk factors for Posttraumatic Stress symptomatology in female and male OEF/OIF veterans. *Journal of Abnormal Psychology*, 120(4): 831.

Vogt, D., Vaughn, R., Glickman, M.E., Schultz, M., Drainoni, M., Elwy, R. et al. (2011). Gender differences in combat-related stressors and their association with postdeployment mental health in a nationally representative sample of U.S. OEF/OIF veterans. *Journal of Abnormal Psychology*, 120(4): 797–806.

Wang, P.S., Lane, M., Olfson, M., Pincus, H.A., Wells, K.B., & Kessler, R.C. (2005). Twelve-month use of mental health services in the United States: results from the National Comorbidity Survey Replication. *Arch Gen Psychiatry*, 62(6), 629–640.

Washington, D.L., Caffrey, C., Goldzweig, C., Simon, B., & Yano, E.M. (2003). Availability of comprehensive women's health care through Department of Veterans Affairs Medical Center. *Womens Health Issues*, 13(2), 50–54.

Washington, D.L., Yano, E.M., Simon, B., & Sun, S. (2006). To use or not to use. What influences why women veterans choose VA health care. *J Gen Intern Med, 21 Suppl 3*, S11–18.

Wright, S., Craig, T., Campbell, S., Schaefer, J., & Humble, C. (2006). Patient satisfaction of female and male users of Veterans Health Administration services. *Journal of General Internal Medicine, 21*, S26–S32.

Yano, E.M., Bastian, L.A., Bean-Mayberry, B., Eisen, S., Frayne, S., Hayes, P. et al. (2011). Using research to transform care for women veterans: Advancing the research agenda and enhancing research-clinical partnerships. *Women's Health Issues, 21*(4, Supplement), S73–S83.

15 Health, aging, and the post-service life cycles of US veterans

Alair MacLean and Ryan Edwards

Introduction

Veterans constitute approximately 8 percent of the US population, or roughly 23 million people (US Census Bureau 2010). For the majority of these veterans, the period of military service is a relatively brief but important segment of the life course. The average length of service among respondents in the 2001 National Survey of Veterans was about 6.5 years, or a little over 10 percent of their roughly 61 years lived on average (MacLean and Edwards 2010). The majority of living veterans have served during periods of major warfare, while only approximately a quarter served during peacetime (US Census Bureau 2010). In addition, 39 percent of respondents to the 2001 National Survey of Veterans reported having served in a combat or war zone, while 36 percent reported exposure to dead, dying, or wounded people (Department of Veterans Affairs 2002).

Exposure to the physical and psychological harms of combat is the clearest channel through which military service may harm physical and mental health. The ultimate shock to health, death itself, can occur as a result of combat or service-related accidents, and sometimes war-related deaths occur many years after the formal close of hostilities. But there are many other ways in which military service can affect health. More indirect channels include the development of healthy or unhealthy behaviors such as regular exercise or smoking that may arise either in response to the stresses of combat or the command structure, or more or less independently while the individual is engaged in military service. People face different risks of diseases and accidents when they are serving compared with those they face in their civilian lives. Yet the net effect of these changes in risks on health and mortality could be positive or negative depending on the level of hostilities.

Military service may also affect health by independently changing the life-cycle paths of earnings and wealth. Veterans' health may also be directly or indirectly shaped by educational attainment, which is heavily subsidized for many although not all veterans. It may also affect health by means of its effects on family formation and quality. Many of these influences are likely to have lasting effects on health and well-being throughout the life cycle. But isolating the effects of military service per se on post-service health and other outcomes is, in general, a very challenging task.

According to previous research, veterans may have better or worse physical and mental health than non-veterans, as well as different rates of mortality, though these associations may stem not from service per se, but rather from selection into the armed forces and into military positions and experiences. In this chapter, we summarize and discuss the literature examining the health of aging veterans and the relationships between military service and later-life health and well-being. We outline the challenges to assessing whether and how military service affects health and discuss some basic demographics of US veterans, who are a diverse group especially along the dimension of birth year. We also discuss trends in the experiences of surviving veterans from a bird's eye perspective focusing on shifts in war and peace and survey the literature on the effects of military service on veterans' mortality and health. Finally we provide a summary, an outline for future research efforts, and some concluding remarks and policy recommendations. This chapter builds on our previous empirical work examining the impact of rank on mortality (Edwards 2008) and health (MacLean and Edwards 2010), as well as the impact of combat on disability (MacLean 2010).

Challenges to assessing the effect of military service

In order to evaluate whether and how service affects the health of veterans, scholars and policy-makers must address the possibility that any differences we observe in the health of veterans versus that of non-veterans could reflect other factors. If recruits have better or worse health than civilians before they serve, then the association between military service and observed health in later life will be spurious unless we control for those pre-existing conditions. Earlier researchers have argued that there is health selection into the military, leading people to enter the military at least partly on the basis of their pre-existing health. The armed forces have typically rejected recruits who have poor health, leading service members to be healthier than civilians.

In addition, the armed forces reject recruits who have other characteristics that are probably associated with or may be proxies for poor health. The services typically exclude people, for example, who are at the bottom of the distribution of what sociologists and economists call "ability," meaning those who have the lowest cognitive test scores. People with low test scores also tend to have worse health than those with higher scores (Singh-Manoux, Ferrie, Lynch, and Marmot 2005). At the top of the cognitive distribution, people are less likely to join the military and more likely to go on to college (MacLean and Parsons 2010). They are also less likely to join the military if they come from families with high socioeconomic status (MacLean and Parsons 2010). Research has also shown people who are more educated and have a higher socio-economic status are healthier than individuals who are less educated and come from less advantaged backgrounds (Elo 2009). Thus, the health of service members will tend to differ systematically from the health of civilians in a manner that is totally unrelated to military service but based instead on their pre-service characteristics.

Especially today, in the context of the current all-volunteer force, untangling the causal effects of military service from selection is a daunting task. We would expect that today's volunteer service members are likely to be healthier than their civilian counterparts at least initially, because of entrance standards (Cawley and Maclean 2012) and the demands of basic training. Except during times of economic recession such as we are experiencing today, volunteer soldiers may also come from less advantaged backgrounds, given how military pay typically lags its civilian counterpart for a given educational background. Seeking educational subsidies is another motivation for enlistment that is likely to reveal initial differences between veterans and non-veterans. Perceptions of and tastes for risk may be important in determining who signs up for a very risky occupation, even if it is temporary, and those preferences are probably also important for health outcomes.

Once in the military, service members may be assigned to positions or experiences on the basis of their health or correlated characteristics. Service members are more likely to become officers if they have college degrees than if they do not. Researchers have also discovered that the armed forces send service members into combat if they have better health, leading to the "healthy warrior" effect (Armed Forces Health Surveillance Center 2007). Due to this effect, combat veterans may have worse health than they would have otherwise, but they still look healthier than veterans who did not see combat.

The VA takes a very time-consuming but direct approach to assessing service-related disability or health by identifying specific conditions "acquired or aggravated" by specific events occurring during service (Institute of Medicine 2007). But the disability claims process can be long and onerous, at least in part because the standard for identifying service-related disabilities is set relatively high, requiring a medical examination and service documentation. Not all disabled veterans have acquired a VA disability rating, and furthermore veterans may have conditions about which they are unaware. Finally, any protective effects of service on later-life health would never be captured by VA disability ratings.

A far broader class of health impacts than is encompassed by VA disability ratings is likely to emerge if one were able to adopt a counterfactual perspective and compare outcomes against what would have happened to individuals if they had never served. Although by no means the only relevant perspective for policy, this perspective has gained traction over the last several decades in the social sciences. It resembles the motivation behind conducting randomized controlled trials (RCTs) to establish causality between a treatment and an outcome, holding all other relevant characteristics fixed.

In several cases, researchers have been able to exploit the use of the draft during these periods as a source of plausibly exogenous assignment into treatment and control groups. In some historical periods, force strength was significantly bolstered for fighting major wars through conscription. This type of study would provide the most unbiased estimate of the total effect of military service on outcomes, and several efforts have successfully explored the impact on earnings. But to date, this type of approach has produced ambiguous results regarding the net effects on health, possibly because there are many countervailing influences of military service on physical and mental health, on healthy behaviors, and on socioeconomic status. What is apparently needed to guide further research in this area is a careful decomposition of the array of influences running between military service and health that motivates new tests using new structural approaches. In this chapter, we aim to provide precisely that, drawing on the many observational studies that explore the relationships between military service and health in addition to examining the relatively thin body of research that is able to compare several types of outcomes among treatment and control groups.

We view identifying causal impacts of service on older-age health as an ideal that should become more attainable with a careful review of observational studies, and by no means as the only worthwhile investigation. If the association between military service and health is direct, veterans are likely to experience better or worse health than non-veterans because of experiences they have while in the armed forces. They may suffer worse health than non-veterans because they experienced more stress when they were in the armed forces than did comparable people in civilian society. They may also experience better or worse health because the military leads them to learn healthy or unhealthy behaviors. Some researchers have shown, for example, that veterans are more likely than non-veterans to smoke. Indeed the military provided troops with cigarettes during their service in World War II (Bedard and Deschenes 2006). In addition, veterans may be affected by environmental exposures, such as those encompassed by the term, "Gulf War Syndrome" (Institute of Medicine 2006).

The benefits of a proactive, aggressive plan of research on the broader health effects of service are made clear by the ongoing conflicts overseas, which have produced more than 2 million new wartime veterans (Institute of Medicine 2010). The costs of treating even currently known conditions associated with war injuries among this cohort are likely to be large (Congressional Budget Office 2010; Stiglitz and Bilmes 2008). Comprehensive new research efforts such as the Millennium Cohort Study will reveal much about the unfolding dynamics of health and well-being among service members that we do not yet know (Ryan et al. 2007). But the immediacy and scope of the challenges motivate research-driven interventions in the near term, probably long before causality could be definitively established.

The social, economic, and demographic characteristics of veteran cohorts

Veterans differ from non-veterans on the basis of a number of demographic characteristics that are associated with health and mortality, particularly age, race, and gender, as well as socioeconomic background. Scholars have argued that military service represents a hidden variable in the aging of cohorts (Settersten and Patterson 2006). Historical factors have altered the experience of military service and therefore, potentially, of aging and of the relationship between military service and health. Veterans represent different shares of the population at different ages, and these shares change over time. Today, veterans are close to a quarter of the population over the age of 65 (Wilmoth and London, in press). Among people at younger ages, they constitute much smaller shares of the population. They represent slightly more than a tenth of those aged 45–65. Among those aged 25–44, only 4 percent are veterans. In the year 2030, therefore, veterans will constitute only 10 percent of those over the age of 65 (Wilmoth and London, in press).

As these differences reveal, not all veterans served in the same era. In 2010, for example, about 10 percent of veterans had served in World War II, while 33 percent had served in the Vietnam war. A relatively small share, 38 percent, have served in the 38 years since the beginning of the All-Volunteer Force era (Wilmoth and London, in press). Because they served in different eras, veterans have typically had very different experiences during service. Some veterans served during wartime and were therefore likely to experience combat, while other veterans served during peacetime and had little chance of fighting. More than half of World War II veterans who served saw combat, while only 15 percent of veterans who served between 1974 and 1994 saw combat (MacLean 2011). As current veterans die, and current service members become veterans, these proportions and those related to different experiences in the military will change.

The types of people who serve in the military have also changed over time, meaning that veterans have different average characteristics today than they did in the past. Today, for example, women serve at greater rates than they did forty years ago (Segal and Segal 2004). In 1970, women constituted less than 5 percent of the armed forces. Today, they account for more than three times as large a share, or 15 percent (Segal and Segal 2004). Blacks were under-represented in the armed forces during the World War II and Vietnam eras. Today, they are over-represented (MacLean and Parsons 2010). Younger veterans are therefore much more likely to be female or black than are older veterans.

Socioeconomic characteristics of veteran cohorts have varied, but two consistent patterns appear to be that military service has never drawn exclusively from the upper or lower end, and pre-existing socioeconomic differences between the average service member and the average civilian tend not to be overwhelmingly large (Bachman et al. 2000; Janowitz 1960; Segal and Segal 2004). Still, there appears to be variation in patterns of selection and the effects of military service on earnings across veteran cohorts, and these have implications for relative socioeconomic well-being and thus probably also for health. Angrist and Krueger (1994) show that veterans of World War II were a select group with consistently higher earnings relative to their non-veteran peers through the 1980s. After controlling for the selection of higher ability individuals into military service, they discovered either a zero or small negative effect of World War II-era military service per se on earnings.

Angrist (1990) revealed a similar selection dynamic but a larger negative effect of military service on the earnings of Vietnam-era veterans in the 1980s. The Vietnam-era armed forces may have drawn service members from more disadvantaged strata than did those of the Second World War, perhaps because the war was more unpopular. Alternatively, veterans may have been more negatively affected by serving during the Vietnam era than by serving during World War II. These findings appear to lend more support to the second hypothesis,[1] but more recent research on the Vietnam cohort finds that the negative effect of service on earnings later in life, in their fifties as opposed to their thirties, seemed to have dwindled away to zero (Angrist and Chen 2007; Angrist et al. 2011). Earnings would be negatively affected by lost labor market experience unless military service is a perfect substitute for civilian labor market experience, but other consequences of military service for earnings might also be important.

Earnings respond strongly to education, and the educational attainment of veterans is interesting for at least three reasons. First, since the Second World War, Congress has consistently offered generous educational benefits to wartime cohorts under the GI Bill, which raised the educational attainment of participants (Angrist 1993; Angrist and Chen 2011; Bound and Turner 2002; Stanley 2003). Second, during the Vietnam era, college deferments were a mechanism used by some to avoid the draft, raising the educational levels of those non-veterans above what they otherwise would have been (Card and Lemieux 2001). Third, a large body of literature explores the relationship between education and health, with evidence that causality runs in both directions (Elo and Preston 1996; Kitagawa and Hauser 1973; Lleras-Muney 2005). With the generous Post-9/11 GI Bill now in effect for the current war cohort, the impacts of additional education on earnings and later-life health outcomes are clearly of great current interest and are a promising focus for research. A current view in the literature (Angrist and Chen 2011) is that the net effect of service on earnings may be zero in the long-run because of offsetting effects of missed experience (negative) and increases in education (positive). How these may translate into health impacts, if at all, is less clear.

Just as characteristics of individual veterans are interesting and likely to be important for later-life health, so too are family characteristics and social networks. A vast literature associates the strength of social networks such as families and kinship to health outcomes (Seeman 1996). Costa and Kahn (2010) demonstrate this in a plausibly causal sense by showing that greater social cohesion within units of Union Army soldiers resulted in lower later-life mortality. There have been substantial changes over the last several decades in the family structure of service members (Segal and Segal 2004). Today's all-volunteer military consists of more careerists with families, and military policies aimed at encouraging retention have facilitated that development. Trends in the family status of veterans per se are somewhat less clear. A great unknown in the current overseas conflicts is precisely how accelerated deployment cycles and reduced dwell times have strained military families (Institute of Medicine 2010; MacDermid and Riggs 2011).

The varying demographic characteristics of veteran cohorts imply that the answer to the question of how service has impacted health will probably depend on which cohorts we are talking about, and whether we are comparing veterans to other veterans or to non-veterans. There are well-known gradients in health according to basic demographic characteristics, as well as through socioeconomic status as measured by education, income, or wealth. In general, we define health *disparities* associated with military service as those differences in health that are correlated with service but that are not explained by other well-known factors. But a complicating factor in attributing causality to military service is that service itself may well have changed many other characteristics subsequently. As we have seen, a chief candidate is education. In that case, comparing a veteran's health outcome with the clearest counterfactual will produce an estimate of the health disparity associated with service that may include any health returns to education.

The most direct influences on the health of veterans have relatively little to do with their demographic characteristics in any direct sense, however. The risk environments in which service members find themselves are highly variable and can be deadly, and even when not fatal, these characteristics are likely to have long-reaching consequences for health and well-being. Each conflict in history tends to be not only unique but also can include many unanticipated characteristics, but aggregate casualty statistics imply some general trends in the nature of US warfare and military medicine that are surely important.

Warfare, technology, survival, and disability

Not all veterans serve during wartime, not all wartime veterans see combat, and not all combat veterans are injured. But there are aggregate trends in the nature of military conflict and military medicine that are important for understanding the health and well-being of veterans. We briefly explore these trends in this section.

Offensive and defensive warfare technologies and techniques have continuously evolved throughout the course of human history leading to potentially contradictory effects on veterans' health. Especially since the advent of the modern era, developments in military medicine have brought vast improvements in the probability of survival faced by wounded soldiers. The net effects of trends in these dueling technologies are roughly revealed by aggregate casualty statistics and the probabilities they indicate of being wounded if serving and of being killed if wounded.

Comparing statistics over broad stretches of time can be problematic because of changes in definitions and reporting habits, yet a basic look at aggregate casualty statistics reveals that service members may be more likely to return with serious physical wounds today than they were in the past. Proper measures of relative risk require a careful unpacking of raw manpower statistics into periods of exposure rather than simple headcounts. Table 15.1 is reprinted from Edwards (2010), who lists simple headcounts reported by the US Department of Defense (DoD) and calculates several simple ratios. Deaths attributable to war are surely the most consistent measure provided by the DoD, but even there definitions may have changed over time for deaths not occurring on the battlefield. The Pentagon's category of "Wounds Not Mortal" (WNM) is the most readily available category measuring the prevalence of war wounds. But as Goldberg (2010) notes, an

Table 15.1 Participants, deaths, and wounded in major US wars

Conflict	Participants	Killed	Wounds Not Mortal	Surviving Veterans	Wounded per Participant	Wounded per Survivor	Wounded per Killed
Revolutionary Wars (1775–1783)	217,000	4,435	6,188	212,565	0.029	0.029	1.395
War of 1812 (1812–1815)	286,730	2,260	4,505	284,470	0.016	0.016	1.993
Mexican War (1846–1848)	78,718	13,283	4,152	65,435	0.053	0.063	0.313
Civil War (1861–65)	3,277,556	622,511	478,968	2,655,045	0.146	0.180	0.769
Confederate	1,064,193	258,000	197,087	806,193	0.185	0.244	0.764
Union	2,213,363	364,511	281,881	1,848,852	0.127	0.152	0.773
Spanish American War (1898)	306,760	2,446	1,662	304,314	0.005	0.005	0.679
World War I (1917–1918)	4,734,991	116,516	204,002	4,618,475	0.043	0.044	1.751
World War II (1941–1945)	16,112,566	405,399	671,846	15,707,167	0.042	0.043	1.657
Korea (1950–1953)	5,720,000	36,576	103,284	5,683,424	0.018	0.018	2.824
Vietnam (1964–1972)	8,744,000	58,200	153,303	8,685,800	0.018	0.018	2.634
First Gulf War (1990–1991)	2,225,000	383	467	2,224,617	0.000	0.000	1.219
Iraq and Afghanistan (OEF/OIF) (2001–)	2,100,000	5,376	36,906	2,094,624	0.018	0.018	6.865

Note: For sources, see Edwards (2010).

additional 150,000 troops in Vietnam were wounded but returned to duty within 72 hours. They were not included in the WNM measure during the Vietnam conflict but would be today if they were wounded in Iraq.

Based on the official WNM measure, the ratio of forces wounded to killed has climbed considerably throughout the history of the nation. Gawande (2004) cites these statistics and attributes the rapid rise in the survivability of war wounds to breakthroughs in military medicine, in particular "forward surgical teams" of physicians deployed practically to front lines. Goldberg (2010) finds that survival probabilities have indeed risen since Vietnam, although not quite as rapidly as these raw statistics suggest. He cites a survival rate of 90.4 percent for wounded troops in Iraq before the surge compared with 86.5 percent in Vietnam.

There are other interesting findings that emerge in the simple data. The shares of overall forces or survivors who were wounded display scant evidence of any trends. To the extent that overall force size might adapt to the course of conflicts, this could be evidence of Pentagon policy reactions to the course of conflicts, either through recruiting or conscription.

These two trends imply different things about the health of surviving veterans. On the one hand, the share of surviving veterans of conflicts who were officially wounded has apparently not risen or fallen in any consistent way. But on the other hand, wounded veterans of later conflicts are much more likely to have survived their wounds than wounded veterans of earlier conflicts. This probably represents a net improvement in human well-being, but it may also mean that younger cohorts of veterans who have survived their wounds may be less healthy and more disabled than were older cohorts. As discussed by Edwards (2010), survey data on average VA disability ratings among surviving cohorts of veterans lend some support to this perspective but are far from definitive.[2] Angrist et al. (2010) argue that increasing disability compensation claims among Vietnam veterans in the 1990s may have been driven by the work disincentives in the benefit program more than underlying disability.

Estimates of the effect of military service on mortality and health

Scholars have documented a number of links, primarily using observational techniques, between military service and mortality and mental health, while a smaller number of researchers have shown that military service may be linked with measures of physical health. Physical health, mental health, and mortality are all inter-related. We would typically expect to see any influences that may affect one of them affecting the other two as well, at least in the long run. But over shorter horizons, the links between these may be considerably looser and external events and behaviors may affect these three outcomes very differently. Several additional considerations further motivate the separate examination of these outcomes. Veterans as a group are likely to have begun their adult lives in better physical health than the average non-veteran. They may also have begun with better mental health, but in both cases, military service may have exposed them to greater stressors than those faced by non-veterans. Finally, several causes of death are of special interest here: external causes, such as accidents and suicides, and smoking-related deaths. Especially in the case of accidents, mortality outcomes may completely diverge from measurable physical and mental health outcomes.

Another motivation for a multifaceted approach is that like earnings, mortality is relatively easy to measure in large samples. At around 23 million, veterans are by no means a small subgroup in aggregate, but particular veteran cohorts, whose characteristics can differ markedly, are smaller. Analyses may suffer from lack of power if they focus on individual veteran cohorts within national health surveys like the National Health and Nutrition Examination Survey (NHANES) or the National Health Interview Survey (NHIS), which are of smaller scale than census or administrative data. Similar difficulties complicate analyses of veterans in detailed panel datasets like the *Health and Retirement Study* (*HRS*) or the Panel Study of Income Dynamics (PSID), which are smaller still. The VA conducts surveys of veterans with good coverage of cohorts, but such datasets typically do not include non-veterans as a comparison group. An exception is the relatively unique National Vietnam Veterans Readjustment Study (NVVRS).

Service and mortality

Excess mortality among veterans

A paramount concern about military service is that veterans may die younger than comparable non-veterans, even if they survive their wartime experiences. As we will discuss, the answer to the question of whether veterans die earlier than non-veterans appears to depend on what causes of death we are talking about, which is closely related to age, and on whether the veterans served in wartime. Accordingly, some researchers have shown that particular types of veterans die at younger ages, while other researchers have shown that other types of veterans die at older ages, and still others have demonstrated that veterans die at the same ages as do non-veterans.

Some have argued that veterans die at younger ages because military service harms health. Cohorts in which a greater share of the members are veterans have higher mortality rates than those in which a smaller share of the members are veterans (Bedard and Deschenes 2006). The association between service and mortality increases as cohorts age. According to this research, veterans die at younger ages because they are more likely than non-veterans to smoke (Bedard and Deschenes 2006). Among those who enlisted when they were younger or older than the average, veterans died at younger ages than did comparable non-veterans (London and Wilmoth 2006).

Some researchers have found that veterans are more likely than non-veterans to die of external causes, such as suicides and accidents. In the 1980s, researchers estimated instrumental variable regressions based on the fact that the government operated a lottery that determined the odds that a man would be drafted during the Vietnam War based on birthdate (Hearst et al. 1986). In regressions with birthdate as an instrument, men who were more likely to have been drafted during the Vietnam War were also more likely to die of external causes, such as accidents and suicides, before reaching their 40s (Hearst et al. 1986). But McLaughlin et al. (2008) conducted a meta-analysis of 12 studies and reported the opposite finding, that veterans in general were 10 to 20 percent less likely to die from external causes as were comparable civilians.

There is some evidence that military service may be associated with reduced mortality, which could reflect the fact that the armed forces exclude people with poor health, or possibly that military service directly enhances health. According to a meta-analysis by McLaughlin et al. (2008), veterans from a wide array of time periods experienced on average 20 to 25 percent lower all-cause mortality rates than did comparable civilians. Their analysis may have been disproportionately influenced by a large-scale study of veterans of the first Persian Gulf War, who were observed for only a few years after they finished their service. It is striking that even external-cause mortality appeared to be lower on average among veterans, but the average hid substantial heterogeneity in results across studies. Several of the examinations of mortality among Vietnam-era veterans showed precisely the reverse outcome, that mortality was higher among veterans, both for external and cancer mortality. Another difficulty with the McLaughlin et al. meta-study is that it is unclear whether the individual studies were observational, or attempted to control for selection, or a mix of the two. The approach and title of the meta-study, which emphasizes how selection produces healthy warriors (even though service may make them less healthy than they otherwise would have been) suggests that the constituent studies are all observational.

Excess mortality among certain veterans

While the preceding findings just compare veterans with non-veterans, other researchers have assessed how veterans are affected by particular types of military experiences, such as combat and rank within the military. Whether it ultimately results in physical wounds or not, combat is a high-intensity, stressful event that may produce lasting mental health trauma. Regardless of how it may have developed, post-traumatic stress disorder (PTSD) is associated with higher levels of post-service mortality (Boscarino 2006). Elder et al. (2009) find that veterans who reported combat exposure during World War II died at younger ages than similar veterans who had remained stateside during the conflict (Elder et al. 2009). Interestingly, Boscarino (2006) reports similar effects of PTSD on the mortality of Vietnam veterans regardless of deployment to the war zone. But the prevalence of PTSD measured roughly at age 40 was considerably higher among veterans who went to Vietnam than among those who did not: 10.6 percent compared with 2.9 percent. Combat or deployment to a war zone is not a prerequisite for PTSD but appears to raise mortality through triggering PTSD. Researchers have shown that there is an association between military service in war zones and mortality. Among those who served in the Vietnam era, veterans had higher rates of mortality if they went to Vietnam than if they did not. They were most likely to die from external causes, such as suicide or accidents, in the first five years after finishing their service (Boehmer et al. 2004).

Other researchers argue that combat does not appear to increase particular types of mortality later in life. Among World War II, Korean and Vietnam veterans, men who saw combat were no more or less likely than those who did not to die of heart disease in the 36 years after entering service (Johnson et al. 2010). According to some studies, combat veterans appear to have a lower than expected likelihood of dying from external causes (McLaughlin et al. 2008).

Veterans may also live longer than comparable non-veterans if they are black (London and Wilmoth 2006). Previous researchers, however, have argued that black troops may have been disproportionately likely to be killed during the Vietnam War (Binkin 1993), which could have led to under-estimates of black mortality among surviving veterans.

Some researchers have evaluated the relationship between rank and mortality, finding that veterans die at older ages if they served at higher ranks. Among enlisted men, for example, those who were of a lower rank when they left the armed forces died when they were younger than those who were of higher rank (Keehn 1978). Military retirees experienced similar mortality differentials through rank between 1974 and 2003. They are a highly select group who typically served 20 years on active duty. Among these retirees, men who finished their service in the enlisted ranks faced higher mortality rates and died at younger ages than those who had served as officers, and the slope of the gradient through individual pay grades was fairly constant (Edwards 2008). An O-5 typically faced a better post-service mortality environment than an O-1 through O-4, and also better than that faced by an E-9 and below.

These results are reminiscent of the famous Whitehall studies of British civil servants, which have revealed steep gradients in mortality, health, and unhealthy behaviors through grade or rank of employment (Marmot et al. 1991). In this literature, scholars have proposed the hypothesis that inequalities in the work environment harm health by producing psycho-social stress. One of the key questions for this literature is whether other well-known socioeconomic characteristics that tend to vary with rank or position, such as income or education, might be driving the results. In Keehn's study of military rank and mortality, he reports that education at entry cannot be responsible for the differentials, but Edwards (2008) is unable to control for education in the payroll data he examines. In both cases, there are clear gradients through rank in earnings and potentially pensions, either of which could also contribute to health differentials. MacLean and Edwards (2010) report disparities in self-reported health associated with rank even after controlling for education, income, and other covariates across four datasets. Studies have shown that self reports of health tend to correlate with mortality (Idler and Benyamini 1997), but more conclusive evidence of an independent link between mortality and rank awaits future research with better data.

Service and other measures of health

Mental health

With the exception of the preceding research on mortality, researchers have been much more likely to assess how military service, particularly combat, affects mental health than to evaluate whether it affects physical health (Levy and Sidel 2009). Researchers have explored how combat affects health from the perspective of different disciplines, including psychiatry, medicine, and epidemiology. Service members experience greater stresses in combat, which may worsen both mental and physical health. Researchers have begun to explore the dimensions of PTSD, which was not a formal psychiatric diagnosis until the early 1980s (Kulka 1990). But at least since the Civil War, observers have continuously remarked that some veterans seemed to experience negative effects of combat, however those symptoms may have been described or attributed (Dean 1997).

Scholars have often shown that veterans suffer worse mental health if they were deployed to a war zone or experienced combat than if they did not have combat experience. They have shown that veterans had symptoms of PTSD years or even decades later. Service members can suffer PTSD for short or long periods of time. They can also suffer symptoms that stop and start again. For these reasons, analysts often distinguish between lifetime and current prevalence of the disorder, and estimates vary depending on the instrument that is used to assess the disorder.

Among Australian veterans of the Korean era, men had worse mental health if they experienced combat. They were more likely to be depressed or to have PTSD (Ikin et al. 2007). Within the US population, combat veterans have been shown to suffer greater rates of PTSD, depression, and substance abuse (Prigerson et al. 2002). According to these findings, cohorts with greater shares of combat veterans should also have higher rates of mental disorders as they age. According to one estimate based on the US population, approximately 8 percent of people suffer from PTSD. Approximately one third of these cases are believed to stem from combat exposure (Institute of Medicine 2008). Among veterans of the wars in Iraq and Afghanistan, nearly one fifth report symptoms of one or more mental health diagnoses (Tanielian and Jaycox 2008). Other scholars have suggested that PTSD may reflect not the impact of combat, but of pre-existing trauma. Veterans were, indeed, more likely to report having PTSD if they had experienced childhood abuse (Clancy et al. 2006).

Rohlfs (2010) examines social outcomes linked to psychological trauma, namely rates of violent crime among Vietnam-era veterans in the NVVRS. His identification strategy draws from plausibly exogenous variation in rates of combat exposure by quarter of birth, similar to the method of Angrist and Krueger (1994) of examining World War II-era military service by birth cohort. In addition, the NVVRS measures self-reported combat exposure, for which the quarter-of-birth data provide a good instrument. Rohlfs reports that combat exposure significantly raised violent acts committed by black men and may also have raised crime committed by white men.

Physical health

Other researchers have examined the effect of military service in general on physical health. Teachman (2010) reports that veterans of the all-volunteer force (AVF) rate their physical health worse than expected. Self-reported health is a ubiquitous metric that surely reflects some elements of psychological health. But it is also known to be a good predictor of mortality outcomes independent of objective health measures (Mossey and Shapiro 1982). Physical and mental health are also thought to be connected (Prince et al. 2007) and military service could affect physical health indirectly through its impact on mental health. Schnurr and Spiro (1999) observe that veterans were more likely to rate their physical health as poor if they had worse mental health, which could reflect a connection between the two.

One of the great shortcomings in this literature stems from the difficulty involved in establishing causality and thus isolating a treatment effect of military service on physical health in general. A subset of service-related shocks to physical health, most notably lost limbs and bodily functioning stemming from combat wounds, are relatively overt and easy to establish as having stemmed from service. The same may be true for some mental health trauma, but the challenges there are twofold: the objectivity of diagnosis is often in question, and the causal association with service is unclear. A broader set of potential health effects associated with service, both positive and negative, may exist but are much more difficult to connect to service as opposed to pre-existing sources. Here, as with mortality studies, the most convincing treatment analysis emerges from examining how health varies in response to an instrumental variable that determines military service.

In a recent study, Dobkin and Shabani (2009) examine health status among the Vietnam-era cohort (men born between 1950–1952) observed in the National Health Interview Surveys (NHIS) using the same identification technique as Hearst et al. (1986), the Vietnam draft lottery. They document significant health disparities associated with military service among survivors that emerge from standard multivariate analysis, without adjusting for the selection effects. Self-reported health grew worse and activity limitations rose among veterans as they aged, and depression or anxiety was more common throughout the life cycle.

But when they compare draft-eligible men with the rest of the cohort, Dobkin and Shabani find that the statistical significance of their results falls away. Although the draft lottery predicts military service very well, it apparently does not predict physical and mental health outcomes well. This could be because military service itself does not constitute a nonzero net treatment on health, perhaps because service primarily reflects selection on other characteristics, or there actually are multiple health treatments that are countervailing and offsetting. Or it could be that the draft lottery does not predict the key treatments associated with service, like smoking and combat exposure. It is unlikely that small sample size is a problem given the scope of the NHIS.

Conclusion

There are many overt influences of military service on later-life health, but there are probably also many more that are much less apparent. Combat-related physical injuries present clear burdens for veterans, and many of these are long-lived, chief among them being major limb amputations, disfigurements, and probably also brain trauma, although much less is known about the long-term effects and persistence of TBI, the signature wound of the conflicts in Iraq and Afghanistan this past decade (Institute of Medicine, 2010). Psychological wounds have been a persistent element of warfare throughout human history, but only recently have we begun to develop more consistent methods of diagnosis and treatment, and much work remains to be done. The focus on service-connected wounds, disabilities, and associated challenges is altogether appropriate and deserving of continued attention and research.

But we feel it is our duty as social scientists to highlight a broader view of the effects of military service on health and other outcomes that may not be limited to disabilities or health conditions formally diagnosed by the VA. It is self-evident that military service has far-reaching influences on the minds and perspectives of all veterans whether they saw combat or not, and whether or not they were wounded. A far more difficult question to answer is whether and how military service may have exerted a treatment effect on the health of the average veteran independent of measurable service-related trauma, by which we mean an influence that would not have otherwise occurred in the absence of service and is not already measured by the standard method in veterans' care, the VA disability rating.

As we have shown in this review of the literature, there are partial answers to these questions, and there remain many open questions. One prevailing theme that emerges from the economics literature on the effects of selection is that different cohorts of veterans are select in different ways, but all are select groups. Unadjusted comparisons of veterans with non-veterans are therefore interesting but unlikely to be informative about the causal impacts of military service on outcomes.

Emerging themes appear to be that broadly speaking, military service may have raised smoking behavior, whether because of price subsidies, stress, or the influence of social networks; it probably increased educational attainment through subsidies; it exposed some service members to the physical and psychological trauma of combat; and it kept service members out of the civilian labor force for a time. It is easy to see how these countervailing influences on later-life health may produce no clear net effect on the health of the average veteran, a finding that is not uncommon in this literature. The relevant question becomes whether these individual influences are themselves either small or unsystematic, or large, focused, and just offsetting; either story is consistent with the evidence on the sum of these effects.

Given the preponderance of evidence on diagnosed service-related injuries and their long-lived impacts, our view is that the latter story is more likely, but a definitive answer awaits further investigation. In particular, we think that combat exposure is probably a key transmission channel. Because less than half of all veterans report seeing combat, it is less surprising that the effect of military service on health might be much more attenuated. Recent work by Rohlfs (2010) and others that plausibly addresses the selection problem through the use of instrumental variables or other quasi-experimental methods should be a guide for future studies.

Data limitations are binding constraints for causal and observational studies alike. Even if they could control for every observable characteristic of veterans that is relevant for service and for health, many observational studies still cannot convincingly control for variables that we know are unobservable and that we suspect are important for service and probably also for health. Granted, this is more important for studies of the effect of military service on health more broadly than for studies of combat-related trauma among veterans, which can rely on VA assessments of service-related health conditions, among other things. To date, causal inference has typically relied on a single, if high-quality, source of exogenous variation in military service, which typically requires large-scale datasets to draw statistical power. These large datasets, often drawn from census sources, typically do not provide high enough resolution about key details like combat exposure and other characteristics of military service that might be relevant. In the case of Rohlfs's (2010) work, he gained considerable leverage from the unique data in the NVVRS and employed an instrumental variables strategy to reveal implied mental health effects of combat.

Enhanced resolution of military careers might provide more insights through the analysis of richer data, but the challenges to acquiring such data are considerable. Socio-demographic surveys of veterans and non-veterans typically do not have time to allot to extended questions about military service. The 1994 wave of the Panel Study of Income Dynamics, examined by MacLean and Edwards (2010), is an exception, but many in the military subsample were subsequently dropped in the sample redesign, hampering detailed analysis. Surveys of veterans are much larger in scale and scope but typically do not provide longitudinal detail. Administrative data exist in the form of military service records, but those require a formal request under the Freedom of Information Act, and acquisition may be a lengthy undertaking.

One of the great unknowns is precisely how individuals develop during military service, and it seems likely that formulating new understanding in this regard could inform research about the effect of service on health. It is often said that military service "straightened out" wayward youths in need of discipline. This should be a testable hypothesis, and it is practically inconceivable that any change in attitudes and behavior would not also affect later-life outcomes including health. But the data requirements of such a study are immense. The National Longitudinal Study of Adolescent Health, which covers cohorts born around 1980, asks fairly detailed questions of its military subsample and may ultimately provide suitable insights.

Future work can also extend knowledge about the health of veterans by examining differences by sex and race in greater detail. Previous efforts have assessed the average associations between service and health, but these associations may differ for women and men, and for whites and non-whites, as for example Rohlfs (2010) shows in his study of post-combat violent crimes. Over the last 40 years, women and non-whites have become increasingly likely to serve in the armed forces. Indeed, some scholars have begun to assess whether female veterans suffer different health pressures and stresses than do male veterans (Goldzweig et al. 2006). Research should also assess how the effects on mortality may differ by gender. Blacks are affected differently by their service in terms of their marital outcomes and work satisfaction (Lundquist 2004; 2008). Yet apparently no researchers have evaluated whether black veterans have different average health from black non-veterans or from white veterans.

After a decade of vastly expanded responsibilities for service members and their families, which has occurred simultaneously with the aging of the Baby Boom and its Vietnam-era veterans, the salience of research into the lifelong well-being of veterans is more clear than ever before. Results with the most value-added in terms of policy implications will derive from well-designed studies with rich data and appropriate identification strategies.

Policy implications

Improving our understanding of the lifelong health impacts of military service would improve our knowledge about the determinants of good health and health disparities among human populations more generally. These are not the motivations or charges of DoD or VA, but both groups should be directly interested in the health impacts of service, whether for planning purposes, for designing preventive measures to minimize costs and personnel losses, or for harnessing the productive potential of any positive influences. A challenge is that positive influences of military service on health and well-being have been difficult to fathom with available data. Veteran subsamples in civilian datasets typically do not answer many questions that shed light on their military experiences. It is in the best interests of policymakers and researchers alike for there to be enhanced access to data that can inform new inquiries into the causes and consequences of military service.

A relatively easy step would be to grant selective access to restricted versions of publicly available datasets like the National Survey of Veterans in which there are individual-level identifiers of some type that simultaneously safeguard the privacy of participating veterans while enabling researchers to conduct quasi-experimental studies through exploiting exogenous variation based on geography, birthdate, or other characteristics.

A bolder move would be for the DoD to de-identify and release data that is not public such as the Pre-Deployment Assessment (PDA), the Post-Deployment Health Assessment (PDHA), or the Post-Deployment Health Reassessment (PDHRA). The ideal dataset is a longitudinal follow-up of veterans whose characteristics were measured prior to service or deployment. Assembling such data is by no means easy, but the use of retrospective questions in a survey that is linked to administrative data could suffice. The recent National Survey of

Veterans 2010 was recently fielded too late to incorporate these suggestions, but future studies might.

In an era when burdens of deployment are rising, policymakers should take a proactive stance toward measuring their effects. To best inform support policies for new veterans of the wars in Iraq and Afghanistan, this may well involve understanding the effects of deployments among older veteran cohorts first.

Notes

1 Our reasoning here is the following. If Vietnam veterans were less selected than WWII veterans, one would expect to see less of a difference between ordinary least squares estimates, which cannot correct for selection, and instrumental variables estimates. Instead, we see a similar wedge between them in the same direction for both cohorts. That evidence is more supportive of a larger negative impact of service during the Vietnam era on earnings.

2 The data show higher average VA disability ratings among younger cohorts of veterans earlier in their lives compared with older cohorts. But it is unclear whether that is the result of greater average disability. Other candidate explanations include increasing generosity in VA disability programs, greater knowledge and thus accelerated acquisition of VA disability ratings, trends in social mores regarding health or public benefits, or other factors.

References

Angrist, Joshua D. 1990. "Lifetime Earnings and the Vietnam Era Draft Lottery – Evidence from Social-Security Administrative Records." *American Economic Review* 80(3):313–336.

Angrist, Joshua D. 1993. "The Effect of Veterans' Benefits on Education and Earnings." *Industrial and Labor Relations Review* 46(4):637–652.

Angrist, Joshua D. and Stacey H. Chen. 2007. "Long-Term Consequences of Vietnam-Era Conscription: Schooling, Experience, and Earnings." *NBER Working Paper* 13411, September.

Angrist, Joshua D. and Stacey H. Chen. 2011. "Schooling and the Vietnam-Era GI Bill: Evidence from the Draft Lottery." *American Economic Journal-Applied Economics* 3(2):96–118.

Angrist, Joshua D. and Alan B. Krueger. 1994. "Why Do World-War-II Veterans Earn More Than Nonveterans?" *Journal of Labor Economics* 12(1):74–97.

Angrist, Joshua D., Stacey H. Chen, and Brigham R. Frandsen. 2010. "Did Vietnam Veterans Get Sicker in the 1990s? The Complicated Effects of Military Service on Self-Reported Health." *Journal of Public Economics* 94(11–12):824–837.

Angrist, Joshua D., Stacey H. Chen, and Jae Song. 2011. "Long-Term Consequences of Vietnam-Era Conscription: New Estimates Using Social Security Data." *American Economic Review* 101(3):334–338.

Armed Forces Health Surveillance Center. 2007. "'Healthy Deployers': Nature and Trends of Health Care Utilization During the Year Prior to Deployment to OEF/OIF, Active Components, U.S. Armed Forces, January 2002–December 2006." *Medical Surveillance Monthly Report* 14(3):2–5.

Bachman, Jerald G., David R. Segal, Peter Freedman-Doan, and Patrick M. O'Malley. 2000. "Who Chooses Military Service? Correlates of Propensity and Enlistment in the US Armed Forces." *Military Psychology* 12(1):1–30.

Bedard, Kelly and Olivier Deschenes. 2006. "The Long-Term Impact of Military Service on Health: Evidence from World War Ii and Korean War Veterans." *American Economic Review* 96(1):176–194.

Binkin, Martin. 1993. *Who Will Fight the Next War? : The Changing Face of the American Military*. Washington, DC: Brookings Institution.

Boehmer, T.K.C., D. Flanders, M.A. McGeehin, C. Boyle, and D.H. Barrett. 2004. "Postservice Mortality in Vietnam Veterans – 30-Year Follow-Up." *Archives of Internal Medicine* 164(17):1908–1916.

Boscarino, Joseph A. 2006. "Posttraumatic Stress Disorder and Mortality among US Army Veterans 30 Years after Military Service." *Annals of Epidemiology* 16(4):248–256.

Bound, J. and S. Turner. 2002. "Going to War and Going to College: Did World War II and the G.I. Bill Increase Educational Attainment for Returning Veterans?" *Journal of Labor Economics* 20(4):784–815.

Card, David and T. Lemieux. 2001. "Going to College to Avoid the Draft: The Unintended Legacy of the Vietnam War." *American Economic Review* 91(2):97–102.

Cawley, John and Johanna Catherine Maclean. 2012. "Unfit for Service: The Implications of Rising Obesity for U.S. Military Recruitment." *Health Economics* 21(11): 1348–1366.

Clancy, C.P., A. Graybeal, W.P. Tompson, K.S. Badgett, M.E. Feldman, P.S. Calhoun, A. Erkanli, M.A. Hertzberg, and J.C. Beckham. 2006. "Lifetime Trauma Exposure in Veterans with Military-Related Posttraumatic Stress Disorder: Association with Current Symptomatology." *Journal of Clinical Psychiatry* 67(9):1346–1353.

Congressional Budget Office. 2010. *Potential Costs of Veterans' Health Care*. Washington, DC: Congressional Budget Office.

Costa, D.L. and M.E. Kahn. 2010. "Health, Wartime Stress, and Unit Cohesion: Evidence from Union Army Veterans." *Demography* 47(1):45–66.

Dean, Eric T. 1997. *Shook over Hell: Post-Traumatic Stress, Vietnam, and the Civil War*. Cambridge, MA: Harvard University Press.

Department of Veterans' Affairs. 2002. *2001 National Survey of Veterans (NSV) Final Report* Retrieved August 12, 2011 (http://www.va.gov/VETDATA/docs/SurveysAndStudies/NSV_Final_Report.pdf.).

Dobkin, Carlos and Reza Shabani. 2009. "The Health Effects of Military Service: Evidence from the Vietnam Draft." *Economic Inquiry* 47(1):69–80.

Edwards, Ryan D. 2008. "Widening Health Inequalities among U.S. Military Retirees since 1974." *Social Science & Medicine* 67(11): 1657–1668.

Edwards, Ryan D. 2010. "U.S. War Costs: Two Parts Temporary, One Part Permanent." in *NBER Working Paper*. Cambridge, MA: NBER.

Elder, G.H., E.C. Clipp, J.S. Brown, L.R. Martin, and H.S. Friedman. 2009. "The Lifelong Mortality Risks of World War II Experiences." *Research on Aging* 31(4):391–412.

Elo, Irma T. 2009. "Social Class Differentials in Health and Mortality: Patterns and Explanations in Comparative Perspective." *Annual Review of Sociology* 35(1): 553–572.

Elo, Irma T. and S.H. Preston. 1996. "Educational Differentials in Mortality: United States, 1979–85." *Social Science & Medicine* 42(1):47–57.

Gawande, Atul. 2004. "Casualties of War – Military Care for the Wounded from Iraq and Afghanistan." *New England Journal of Medicine* 351(24):2471–2475.

Goldberg, Matthew S. 2010. "Death and Injury Rates of U.S. Military Personnel in Iraq." *Military Medicine* 175(4):220–226.

Goldzweig, C.L., T.M. Balekian, C. Rolon, E.M. Yano, and P.G. Shekelle. 2006. "The State of Women Veterans' Health Research." *Journal of General Internal Medicine* 21:S82–S92.

Hearst, Norman, Thomas B. Newman, and Stephen B. Hulley. 1986. "Delayed Effects of the Military Draft on Mortality." *New England Journal of Medicine* 314(10):620–624.

Idler, E.L. and Y. Benyamini. 1997. "Self-Rated Health and Mortality: A Review of Twenty-Seven Community Studies." *Journal of Health and Social Behavior* 38(1):21–37.

Ikin, J.F., M.R. Sim, D.P. McKenzie, K.W.A. Horsley, E.J. Wilson, M.R. Moore, P. Jelfs, W.K. Harrex, and S. Henderson. 2007. "Anxiety, Post-Traumatic Stress Disorder and Depression in Korean War Veterans 50 Years after the War." *British Journal of Psychiatry* 190:475–483.

Institute of Medicine. 2006. *Health Effects of Serving in the Gulf War*. Washington, DC: National Academy Press.

Institute of Medicine. 2007. *A 21st Century System for Evaluating Veterans for Disability Benefits*. Washington, DC: National Academies Press.

Institute of Medicine. 2008. *Physiologic, Psychologic, and Psychosocial Effects of Deployment-Related Stress*. Washington, DC: National Academy Press.

Institute of Medicine. 2010. *Returning Home from Iraq and Afghanistan: Preliminary Assessment of Readjustment Needs of Veterans, Service Members, and Their Families*. Washington, DC: National Academies Press.

Janowitz, Morris. 1960. *The Professional Soldier, a Social and Political Portrait*. Glencoe, IL: Free Press.

Johnson, A.M., K.M. Rose, G.H. Elder, L.E. Chambless, J.S. Kaufman, and G. Heiss. 2010. "Military Combat and Risk of Coronary Heart Disease and Ischemic Stroke in Aging Men: The Atherosclerosis Risk in Communities (Aric) Study." *Annals of Epidemiology* 20(2):143–150.

Keehn, Robert J. 1978. "Military Rank at Separation and Mortality." *Armed Forces & Society* 4(2):283–292.

Kitagawa, Evelyn M. and Philip Morris Hauser. 1973. *Differential Mortality in the United States: A Study in Socioeconomic Epidemiology*. Cambridge, MA: Harvard University Press.

Kulka, Richard A. 1990. *Trauma and the Vietnam War Generation: Report of Findings from the National Vietnam Veterans Readjustment Study*. New York: Brunner/Mazel.

Levy, B.S. and V.W. Sidel. 2009. "Health Effects of Combat: A Life-Course Perspective." *Annual Review of Public Health* 30:123–136.

Lleras-Muney, Adriana. 2005. "The Relationship between Education and Adult Mortality in the United States." *Review of Economic Studies* 72(1):189–221.

London, Andrew S. and Janet M. Wilmoth. 2006. "Military Service and (Dis)Continuity in the Life Course: Evidence on Disadvantage and Mortality from the Health and Retirement Study and the Study of Assets and Health Dynamics among the Oldest-Old." *Research on Aging* 28(1):135–159.

Lundquist, Jennifer Hickes. 2004. "When Race Makes No Difference: Marriage and the Military." *Social Forces* 83(2):731–757.

Lundquist, Jennifer Hickes. 2008. "Ethnic and Gender Satisfaction in the Military: The Effect of a Meritocratic Institution." *American Sociological Review* 73(3):477–496.

MacDermid, Shelley and David S. Riggs. 2011. *Risk and Resilience in U.S. Military Families*. New York: Springer.

MacLean, Alair. 2011. "The Stratification of Military Service and Combat Exposure." *Social Science Research* 40:336–348.

MacLean, Alair and Ryan D. Edwards. 2010. "The Pervasive Role of Rank in the Health of US Veterans." *Armed Forces & Society* 36(5):765–785.

MacLean, Alair and Nicholas Parsons. 2010. "Unequal Risk: Combat Occupations in the Volunteer Military." *Sociological Perspectives* 53(3):347–372.

Marmot, M.G., George Davey Smith, Stephen Stansfeld, Chandra Patel, Fiona North, Jenny Head, Ian White, Eric Brunner, and Amanda Feeney. 1991. "Health Inequalities among British Civil Servants: The Whitehall II Study." *Lancet* 337(8754):1387–1393.

McLaughlin, Ruth, Lisa Nielsen, and Michael Waller. 2008. "An Evaluation of the Effect of Military Service on Mortality: Quantifying the Healthy Soldier Effect." *Annals of Epidemiology* 18(12):928–936.

Mossey, Jana M. and Evelyn Shapiro. 1982. "Self-Rated Health: A Predictor of Mortality Among the Elderly." *American Journal of Public Health* 72(8):800–808.

Prigerson, Holly G., Paul K. Maciejewski, and Robert A. Rosenheck. 2002. "Population Attributable Fractions of Psychiatric Disorders and Behavioral Outcomes Associated with Combat Exposure among US Men." *American Journal of Public Health* 92(1):59–63.

Prince, Martin, Vikram Patel, Shekhar Saxena, Mario Maj, Joanna Maselko, Michael R. Phillips, and Atif Rahman. 2007. "No Health Without Mental Health." *Lancet* 370(9590):859–877.

Rohlfs, Chris. 2010. "Does Combat Exposure Make You a More Violent or Criminal Person?" *Journal of Human Resources* 45(2):271–300.

Ryan, Margaret A.K., Tyler C. Smith, Besa Smith, Paul Amoroso, Edward J. Boyko, Gregory C. Gray, Gary D. Gackstetter, James R. Riddle, Timothy S. Wells, Gia Gumbs, Thomas E. Corbeil, and Tomoko I. Hooper. 2007. "Millennium Cohort: Enrollment Begins a 21-Year Contribution to Understanding the Impact of Military Service." *Journal of Clinical Epidemiology* 60(2):181–191.

Schnurr, Paula P. and Avron Spiro, III. 1999. "Combat Exposure, Posttraumatic Stress Disorder Symptoms, and Health Behaviors as Predictors of Self-Reported Physical Health in Older Veterans." *Journal of Nervous and Mental Disease* 187(6):353–359.

Seeman, T.E. 1996. "Social Ties and Health: The Benefits of Social Integration." *Annals of Epidemiology* 6(5):442–451.

Segal, David R. and Mady W. Segal. 2004. "America's Military Population." *Population Bulletin* 59(4):3–40.

Settersten, Richard A. and Robin S. Patterson. 2006. "Military Service, the Life Course, and Aging – an Introduction." *Research on Aging* 28(1):5–11.

Singh-Manoux, Archana, Jane E. Ferrie, John W. Lynch, and Michael Marmot. 2005. "The Role of Cognitive Ability (Intelligence) in Explaining the Association between Socioeconomic Position and Health: Evidence from the Whitehall II Prospective Cohort Study." *American Journal of Epidemiology*. 161(9): 831–9.

Stanley, M. 2003. "College Education and the Midcentury GI Bills." *Quarterly Journal of Economics* 118(2):671–708(38).

Stiglitz, Joseph E. and Linda Bilmes. 2008. *The Three Trillion Dollar War: The True Cost of the Iraq Conflict*. New York: W.W. Norton.

Tanielian, Terri L. and Lisa Jaycox. 2008. *Invisible Wounds of War: Psychological and Cognitive Injuries, Their Consequences, and Services to Assist Recovery*. Santa Monica, CA: RAND.

Teachman, Jay D. 2010. "Are Veterans Healthier? Military Service and Health at Age 40 in the All-Volunteer-Era." *Social Science Research*. 40(1): 326–335.

US Census Bureau. 2010. *Statistical Abstract of the United States: 2011 (130th Edition)*. Retrieved August 12, 2011 (http://www.census.gov/statab/www/.).

Wilmoth, Janet M. and Andrew S. London. in press. "Aging Veterans: Needs and Provisions." in *Handbook of the Sociology of Aging*.

16 Veteran care at the end of life

Their last battle

Deborah L. Grassman and Scott T. Shreve

Media images of soldiers dying on a battlefield are familiar to most Americans. Less familiar are the 1,800 veterans who are dying every day (one out of every four deaths in America), years after they leave military service. Many people do not realize that military service influences soldiers in ways that can sometimes complicate peaceful dying, even though their death may not occur until many years after they leave military service. We provide an appendix on the Culture of War to show how some of these complications may depend on the particular war the veteran fought. However, some military influences from any war impact how veterans and their families cope with the dying process and can include:

- The value of stoicism so earnestly and necessarily indoctrinated in young soldiers might interfere with peaceful deaths for all veterans, depending on the degree to which stoicism permeated their later lives;
- Veterans who served in dangerous duty assignments might have their deaths complicated by traumatic memories or paralyzing guilt, depending on the extent to which they were able to integrate and heal traumatic or guilt-inducing memories;
- There is a high incidence of alcohol abuse (Grossman, 1996, p. 260) or other "flight"-type behaviors used either to avoid confronting locked-up feelings or to numb traumatic memories. These factors might contribute to "unfinished business" as veterans face the end of their lives;
- Veterans often acquire wisdom because they have reckoned with trauma, stoicism, and addictions. Understanding these three elements helps access their wisdom and has been referred to as "post-traumatic growth" (American Psychological Association. Post Traumatic Growth Inventory, www.apa.org/ptgi).
- Veterans and their families have unique bereavement needs to consider when providing care.

The above examples highlight just a few of the possible impacts combat experience can have on veterans at end of life. For those charged with caring for terminally ill veterans and their families, the literature is only beginning to evolve in providing guidance for addressing these unique areas of needs. Pharmacologic interventions for select conditions can be helpful but when a provider is faced with a veteran refusing to admit he or she is in pain when the grimace says otherwise, care often extends well beyond the medicine cabinet.

Stoicism at the end of life

Veterans are often non-complaining, "grin-and-bear-it" types who endure their sufferings silently. The few times tears or fears break through their stoic façades, they feel embarrassed, apologize, and quickly re-retreat; these walls offer protection. Unfortunately, their "fight to the bitter end" attitudes sometimes mean just that – fighting until a death that is, indeed, bitter. Their "attack and defend" instincts make death the enemy and dying a battle. Survival-mode mentality interferes with letting go. When backed into a corner, soldiers are not conditioned to surrender; they are conditioned to fight.

The dictionary defines the word *stoic* as: "showing indifference to joy, grief, pleasure, pain" (*Webster's New World Dictionary* 1995: p. 581). Like spores that entomb potential energy and growth, stoicism seals off vitality – separating inward and outward selves. Stoicism sometimes robs people of a peaceful death. It can keep people trapped in isolation, disconnected from their inner selves and from those they love.

Breaching façades can be important because these walls of stoicism contribute to agitation and lack of peace as veterans die. Box 16.1 provides some examples for how to create safe emotional environments to breach stoic façades. Otherwise, veterans will underreport their physical and emotional pain as well as any fear they are experiencing as they face death. For example, one VA Hospice nurse exasperatedly asked, "How much pain does a veteran need to die?" She was frustrated by the stoicism she was witnessing with a veteran who kept refusing pain medication in spite of his suffering.

Stoicism is necessary on the battlefield, as it is in many life situations, but the walls that stoicism erects can outlast its usefulness. The walls keep out necessary feelings – and other people. Stoicism can create protection from untrustworthy influence in anyone's life for a period of time, but as a long-term coping mechanism, it can be stifling. It is the *relationship to* stoicism that often needs modification so that stoicism will not be used inappropriately. Its overuse creates problems as serious as the problems it has been used to counteract. Though it is important to respect veterans' silence when they choose to maintain stoic fronts, it is also important to offer alternatives. Helping veterans use stoicism like a door instead of a wall can be useful. A door can be opened or closed at will and as often as they want, leaving the safety of their stoicism available to them.

Stoicism might be conceptualized as being comprised of three components: pride, control, and independence. Anything threatening pride, control, or independence can incite anger and defensive fight/flight responses. Dying is a humbling experience that challenges all of these. Control is lost, pride takes a blow, and independence is gradually taken away. Sooner or later, the wall has to crumble. Later means fighting to the bitter end; sooner means a weary soldier is finally able to surrender to hope for a peaceful death.

Box 16.1 Creating safe emotional environments with stoic veterans

Help dying veterans feel comfortable emerging emotionally if they so choose. You can do damage if you push; you also do damage by not asking difficult questions. Your job is to open the door without pushing.

Validating suffering

Validating suffering is one of the most important contributions you can make to the veteran's dying process; it helps them acknowledge that there's a problem – not always easy for people who are stoic.

- Resist the urge to tell them "It'll get better," "Count your blessings," "Don't be so negative," or any of the other things that indirectly communicate: "Don't tell me your problems. Don't let yourself feel human. Put up that stoic wall and hide behind it."
- Avoid platitudes about smiling or keeping their chins up. This is just another way of telling them to hide behind a stoic wall.
- Affirm their suffering. Statements such as "You've had a hard go of it" or "It takes a lot to go through all of this" tell the veteran that someone understands how hard their situation is. It lessens their sense of isolation.

Confronting stoicism

Try to open the door for veterans to consider alternatives:

- "I know a lot of veterans put on a macho front and don't want to take pain medication. But pain can consume your energy. You need your energy for other things now."
- Encourage veterans to consider softening prideful ways so transitions can be navigated as they near the end of their lives:
- Encourage them not to confuse stoicism with courage: "Anyone can hide behind a stoic wall of silence. It takes courage to reach out to connect with others or say 'I'm sorry' or 'I'm wrong'."
- "Sounds like pride might be keeping you stuck – getting in the way of things going better for you."
- "Most of us have a hard time owning our mistakes. Do you sometimes find it difficult to own your mistakes?"

Recognize the opportunity to penetrate stoicism by acknowledging their lack of control. Encourage coming to peace with the helplessness of dying by asking them to consider what they need to let go of and what new things might they want to hold onto now that their situation has changed:

continued…

Box 16.1 continued…

- "Your world has changed a lot. It's really shrinking."
- "I find it hard to accept that some things are beyond my control. Tell me how you're doing with that."
- "It can be hard to wait for death to come – to know it's not on your timetable."
- "It's tough to realize we can't control the world – that we're not God."
- "Sometimes veterans tell me that feeling helpless makes them angry. I imagine it's hard for a soldier to learn how to surrender – to let go."

Don't try to affirm their self-sufficiency any more. It only reinforces independence they no longer have as they are dying. Instead, validate their suffering and en-courage reckoning:

- "It's hard to not be able to do things for yourself anymore."
- "It's not easy to be at the mercy of others now."
- "Some veterans tell me asking for help is humiliating. Tell me how helplessness makes you feel."
- "Are you the kind of person who can accept things are changing and ask for help – or do you sometimes try to pretend nothing has changed and things can go back to the way they used to be?"

Counteract pride, independence, and control by helping veterans value qualities they have which will transform stoicism:

- "It takes a lot of courage to open yourself to your emotions and fears. I admire that."
- "I appreciate your honesty with yourself and with me. It's refreshing."
- "You're accepting life on its own terms now rather than trying to impose your own. It's a humbling process. Humility is a good thing. It's an honorable quality I see in you."
- Veterans can often talk about their feelings; they have a more difficult time feeling their feelings. Give them permission to feel:
- "I know it can be hard for veterans to express their feelings. But, now may not be a time to pretend like nothing is going on or that nothing has changed."
- "It may be difficult to express the hurt you might be feeling. It may be tempting to try to hide it and act like everything is going on like normal. It takes a lot of energy to pretend."
- "Now is a time when you might want to consider letting yourself be honest with yourself…and maybe with a few others you trust too."
- "There's no shame in feeling your feelings. Feelings have vitality. They're meant to be shared with those who love you. It's okay to recognize your needs when you have them and ask for help when you need it."

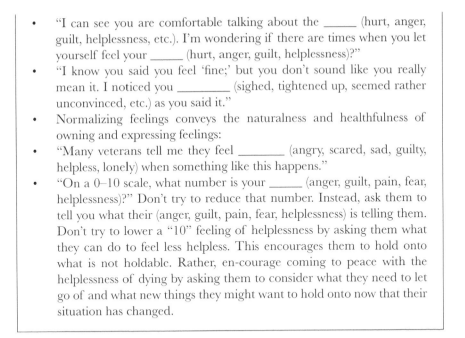

- "I can see you are comfortable talking about the _____ (hurt, anger, guilt, helplessness, etc.). I'm wondering if there are times when you let yourself feel your _____ (hurt, anger, guilt, helplessness)?"
- "I know you said you feel 'fine;' but you don't sound like you really mean it. I noticed you _____ (sighed, tightened up, seemed rather unconvinced, etc.) as you said it."
- Normalizing feelings conveys the naturalness and healthfulness of owning and expressing feelings:
- "Many veterans tell me they feel _____ (angry, scared, sad, guilty, helpless, lonely) when something like this happens."
- "On a 0–10 scale, what number is your _____ (anger, guilt, pain, fear, helplessness)?" Don't try to reduce that number. Instead, ask them to tell you what their (anger, guilt, pain, fear, helplessness) is telling them. Don't try to lower a "10" feeling of helplessness by asking them what they can do to feel less helpless. This encourages them to hold onto what is not holdable. Rather, en-courage coming to peace with the helplessness of dying by asking them to consider what they need to let go of and what new things they might want to hold onto now that their situation has changed.

Pride can prevent people from acknowledging failing health, weakness, or other changes. It might mean not listening to one's own body or working beyond the point that the body is saying it is exhausted. Pride keeps people from seeking medical help – ignoring or belittling symptoms until it is too late to do any good. It can even keep people from admitting that they are dying. Helping people let go of pride so new worlds can open can be important.

Control increases the chance of conquering enemies on a battlefield; being vulnerable can also get you killed. However, trying to control people or circumstances off the battlefield sometimes *creates* enemies. Fear of being at the mercy of others causes resistance. When the need to control manifests as a need to conquer, it can create frustration, anger, and bitterness for everyone involved. There is nothing like death to make people realize how little control they have. Yet, once they realize that they are going to die, veterans sometime want to control its timing, getting angry and frustrated with the waiting. "I'm not dead and I'm not alive. If things can't go back to how they used to be, then let's get this over with *now*." Sometimes they want to control death itself.

Fierce independence seldom yields without a fight because nothing is more embarrassing than for a proud and independent veteran to have to ask for help with personal needs. Yet, "I can handle it myself" is simply not always true. At some point, weakness forces realization of the necessity of dependence on others. Nevertheless, veterans have been taught to survive; they pull themselves up by their own bootstraps. Maintaining independence requires strong will power; ultimately, will power must also be surrendered as they are dying.

An inability to let go of pride, control, and independence so that a veteran can reach out for help increases suffering. Physical limitations and emotional displays can embarrass veterans and create fears that others will perceive them as weak. They might feel helpless and vulnerable to attack. Letting go might be viewed as admitting defeat or an act of surrender – something good soldiers do not do. Yet, mature mental health includes identifying needs and asking for help when it is needed. Both require vulnerability. Stoicism often keeps people from saying what they need or allowing others to meet their needs. This mask of invulnerability sometimes will not even allow them to admit they *have* needs. The fear of imposing on others at this time of their lives can frustrate their family members and professional caregivers, who desperately want to do whatever they can to help these "imposaphobics". Fear of vulnerability prevents veterans from seeking Hospice or Palliative Care services or accepting help for depression or Post-Traumatic Stress Disorder.

Though it often takes longer to accomplish, ultimately most dying veterans are able to let go of control, allowing themselves to become completely human, growing in humility as they learn how to ask for help and how to become a gracious receiver, discovering connection and compassion in the process. This takes courage and it is as heroic as facing any enemy in battle.

Traumatic memories or paralyzing guilt as death approaches

One way to conceptualize war is to view it as a black hole with no light of day, no consciousness. Like black holes in the universe that suck life from surrounding space, war sometimes sucks the life out of soldiers. They return home from war and they want to leave the war behind them and get on with their plans for their future. Their ability to do this varies; this variance can be conceptualized along a spectrum of three trajectories (Figure 16.1):

*   true integration and healing of post-war trauma;
*   *apparent* integration of combat trauma with the veteran *seemingly* unscathed until combat memories escape from behind stoic walls as they face personal illness, death, or some other trigger;
*   inadequate integration of trauma (PTSD).

One determining factor of which trajectory is taken may depend on the strength of each veteran's stoic wall to encapsulate, segregate, and isolate them from healing resources within the self. Those on the first trajectory above (the majority) may somehow be able to either not build a stoic wall or to remodel it in such a way that it does not isolate them from themselves or others. People on the last trajectory, on the other hand, might build walls that end up imprisoning themselves. Veterans on the middle trajectory might erect a wall without even realizing it. This unknown barrier is lost in a consciousness that cannot see it, feel it, or find its way through it.

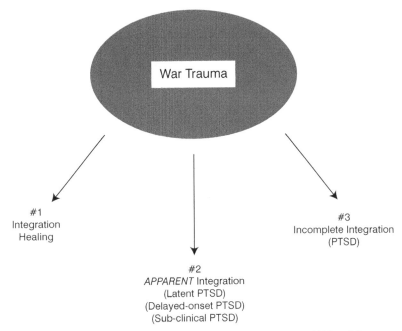

Figure 16.1 Possible trajectories in the aftermath of war (Grassman 2009 p. 61)

Trajectory with integration of trauma

In general, the extent to which veterans reckon with trauma *before* they come to the end of their lives, is the extent to which they will have a peaceful death. Combat veterans of the first trajectory who have struggled and successfully reckoned with their combat experiences have a better end-of-life experience than the civilian population. They have journeyed into a deep part of themselves to reconcile the horrors they faced in the military including confronting their own mortality at an early age. As they face their death, they might say, "I've faced death before in the war. I'm not afraid of it anymore." They say it sincerely without bluster that can arise from stoicism or other attempts to deny fear. They might say other things too:

- "Every day since the war has been a gift – each day a day I didn't think I'd have."
- "But for the grace of God, it could have been me who died in that war. I'm aware of the gift of grace with me now as I'm facing death."
- "I must have been spared in that war for a reason. I've lived my life trying to live up to the reason, to fulfill that meaning. If I didn't do that, it means my buddies died for nothing."

War did not erect a stoic wall in veterans on this trajectory; it tore one down. War brought focus and changed priorities. "It made me see what was *really* important." All else pales after having experienced the worst humankind has to offer. Perspectives shift, and often shift toward a willingness to reckon with any obstacle interfering with peace, including inward obstacles. The cruelty of war taught them how to love and forgive others and themselves. It was a lesson they lived daily. Because they faced death before and lived their lives differently, they live their deaths differently.

Trajectory with apparent integration of trauma

Some people seem to integrate trauma into their lives, but it emerges later when something unmasks the unresolved trauma. Though it might seem to appear suddenly after many years, a review of their lives usually finds PTSD creeping out in subtle ways. For those who have successfully hidden combat memories (even from themselves), turmoil or agitation might surface at end of life because with approaching death the protective mechanisms of the conscious mind may no longer be able to conceal memories of war. This delayed-onset PTSD may be particularly overwhelming and frightening, requiring intense support because these veterans have built especially strong defensive walls. However, when they are able to push through their defenses so they can recover scattered pieces of broken self, they become role models for how to redeem suffering.

Trajectory with PTSD

Many veterans with PTSD have successfully suffered war experiences by learning lessons that help them live their lives, deal with trauma, reckon with their PTSD, and face their deaths. If they received PTSD treatment, they can often tell the healthcare provider what helps them feel better. They might already have a PTSD network of friends who can provide support. Family members usually know how to respond to breakthrough episodes of PTSD because it is familiar territory. Other veterans with PTSD have not grown through the experience. They have compartmentalized the trauma, banishing it into unconsciousness. They might have increased difficulty as death approaches – haunted by residual memories or corroding guilt.

When patients with PTSD are admitted to a hospital, they can be anxious, suspicious, angry, or any combination of these. Leaving their home to enter an unknown hospital environment is threatening, increasing their feelings of danger. The hospital environment itself can act as a trigger with its militarized processes. Their own anticipated death can act as a PTSD trigger. PTSD, especially when combined with alcohol abuse, may have taken its toll on their relationships, leaving unfinished business to be resolved for a peaceful death to ensue. PTSD, however, can be a redeeming factor. Veterans with PTSD often have a resiliency because of what they have been through; they have been able to laugh, relate, find hope, share, and stay connected in spite of what they have experienced. They have been victims, and they have also been survivors. Many learn to live from a deeper part within themselves.

Interventions

Even though their wartime experiences were over many years ago, ask combat veterans about their military experience: "Now is a time to look back over your life. Is there anything that might still be troubling you? Anything about the war that might still haunt you?" Then, sit quietly. These are not the kind of answers that can be hurried. Veterans might talk about past experiences with death – deaths that were often violent and mutilating. They bring these experiences with them when they are enrolled in hospice programs. To allay these fears, it can be helpful to discuss the peacefulness of their expected death and the plan for how that will be achieved.

The Diagnostic and Statistical Manual (DSM) identifies how PTSD expresses itself differently in children. Children's dreams may be "frightening without recognizable content" or "trauma-specific reenactment may occur" (American Psychiatric Association 2000: 467–468).

The DSM does not address PTSD in people who are dying. Dying people often express PTSD as children do; they act it out. The reason for acting it out might relate to a more porous connection between the conscious and unconscious mind such that controlling traumatic memories when they arise becomes more difficult. Controlling traumatic memories when they arise from unconsciousness becomes more difficult; agitation (acting out the trauma) sometimes ensues. It is important to distinguish the agitation of PTSD from "terminal restlessness" or delirium. Some of the medications used for terminal restlessness may be ineffective for PTSD at the end of life; for example anti-psychotic medications are often more effective than benzodiazepines. However, before medicating agitation, it is important to determine its source. Pain, full or infected bladders, constipation, dyspnea, PTSD, medication interactions, unfinished business in personal relationships, and terminal restlessness can cause agitation. Treatment is different depending on the cause. An "8 P Assessment" for agitation can be performed: pain, pee, poop, puffing, PTSD, polymedicines, people (unfinished business with), and pre-death (terminal restlessness).

Many of the standard treatments for PTSD are not feasible when veterans are imminently dying. Medications taken for PTSD may no longer be administered by mouth and might be unavailable by other routes. Normal "talk therapy" or groups are not practical. Usual "grounding techniques" may not be effective because the veteran's rational access to his conscious mind is limited. Sometimes, PTSD surfaces for the first time at end of life and is particularly frightening at a time when the veteran is especially vulnerable. Some Hospice organizations and Vet Centers are partnering to develop PTSD Response Teams that can respond to this emergency when it surfaces at end of life in the home setting; certainly, no single healthcare team member should be expected to handle this alone. Not only do staff at the Vet Centers have the expertise and resources to deal with the trauma, but they can provide outreach services to dying veterans who are not enrolled in VA.

It can be important to eliminate as many "triggers" for PTSD as possible. Coming into a hospital (especially a VA hospital) can trigger past military memories of barracks, procedures, unsafe environments, past combat hospitalizations, and visiting injured comrades. A government hospital and its employees may not be trusted by Vietnam vets. On the other hand, a VA might be a source of comfort, belonging, security, and camaraderie, especially if the veteran previously received care there.

Loud or unexpected sounds will startle people with PTSD, so they should not be touched without first calling their name or letting them see you. The use of bed alarms should be limited; they exacerbate the startle response. Restraints should also be avoided; even tight bed clothes or linens can trigger memories of being confined in prison if the veteran is a POW.

Farewell to arms: coming to peace at the end of life

Veterans who have served in dangerous duty assignments not only sustain physical injuries, they sustain mental, emotional, social, spiritual, and moral injuries. Some of the non-physical injuries arise from issues surrounding having killed other people. Some sources even report that the act of killing is the single most important factor generating PTSD (Baum 2005). Experiencing or witnessing violence can cause PTSD in anyone; the difference with veterans is that they often *committed* this violence as part of their military mission. This is a deeper level of traumatization. It should not be surprising that these kinds of spiritual and moral wounds surface when veterans are getting ready to "meet their Maker" as they come to the end of their lives.

Veterans may carry guilt or shame for things they have seen and done. This can interfere with peace of mind and peace of heart. Some veterans feel guilty about having killed other people. Others report that they loved the rush of the killing and later have guilt for having enjoyed it. Some veterans do not even want to acknowledge the awards they received for marksmanship. Others have guilt for killing women and children. Killing enemy soldiers can at least be justified; civilians' deaths cannot, nor can the accidental killing of comrades in what is called "friendly fire." Intentionally killing officers who consistently made poor judgments that jeopardized lives of those they commanded also produces guilt. Other veterans feel guilty for *not* killing: "They had to take me off the front lines. I was such a coward." Some veterans suffer survivor's guilt. Non-combat veterans sometimes feel guilty when they have seen fellow soldiers volunteer for dangerous missions. Nurses and medics sometimes express guilt about the life and death decisions they made. There may be shame for "leaving a buddy behind" so escapes could be made more quickly. War protestors sometimes feel guilty for the harm their actions caused soldiers.

It is essential that healthcare providers know how to respond to veterans' guilt and shame. It is tempting to try to soothe the guilt with rationalizations: "That was a long time ago" or "You were just obeying orders and doing your duty." These dismissive responses do not help; they essentially communicate to the veteran that the healthcare provider does not want to hear about their guilt. What veterans need is to have the guilt acknowledged and accepted so that they can forgive themselves. To begin the process, ask an open-ended question when initially assessing trauma. Afterward, sit quietly in silence for several seconds, shifting into a low, quiet energy. Sample questions and statements include:

- "Some combat veterans have told me they lost their soul in that war. Did anything like that happen with you?"
- "Many veterans who've not been in combat have sustained other kinds of trauma. Are there any traumas you've sustained that might still be troubling you a bit?"
- "You've had to carry a lot of burdens. Fitting back into the world after war isn't easy."
- "I would think the world was pretty confusing after you returned from war. All the rules had changed; much of what you were taught was violated."
- "Sometimes combat veterans tell me that when they killed others, they killed a part of themselves. Did you experience anything like that?"
- "I would guess there have been times when you've been pretty angry at God for allowing the world to have war in it, for not intervening to protect people from cruelty."

Families are also a source for veterans' experiences of war. A door can be opened by offering a quote heard by other family members:

- "Some families have told me 'Most of my brother remained in Vietnam.' Did anything like that happen with your loved one?"
- "Some family members have told me that their loved one was like a stranger, just a shell of the person they used to know. Have you experienced anything like that with your loved one?"

Guilt should teach not punish. Try to help veterans sort through what they can learn from their guilt so they can enter the work of forgiveness. There may also be irrational guilt that they need to let go of because they are trying to control something they had no control over; they may need to forgive themselves for not being God (they are not omniscient and omnipotent). Though it is true that the past cannot be changed, the *relationship to* the past can be changed, and forgiveness is the means whereby that is accomplished.

Forgiveness could even include forgiving soldiers on the other side – the "enemy." Many have been able to do that early in their civilian lives; others harbor hatred that sometimes complicates peaceful dying. Some Vietnam veterans struggle with forgiving the government for using and betraying them. Korean and Vietnam veterans may need to forgive the American public for ignoring or scorning them. Forgiveness is not just between people either. Soldiers may have the need to forgive the world for being unfair and for having cruelty and war in it; they may have a need to forgive God for allowing the world to be like it is.

If self-forgiveness seems like a lot to expect, it is, but it is also essential; to withhold forgiveness means to cut oneself off from a compelling force deep in the soul that seeks it. If that forgiving force is denied, vitality and peace remain elusive. If someone is unable to achieve forgiveness, they might arrive at the end of life filled with bitterness. Stockpiling transgressions of others (blame) or self (guilt) is the recipe for making bitterness. Bitterness is a poison that greatly complicates peaceful dying.

Rituals of forgiveness can be developed to restore integrity. Chaplains are another important resource; they are usually trained in both the process of forgiveness and the value of rituals. Healthcare providers can also help precipitate the process with veterans who report mistreatment, such as Vietnam War vets: "I wish our country could have shown greater respect for the service you provided. I wish you didn't have to experience the indignities you've had to suffer because of people's ignorance. I want you to know that you *are* honored now and should have been considered a hero. And *unsung* heroes are the *most* worthy kind." Tears often well up in the veteran. More importantly, a soldier is brought home from war as the forgiveness process is precipitated.

Behaviors that avoid confronting feelings or memories

The brother/sisterhood that saw veterans through danger is often called into action when a buddy is dying. Veterans come to the bedside to care for their falling comrade. And after death, they often check on their fallen comrade's family to make sure their needs are being met. On the other hand, there is a high incidence of alcohol abuse (Grossman 1996 p. 260) or other "flight"-type behaviors that veterans sometimes use either to avoid confronting locked-up feelings or to numb traumatic memories or anything associated with death. These factors might contribute to "unfinished business" as veterans face the end of their lives.

Stoicism, PTSD, and alcohol abuse can all lead to estrangement of families and the need for forgiveness. Any of these problem areas can complicate peaceful dying and effective grieving. This kind of "unfinished business" often surfaces as people face death because perceptions of time change. This is reflected with people who survive a potentially fatal accident when they say, "My whole life flashed before me." In that moment, past, present, and future are no longer experienced as sequential; rather, time is compressed into the ever-present now. Experiencing the eternity of the ever-present now is one of the gifts death offers. It is an inward space where past, present, and future *coexist*. This experience is very different from trying to block the past or defer plans for the future in order to live in the "present moment." People who are aging often experience the eternity of the ever-present now not in a flash, but in a process of reflection. Elders do not "live in the past;" the past lives in the now, offering opportunities for insight and healing. They review their lives to see what lessons they have learned or what meaning their life contains. It is a natural search for meaning and insight before they let go of their earthly existence.

During this life review, there is opportunity to guide veterans in seven steps that facilitate inner peace (Byock 1997). These steps include saying:

- Forgive me
- I forgive you
- I love you
- Thank you
- Good bye.

This is followed with encouraging them to do the last two steps (Grassman 2009 p. 201):

- Let go
- Open up.

Providing guidance in the above steps and giving veterans considerations for reflection can be important. The discussion might be introduced like this: "All of us have done things to hurt each other; none of us are saints. Now is a time to reflect on people you may have hurt and consider asking for forgiveness. Think about those who have hurt you, as well as any hurts you may be holding onto. Consider letting them go, offering forgiveness. Think about whom in your circle of friends and family may benefit from an expression of your love. Think about those people who have impacted your life. Who might benefit from an expression of gratitude for having touched your life?" Encourage the veteran to be as specific as they can in these contemplations. Affirm they can do this privately and that it is a process that takes time.

Continue dialogue with them regarding the last steps: "The next thing is the hardest but probably the most important and that is to say goodbye to all those you love and want to hold onto, to say goodbye to this world and everything in it, to say goodbye to all that has been the same. Let yourself grieve. After you've done this, then your new job is to relax and let go of all that is familiar – to open up to all that is new and different that is coming." Family members should also be encouraged to do the process with their dying loved one.

Veteran wisdom

Veterans often acquire wisdom produced from having reckoned with trauma, stoicism, or addictions. The following story highlights this kind of wisdom. In her book, *Peace at Last: Stories of Hope and Healing for Veterans and Their Families*, Deborah Grassman (2009) writes about veteran wisdom as she describes her encounter between two veterans: one who had wisdom and one who was willing to learn how to become wise.

They had been strangers until fate found them in the same room on our Hospice unit. Luke was a quiet, gentle man. He was paralyzed by a spinal cord compression caused by prostate cancer. He was down to 100 pounds and his body was contorted like a pretzel. He was also blind from glaucoma.

Yet, he emanated serenity. He had a wonderful sense of humor and a youthful giggle that invited everyone into light-heartedness.

He also emanated gratitude. He was grateful to be alive, grateful to receive care, grateful even to be dying because he knew he would soon be home with "my Lord." As an elder in his church, Luke was well known and well loved in the town's African-American community. Now that he could no longer go to church, his family brought church to him: hymns, communion, scripture, and prayer. When none of his family was around, staff members would play recordings of the Bible or of Mahalia Jackson.

There was a genuine holiness in Luke; whenever he spoke, everyone in his presence felt this holiness. Everyone, that is, except his roommate.

Arthur was a gruff ex-Marine Corps sergeant. He admitted to being in pain, but usually refused medication. Instead, he paced. The effects of frostbite from inadequate uniforms in the cold regions of Korea had caused some painful nerve damage to his feet; nevertheless, he was grateful that he hadn't had an amputation the way some of his comrades had.

As Luke had brought everyone into his serenity, Arthur brought everyone into his misery. He was a surly man with little tolerance for anyone's ways except his own. Divorced four times, he claimed all his wives had been stupid. He was estranged from his children. But his 41-year-old son, Frank, began to visit him. Not having seen his father for 30 years, Frank wanted one last chance to know him. Arthur frequently snarled and cursed at Frank. Yet, Frank remained undaunted and stayed faithfully at his father's side.

I made an effort to reach Arthur. "You seem so angry," I said. "It worries me to see how you're pushing everyone away from you."

He shrugged. "They're all morons, that's all," he said contemptuously.

"Is it possible," I asked lightly, "that *you're* the one being moronic at the moment?"

He scowled, but he didn't push me away.

"You really want everything to go your way," I continued. "Anyone who has other ideas is wrong."

"Yeah," he grunted. "You gotta problem with that?"

"That was important in the military. It worked well then. You were a sergeant and you needed your men to do what you told them to do. But I don't know about now. You might be facing the end of your life in the next several months," I said soberly. "Everything's changing. You might want to think about doing things a little differently now so you can get ready to have a peaceful death – a death *without* fighting."

Arthur didn't say anything, but I could see him mulling it over. "Maybe…" he said grudgingly and then quickly changed the topic. Motioning toward Luke's bed, he asked to have his room changed. When I asked why, he described a racial incident in the Marine Corps in which he had been reprimanded when a subordinate "played the race card against me." We talked about how this had intensified his racism. He said he had little use for a blind, paralyzed black man.

I had to resist the urge to move Arthur. It would easily resolve the problem, but it would avoid an opportunity for making needed inward changes.

"I'll ask Luke and see what *he* says," I replied. Arthur was used to calling the shots. I wanted him to know that Luke had a voice in this too. I didn't want Arthur's prejudice to affect Luke, but I also knew Luke could be a healing influence on Arthur.

I spoke with Luke. He was not fazed by Arthur's mean-spirited assaults. Used to bigotry all his life, Luke shrugged off Arthur's ill temper and laughed with understanding at the proposed room change. Though Arthur didn't like it, I decided not to move him to another room.

Over the ensuing weeks, Luke's aura of holiness slowly infiltrated Arthur's side of the room. Arthur complained less about having Luke as a roommate. Gradually, Arthur started seeking the peace he saw in Luke. In the middle of a lonely night, Arthur called to Luke:

"You awake, Luke?"

"Yep."

"How about a prayer?"

Luke prayed and Arthur seemed to surrender some of his anger and bitterness. The wall that had shielded his tender, vulnerable feelings was slowly crumbling. Arthur became more mellow with fewer bursts of temper.

Luke and Arthur began sharing other things. When Luke's family brought communion, Arthur had communion too. When Arthur went home on the weekends, he would bring back food to share with Luke. Frank talked to the staff to get approval to use the stove in the kitchen on the unit so he could make breakfast for his father; Arthur asked him to make enough for Luke too. When Frank fixed breakfast the next week, Arthur invited the other eight patients on the unit. Mahalia Jackson and the smell of bacon called everyone within hearing and smelling distance into satisfying repast. Soon the weekly event outgrew Frank's capabilities; volunteers and the Hospice chaplain and physician were recruited into cooking, singing, and praying. Word of good food and fellowship spread throughout the Medical Center. Each week new faces from other wards eagerly appeared. (A tradition was born that 12 years later, continues to thrive and has had the surprising effect of providing "pre-Hospice" care for non-Hospice patients.)

The friendship between Luke and Arthur deepened over their weeks together. Possibly for the first time, Arthur was caring about someone other than himself. When Luke needed something, Arthur was there to get it. Conversation drifted between their beds at all hours. A synchrony emerged as though they were still soldiers bonded in the same trench.

One morning as the sun was rising, Luke called out, "You awake, Art?"

"Yeah. What do you need Luke?"

When Luke didn't respond, Arthur sat up so he could see him more clearly. Luke lay there with his hand outstretched toward Arthur. "I'm dying Art. The Lord is here for me."

"I'll get someone," Arthur said in a panic. Hurrying from the room, he returned with the housekeeper, Margurite. Luke smiled as the three joined hands. Arthur asked Margurite to pray. When they opened their eyes after the prayer, Luke had died.

Arthur was heart-broken. He beckoned to me as I came down the hallway. "Luke died Deborah. I can't believe it. He died." He told and re-told their last moments together as if to convince himself of the reality. I put my hand on Arthur's shoulder and said nothing. After a while, he spoke again but he wasn't speaking to me or to anyone in particular. "Tell Luke I'll be joining him soon."

Arthur was given time alone with Luke, but at last it was time to prepare Luke's body for the morgue. Arthur's fierce Marine loyalty would not allow him to leave the room.

"I'm staying right here with him. I'm not going to abandon him now." The room was a foxhole from which these two had faced death together. Luke had carried Arthur through its fire. Now, it was Arthur's turn.

Arthur lingered at the doorway, watching as Luke's body was placed on a morgue cart. As Luke's body passed, Arthur raised his hand into a stiff salute. "There goes my best friend," he said, tears streaming down his face as the cart clattered down the hall. "Who would have ever thought…," he added, his voice trailing off.

I could only remain silent, tears in my eyes, beholding the moment. I was filled with admiration for Arthur's courage and humility. I felt awed by the crumbling walls of prejudice Luke had penetrated. I had witnessed this kind of heroism in many veterans, but still I remained filled with wonder.

Arthur was now inconsolable. "How could Luke leave me?" he moaned despairingly.

Over the next few days, Arthur erected his wall again, becoming gruff and demanding. Nothing satisfied him – including his new roommate. No matter what his roommate said or did, it was wrong; it was not Luke. The roommate was moved and the bed kept empty for awhile to help Arthur focus on his grief. The empty bed seemed to contain Luke's spirit so that the Arthur that Luke had so lovingly coaxed from hiding, gradually re-emerged.

Arthur's condition stabilized and he was discharged to the Medical Center's community living center. Each week he reappeared for breakfast on the Hospice unit – usually with a few new buddies. Making new friends was no longer difficult; caring for other people was no longer foreign. Black or white, rich or poor, Arthur befriended everyone around him. His relationship with Frank grew tender; he had become the father Frank always wanted.

A year later, Arthur was re-admitted to the Hospice and Palliative Care unit for end-of-life care. With Frank at his side, he died peacefully. It had been a year of change – a year with kinship and camaraderie because Arthur had discovered the meaning of fatherhood and life without the specter of bigotry foreshadowing his perceptions. It had been a year of healing.

Bereavement care for veterans and their families

Veterans have much unresolved grief. On a battlefield, there is no time or space to grieve. A comrade dies and grief must be numbed so fighting can continue. Attention and energy are needed for survival; grief is a distraction that could be fatal. With grief on hold, their bereavement needs may stagnate. Facing their own death decades later or the death of a loved one, however, can trigger PTSD or activate grief from the many past losses during combat – deaths which were often mutilating or guilt-laden. When this occurs, there may be a disproportionate grief response. This exaggerated grief response is good if the veteran uses it as an opportunity to go back and mourn the deaths of his comrades. If he does not, he can become depressed instead.

Veterans may be aware that they have unresolved grief. This awareness can cause a fear of grieving when a member of their own family dies. "If I start crying, I may not be able to stop." This fear compounded by the stoic culture of the military sometimes interferes with veterans' willingness to receive bereavement services. They might fear being a "cry baby," losing control, or becoming vulnerable. Bereavement groups are sometimes viewed as a "pity party" that they want no part of. One-on-one approaches or providing bereavement groups strictly for veterans may be more effective.

Veterans might have other issues that interfere with effective grieving. They may feel angry or bitter about medals they did not receive, service-connected disabilities they did not get, pensions they did not receive, or Agent Orange damage that went unacknowledged. Anger sometimes shields them from effectively encountering their need for grieving. If the veteran has PTSD, he probably does not trust easily or is reticent to reach out to strangers trying to provide bereavement care. They might cope with grief by isolating or "bunkering down," which is often counterproductive. Initial approaches by bereavement counselors may need to be modified, focusing on gaining trust. For veterans who have a mental illness, the mental illness might become exacerbated when there is a death in their family. Bereavement programs need to be an integral part of mental health programs for veterans.

Suppressing grief as they are facing their own death or a loved one's death can be stifling. Downplaying their suffering and ashamed of "weak" feelings, veterans often confuse stoicism with courage. Helping them see another kind of courage – the courage to face uncomfortable emotions head on – can help them express their grief. However, the goal is not to make veterans cry; the goal is to help them grieve in whatever way they can. Sometimes actions such as planting a memorial tree, visiting the surviving family members, or going to a grave site may be more effective. However, it is still important to give veterans permission to cry so they can feel free to do so. For example:

- "I see you choking down tears. I want you to know that it's okay to cry. We say here that the only bad tears are uncried tears."
- "It's good to see your tears; they're safe here."
- "This is a very sad time. Tears are welcome here."

Some bereavement issues are not emotional, but practical. Veterans who are receiving a pension that stops with their death, might fight hard to stay alive for their spouse's financial welfare. This concern can cause veterans to want resuscitation or to not want hospice services, even though focusing on futile medical treatments can interfere with anticipatory grieving for their own life. It also prevents essential dialogue with family, leaving family members with regrets for things left unsaid or undone. Military funerals include presenting an American flag to a family member. Disputes within families or divorces with multiple blended families might cause issues surrounding "Who gets the flag?" The resulting anger can complicate bereavement. Identifying these issues early and arranging to have more than one flag helps prevent this complication.

It can be important to inform veterans of their burial benefits. Veterans and their spouses are eligible for free burial at the closest national cemetery. This can ease financial burdens and facilitate "good grief" for both the veteran and the family.

Bereavement for families of veterans

Stoicism can affect whole family systems. Grief might be hidden by a silent or angry façade. If the veteran was "career military," the family may have lived in numerous places for short periods of time. This can have different effects on bereavement. Because they have no established roots, there may not be a network of support that facilitates effective grieving. On the other hand, because of frequent moving, families of veterans may readily reach out for support because they have learned how to ask for help and form new bonds quickly.

If the veteran had PTSD, especially if it became exacerbated during their dying process, the family caregivers may be exhausted and not have the energy required for grief work. They may have become so consumed with caregiving that they lost their own life or sense of self, which makes grief recovery more difficult.

If PTSD is identified for the first time as a veteran is dying, the impact on the family needs to be factored into their bereavement needs. Some feel relieved saying, "I'm so glad to know it has a name. I knew something was wrong but I didn't know what. Now this makes sense." Others might feel guilty. "I wish I would've realized this sooner, I would have _____(listened more carefully, gotten him help, been more patient and understanding, etc.)."

Writing a condolence letter to a veteran's family can be helpful, especially if it acknowledges the influence that the military exerted on the family, such as the one cited in Box 16.2. Providing veteran-centric memorial services can also effectively respond to the bereavement needs of families. Vet Centers are located throughout the country. They were established after the Vietnam War by veterans dedicated to providing services to veterans who were reticent to come to government facilities to receive care. Vet Center staff also care for the veteran's family. Staff are trained in bereavement care and, in addition to community and VA hospice programs, are a good resource for families.

Box 16.2 Example of bereavement letter to veteran's family

Dear Susan, Greg, Jane, Paul, and Amy,

As I came away from the funeral service last night, I was left with a desire to share my own story about your Dad. I have known your Dad for the past 10 years as part of our church community. He started a small group in his home and we have been meeting monthly since. Your Dad was careful to say in the first meeting that this would not be the kind of meeting where people "spill their guts" – and your Dad kept his word about that for five years. But one night, your Dad started talking about the death of your sister. As he spoke, it became apparent that the death of this daughter at age five had been deeply disturbing, though he had never let himself grieve. Instead, he had boxed up his pain, hoping it would go away. Now, 40 years later, here it was again. This time though, he let himself feel his pain. He told of his despair over losing a child at that tender age, and he let himself cry. He was embarrassed at first. But soon the emotion gave way to the sobs of tears he had held back so long. Your Mom said it was the first time she'd ever seen him cry. I think your Dad was a little different after that day. A part of his heart was unlocked and his sharing became more open, his feelings expressed more freely.

I also think of your Dad at our 4th of July party. We did a tribute to the veterans for the freedom we were celebrating that day. I called the three veterans who were at the party to the front of the group and seated them in places of honor. Then we sang *God Bless America* and saluted them. That meant a lot to your Dad. Your Dad sacrificed a lot for his country. He bore a lot of physical and emotional scars from the war. Those scars are what I thought of last night when I saw the flag draped across his coffin.

I learned more about your Dad's struggles after the war when I visited him in the hospital last week. He wasn't taking any painkillers for his pain. He said he wouldn't have anything to do with morphine. Then, he told me the story of how he had become addicted to it with his injuries during the war. He said that during wartime, there weren't facilities for fixing the injury. Instead, he said the soldiers were "doped up" until medical services could be provided. After being on morphine for many months, he got hooked on it. After his injuries were repaired and healed, he continued on it. He told me about a time when he beat up a pharmacist friend of his to get more. He said that was about the "stupidest" thing he ever did and was deeply ashamed. But, it served as the wake-up call to kick his habit. And he kicked it the only way he knew how. He went off into a cabin in the woods. He stayed there by himself and sweated it out. Your Dad said it was pure hell. He sat with a loaded gun to his head and his finger on the trigger for many of those days. I think it was a combination of will power on your Dad's part, defiance toward his father, and faith in God that kept him from pulling that trigger. At any rate, as I listened to your Dad's story, my respect for him deepened. I had a greater appreciation of his stoicism. I had a deeper sense of who he was and why he was. My hope is that through his death, you will have a deeper sense of his life, a deeper sense of his love for you, and a deeper sense of yourselves.

Interventions for community agencies or partnerships

Helping veterans at the end of life is important because it is one last opportunity to help them find peace before they leave their earthly journey. To accomplish this, Congress passed a law allowing all enrolled veterans to have access to hospice and palliative care services as part of their uniform benefits package (38 CFR 17.36 and 17.38). Through this legislation, enrolled veterans in all settings regardless of service-connected status and deemed by a VA physician to require these services will be offered these services purchased or provided by VA. Helping veterans enroll in VA by getting their military discharge papers to the eligibility office facilitates the process. "Death with honor" has been a code the military has lived by. It is a code that is worthy to be maintained after they leave the military.

Because 96 percent of veterans die outside VA's healthcare system, the Department of Veterans Affairs has partnered with NHPCO (National Hospice and Palliative Care Organization) to establish the "We Honor Veterans" campaign to engage hospice and palliative care programs throughout the nation to assist veterans in achieving a peaceful death. Hospice Veteran Partnerships (HVPs) have been formed in communities to promote effective end-of-life care for veterans. These partnerships collaborate to provide care, overcome interagency barriers, and provide educational forums for veterans and staff caring for them. Members of the HVPs include veterans as well as staff from state hospice associations, VA Medical Centers, VA clinics and home-health programs, Vet Centers, and Veteran Service Organizations.

One of the goals of the We Honor Veterans campaign is that every veteran is identified upon admission into a hospice or palliative care program so their unique needs can be met. Admission forms should include questions asking about military service. Some veterans, however, do not call themselves "veterans," a title they reserve for those veterans who have service-connected injuries or veterans who have been in combat. When asked if they are a veteran, they might reply "No." Instead, ask if they have served in the military.

There are other issues to consider when assessing veterans at the end of their lives. Healthcare providers should not assume that all non-combat veterans did *not* sustain trauma. Many served in dangerous assignments. Rather than asking a veteran if they are a combat vet, ask them if they served in a "dangerous duty assignment." On the other hand, when assessing military history, do not assume all combat veterans sustained trauma; some had relatively "safe" assignments. Equally important, do not assume that those who sustained trauma have PTSD; most do not.

Ask open-ended questions that give the veteran control over how much or how little they choose to reveal. *How* the question is asked is more important than *what* is asked because it reveals your intent:

- "Tell me a little bit about how things went for you in the military."
- "How did your experiences in the military mold and shape your life?"

The We Honor Veterans campaign encourages agencies to express appreciation to veterans for service to their country. There are many ways to do this. Certificates can be posted above a veteran's hospital bed. An official looking document, the certificate might cite the veteran's name, years served in the military, seal of the service branch to which they had belonged, and words such as, "We appreciate our Veterans." In home-hospice agencies, the certificate acts as a reminder for all healthcare providers coming into the home that they are in the presence of a veteran. The certificates are also important to families. Families often want to frame the certificate, especially after the veteran dies.

"Thank you for serving our country" is a small thing to say but it can make a big impact. It requires sincerity however; words become trite and perfunctory when they do not come from personal exploration and development of awareness of the sacrifices veterans have made. Veterans often downplay that sacrifice, saying "I just did what needed to be done." When posting a certificate, reach out to shake the veteran's hand. Tell them you appreciate their service. Although some veterans will shrug it off nonchalantly, a tearful chord will be struck with many others. They might say: "No one's ever said that to me before," "I didn't know anyone cared any more," or "Thank you. It means so much that you haven't forgotten."

Some hospices purchase American flag lapel pins or other symbols that honor veterans. After speaking about their military service, ceremonially pin the veteran and say something that reflects your appreciation, such as: "Each time you look at this pin, may you know how much I appreciate *my* freedom. I know that it comes with a price and that you helped pay that price." Pins and certificates often invite stories about military service. Some hospice agencies go even further; they send a team to record the veteran's military history as well as the lessons they learned. Equally effective is identifying hospice volunteers who are veterans and assigning them to patients who are veterans. Camaraderie surfaces quickly. All agencies caring for dying people are encouraged to transport their veteran patients to the morgue or funeral home under an American flag quilt. It is one last opportunity to pay respect to a fallen hero.

Inpatient hospice facilities are encouraged to decorate one section with military décor or symbols for veteran patients. Facilities are also encouraged to consider placing veterans in a two-patient room with another veteran. There is great camaraderie as they care for each other. Family members of the veterans often become mutually supportive as well. Grief can also be facilitated as staff support a veteran as he grieves his roommate's death.

Community hospices and VA agencies often have veteran recognition or other kinds of acknowledgement for veterans on Memorial Day, July 4th, and Veterans Day. The Hospice–Veterans Partnership toolkit and the NHPCO "We Honor Veterans" website (www.wehonorveterans.org) provide many relevant resources that foster the care of veterans at the end of their lives.

Families are often unsung heroes because the sacrifices they have made go unacknowledged. If the veteran experienced trauma, PTSD likely impacted the entire family system. If there were frequent moves because of military reassignments, family life was disrupted. Ceremonially providing symbols that acknowledge their sacrifices can be very meaningful to family members. Some hospices are now providing support groups for families with loved ones in current wars. Other hospices are partnering with the Red Cross to provide bereavement services to family members of soldiers killed in action. Many hospices partner with VA Medical Centers to provide bereavement groups to veterans and their families.

Summary

Veterans and their families often have unique end-of-life needs that are distinct from their civilian counterparts. Many healthcare providers and hospice agencies are joining forces to meet the needs of dying veterans so that the men and women who served our country will receive the honor they earned when they joined the military.

Appendix: culture of war – Deborah Grassman

Another important lesson my patients taught me was that each war was different. Each had its own culture that exerted a different influence on young soldiers.

World War II was enthusiastically supported by Americans. Many veterans have told me they joined when they were 16, lying about their ages so they could fight. When one veteran told me he had been 14, I could only shake my head in wonderment.

Virtually everyone sought a way to support the war effort. People grew "victory gardens" and the Red Cross sent pictures of them to the soldiers so they could see their country's support. Women worked in munitions factories while others stayed home and made clothing for the soldiers. No one was left untouched.

Without televisions, the public could be shielded from war's brutality. War could be glamorized, which increased its appeal and fostered further national unity. The mission of World War II enhanced this unity; it was clear and largely undisputed – especially after Pearl Harbor. And the soldiers knew they were in the war for its duration. This fostered cohesion and a determination to get the mission accomplished – a "we're in this together until the job gets done" attitude. When the war was over, troops came home *together*. They were greeted as heroes by a public eager to hear their victorious wartime stories.

While the adulation was gratifying, the soldiers needed more from their friends, families, and the media. They had been through horrors they could not have imagined; they had done things they never thought they would do. They needed the approval they were getting, but they also needed to give voice to the traumas they had suffered. But the awaiting public only wanted to hear about acts of bravery and heroism, not of trauma and moral confusion. The soldiers, themselves, often downplayed their acts of courage: "The *real* heroes were those that didn't come home" or "I was just doing my duty." This kind of reticence was sometimes taken for modesty. But some have told me that it's not modesty. They don't feel like heroes because they knew the ugly, despairing, or cowardly acts of war: "If you knew what I did, you wouldn't think I was so heroic." These stories often remained untold, lurking in the veterans' consciousness; they often hid guilt and shame.

The Korean War was different. My Korean War veterans are often more tight-lipped. Known later as the "Forgotten War," it was never an officially-declared war; rather, it was called a "Conflict" or "Police Action." There were no ticker tape parades for these returning soldiers; this was the happy 1950s and people wanted to forget about war and focus on growing prosperity. Korean soldiers' trauma had been minimized or neglected and their combat contributions sometimes forgotten.

If Korea taught us how to ignore soldiers, Vietnam taught us how to shame and dishonor them. There was extensive television coverage from Vietnam. Americans now understood the brutality of war and were at odds with its politics. Protests were organized across college campuses. Actress, Jane Fonda, sent much-publicized cookies to the enemy – an act that symbolized a divided nation.

Many young men had mixed feelings about the Vietnam War, and some opposed it. The draft forced these and others into military service and then into combat. Also, imposed beliefs from fathers who were World War II veterans sometimes prompted unwilling sons to volunteer for Vietnam. For others, sons sought the hero status their World War II fathers had held in the family (and usually came back disappointed, I notice).

These soldiers often became more cynical by their experience in Vietnam, and their cynicism affected the soldiers who believed the war was necessary. This prevailing mood is depicted by a caption on a painting in the National Vietnam Veterans Art Museum in Chicago. It reflects the bitterness I often saw corroding the souls of some veterans. It read:

> We the willing
> Led by the unknowing
> Do the necessary
> For the ungrateful

In addition to political influences, there were pragmatic factors. Though they could volunteer for more, soldiers were required to do only one-year tours in Vietnam. Rather than the "we're in this together until we get the job done" attitudes of the World War II soldiers, they tended to think in terms of "I'm just rotating through until my tour's up." Reports of anti-war protests at home shook their confidence in the war as well.

Frequently-rotated new troops also meant fewer available seasoned troops: "You couldn't trust new soldiers to cover your back," a Vietnam vet told me. He said green recruits were also more trigger happy. "They were more likely to kill other soldiers who they mistook as enemy soldiers" – the famously named "friendly fire."

War tactics also were different in different wars. Before Vietnam, there was a certain level of safety "behind the lines" (if there can be any safety in a war), which allowed a small degree of mental and emotional recuperation between battles. In Vietnam, it was guerilla warfare which meant there was no safe place to let defenses down. The enemy easily infiltrated, making it difficult for soldiers to distinguish friend from foe. Soldiers were on guard even in their sleep. Explosives were sometimes hidden on dead bodies, blowing up when soldiers came to retrieve them. Commonly, I've heard stories of soldiers carrying candy on them so they could give them to village children; but this could be used against them. Sometimes, the children were booby-trapped to explode while in the soldiers' midst!

Chemical warfare with Agent Orange defoliant was being used by American soldiers against the Vietnamese. Years later, when soldiers started experiencing effects from Agent Orange, the government disregarded their complaints. Vets had to organize and fight to receive attention, treatment, and compensation. The memorial wall in Washington DC does not include the names of these soldiers who died from the effects of Agent Orange; Vietnam vets sometimes experience this as one more reminder that their service was not valued nor their sufferings understood.

As important as any of the military factors, is how the non-military public treated Vietnam veterans. Unlike World War II veterans, these men and women did *not* return as heroes. Often they weren't even welcomed home. Anti-war protests had grown and people who had advocated bringing the soldiers home now turned their anger against the soldiers themselves. They greeted returning soldiers at the airports by spitting on them and shouting "baby killers" or "murderers." As a result, soldiers often hid their history about Vietnam like a dirty secret.

I've often speculated about how differently our soldiers would have been treated had there been a convincing victory in Vietnam. But the reality is that Americans don't like losers, even in war, even when it may not have had anything to do with the warriors. We didn't want to hear; we wanted no reminders. As a result, soldiers' stories had no where to go. They couldn't even talk with each other much of the time. Unlike World War II soldiers who often came home in boats or trains that gave them time to share their experiences and "de-brief" each other along the way, Vietnam soldiers were flown home into a hostile civilian culture in a single day – their suffering never validated, their souls left burdened, their stories left untold because we didn't want to hear them.

I've often watched World War II veterans rightfully swell up with pride when Hitler is mentioned. "We got him," they'll say, feeling the satisfaction of being part of a successful campaign to protect the world from evil. Vietnam veterans rarely feel this kind of satisfaction. Uncertainty and ambiguity about the goals and outcomes of the war often erode any sense of achieved purpose. Without a convincing victory, veterans felt their sacrifices had been meaningless. The political nature of the war added to their sense of injustice: "We could have won that war if the politicians had stayed out of it," some vets have told me. "They never financed the war so that we could have the resources to do what needed to be done," others have told me. This sense that their sufferings had been futile could linger for years, corrupting their civilian lives and even their deaths years later.

When I started seeing how isolated Vietnam veterans were, I often encouraged them to join the Veterans of Foreign Wars, American Legion, or Disabled American

Veterans organizations. "We're not welcome there," I was told sometimes. "They don't understand us either." Some World War II vets couldn't comprehend that Vietnam was different. Some viewed these soldiers as "wimps" who had "lost" the war. I remembered all the quips TV's Archie Bunker made about the superiority of World War II: "the *big* one" (i.e. the *only* one). The generational clash and the war culture clash interfered with communication and support. Initially, the Veterans of Foreign Wars posts did not allow Korean or Vietnam vets to join because those wars were not *declared* wars. Though that is no longer the case, it has taken years for the American public to register more understanding and acceptance; for most Vietnam vets, the damage had already been done.

Prisoner of War camps for each war also had their own cultures depending on the country they were in, the conditions they were subjected to, and the tortures used to extract information. I have heard horror stories from some of them. Perhaps most horrifying was the one told me by a veteran who survived the Bataan Death march. As he and the other prisoners were walking past a field, a pregnant farm woman threw them some food she was picking. One of the guards walked over to her, pulled out his knife, and cut the baby out of her body as the helpless prisoners watched!

References

American Psychiatric Association, 2000, *Diagnostic and Statistical Manual of Mental Disorders*, 4th edn. Washington, DC: APA, 467–468.

Baum, D., 'The Price of Valor', *The New Yorker*, July 2005.

Byock, I., *Dying Well*. New York: Riverhead Books, 1997.

Grassman, D., *Peace at Last: Stories of Hope and Healing for Veterans and Their Families*, St. Petersburg, FL: Vandamere Press, 2009.

Grossman D., *On Killing: The Psychological Cost of Learning to Kill in War and Society*, New York: Little, Brown, 1996, p. 260.

Webster's New World Dictionary, New York: Simon & Schuster, 1995.

Index

Italic page numbers indicate tables; bold indicate figures.